dBASE III® PLUS

A COMPREHENSIVE USER'S MANUAL

dBASE III® PLUS
A COMPREHENSIVE USER'S MANUAL

KERMAN D. BHARUCHA

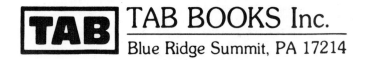

TAB BOOKS Inc.
Blue Ridge Summit, PA 17214

FIRST EDITION
FIRST PRINTING

Copyright © 1986 by TAB BOOKS Inc.
Printed in the United States of America

Reproduction or publication of the content in any manner, without express
permission of the publisher, is prohibited. No liability is assumed with respect to
the use of the information herein.

Library of Congress Cataloging in Publication Data

Bharucha, Kerman D.
dBASE III PLUS—a comprehensive user's manual.

Includes index.
1. dBASE III PLUS (Computer program) I. Title.
II. Title: dBASE three PLUS—a comprehensive user's
manual. III. Title: dBASE 3 PLUS—a comprehensive
user's manual.
QA76.9.D3B5   1986   005.75′65   86-5925
ISBN 0-8306-9454-4
ISBN 0-8306-2754-5 (pbk.)

Contents

Acknowledgments

A t the time of publication of my first book on dBASE, I was rather remiss on acknowledgments, being, at the time, somewhat ignorant of the processes of publication. I would like to make up for this now.

I acknowledge, with gratitude and thanks, the assistance of Mr. Kevin Burton, who has been my constant liaison on this project, and without whose help the publication of the book would have been delayed considerably.

I also wish to thank Mr. Robert Ostrander, Managing Editor, Senior Computer Editor Marilyn Johnson, and the TAB editorial and production staffs for their time and input into the process of finalizing the manuscript.

Introduction

d BASE III PLUS is the name of a software package marketed by Ashton Tate, Inc., and is a powerful development tool for microcomputer business applications. If you utilize a microcomputer for personal or business needs but have never had the level of knowledge required for working with dBASE III PLUS, or if your attempts at working with dBASE III PLUS through the technical manual have proven frustrating, then the solution to your problem is contained in this book.

dBASE III — PLUS A Comprehensive User's Manual discusses version 1.0 of product, which is the latest release, and has been written for the person who wants to get started on the serious development of business applications, without going through the hassle and frustration of reading the technical manual on dBASE III PLUS. The overall emphasis in this comprehensive work is on the logical approach. You will begin with the study of some fundamental computer concepts, including a general discussion on databases, before beginning your study of dBASE III PLUS. Within the dBASE III PLUS environment, you will learn, in logical order, how to create a database, display the data from many different points of view, edit or modify the database so as to guarantee the integrity of both data and structure, sort and index the data to rearrange it for reporting, pull off reports from the data, and write your own computer programs in dBASE, thereby gaining much more power and flexibility with dBASE III PLUS.

Obviously, no attempt has been made at any time to replace the manuals, and while the full use of this book will take you a very long way towards effectively utilizing this powerful software, access to the most complete repertory of commands is provided only by the dBASE III PLUS technical manuals. The study of this book will guarantee your ability to understand, without further external assistance, any specific commands from the manuals not explicitly covered here.

As each command is discussed, several "What-If" types of possibilities are explored for that command, so that you are not left in any doubt at all as to the multiple choices of actions available, or their outcomes. Specific instructions are covered in one area of the book so you will not have to search through the whole book for answers.

Literally zero data processing knowledge is presumed, and the approach taken has been that of guiding a novice through the paces of running and effectively utilizing dBASE III PLUS. The book has been formatted in three sections. Section 1 discusses some fundamental computer concepts and database concepts. Section 2 starts off with the study of dBASE III PLUS basic features, and you will learn how to create, modify, display, edit, sort, index, and report from any database. Section 3 is the advanced features section. In this section you learn to write your own programs in dBASE III PLUS, starting with the simplest of programs and working your way up to a high degree of programming sophistication.

If you feel that you already know some dBASE III PLUS, then follow through the table of contents down to the logical point you wish to pick up from. Reading all the preliminary material, however, will virtually guarantee that even the experienced dBASE III PLUS user will absorb additional, useful information on this subject.

> **Note:** dBASE III PLUS can be used either as a stand-alone system for a single-user, or it can be networked in a multiuser local-area network (LAN) environment. This book is entirely geared towards making you a dBASE expert in the single-user world and will not address the LAN environment. You will need to know the single-user environment thoroughly before you can begin to explore the multi-user environment.

Part 1

Fundamentals

1. Data Processing Fundamentals

I n this chapter, I will introduce some definitions, explain some procedures, and answer some questions. If you are generally familiar with microcomputers and if you already use dBASE III PLUS, you may prefer to skip all preliminary information and scan the table of contents for specific topics of interest.

Data Processing. *Data processing* is the systematic *collecting, analyzing, summarizing* and *reporting* of data. The function of data collection is, by far, the costliest of these four functions, and the most time-consuming, since it requires substantial human input into the process. Subsequent functions, of course, are purely mechanized by way of the computer.

Computer Program. A *computer program* is nothing more than a series of instructions to a computer. These instructions are, for the most part, *sequential* in nature. If you can manage to write a few instructions, in any computer language, and if you can manage to store these instructions on an external device (say, a floppy diskette), then you have created a computer program.

A portion of a computer program could be represented by the following lines:

```
              ----------------
              ----------------
STEP5         READ A RECORD
              ADD 1 TO RECORD-COUNTER
              PRINT OUT THE RECORD
              GO TO STEP5
              ----------------
              ----------------
```

In this over-simplified example of a computer program, you can appreciate that the program is reading each record and printing it out, while keeping track of the number of records read. Computer programs can range from trivial to super-sophisticated, depending on the output requirements of the programs, and the number of lines of program code could range from just a few to several thousand.

It is important to understand that a computer program provides instructions to the computer, making it perform one or more *tasks*. Without a program (the set of instructions) to guide it in its tasks, a computer can do nothing at all.

Module. A computer program is also known as a *module*. Some argument of theoretical interest could be made by programmers that a module is a subportion of a program, and not the whole program. Entire programs however, can be made to function as subsections of other programs, and so in this book I will follow the convention that the word *module* is completely synonymous with *computer program*.

Hardware. The term *hardware* refers to the physical computer itself. Anything you can see and touch, the electronics of the machine, the various peripheral devices such as CRT (screen), keyboard, disk drives, printer, and modem are all encompassed in the term hardware.

Software. *Software* refers to the computer program or programs that control a computer system at any point in time. The microcomputer usually runs only one program at a time, but in the case of mainframe computers, several hundred programs or modules could be executing "simultaneously."

CPU. The basis of any computer system is the piece of hardware known as the *central processing unit* (CPU). This piece of hardware contains all the electronic circuitry required to perform the functions of *arithmetic, logic and control*. It is the brains of the microcomputer system.

At any point in time, the CPU performs one of the following three functions:

1. It *obtains* the *next sequential instruction* from the computer program.
2. It *interprets* that instruction.
3. It *executes* that instruction.

The cycle then repeats, beginning again at step 1 for the next instruction. This cycle repeats, until the computer encounters that instruction telling it to stop the run.

It is important to understand that the CPU is being fed its instructions one by one from the computer program that is currently executing in the system.

Memory. Another piece of hardware in a computer system is that known as the *main memory structure* of the system. For now, it is useful to visualize memory as being comprised of individual cells, like post office boxes, with each box being capable of containing one character.

The term *character* refers to a digit (0 through 9), a letter (a through z or A through Z), or a special character (such as the @, #, $, %, & , and *). The CPU has direct access to any memory cell at random, and hence the main-memory structure is known as *random(ly) access(ible) memory* or *RAM*.

Since the CPU goes through life obtaining, interpreting, and executing instructions, it stands to reason that the computer system must have a way of providing these instructions to the CPU. This is the function of main memory. In the case of a microcomputer system, the entire module that is currently executing needs to be in main memory, so that the instructions from the program can be accessed by the CPU. Also, main memory contains that portion of the data that the program is currently working on.

Conceptually, the layout can be shown as follows:

```
                         ---------
                        | C.P.U.|
                         ---------

(main memory - RAM)
    -------------------------------------------------------------
    |    |     |     |      |     |     |     |     |     |     |
    |<-------------------program------------><-------data----->
    |    |     |     |      |     |     |     |     |     |     |
    -------------------------------------------------------------
```

Input/Output. Any flow of data into computer memory comprises an *input* operation. Any flow of data out of computer memory comprises an *output* operation. The terms *input/output* are used in conjunction with main memory, not in conjunction with any external device.

For example, if you write information out to any device, the information could only have come out of main memory, and so the *write* operation constitutes an *output* operation. If you read information off of a device, that information can only be read into main memory, and so the *read* operation constitutes an *input* operation. Any flow of data to and from any device can only be accomplished via main memory. Any computer program worth a dime performs some kind of input/output (read/write) operations geared towards achieving a specific data-processing objective.

Peripherals. Surrounding the CPU and RAM are the external devices for permitting data to flow into and out of the computer system. The *keyboard* is the basic input device for placing information directly into a reserved area of memory. The *screen* is the basic output device for visual display of a reserved area of memory. The *disk drives* are used for permitting access to floppy diskettes on which information can be magnetically stored, or from which information can be retrieved. The *printer*, of course, is the basic output device for hard-copy displays.

Characters. If you want to store your name in a computer system, you will have to provide the system with the letters comprising your name. These letters are the individual CHARACTERS in your name.

Suppose you also want to store your address in the computer system. You will have to supply to the system all the individual characters (letters and numbers) comprising your full address. So also, for your employee number, organization, salary, or any other *piece of information* you want to maintain for yourself.

Field. Each piece of information created through the use of characters is called a *field* of information. Thus, you may have created your name-field, your organization-field, and your salary-field with the use of the appropriate characters.

Record. Now, if you have stored all the information you may want about yourself in the form of fields of information, you have managed to create one *record* of information about yourself.

File. As you may have guessed, if you can do the same for some of your colleagues working in the same department, you will have managed to create a *file* of information, comprising several records of information.

The last four definitions pertain to computer data, and can be summarized as follows:

A *file* is made up of individual records of information.
A *record* is made up of individual fields of information.
A *field* is made up of individual characters of information.
A *character* is any number, letter or special character.

2. Operating System Fundamentals

An operating system is a collection of specialized programs (or modules) that provide, among other things, an *interface* (a support) for input/output operations. For example, your program has started execution, and at some point in time, it issues a read request to read information off of a disk. The operating system's module takes over, since it has to figure out where on the face of the disk the next block of data is located; having obtained that information, it has to complete the task of loading that block into computer memory then and handing control back to your program.

Your program continues churning away until it comes to a request to write information to disk. Once again, the operating system takes over. It has to figure out where on the face of the disk there is space for the next block of information to be stored, and having figured that out, it has to complete the output operation by writing the block out from memory to disk, and then hand control back to your program.

Each time your program requests any kind of input or output operation to be performed, the modules of the operating system take over and perform that task. This is how the operating system *interfaces* between your program's logical input/output requests and the physical aspects of carrying out the input or output request. Apart from providing this area of commonality for input/output for all programs, the operating system also handles disk-file maintenance and access procedures, and the physical loading and execution of programs. It also provides common utilities that can, for example, make copies of files, format disks, and copy the operating system itself. This, of course, is a very simplified explanation of some of the workings of an operating system, and depending on the computer system you are using, the operating system could be anything from basic to super complex.

Several operating systems for microcomputers are available; they have names such as CP/M, CP/M-86, PC-DOS, MSDOS, TRSDOS, Concurrent CP/M, CDOS, CROMIX, UNIX, and XENIX.

Obviously, the main programs of the operating system itself would always have to be resident in memory so that your program's read/write requests can be carried out. It stands to reason, therefore, that regardless of the brand of business computer system in use, you will first have to load the operating system into memory, before executing any other program. The process of loading the operating system into memory is also known as *booting* the system.

Loading your computer system's operating system into memory is usually a very simple task. The exact mechanics of the loading process differs for different computers. Some computers self-load the operating system: that is, as soon as you have powered on, the computer accesses the operating system disk, and within a few moments the operating system has been loaded and it is ready for usage. These systems are often equipped with a *hard disk*, and the system self-boots from the hard-disk on power up. Many systems with floppy disk drives require that you first power-up, then place a diskette containing the operating system into the A drive, and then type L (or some combination of keys) to start the load process. Please consult your computer system's manual for the exact process of loading your operating system into memory.

When the operating system has been successfully loaded, you should see something like a C> (if you loaded from the hard-disk) or A> (if you loaded from the A floppy drive) symbol on the screen. This means that the operating system is "hooked onto" the C or A drive, and is asking you something to the effect, "Now What ?" and is waiting for you to enter a command to be executed.

3. Databases and dBASE III PLUS Fundamentals

A database is a central repository of related information. To paraphrase this, a database is a *physical grouping* of a collection of individual, but related, bits and pieces of *information*.

As an example, if you want to maintain information about each and every individual employed in your organization, you will need to create a *base of data* about all your employees. This base of data could contain, for example, information about each employee's employee-number, name, salary, year of hire, and date of last promotion. This base will subsequently provide you with immediate access to the type of information you are seeking. Databases can and are being maintained for every subject from astronomy to zoology. Computers, because of their speed and accuracy, are the information processors, the physical means, of creating and subsequently accessing these databases.

RELATIONAL DATABASES

A *relational database* is one in which the data is arranged in the form of a *matrix*, with the rows of the matrix forming each individual record in the database, and the columns of the matrix forming the individual fields of information, across all records. An example of the structure of such a database follows:

	field-1	field-2	field-3	field-4	field-5
	(EMP_NUM)	(EMP_NAME)	(ORG)	(TOWN)	(YR_HIRE)
record-1	80085L	JOHN JONES	BSG	ROCHESTER	1980
record-2	3647A	ADAM SMITH	RBG	PENFIELD	1975
record-3	xxxxx	xxxxxxxx	xxxxx	xxxxxxx	xxxxx
record-4	xxxxx	xxxxxxxx	xxxxx	xxxxxxx	xxxxx

The fields of information can, of course, be just about any field conceptualized by the user of dBASE. The EMP_NUM, EMP_NAME, and other field names have been provided just as examples.

Using such databases, you can establish a *relationship* between two or more databases, by using a common *key* field of information. You can, for example, access an Inventory database, and using the PART NUMBER as the key for each inventory record, list out all the transactions for this PART NUMBER from a Transactions database. As another example, you can access a Personnel-Master file and a Payroll-Master file via the (common) social-security field to produce paychecks. If you are creating another file using a relationship, then for the structure of the new database, you can specify any combination of fields from the input databases. You can even build entirely new fields, using the data from the input databases. A management system that permits such interaction between databases is a *relational database management system*.

THE dBASE III PLUS SYSTEM

So where does dBASE III PLUS fit in with all of the previous concepts and definitions ?

dBASE III PLUS is the name of a software package (a collection of computer programs), marketed by Ashton Tate, Inc., of Culver City, California; it is a very powerful tool for the development of microcomputer business applications.

dBASE III PLUS is a data manager. It is a piece of software that lets the user have full freedom in the conceptualization and creation of databases for all types of business applications. Since business depends on timely information dissemination, the value of a powerful, programmable utility for database generation, maintenance, and query cannot be overstated.

dBASE III PLUS is defined as a *relational database manager*; that is, this software will help you create and maintain relational databases.

dBASE III PLUS can be executed on a variety of microcomputers, under any one of the popular operating systems mentioned earlier. If you are inclined to use dBASE III PLUS for your business needs, but are unsure of the compatibility of your computer system with dBASE, your dealer should be able to help you out.

WHO NEEDS THIS BOOK?

Because dBASE III PLUS is a data manager, anyone who has the need to create and maintain data needs to learn to use a package such as dBASE III PLUS.

This book has been written for the person who wants to use dBASE III PLUS for creating and maintaining and querying business-oriented, or commercial, databases (commercial, as opposed to scientific). If you own or use dBASE III PLUS for personal or business applications but have found the dBASE III PLUS manual too technical in its approach and too cryptic in its format, the study of this book will prove highly rewarding. Every software package demands that you spend some time in its study, and dBASE is no exception. This book will start you off with step-1 and guide you through a very logical path to a high level of dBASE sophistication. Experienced dBASE users, too, stand to gain much valuable information from this book. The experienced dBASE user may prefer to skip all preliminary information and scan the table of contents for specific topics of interest.

WHICH VERSION IS DISCUSSED?

I will be discussing dBASE III PLUS version 1.0, which is the latest release of the software (January 1986) in the dBASE series. In this very dynamic environment of software development, it is quite possible that further releases of dBASE III PLUS may be announced before this book is available in print. However, just as one does not rush out to buy a new car every time a new model is announced, so does one not rush out to pick up every new release of a software package. Ashton-Tate has guaranteed that these releases will all be *upward compatible*, and so whatever you learn for the dBASE III PLUS 1.0 version will hold good for the later versions.

A WORD ON DOCUMENTATION

Let us take a moment here to emphasize that you must be prepared to maintain good *documentation* if you hope to work well with dBASE. This is necessary because, for every database you create under control of dBASE, several supporting files will subsequently have to be produced. For example, assume that you have a good, clean database, and now you are ready to start creating reports from this database. Before you can create any report, your database will have to be either *physically sorted* or *logically indexed* to provide the proper *sequencing* of records for the report; therefore you will have to develop either a *sorted file* or a *logical index* for your master database. This process can result in the creation of quite a few files or indexes, especially if you want several reports, each requiring its own sequencing of records. Also, each type of *report format* you need requires the production of that specific format in the form of a *report format file*. Once again we have the possibility of several format files connected with one master database. As you can appreciate, you will find yourself creating many different types of files in support of just one database, and you need to have a good method of documentation, in order to name and keep track of the various files you create. Obviously, this effect drastically multiplies for each additional database you create. (The terms *sorting, indexing,* and *report-formats* are covered in detail in the appropriate places in the text. Right now, I am merely emphasizing the need for good documentation.)

STARTING UP WITH dBASE III PLUS

If it were not for the fact that dBASE III PLUS is copy-protected software, starting up with dBASE III PLUS would be a very simple matter. As it stands, however, the software is copy-protected, so in order to start functioning with dBASE III PLUS, you have to do the following:

1. Make backup copies of *some* of the disks included in your dBASE package.

2. If you want to be able to load dBASE from a hard disk, create a *subdirectory* on the hard disk and go through an *installation* procedure, which puts an activated copy of dBASE onto the hard disk.

3. If you want to be able to load dBASE from a floppy disk, *prepare* your Systems Disk #1 for this function.

Making Backup Copies

Your original dBASE III PLUS kit is comprised of (a) System disk #1 (copy-protected); (b) System disk #1 backup (copy-protected); (c) System disk #2; (d) a sample programs and utilities disk; (e) an applications generator disk; (f) an on-disk tutorial disk; (g) Administrator disk #1 (copy-protected); and (h) Administrator disk #2 (copy-protected).

Given a choice, you must *never* play around with any original software disk(s), since you can never know exactly when the originals will be required. So at this point in time, please make backup copies of all the nonprotected disks in your kit. If you don't know how to make backup copies of disks, I will (regretfully) refer you to your operating system (DOS) manual for the exact process of making backup copies. I would suggest that you should not proceed beyond this point until you have made the recommended backup copies.

Presuming now that you have made the suggested copies, from now on every subsequent reference to System disk #1 will refer to the original disk, since you could not have made a functioning copy of this disk, and every subsequent reference to System Disk #2 will refer to your backup copy, and not to the original, since you have made a functioning copy of this disk. The same argument will apply to the other (protected and nonprotected) disks. I would suggest that you put aside, in a safe place, all the original disks for which you were able to make copies.

Creating Subdirectories on Your Disk

If you intend working with floppy disks only, you may skip this section entirely and pick up at the section entitled "Preparing to Use Systems Disk #1 for dBASE III PLUS."

I will take for granted that you know enough about MS-DOS or PC-DOS to be able to create a subdirectory on your hard disk drive. If you do not have the knowledge to do this yet, I suggest that you stop reading any further in this installation procedure. Now you can either read the MS-DOS or PC-DOS manual for your computer or study Appendix A of this book where I have explained the workings of the directory structure in MS-DOS—or of course, you can always ask someone to help you out with this process.

For the person who is a novice at computers, I can appreciate that this present "stop-and-go" situation may be discouraging, since it would seem that you need to have some amount of prior computer background to be able to work with dBASE III PLUS. You should, however, realize that dBASE (or any other software package) does not run in a vacuum, and some preliminary steps need to be performed so the software can execute as intended. Making backup copies, and understanding the subdirectory structure is absolutely basic and necessary to the installation of any software onto a hard disk.

At this point, I will presume that you know exactly how to create a subdirectory on your disk. I am now going to emphasize a procedure that you would be well-advised to follow religiously any time you install copy-protected software. This procedure applies equally well to other popular, copy-protected software, such as LOTUS 1-2-3. This recommendation comes from having experienced, first-hand, the problems that could crop up if you have not taken some precautions up front.

Let us suppose that you want to use dBASE III PLUS for several applications, such as a medical system, a dental system, and a stocks system. I would recommend that you create one subdirectory at the root-level called PROJECTS, and under that subdirectory, create other subdirectories called MEDICAL, DENTAL, STOCKS, or any other system you may want to create. The reason behind recommending this two-tier hierarchy is that at some predetermined frequency, you will be doing a BACKUP of the disk (either in entirety or for selected projects). Now if you have performed a BACKUP of the subdirectory called \PROJECTS (in effect, a BACKUP of all of your working disk), and if the system subsequently crashed (a hardware or power failure), when you get on-line again you can safely perform a *restore* procedure on the subdirectory called \PROJECTS, and get back a working-copy of your complete disk. If you have performed a BACKUP of only the \PROJECTS\DENTAL subsystem, you can safely RESTORE the subdirectory called \PROJECTS\DENTAL, if the need arises. (BACKUP and RESTORE are utility programs found on your DOS diskette.)

If you have not taken this precaution of creating subdirectories, then your BACKUP procedure will be done at the root level. While this in itself is fine, should you want to perform a restore procedure at the root level, you will have wiped out the working copy of dBASE III PLUS!!! This is because dBASE maintains hidden files in the root directory (this is the heart of the copy-protection feature), and your restore procedure at the root level wipes out these hidden files. Without these files to give your copy of dBASE the green light, you are unable to load the software subsequently!!

Having a subdirectory called \PROJECTS and sub-subdirectories for the various individual systems (dental, medical, etc.) provides you with the ability of backing up either a specific system or backing up the entire working disk, and of subsequently performing a restore procedure, if need be, without the danger of losing your working copy of dBASE III PLUS. To backup the entire working disk, you would do a backup on the directory called \PROJECTS. To backup say, DENTAL, you would do the backup on \PROJECTS\DENTAL. Your restore procedure, if required, could either restore \PROJECTS (to restore your entire working disk), or restore \PROJECTS\DENTAL (to restore only the DENTAL subsystem). Please ensure that your restore procedure never restores at the root level!

Presuming you know how to create a subdirectory on the hard disk drive (which I shall refer to as C>), let us suppose you have created the subdirectory called \PROJECTS\DB3PLUS. Further, you have made this the *default directory* on the C> drive (hard disk drive). We will be installing dBASE III PLUS into this subdirectory.

Installing dBASE III PLUS on Your Hard Disk

dBASE III PLUS was designed to function on the IBM-PC family of computers, and so the installation of the software onto the hard disk is a fairly straightforward process. The following description applies equally well to any IBM PC-compatible microcomputer.

CAUTION

1. If you already have an earlier version of dBASE III (version 1.x) installed on your disk, you should either uninstall it or install the PLUS version in a completely separate subdirectory.

2. If you already have an installed Developer's version of dBASE III, you must uninstall it before installing the new PLUS version.

3. If you have already installed dBASE ACCESS (for networking), it was installed from the Systems disk #1, whose installation count is now zero. Hence, dBASE ACCESS must be uninstalled, bringing the installation count (on Systems disk #1) back to 0001, before the single-user PLUS version can be installed. (You can only have one installation from the Systems disk #1, either single-user dBASE III PLUS, or the multiuser dBASE III PLUS for local area networking.)

Basically, the installation requires the copying of dBASE from the original disk onto your computer's hard disk drive, into the current subdirectory that has been set up to receive the software (as described earlier). Since the software is copy-protected, this copying involves a two-step process.

Place your System disk #1 in drive A, and make A your default drive. At this point, A is the default drive, and the default directory on the hard disk is \PRO-JECTS\DB3PLUS. Now type in:

A>INSTALL C: <cr>

You have asked the INSTALL program to do its thing, and the screen in front of you now merely tells you to touch any key to go ahead with the installation procedure. When you go ahead, the INSTALL program informs you that 0001 installation is available to you, and if you proceed with the operation, then no more installations will be possible with the Systems disk #1 in the A drive.

When you ask to go ahead, in a short while the program instructs you to place the Systems disk #2 in the A drive and touch any key to continue. In a few more seconds, the copying and installation are complete. At this time, you have a working dBASE III PLUS software system under the default directory called \PROJECTS\DB3PLUS.

You may, now, if you like, make a copy of the Sample Programs and Utilities disk and the On-Disk Tutorial disk in the subdirectory \PROJECTS\DB3PLUS.

One final step is required to complete the installation. You will have to create a file called CONFIG.SYS in the root directory of the hard disk. You can either copy this file over from the System disk #1, as follows: A>COPY CONFIG.SYS C:\ <cr>, or follow the instructions in Appendix-A.

Having created the CONFIG.SYS file, you are ready to start work with dBASE

14

III PLUS. At this point, your hard disk has been prepared for subsequent repeated usage for loading dBASE III PLUS into memory.

Creating Multiple Working Copies of dBASE III PLUS on the Hard Disk

If you have several subdirectories under \PROJECTS (one for each application you may be working on), it is very easy to copy the *installed* dBASE software files over from the \PROJECTS\DB3PLUS subdirectory to the various subdirectories, in effect creating multiple copies of a working dBASE, one for each subdirectory. This facilitates bringing up dBASE III PLUS regardless of which application you are working on. For example, you have dBASE in \PROJECTS\DB3PLUS, and you also want an operational copy of dBASE in \PROJECTS\MEDICAL. All you have to do is type:

C>COPY \PROJECTS\DB3PLUS\DB*.* \PROJECTS\MEDICAL   <cr>

This command will copy over all the dBASE files (five such files) from \PROJECTS\DB3PLUS into \PROJECTS\MEDICAL. Now you have a working copy of dBASE in the \PROJECTS\MEDICAL subdirectory.

Please note that I am not recommending that you make these copies, one for each subdirectory, since, in all probability, Ashton Tate would consider multiple copies on the same hard disk as illegal. Logically, since the intention behind making these copies is not dishonorable, it would seem that a copy in each directory would be permissible. However, I again wish to emphasize that I am not recommending this approach.

A Word of Caution

You should never delete the dBASE software files off of the \PROJECTS\DB3PLUS directory without Uninstalling the software. This uninstallation gives you, again, one valid installation for the future. Failure to adhere to this rule will result in the unavailability of further installations from your Systems disk #1.

This is where the System disk #1 backup copy comes into play. (This is the backup copy of Systems disk #1 that comes from Ashton-Tate). If you encountered a hardware problem in which your dBASE files were inadvertently deleted from the hard disk, you can fall back upon this backup copy to provide you with one installation, when your hardware problem has been rectified. Just use this backup copy as you would have used the original System disk #1 for the installation.

Uninstalling dBASE III PLUS

If, for any reason, you want to uninstall dBASE III PLUS from the hard disk, the process is very simple. Place the System disk #1 in the A drive, make A the default drive, and make \PROJECTS\DB3PLUS the default directory on the hard disk drive. Now type:

A>UNINSTAL C: <cr>

Follow the prompts, and within a few seconds you will see the message that the uninstallation was successful. Now, of course, the dBASE III PLUS on your hard disk is nonoperational, and you have one installation available again from your Systems disk #1.

Please note that if you have several dBASE III PLUS copies, one for each directory as discussed earlier, *all* the working copies are rendered useless because the uninstall procedure renders the hidden files in the root directory nonoperational. A subsequent reinstall procedure for \PROJECTS\DB3PLUS will reinstall only the copy of dBASE in the \PROJECTS\DB3PLUS subdirectory. You will now have to recopy the dBASE files to each of the subdirectories in which you want to use dBASE III PLUS, if you want to follow that route.

Preparing Systems Disk #1 for dBASE III PLUS

You can use one of two methods of loading dBASE III PLUS from a floppy drive, one using a DOS disk, and the other using a prepared version of Systems disk #1. I will show you how to use Systems disk #1 directly, since there is less of a hassle involved here, than in using a DOS disk to load dBASE each time.

In order to use Systems disk #1 to load dBASE, the Systems disk #1 itself will have to be prepared, as follows:

1. DOS must be available on Systems disk #1.
2. The COMMAND.COM file must be on Systems disk #1.

To obtain the above results, proceed as follows:

    1. a   Put your DOS disk in drive A
          b   Put your Systems disk #1 in drive B
          c   Press the Ctrl and ALT keys, and while you have them pressed, press DEL. This causes a *system reset.*
          d   When prompted for the date and time, touch <cr> each time, in effect ignoring these for now.
          e   When you see the A> prompt, enter the following command: A>SYS B: <cr>

    2.   When you see the A> prompt again, enter the following:

          A>COPY COMMAND.COM B: <cr>

At this point, your Systems disk #1 has been prepared for subsequent repeated usage for loading dBASE III PLUS.

The preceding sections explained how to prepare either the hard disk or the Systems disk #1 as the primary medium for loading dBASE. We shall now see to the process of actually loading dBASE from the hard disk or from the floppy disk.

LOADING dBASE III PLUS FROM THE HARD DISK

To load dBASE from your hard disk, reset the system by pressing the Ctrl and ALT keys, and while you have them pressed, pressing the DEL key.

When asked for the system date and time, you may either enter these, or touch <cr> to bypass a date and time entry, if the existing system date and time are accurate.

At the C> prompt type: C>CD \PROJECTS\DB3PLUS   <cr>
                            C>dBASE   <cr>

In a few moments, you will see the Ashton-Tate screen containing the usual welcomes and warnings. There is an approximate 10 second wait, at the end of which you will find yourself in the dBASE Assistant mode. If you don't want to wait the full 10 seconds, you can touch <cr> to proceed directly to the Assistant menu. You can now either continue using the Assistant or touch the ESC key to escape from the Assistant mode and go directly to the dBASE *dot prompt*.

The above start-up procedure presumed that you want to start executing dBASE in the DB3PLUS subdirectory. If you have several working copies of dBASE in your various (project) subdirectories, you could just as easily have done the following:

At the C> prompt type: C>CD \PROJECTS\DENTAL   <cr>
                            C>dBASE   <cr>

Now dBASE would be executed from the DENTAL subdirectory.

LOADING dBASE III PLUS FROM THE FLOPPY DISK

To load dBASE from a floppy disk, put your prepared Systems disk #1 in the A drive and then reset the system, by pressing Ctrl and ALT keys, and while you have them pressed, pressing the DEL key. Enter a new date and time, or accept the current date and time, and touch <cr>, until you get to the A> prompt.

Now type: A>dBASE   <cr>

When the system prompts you, remove Systems disk #1 from the A drive, and put in System disk #2 (*your* copy of the disk—if you remember, you should have made a working copy of this disk), and then touch <cr>. The dBASE Assistant pops up, and you can now either continue using the Assistant or touch ESC to escape from the Assistant mode and go directly to the dBASE *dot prompt*. From now on, you continue using the Systems disk #2 in the A drive. You may, if you like, place a *data* disk (a formatted disk on which you will create and maintain your data) in the B drive.

THE dBASE III PLUS ASSISTANT

dBASE provides you with an Assistant feature that is menu-driven and is supposed to provide the novice with the ability to create data files and other supporting files (format, index, etc.). My own impression of the assistant feature, however, is that the complete novice would be rather confused by the proliferation of terminology shown at the various menu screens, and the Assistant feature seems to be more for someone who has at least casually delved into the subject of dBASE and who has some background in data processing and dBASE "buzz" words, rather than for the complete novice. For example, if you have no idea what *Index* is all about, you cannot be expected to make efficient use of the Assistant. I feel strongly that a good book on dBASE would prove much more beneficial to the first-time user than the Assistant feature would, for actually learning dBASE III PLUS.

When you first invoke dBASE III PLUS, either from the hard disk or from the floppy disk, you start off in the Assistant mode of operation. (You can change this default—more on that, later.) To get out of the Assistant mode, touch the ESC key, and you will be out of Assistant, to the famous dBASE dot prompt.

The DOT Prompt

Any time you see the *dot* staring you in the face, you must know that you are in *native dBASE mode*, and now dBASE is asking you something to the effect of "What Next ?"

At this stage, you may enter one of many commands available under dBASE. As soon as the command is executed, dBASE again presents the dot prompt and waits for the next command. Unless otherwise informed, dBASE will always present you with the dot prompt and wait for the next command.

> **Note:** Never leave off a dBASE session by just powering down and walking away at the dot prompt. If you do that, some of the last few records you had changed or created are still in memory, and your file will have lost these few records, which should have been written out to disk. To exit dBASE, always provide the QUIT command. This will ensure the integrity of the database most recently in use. Once you QUIT, you will find yourself back at the operating system level, at the C> symbol, at which point you may power down and walk away.

THE ESC KEY

There will be times, of course, when you type a command at the dot prompt, and you make an error in the syntax. You can either use the backspace key to back up to the error and make corrections, or use the ESC (escape) key to escape from this command, and restart a new command on the command line. The use of the ESC key wipes out the current command and presents the dot prompt again.

The person who has some slight familiarity with dBASE will encounter times when they forget the format of a specific command and would like a quick reference to the manual. dBASE provides an *on-line assistant* feature, whereby at the dot prompt, you may type in **HELP XXXXX** (where XXXXX is a dBASE command). You will then be provided a description of the command on the screen. This description screen, in turn, lets you specify the next command you may want help with. You can use the ESC key to exit from this on-line assistant mode.

GENERAL EXPLANATIONS AND CONVENTIONS

Before you get started on your study of dBASE, please note a few lines of explanation regarding syntax and other matters important to your clear understanding of some items provided in this book.

dBASE or dBASE III PLUS ?

In this book, I have used the terms dBASE and dBASE III PLUS to mean the same software package, dBASE III PLUS Version 1.0, as marketed by Ashton-Tate.

Syntax

At several places, I have provided the *syntax* of some dBASE commands, an example of which follows:

.COPY TO   <file>   [FOR <condition>]   ....<cr>

The word <file> implies that the name of a file (or database) must be provided in place of <file>, and that without this entry, you will have committed a syntax error.

The phrase [FOR <condition>] specifies that the entire phrase is optional. Any entry in square brackets is an optional entry. Note, however, that within the optional entry, there is an entry like <condition>. This implies that *if* the FOR statement is used, there *must* be a condition provided with the FOR clause.

> **Please Note:** In dBASE III PLUS, any command and/or any parameter of any command can be reduced to the first four characters. You do not have to type out the whole word. Also, you can use any combination of upper- and lowercase characters during the entry of the command. For example, you may specify .MODIFY STRUC-TURE or .MODI STRU to get the same effect.

The <cr> Symbol

The <cr> symbol at the end of any command line refers to the *carriage return* and is your cue that you should press the Enter or Return key on your keyboard. Obviously, if you do not enter a <cr>, the screen will stare right back at you and nothing will happen.

Enter or Return

The words *enter* or *return* have been freely used interchangeably in this book to refer to the <cr> action.

Control Keys

At several places in this book, I have referred to either a dBASE function or a cursor-control movement using the control key with a letter. For example, to instruct you to use a control key and the W key together, I have used Ctrl-W.

Perform this control action by pressing the key marked Ctrl (or CTL or CONTROL) on your keyboard, and while you keep it depressed, press W!

There are several Ctrl-key-and-letter combinations mentioned throughout the book, and they all follow the above routine.

Specific Computer

I mentioned before that cursor-control explanations included in the book require a Ctrl-and-letter type of input from you. These control key combinations will work properly regardless of the computer type used for executing dBASE!

This book was prepared using the COMPAQ DESKPRO 286 computer, which is "100 percent IBM-compatible." I cannot, however, guarantee that all commands mentioned in this book will work exactly as specified on your "IBM-compatible" computer! Some differences in compatibility cannot be ruled out as being possible. (Incidentally, there is no such thing as "100 percent compatibility" across all software products!)

Disk Drive Names

If you are using a floppy disk system, note that in all probability your disk drives have been assigned letters of A and B. If you have a hard disk in your system, the hard disk assignment is C. This book, prepared on the COMPAQ computer system with a hard disk, will show C> to refer to the system prompt. Please make mental substitutions as appropriate for your hardware.

Files and Databases

Throughout the course of this book, the terms *file* and *database* have been used interchangeably as referring to the same physical entity, the *central repository of information*.

File-naming conventions under the CP/M, MS-DOS, and PC-DOS operating systems dictate the following:

1. You must provide a primary name for the file from one through eight characters in length.

2. You may or may not provide a secondary name (or extension). If you do provide a secondary name, it should be from one through three characters in length, and the two names must be separated by a period.

3. You may mention a drive name ahead of the filename as follows: **B:filename**. This would imply that you are accessing (creating, reading from, or writing to) a file called <filename> on the B: drive. If no drive name is indicated, the default drive (A> or C>) is selected.

The following list is an example of valid variations of a filename.

STUDENTS is a valid name for a dBASE database.
STUDENTS.DAT is also valid.
STUDENTS.FIL is also valid.
B:STUDENTS is also valid.

If you do not provide a secondary name for a file, dBASE III PLUS will provide its own default secondary name of .DBF (for dBASE file). Some exceptions to this rule will be outlined at the appropriate places in the book.

Scrolling

The word *scrolling* refers to the rapid movement of data across the face of the screen. If a command in dBASE III PLUS produces the scroll effect, you can momentarily freeze the action on the screen with a Ctrl-S entry. Another Ctrl-S unlocks the freeze. That is, Ctrl-S stops and restarts the scroll movement.

Avoiding the Assistant Upon Loading dBASE

Your version of dBASE (either the installed version on the hard disk or the one on the prepared Systems disk #1) contains a file called CONFIG.DB. When dBASE first loads, it searches for this file and executes any commands there. One of the commands in that file is COMMAND = ASSIST. This causes the Assistant feature to be invoked each time you enter into dBASE III PLUS. For now, I suggest that you delete this file. Without this file, upon loading dBASE, you will be presented directly with the dot prompt. You can delete this file at the C> prompt by going to the appropriate sub-directory (if necessary) by typing:

C>CD \PROJECTS\DB3PLUS   or   C>CD \PROJECTS\DENTAL <cr>

and then erasing the file by typing:

C>DEL CONFIG.DB   <cr>

The above commands will select that subdirectory on the hard disk from which you would like to load dBASE and go directly to the dot prompt and delete the CONFIG.DB file from that subdirectory.

If you are working with the prepared System disk #1, you can type:

A>DEL CONFIG.DB   <cr>

Configuring dBASE III PLUS

Let me mention at this time a feature in dBASE III PLUS that lets you tailor the initial workings of the software to your specific requirements. In other words, suppose you were in the habit of always performing specific *housekeeping* commands each time you entered dBASE. You can have these commands specified "permanently" so that dBASE automatically executes these when it is first loaded.

For obvious reasons, however, it would be quite out of line for me to attempt to describe this process here, since you have yet to begin your study of dBASE and its various commands. The configuration process will not have much meaning for you now, so I shall relegate this description of tailoring dBASE to a much later chapter.

SUMMARY

In this section, you learned some data-processing terminology essential to the under-standing of dBASE. You also learned the processes of installing and uninstalling dBASE from a hard disk and of preparing System disk #1 for use on a floppy-drive system.

Part 2

Basic Features

4. The Creation Process

You are ready to create your first database using dBASE. The process of creation is really the process of translating to dBASE the proposed *structure* of the data you wish to create.

DATA FIELDS

Let us say, for example, that you want to keep track of some information pertaining to the employees in your company. Assume that for each employee, you want to keep track of his/her Employee-Number, Name, Organization, Year-of-Hire, and Salary. Right at this point, you have conceived a *structure* for the information to be maintained for each employee. By deciding upon what fields of information you want to keep track of, you have taken the first step towards formalizing the structure of your proposed database.

For now, let us say that your *conceptual structure* for the data for each employee looks like this:

Employee-Number	Employee-Name	Organization	Yr-of-Hire	Salary

The actual names of the fields in your conceptual structure will be decided later, but for now the above names will suffice. Now you have to go one step further and let dBASE know what the contents of the fields are going to be. After all, the actual names really do not mean too much to dBASE, and it needs to be made aware of the kind of data it is dealing with in each field.

You can define a field as being one of five types: *character, numeric, logical, date,* or *memo*. For now, we will concentrate on the character and numeric types. The other field types will be covered later in this section.

Character and Numeric Fields

Basically a field defined as a *character field* will accept any character of data subsequently entered, whereas a field defined as a *numeric field* will only accept the digits 0 through 9, the decimal point, and the negative sign (–) as data. (Trying to force character data into a numeric field will lock up the keyboard.) There may, however, be ambiguous situations you may have to resolve. Take, for example, the Employee-Number field. Suppose you know for a fact that during actual data entry into this structure, the data going into the Employee-Number field will only be comprised of the digits (0 through 9). That is, there will be no special characters (*, $, @, etc) or letters needed in the Employee-Number fields. Would you now define the Employee-Number field as numeric?

The answer is no, since the only test needed to determine if the type of the field should be numeric as opposed to character is to ask yourself the question; "Do I foresee myself performing any kind of *computation* on this field? Will I ever be adding employee numbers together, or will I ever take an employee's record and add his employee number to his social-security number?" Since the answer to these questions is no, you should define the Employee-Number field as being of the character type.

As another example, take the Year-of-Hire field. Would you define the type of this field as numeric? Again, try and answer the same questions as before. Do you foresee performing any kind of computations against the Year-of-Hire field? The answer here is yes. You may, perhaps, decide that you want to subtract the Year-of-Hire from today's date to obtain an employee's longevity in service. Since there is a possible computation in this case, the Year-of-Hire field should be defined as being numeric.

Other examples are a Social-Security field, which should be of the character type, and a Salary field, which should, of course, be defined as numeric.

At this stage, your conceptual structure looks like this:

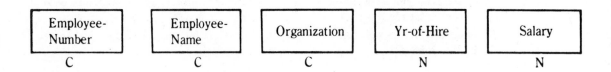

One more piece of information needs to be provided before the proposed structure for each record of information is complete. As you may have guessed, you have to inform dBASE how large each of these fields is going to be. How many characters of information do you foresee going in as data, for each employee number or each employee-name? etc.

Let us say that each entry in the Employee-Number field will not contain more than six characters of data; the Employee-Name field can contain up to 15 characters of data, and the Organization field up to 3 characters of data. The Year-of-Hire field can contain four characters of data (for data being entered as 19xx).

The Salary field needs to be looked at carefully. Suppose you visualize the actual data being entered into the salary fields as being of the form 99999.99 (That is, five digits before the decimal and two after). This is, of course, adequate for salaries up to $99,999.99 per year and will serve for the average salary. Now the length of this field should be defined as 8,2 (a total of 8 characters, inclusive of the decimal point, and including two decimal places).

As a further clarification of this point, let us introduce a field that will not make any logical sense in the type of database we are considering, but has definite applications elsewhere. Let us consider a field like the Debit/Credit type of field used in financial applications. In order to determine the length of this field, you again have to consider the kind of data that field will actually contain. As an example; suppose the field is to be designed to contain up to three digits before the decimal and two decimal places, and could possibly have negative values put in during data entry. That is, you could possibly have a value such as -999.99. The length of this field should be defined as 7,2 (a total of seven characters with three before the decimal, two after the decimal, one decimal point and one (possible) minus sign).

In our example, the formalized structure now looks like this:

Employee-Number	Employee-Name	Organization	Yr-of-Hire 19xx	Salary (5) . (2)
C	C	C	N	N
6	15	3	4	8,2

This, of course, is still our conceptual structure. We have not actually defined anything to dBASE yet.

You may define the Employee-Number field as ENO, if you like, but while this may make a lot of sense to you, it may make no sense at all to someone else picking up after you. So you may decide upon EMPNO. This is, of course, more readily comprehensible than ENO for employee number, but to make it precise, you should try something like EMP_NUM.

As another example, for the Year-of-Hire field, you may try something like YR_OF_HIRE, instead of YRHR. To break up the words for ease of reading, the *underscore* character is accepted. The *space* character, if used, will result in an error.

The only rule to be satisfied is that the total length of the name itself cannot be more than 10 characters, inclusive of the underscores. Do not confuse the length of the field name with the length of the field itself. For example, the field called EMP_NAME has been defined as being 15 characters long, but the word *EMP_NAME* itself is only 8 characters long.

Logical Fields

A logical field is one which is of a predefined length, 1 character, and will accept as input either the letters T or Y (for TRUE/YES) or the letters F or N (for FALSE/NO). The actual data is stored exactly as entered, but will be displayed on the screen or the printer as .T. or .F. only. If no data is entered, the default is .F.

For example, if a field called EXEMPT is defined as a logical field, you may want to enter T into the EXEMPT fields of all exempt employees, letting the EXEMPT fields of other employees default to .F. Because the nature of the field is logical, you can now access such fields for information without the use of any logical operators.

As an actual example of a dBASE command using a logical field called EXEMPT as described above, let us say you want a listing of all exempt employees.

.LIST FOR EXEMPT   <cr>

will do the trick.

Contrast this with the situation in which the EXEMPT field was defined as a character field, and you had entered a T as data in that field for all exempt employees. In this case, the above command would have to be entered as:

.LIST FOR EXEMPT = 'T'   <cr>

Notice that now the relational operator (equals) had to be used to clarify the meaning to dBASE.

Date Fields

A *date-field* is also of a predefined length, eight characters, and dBASE presumes that you will be subsequently entering a date of the format MM/DD/YY. At the time of actual data entry into this field, dBASE automatically checks for the accuracy of the data entered. For example, an entry of 12/35/85 would invoke a beep and an error message. The built-in edit even checks for a leap-year! Date fields are very useful in that they reduce the amount of programming effort needed for routines computing time lapses, since you can add numbers to or subtract numbers from, date fields, or you can add or subtract two date fields directly. The actual mechanics of using the date fields will be described later.

Memo Fields

A memo *field* is also of a predefined length, 10 characters in the file itself, and automatically contains the word *memo* for data. Through the use of this field, you can maintain memos for individual records. Each memo could be up to 4000 characters long if the built-in dBASE word processor is used, or can be of any length if it is set up with a commercial word processor. As an example, consider a dental office, where the office manager may use dBASE to write out a short memo to a patient. This memo would then appear on the next bill to the patient. Using the memo field, you can maintain different memos to be sent later to different individuals. Although a memo field itself is only 10 characters wide in the database file, dBASE makes use of an external file in which it stores the contents of the individual memos, and hence the memo can have the capacities mentioned earlier. This external file will have the same primary name as the dBASE file, but will have the .DBT extension for the secondary name. dBASE maintains this file in an internally usable form. The actual mechanics of using the memo field will be described later.

CREATING A DATABASE STRUCTURE

We shall now look at the mechanics of defining the structure of database to dBASE. Once you have entered dBASE, the dot prompt is the signal that dBASE is waiting for you to enter a command. The command for creation of a structure is CREATE.

> **Caution:** If you tell dBASE to create a file, and by error you enter the name of an existing file, dBASE will provide you with a warning message. If you fail to heed the warning, dBASE will overlay the file with the new structure that you will be creating, in effect destroying your previous file (structure and data). Obviously, you should take the opportunity to exit gracefully from such a situation.
>
> If you elect to go ahead and overlay an existing file definition with a new one, and then if you have a change of mind, it is too late! Please note that at this point, your change of mind does not give you the previously existing file back! So think twice before overlaying an existing file definition.

Directory Listings

You may want to avoid the situation in which you accidentally use the same name of an existing file, so before we go forward with the study of the CREATE command, let us make a small detour and see how dBASE will let you make a check of the directory listing of a disk to see the names of the files currently existing on that disk. Before you list the filenames on the screen or at any time while you are using dBASE commands, you can clear the screen, by typing the dBASE command:

```
.CLEAR        <cr>
```

This will "wipe off" the screen. The dot prompt will appear at the bottom left of the screen, and you can proceed with another command. Note that CLEAR only cleans up the screen and does nothing else.

To see a list of files on the screen, you could enter one of the following commands:

```
.LIST FILES                  <cr>
.LIST FILES ON B             <cr>
.LIST FILES ON B:            <cr>
```

The first option will produce a listing of all the files on the C-drive (the *logged-in* drive) that have a secondary name of .DBF (for dBASE-formatted file).

The second and third options, of course, will provide a listing of all the .DBF files from the disk in the B drive.

If you want to see *all* the files on any drive, regardless of the names of the files, enter one of the following commands:

```
.LIST FILES LIKE *.*         <cr>
.LIST FILES ON B LIKE *.*    <cr>
.LIST FILES ON B: LIKE *.*   <cr>
```

This will produce the required listings from the drive mentioned in your command.

If you want to see a particular group of files, for example, all the index files, you can use one of the following commands:

```
.LIST FILES LIKE *.NDX              <cr>
.LIST FILES ON B LIKE *.NDX        <cr>
.LIST FILES ON B: LIKE *.NDX       <cr>
```

Here, the *.NDX is the *mask*, defining the type of files you want a directory listing of.

In place of LIST FILES or LIST FILES LIKE, you can also use the DIR command. For example:

```
.LIST FILES
```

is equivalent to

```
.DIR
```

and

```
.LIST FILES LIKE *.NDX
```

is equivalent to

```
.DIR *.NDX
```

Notice that the LIST FILES and the DIR commands both provide information on the amount of available space on the drive.

In case some disk clean-up is required, you can use the commands described below. To delete some files, if necessary, use:

```
.DELETE FILE XXX.YYY         <cr>
```

This will delete that specific file.

> **Note:** You can only delete files with *status-codes* or *attributes* of *read/write*. Files with the status-codes or attributes read only cannot be deleted! Status codes and attributes are explained in your operating system reference handbook. Also, if you delete a dBASE file that has a memo field in its structure, the associated memo file (the .DBT file) is not automatically deleted. It is, however, useless since it cannot be used except if referenced through a dBASE file.

To rename files use this command:

```
. RENAME  ABC.F1    TO  XYZ.F2       <cr>
```

This will rename the file exactly as specified. Please note that rename also works on protected files! Also, if you rename a dBASE file that had a memo field in the structure, the associated memo file (the .DBT file) is not automatically renamed, and your next attempt to use the renamed file will fail, because dBASE will tell you that its memo file cannot be opened. You will therefore have to rename the memo file as well before you can use the renamed dBASE file.

The DOS Interface

dBASE provides you with the ability to execute commands at the operating-system level. That is, while in dBASE you can execute DOS commands. This interface with DOS is provided through the use of the RUN command. For example:

. RUN DIR	is the same as executing the DIR command at the C> prompt; that is, it is the same as C>DIR <cr>.
. RUN DIR *.DBF	provides a listing of the .DBF files.
. RUN DIR *.NDX	provides a listing of the .NDX files.
. RUN DEL XXX.YYY	will delete that specific file.
. RUN REN ABC.F1 XYZ.F2	will rename the file exactly as specified.

Note that the .RUN DIR commands also provide you with information on the amount of available space on the drive.

Note that there are slight differences in the formats of the DELETE and RENAME commands, depending on whether these are specified at the DOS level or at the dBASE level. Remember that you can execute any DOS command using the RUN interface command.

Software and Data Handling

If you have a floppy disk system, you would be well-advised to maintain your software and your data on separate disks. That is, do not get into the habit of creating your data on the same disk that contains the dBASE software, if for no other reason than that you may need the extra space on your disk, if you have several applications under dBASE. This recommendation is, of course, based also on logical and esthetic reasoning that dictates that software and data should be distinct and separate, which is how I have always proceeded when using a floppy-disk system. An argument could also be made to the effect that if one has software and data on the same disk, one only needs to carry one disk instead of two. To which, again, a counter can be made that the space requirement for two disks is virtually the same as that for one disk. Besides, if you are going to be at all serious about dBASE, you will find yourself requiring many more than just a couple of disks, and your dBASE software disk should be kept free of all data. The hard-disk user, of course, is freed from this space constraint.

Proceed as you wish, and use the appropriate version of the LIST command to find out what dBASE files you already have on your data-disk.

Note: If you do decide to keep to the recommendation of separating your software and your data, there is a useful feature in dBASE, which, if invoked, lets you *log-on* to the B drive for data, but still access the dBASE software modules from the load drive as and when needed. The following command invokes this feature:

.SET DEFAULT TO B   < cr >

or

.SET DEFAULT TO B: < cr >

From now on you can refer to all your data files (and other files you will create later on) on the B drive without having to key in B: for each reference. The dBASE software itself will continue to operate from the load drive.

Creating Your Database

So much for our detour . . . Now having decided on a file name and having ensured that this filename for the proposed structure does not currently exist on the target disk, you may now enter:

.CREATE   < cr >

or

.CREATE < filename >   < cr >

If you do not enter a filename in the command line itself, dBASE will prompt you for it in an intermediate step. Also, if you have not used .SET DEFAULT TO B: then you will have to mention B:< filename >, if you want to create your file on the B: drive.

Suppose we name our proposed file PERSNL. After creation of this structure, its actual name in the system will be PERSNL.DBF, since dBASE will provide the .DBF secondary name.

.CREATE PERSNL   < cr >

The effect of this action is that dBASE sets up the following screen layout, expecting your file-definition entries:

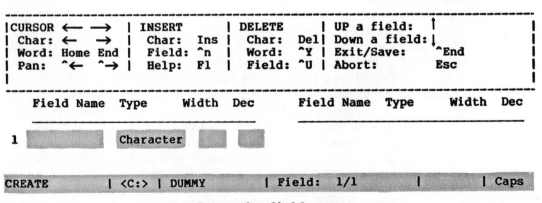

```
                                                    Bytes remaining: 4000

---------------------------------------------------------------------------
|CURSOR ←  → | INSERT        | DELETE       | UP a field:   ↑            |
| Char: ←   → | Char:  Ins | Char:   Del| Down a field:↓             |
| Word: Home End | Field: ^n | Word:  ^Y | Exit/Save:    ^End         |
| Pan:  ^←  ^→ | Help:  F1 | Field: ^U | Abort:        Esc          |
|                                                                         |
---------------------------------------------------------------------------

    Field Name   Type     Width  Dec      Field Name   Type     Width  Dec
    _____      _____

 1  [        ]   Character  [   ]  [   ]


CREATE          | <C:> | DUMMY          | Field:  1/1          |     | Caps
```

Enter the field name.
Field names begin with a letter and may contain letters, digits and underscores

32

At this point, dBASE wants you to specify the *name* of each field you want to define, the *type* of the field, the *length* of the field, and the number of *decimal* places, if the field is a numeric field.

Notice the *status line* at the bottom of the screen. It reminds you that you are executing the CREATE command in order to create a database file called PERSNL(.DBF) on the C drive, that you are about to describe FIELD 1, and that your keyboard is locked in the CAPS (ON) mode.

> **Note:** Having asked to CREATE a file, you may, of course, change your mind on this creation, simply by hitting <cr> on the first blank field of the structure. dBASE will ask for a confirmation of the action, then delete this file.

Let us define the fields of information for our proposed structure, as follows. Please go along with the creation of the file called PERSNL(.DBF), as I explain it in this book. I will be using this file throughout the book for examples.

```
                                              Bytes remaining: 3946

------------------------------------------------------------------------
|CURSOR <-- -->  |  INSERT       |  DELETE       | UP a field:   (Up-arrow)   |
| Char: <-   ->  |  Char:   Ins  |  Char:   Del| Down a field: (Dn-arrow)   |
| Word: Home End |  Field:  ^n   |  Word:   ^Y | Exit/Save:    ^End         |
| Pan:  ^<-  ^-> |  Help:   F1   |  Field:  ^U | Abort:        Esc          |
|                                                                            |
------------------------------------------------------------------------

      Field Name   Type      Width  Dec      Field Name   Type     Width  Dec
      _____  _____   _____  ___      _____   _____   _____  ___

 1    EMP_NUM      Character    3
 2    EMP_NAME     Character   13
 3    TOWN         Character    9
 4    ORG          Character    3
 5    DT_OF_HIRE   Date         8
 6    SALARY       Numeric      8     2
 7    NOTE         Memo        10
 8                 Character


CREATE        | <C:> | DUMMY      | Field:  1/1        |        | Caps
```

Enter the field name.
Field names begin with a letter and may contain letters, digits and underscores

Observations Concerning the CREATE Command

1. You can ask to define a file either on the floppy drive or on the hard disk drive. See the preceding paragraphs for a review of this option.

2. If you ask to CREATE <filename>, and <filename> already exists on the

same disk as your intended file, dBASE provides a warning message, which you should heed.

3. You can change your mind about creating a new file, by touching <cr> on the first field when dBASE asks you to define the structure.

4. dBASE comes up with a default of *Character* for a field type. If you are defining a character field, simply press <cr> to move the cursor to the LENGTH field and carry on with the definition. If you want to define a numeric field, simply type N for the first character. This changes the definition to *Numeric*, and the cursor moves on to the LENGTH field. If you type in L for LOGICAL field, dBASE gives it a default length of 1, and moves the cursor for the next field definition. In a similar manner, D for DATE provides a default of 8 characters, and M for MEMO provides a default of 10.

5. As you are creating the structure, you may move the cursor using the arrow keys and make changes to fields previously entered, if required. The top of the screen provides a special menu to show how you may move the cursor and make changes:

Use the arrow keys as you normally would, to move up/down, left/right.

Use Ctrl-N to open up space for a new field definition where the cursor is located.

If you have defined a long structure (maximum 128 fields), you can use the PgUp and PgDn keys for backward and forward scrolling.

Other keyboard controls have been provided, but you may or may not find these useful, depending entirely on your typing ability. These controls would be used to make changes to existing field names.

Ctrl-G or the DELETE key. While in the middle of a field, each time you hit Ctrl-G or the delete key, you will delete the character under the cursor (the cursor does not move), and the other characters to the right of the cursor will move left by one position.

Ctrl-Y. While in the middle of a field, if you hit Ctrl-Y, you will erase the field from the position of the cursor up to the end of the field, (an *erase-end-of-field* effect).

Ctrl-V or the INSERT KEY. These keys are used for the *insert* function. Suppose one of the fields was named EMP_NM instead of EMP_NUM as you had intended. You now want to insert the U ahead of the M. (You could, of course, just retype the whole name again, but the idea is to show the insert function, here). Bring the cursor up to the M using the features previously described, and enter Ctrl-V or INSERT. Notice the word INSERT appears at the bottom of the screen in the status line. This means that you are in the insert mode, as opposed to being in the over-write mode of operation (which, of course, is always the default). Now key in the letter U and you will see it inserted into the field, that is, the other characters are moved over to the right to make room for this character to come in. If you insert too many characters into a field, characters will start spilling over, into no man's land. Try inserting a few characters to see the whole effect of the insert function. To get out of the insert mode, use Ctrl-V or INS again. Ctrl-V or INS is a *toggle* switch to get you in and out of the insert mode.

The BACKSPACE key. The use of the BACKSPACE key once will cause the cursor and the character under the cursor to move one character position to the left, overlaying, and thus deleting, that character. All other characters to the right of the cursor also move accordingly. Holding this key down will create a multiple, ripple effect, with the cursor running to the left, deleting characters in its path.

Please note that you can turn the cursor-control menu at the top of the screen ON or OFF through the use of the F1 key.

6. If you enter the same field on two different lines (in effect trying to create the same field again), dBASE prompts you with a beep.

7. The maximum length allowed for character fields is 254.

8. The maximum length for numeric fields is 15 digits of accuracy. You may ask for a numeric field up to 19 digits in length, but the accuracy of the data is guaranteed for only 15 digits, regardless of whether these digits are before and/or after a decimal point, and regardless of the minus sign, if any. Hence the term *15 digits of accuracy* is used.

9. You can define a maximum of 128 fields, for the structure of any one database.

10. Within the limitation of 128 *fields* of data, you can only define a maximum of 4000 *characters* of data. For example, in the seven fields already established, we have defined a total of 54 characters of data (3 for EMP_NUM + 13 for EMP_NAME + 9 for TOWN + 3 for ORG + 8 for DT_OF_HIRE + 8 for salary + 10 for NOTE).

11. When you want to wrap up the definition of the structure, press <cr> on a blank line.

Let us wrap up the definition of our structure, for now, by pressing <cr>. dBASE will ask you if you want to enter data into this structure at this point. Usually the answer should be N, for No, since you would normally want to review your structure and make changes to it, before you actually go ahead and input data into this structure.

Please enter N for NO. We will input data at a later stage.

Having CREATEd your database structure, you may want to review the structure for accuracy, before you actually go ahead and put data into it. Also, you will want to keep a hard copy of the structure for your own documentation.

Displaying and Documenting the Structure of the File

Because our file called PERSNL.DBF has just been created (structure only, no data yet), it is already in USE and under control of dBASE. So you can proceed with further commands against this file immediately. Normally, if you were working on another file and then wanted to bring PERSNL into use, you would have to provide the command:

.USE PERSNL

At the moment, as explained earlier, the file is already in USE, because its structure was just created.

Now to display the structure of this file, type in:

.DISPLAY STRUCTURE   <cr>

or

.DISP   STRU   <cr>

This will bring the structure of the file up on the screen.

```
Structure for database : C:PERSNL.dbf
Number of data records :      0
Date of last update    : 02/10/86
Field  Field name   Type        Width     Dec
    1  EMP_NUM      Character      3
    2  EMP_NAME     Character     13
    3  TOWN         Character      9
    4  ORG          Character      3
    5  DT_OF_HIRE   Date           8
    6  SALARY       Numeric        8        2
    7  NOTE         Memo          10
** Total **                       55
```

Reminder: In dBASE, any command and/or any parameter
of any command can be reduced to the first four characters.

In the case of a long file structure, dBASE will display 16 fields at a time on the
screen and then wait for any entry from you, before displaying the next 16 fields.

If you want this structure to be printed out, you can specify:

. DISP STRU TO PRINT   <cr>

Notice that the structure display shows how many records are in the file, along
with the date of last update.

Modifying Structures

Having reviewed the structure of the file you have just created, it is logical for
us to take the following stand: If you do want to make some kind of change to the structure of the database, now would be the time to do so, before you start putting in data.
Perhaps, the type of change you envision entails the insertion of another field between,
say, the ORG and DT_OF_HIRE fields; or perhaps you want to change the structure of one of the existing fields, (maybe a name change, a type change, or a length
change); or perhaps you want to delete one of the defined fields from the structure.
Regardless of the kind of change you want, as you already know, it would be logical
to make changes now. This does not mean, however, that you cannot alter the structure of an existing database that contains data records. You can change structures at
any time, in any database.

A Word of Caution

If you are modifying the structure of an existing database that has data-records
in it, note that you should choose your modification cautiously. Consider the following
situation. Suppose you have a character field called EMP_NUM that has, as data,
a combination of digits and characters, starting with digits, and you want to change
its type to numeric. Since dBASE will not retain character data in a numeric field, at
the end of the modification you will have lost all your character data from that
EMP_NUM field! Only the leading numerics will be retained in the (new) numeric
field. If the original data had leading characters instead of numerics, nothing would
have been retained.

36

If you change a field name and a field length at the same time, (either in the same or different fields), note that you will lose the data for the field(s) with the name change! Since dBASE cannot handle this dual-change at the same time, make one of the changes first (either one) and then make the other change to the modified structure.

If you change the name of a field (only), and you want to save this new structure, dBASE will ask you a question (near the status line): "Should data be COPIED from backup for all fields? (Y/N)". What this means is that, by default, when you change the name of a field, you will lose all your data from all the records for that specific field, at the end of the modification. By responding with a **Y** to this question, you can retain all your data for all the records for that field, at the end of the name-change modification. (This has to do with an internal APPEND that dBASE goes through. The APPEND command is explained in detail at its appropriate place in the book.)

At the moment, of course, since you have just created your PERSNL.DBF file and there are no data records in it, you can modify its structure at will, without any adverse effects.

To modify the structure of the database you have just created, enter:

.USE PERSNL	<cr>	(Not necessary if the file is already in use.)
.MODIFY STRUCTURE	<cr>	or
.MODI STRU	<cr>	

This brings up the structure of the file on the screen. The format is identical to the one you saw at the time of structure creation. Cursor controls are also identical to those discussed in the creation section!

When you have made the required changes to your structure, you can either enter Ctrl-W or Ctrl-END to save the new structure, or enter Ctrl-Q or ESC to change your mind on the changes made.

Using the combination of cursor controls you have been introduced to so far, modify the structure of the file called PERSNL.DBF to include a new field called **EXEMPT   L** (a *logical field*) after the ORG field. This field will be used to keep track of the employee's Exempt/Nonexempt status. Note that this logical field has an *implied length* of one character. Enter a Ctrl-W to *save* the new structure of the file. (A Ctrl-Q, of course, would keep the original structure intact.) At the end of the save process, dBASE comes up again with the dot-prompt. To ensure that the change has taken place, and again, for the sake of documentation type:

.DISP   STRU   <cr>

or

.DISP   STRU   TO   PRINT   <cr>

and you will see:

```
Structure for database : C:PERSNL.dbf
Number of data records :       Ø
Date of last update    : 1Ø/29/85
Field  Field name  Type       Width   Dec
    1  EMP_NUM     Character      3
    2  EMP_NAME    Character     13
    3  TOWN        Character      9
    4  ORG         Character      3
    5  EXEMPT      Logical        1
    5  DT_OF_HIRE  Date           8
    6  SALARY      Numeric        8      2
    7  NOTE        Memo          1Ø
** Total **                     56
```

At this point in your study of dBASE, you should be able to CREATE a structure, and if need be, MODIFY the structure to come up with the exact database format you want.

The Extra Field

Look at the structure of the file again. Is there anything you see about the structure that does not quite click? (Try to find the discrepancy, before you read ahead.)

You may have noticed that dBASE informs you that your record structure is a total of 56 characters long, but you can swear that the individual field lengths only add up to 55. That is, dBASE says that the length of all subsequent data records entered into this structure will be 56 characters, but you know you have only defined 55 characters in the structure. Why is dBASE obviously giving you an extra character position?

Suppose you had entered some data records into the structure and then later decided that you did not like the looks of a particular record. You could ask dBASE to DELETE that record. Now a delete request to dBASE does not result in that record being physically zapped out right away, but rather in its being *logically* deleted; that is, the record is *flagged* as being deleted. dBASE uses an * ahead of the record to mark it as being deleted. Without an extra character position into which to place an *, dBASE would have no other option but to put the * in one of the existing data fields.

This capability of logically deleting records affords the user the luxury of a change of mind on a deleted record: the user can always ask dBASE to reactivate any or all deleted records. dBASE obliges by simply removing the * from its position ahead of the record.

In summary, the extra character position is provided by dBASE to handle a possible *delete indicator* (the *) should the need arise to delete and/or reactivate records. (You may rest assured this need will arise.)

I mentioned before that you can define a maximum of 4000 characters of data for a record structure. This does not include the extra position created by dBASE to handle deleted records. You, as a user, may define a full 4000-character structure for your database. The field to handle the delete indicator is a plus, from dBASE.

Closing a File

The statement .USE FILEA brings the file with that name under the control of dBASE;

that is, the file is *open* in a work area. If you now say .**USE FILEB**, you have automatically closed FILEA from the work area, and FILEB is now open in the same (primary) work area. Now if you enter .**USE FILEC**, FILEB will automatically be closed, and FILEC will be open in the primary work area. You will always have one file open in the primary work area.

To close the file last in USE, without opening any other files, you must specify:

.**USE**   <cr>

The USE statement, without any parameters, closes the file in use.

> **Note:** As you will see later, dBASE will let you specify up to 10 work areas, in which you can have up to 10 databases open simultaneously. The word simultaneously simply means that dBASE will maintain separate and independent pointers for the *current record* in *each* of the separate work areas. The concept of the current record will be explained a little later. At the moment, I am emphasizing the point that if you do have more than one file open simultaneously, the .USE command will only close the file in use in the *current* or *active)* work-area! The other file(s) in the nonactive work area(s) will still remain open.

The concept of multiple files in multiple active and nonactive work areas will be explained at a more appropriate place in the book.

THE APPEND COMMAND

Now that you are familiar with the mechanics of creating a structure and modifying it to suit your purpose, we shall proceed with the mechanics of entering data into the structure of the file.

Please read through the following discussion before you go ahead and try the APPEND command. There are several points to be highlighted, before you actually start entering data.

The APPEND command is used for entering data into a database. You use this command whether or not the database currently contains data. That is, you can start entering data for the first time by using the APPEND command and enter additional data on subsequent occasions by using the APPEND command. The new records are simply added on to the end of the existing data records.

To begin to enter data into the PERSNL database type:

.**USE PERSNL**   <cr>   (if not already in USE)
.**APPEND**   <cr>

This will bring up the blank structure (*mask*) of the PERSNL file on the screen, as follows:

```
-------------------------------------------------------------------
I                                                                 I
I                    (CURSOR CONTROL MENU)                        I
I                                                                 I
-------------------------------------------------------------------
EMP_NUM      ▓▓▓▓▓▓▓
EMP_NAME     ▓▓▓▓▓▓▓▓▓▓▓▓▓▓▓▓
TOWN         ▓▓▓▓▓▓▓▓▓▓▓▓▓▓▓
ORG          ▓▓▓▓▓▓
EXEMPT       ▓▓▓
DT_OF_HIRE▓▓▓▓▓▓
SALARY       ▓▓▓▓▓▓▓▓▓▓▓
NOTE         Memo
```

This is merely the *shell* (or *mask*) of the new record. You could now start entering data into it. The field names are, of course, the names you had provided when you had created the structure. The lengths of the various fields are outlined by the inverse video display. The record number at the top indicates which record you could currently enter data into.

Appending Common Information

If you want to enter a lot of common information across the records (for example, most of the employees are in the same organization and in the same town, and it would be ridiculous to have to key in 'GSD' and 'ROCHESTER' across 300 records), you can make use of a feature that will help you maintain common information across records. This feature is to be invoked, *before* you enter the APPEND mode, by typing:

```
.USE PERSNL                    <cr>
.SET CARRY ON                  <cr>
.APPEND                        <cr>
```

Now, instead of the blank structure of the next record coming up on the screen, the mask comes filled in with whatever had been keyed into the preceding record! (For the very first record APPENDed into an empty database structure, the mask is always blank.) You can now go through the record, making changes to the data, as necessary, and skipping those fields that contain the common information.

Note that if you start off with invalid or false common information, you could end up with a couple of hundred records having to be subsequently edited! Also, you cannot pick and choose the fields on which you want the CARRY ON to function. It's an all-or-nothing proposition.

In either case, with or without the SET CARRY ON feature, we are in full-screen edit mode, and the cursor-controls you learned previously apply here, with one exception: If you use the <cr> key when the cursor is in the first position of the first field, and no key depression has been made in the record, dBASE assumes you are through APPENDing and gets you out of the APPEND mode. This is true even if you have

SET CARRY ON. When this happens, the record currently on the screen is *not* saved. Records entered previous to this one, of course, will have been saved.

If you use the <cr> key when the cursor is in the first position of the first record, and data had been entered elsewhere in the record, dBASE *saves* that record and presents the structure of the next record. This is true even if you have used SET CARRY ON.

Please read all the observations concerning the APPEND command, before you start entering the data into the database. The record number at the top of the screen tells you which record you are currently working with.

Observations on APPEND

1. If you attempt to key in character data (letters or special characters) into a numeric field, the keyboard will be locked ,up and a bell will ring at the console. The *default* value (the contents if nothing is entered) of a numeric field is zero.

2. When the cursor gets to the end of any one field, it automatically drops down to the start of the next field and a beep is sounded.

3. When the cursor is moved beyond the end of the last field, the record is saved, and the mask of the next record is displayed for data entry.

4. You can make any number of changes to the data of the current record on the screen, by moving the cursor back and forth across the fields, using the cursor controls shown in the menu at the top of the screen. Remember that you can use the F1 key to toggle this menu on or off.

5. You don't have to get the cursor to the very end of the last field in order to save a record. You can enter data into only a few chosen fields, and when you want to save that record, you can enter a Ctrl-C or the PgDn key. This saves the partially filled-in current record and presents the shell of the next record.

6. dBASE can handle up to a *billion* records in any one database. Needless to say, I have not had the opportunity to either prove or disprove this assertation by Ashton-Tate.

7. Once a record has been saved and the blank structure (or filled-in structure, if SET CARRY ON was used) of the next record has been presented to you, you can always go back to previous records by using the PgUp key and then go forward again using the PgDn key. You can only page up as far as record number 1. If you try to page down beyond the last record and you have not SET CARRY ON, you will find yourself out of the APPEND mode and back to the dot prompt. If you have SET CARRY ON, however, your attempt to PgDn beyond the last record will only serve to create duplicates of the last record! If you have accidentally fallen out of APPEND, you can get back in again by using the APPEND command.

8. To enter data into a Memo field, bring the cursor down to the field and press Ctrl + PgDn; you will find yourself in the dBASE word processor. Enter your memo into the *word-processing scratch pad* provided, using the controls as shown in the menu at the top of the screen. Remember that the F1 key can turn this menu on or off.

Although a memo field itself is only 10 characters wide in the file structure, the contents of the memo are stored in a separate file. For example, the actual contents of the memos for the PERSNL.DBF file will be stored in a file called PERSNL.DBT, in a form internally converted by dBASE.

A word of advice: If you intend to write only a few lines as memos for individual records, it is better to define the field as a character field rather than as a memo field. After all, a character field up to 254 characters in length can be defined for a memo, if required. The advantage is that you don't have to enter the dBASE word processor to input data into that field. A greater advantage is that data from a character field can be displayed in any form of the DISPLAY command, which will be studied later.

Also, each time you change (and save) the contents of a memo file, dBASE uses up more space on the disk and does not utilize existing memo-file space. If you have been making many changes in your memo file records, you would be well-advised to make a COPY of the database, so as to release all memo space occupied unnecessarily. The COPY command is explained in detail at a more appropriate place.

9. A logical field will initially show up with the ? character in the APPEND phase; however, it can only accept T, F, Y, or N as input, and its contents will be displayed on the screen or the printer as either T or F only. For example, in your file you have defined a logical field called EXEMPT. Employee records of EXEMPT employees should contain T (true) for the EXEMPT field. NONEXEMPT employees should have an F (false) entered in the EXEMPT field. The default (if nothing has been entered) is F.

10. Dates entered into a date field will be automatically edited for accuracy, and dBASE will even check for a leap-year. The entry will be presumed to be in the format MM/DD/YY, which is how the date should be entered.

11. When you have made the last APPEND for the day, and dBASE has again placed the blank (or filled-in) structure of the next record on the screen, you may leave the APPEND mode in one of several ways:

a. I mentioned before that the use of the <cr> key, when the cursor is in the first position of the first field, will get you out of the APPEND mode. This is also true if you were using the SET CARRY ON feature.

b. You can enter a Ctrl-W. While a Ctrl-W is used in dBASE to save what you were doing, if you use the Ctrl-W on a blank structure, dBASE takes you out of the APPEND mode, since there is nothing to save. This works in the same manner when you are using the SET CARRY ON feature.

c. You can always use Ctrl-Q (change your mind) when the next record is presented and get out of the APPEND mode. This also works when you are using the SET CARRY ON feature.

12. You don't have to save the last record being worked on in order to get out of the APPEND mode. If you have been entering data in a particular record, and you want to get out without saving this record, you can always use Ctrl-Q to do this.

13. If the record has many fields in the structure (maximum 128), it is possible that the entire structure may not be visible on the screen all at once. When you enter the last character of the last field visible on the screen, the rest of the record structure appears. If you want to skip a few fields when entering data, you can use PgDn and

PgUp to scroll forward and backward in order to bring other fields into view.

14. If necessary, at the end of the APPEND process, do not forget to use .SET CARRY OFF; if you forget, this mode remains active, regardless of the file in USE.

15. During data entry, if you find the beeps annoying, you should get out of the APPEND mode and back to the dot prompt (see #11), then type in .SET BELL OFF <cr>, and then get back into the APPEND mode again.

Please proceed with the APPEND command, and enter data records into the PERSNL.DBF database. Use the following 15 data records, since we will be using this data for examples throughout the book.

Note that some of the data has been shown as a mixture of upper and lowercase characters. Please enter them exactly as shown. The numbers to the left are the record numbers, which will be automatically provided by dBASE, as you proceed to APPEND the data.

I will presume that you will enter your own data into one or more MEMO fields as desired. Subsequent DISPLAY command examples will show some memos that I have used as examples.

Data Records to Be Entered into the File

Record#	EMP_NUM	EMP_NAME	TOWN	ORG	EXE	DT_OF_HIRE	SALARY	NOTE
1	005	NINA BHARUCHA	WEBSTER	BSG	.T.	05/24/80	25000.00	Memo
2	010	PETE JOHNSON	brighton	BSG	.T.	02/03/76	27590.00	Memo
3	015	GLORIA PATEL	FAIRPORT	RMG	.T.	07/16/82	27500.00	Memo
4	020	MAX LEVINSKY	HENRIETTA	RMG	.F.	04/13/69	27550.00	Memo
5	025	KIM BRANDT	FAIRPORT	RMG	.F.	04/04/77	36000.00	Memo
6	030	TIM MONTAL	ROCHESTER	RBG	.F.	07/07/81	41900.00	Memo
7	035	WILLIAM PATEL	penfield	GSD	.F.	08/17/71	28900.00	Memo
8	040	JAMES JAMESON	ROCHESTER	GSD	.T.	10/21/77	29800.00	Memo
9	045	MORRIS KATZ	webster	BSG	.F.	09/14/80	23450.00	Memo
10	050	PAUL BHARUCHA	BRIGHTON	BSG	.T.	05/23/73	29100.00	Memo
11	055	PHIL MARTIN	WEBSTER	RMG	.F.	07/19/80	31000.00	Memo
12	060	JOHN PETERSON	BRIGHTON	RBG	.T.	04/17/79	31480.00	Memo
13	065	JOY HARDY	fairport	RBG	.F.	01/19/79	34200.00	Memo
14	070	JAN MOREY	ROCHESTER	GSD	.T.	04/23/67	18190.00	Memo
15	075	JOHN JONES	rochester	GSD	.T.	04/04/70	25100.00	Memo

At this point in your study of dBASE, you should be able to CREATE a structure, MODIFY the structure if need be, DISPLAY and document the structure, and APPEND data into the existing structure.

THE DISPLAY COMMAND

Having put in some data into your database, you now want to be able to see that data in various shapes and forms, and to that end, we are going to look at a very powerful command in dBASE—the DISPLAY command.

Through the use of this command, you can display the following on the screen or on paper:

All the data from a database   or

A single record from the database   or

A group of records from the database   or
Specified fields from selected records   or
Records that fulfill a simple condition   or
Records that fulfill a complex condition   or
Combinations of the above!

As you can see, this command is very useful in all its creativity. Please follow closely on this section, because apart from being very useful and interesting, the parameters we shall be studying appear across the board in many other dBASE commands, and understanding them here will guarantee your quick familiarity with their use in the other commands as well.

The general format of the DISPLAY command is:

.DISP   [scope]   [field-list]   [FOR <condition>]
                                   [WHILE <condition>]
                                   [TO PRINT]   [OFF]

As you can appreciate, all the parameters of this command are optional. This command is free form; the number of spaces between parameters is immaterial, provided you have left a minimum of one space.

The first point to be emphasized is that the DISP command, without any parameters, will always display the entire record that dBASE happens to be pointing to when the command is entered. The record that is currently being pointed to by dBASE is called the *current record*.

If the record length is greater than screen size, the record will wrap around on the screen.

You can use the following combination to display the first record in the PERSNL database:

.USE   PERSNL   <cr>
.DISP   <cr>

The USE command opens the PERSNL database and puts dBASE in control over the first record (i.e., dBASE is pointing to the first record). The DISP command will display the first record:

```
Record#  EMP_NUM EMP_NAME      TOWN      ORG EXE DT_OF_HIRE   SALARY NOTE
      1   005     NINA BHARUCHA WEBSTER   BSG .T. 05/24/80   25000.00 Memo
```

Moving the Record Pointer

You can make this record pointer move to any record you want. The following commands can make the pointer move.

.SKIP   <cr>   will move the pointer to the next record in this case, to record #2.

.DISP   <cr>

Record #2 is displayed:

```
Record#  EMP_NUM EMP_NAME      TOWN      ORG EXE DT_OF_HIRE   SALARY NOTE
   2     010     PETE JOHNSON  brighton  BSG .T. 02/03/76    27590.00 Memo
```

.SKIP 5   <cr>   will move the pointer from record #2 to record #7.

. DISP   <cr>

Record #7 is displayed:

```
Record#  EMP_NUM EMP_NAME       TOWN      ORG EXE DT_OF_HIRE   SALARY NOTE
   7     035     WILLIAM PATEL  penfield  GSD .F. 08/17/71    28900.00 Memo
```

.SKIP -3   <cr>   will move the pointer from record #7 to record #4.

. DISP   <cr>

Record #4 is displayed:

```
Record#  EMP_NUM EMP_NAME      TOWN       ORG EXE DT_OF_HIRE   SALARY NOTE
   4     020     MAX LEVINSKY  HENRIETTA  RMG .F. 04/13/69    27550.00 Memo
```

Note that the DISP command simply displays the entire record that the pointer happens to be pointing to.

If you knew which record number you wanted to transfer control to, say, record number 15 you could use the following commands:

.GOTO 15   <cr>
.DISP   <cr>

Record #15 is displayed:

```
Record#  EMP_NUM EMP_NAME    TOWN       ORG EXE DT_OF_HIRE   SALARY NOTE
  15     075     JOHN JONES  rochester  GSD .T. 04/04/70    25100.00 Memo
```

.GO 10   <cr>
.DISP   <cr>

Record #10 is displayed:

```
Record#  EMP_NUM EMP_NAME       TOWN      ORG EXE DT_OF_HIRE   SALARY NOTE
  10     050     PAUL BHARUCHA  BRIGHTON  BSG .T. 05/23/73    29100.00 Memo
```

```
.7              <cr>      This is the easiest way!
.DISP           <cr>
```

Record #7 is displayed:

```
Record#  EMP_NUM EMP_NAME        TOWN      ORG EXE DT_OF_HIRE   SALARY NOTE
      7  035     WILLIAM PATEL penfield   GSD .F. 08/17/71   28900.00 Memo
```

Any one of the above will transfer control to the appropriate record. The subsequent DISPLAY command will display the record.

To transfer control very quickly to the first record in the database, use the following commands:

```
.GO TOP         <cr>
.DISP           <cr>
```

The first record is displayed:

```
Record#  EMP_NUM EMP_NAME        TOWN      ORG EXE DT_OF_HIRE   SALARY NOTE
      1  005     NINA BHARUCHA WEBSTER    BSG .T. 05/24/80   25000.00 Memo
```

```
.GOTO TOP       <cr>
.DISP           <cr>
```

Again the first record is displayed:

```
Record#  EMP_NUM EMP_NAME        TOWN      ORG EXE DT_OF_HIRE   SALARY NOTE
      1  005     NINA BHARUCHA WEBSTER    BSG .T. 05/24/80   25000.00 Memo
```

```
.1              <cr>
.DISP           <cr>
```

Since the first record will always be record #1, this is the easiest way to get to the TOP of the file.

Once more the first record is displayed:

```
Record#  EMP_NUM EMP_NAME        TOWN      ORG EXE DT_OF_HIRE   SALARY NOTE
      1  005     NINA BHARUCHA WEBSTER    BSG .T. 05/24/80   25000.00 Memo
```

To get to the bottom of the file very quickly, a similar format is used:

```
.GO BOTTOM      <cr>
.DISP           <cr>
```

Record #15 is displayed:

```
Record#   EMP_NUM EMP_NAME        TOWN      ORG EXE DT_OF_HIRE   SALARY NOTE
    15    075     JOHN JONES       rochester GSD .T. 04/04/70   25100.00 Memo
```

      .GOTO BOTT   <cr>
      .DISP   <cr>

Record #15 is displayed:

```
Record#   EMP_NUM EMP_NAME        TOWN      ORG EXE DT_OF_HIRE   SALARY NOTE
    15    075     JOHN JONES       rochester GSD .T. 04/04/70   25100.00 Memo
```

      .GO BOTT   <cr>
      .DISP   <cr>

Once more Record #15 is displayed:

```
Record#   EMP_NUM EMP_NAME        TOWN      ORG EXE DT_OF_HIRE   SALARY NOTE
    15    075     JOHN JONES       rochester GSD .T. 04/04/70   25100.00 Memo
```

Again the point has to be emphasized that in the absence of any of the parameters, the DISP command will always display the entire record that dBASE happens to be pointing at when the command is issued.

Note: If you try the following stunt:

.10	<cr>	This places the pointer at record 10
.SKIP 9999	<cr>	Since you don't have this many records in your database, dBASE moves the pointer beyond the last record in the file. This is an end-of-file condition.

Record no.   16

      .DISP   <cr>

You see the following:

```
Record#   EMP_NUM EMP_NAME        TOWN      ORG EXE DT_OF_HIRE   SALARY NOTE
```

In effect, there is nothing to display!

If you try something like:

      .10   <cr>
      .SKIP –9999   <cr>   Now dBASE points to record #1.

Record no.   1

      .DISP   <cr>

Record #1 is displayed:

```
Record#   EMP_NUM EMP_NAME        TOWN      ORG EXE DT OF HIRE    SALARY NOTE
      1   005     NINA BHARUCHA WEBSTER     BSG .T. 05/24/80    25000.00 Memo
```

At this point, it is interesting to note that dBASE can be made to react in a conversational manner. The command ? can be read as "WHAT IS . . . ?"

For example:

```
.? 5 + 4            <cr>        results in the value 9.
.? 5 * (10 / 2)     <cr>        results in the value 25.
```

(The * implies multiplication. / is for division)

If a file is in USE, such as in this case, try the following:

```
.? EMP_NAME        <cr>         will display only the employee name
                                of the current record.
```

We shall now proceed with the rest of the parameters of the DISPLAY command. Please note that the DISPLAY command displays the data along with column headings.

The generic format of the DISPLAY is as follows. Note that all parameters are completely optional (given in square brackets).

```
.DISP  [scope]  [field-list]              [FOR <condition>]
                                          [WHILE <condition>]
                                          [TO PRINT]  [OFF]
```

A generic example may be depicted as follows. (Many detailed examples follow.

```
.DISP  (   ALL            (EMP_NUM, FOR TOWN = 'ROCHESTER'   )
       (                  EMP_NAME, WHILE TOWN = 'ROCHESTER'  )
       (   RECO n         ORG)                                )
       (                                                      )
       (   NEXT n                                             )
       (                                                      )
       (   REST                                               )
                      TO PRINT    OFF
```

At this point, let me remind you of the use of the ESC (escape) key. Having typed in a command at the dot prompt, you may either use the back space key to back up to any parameter to be corrected, or you can restart the entire command. To restart, touch ESC to delete the existing command on the command line, and retype the new command.

48

The Scope Parameter

The [scope] parameter tells dBASE what the scope of the operation is supposed to be; that is, how many records you want included in the DISPLAY.

You may have one of four entries for the scope field:

ALL. Obviously, this means that you want all the records displayed. However, a DISPLAY ALL command will only display 19 records at a time on the screen, and then dBASE will wait for you to press any key, at which point it will display the next block of 19 records, and so on.

If the record-length is longer than the screen size, each record will take up more than one line across the screen.

The movement of the records across the screen is called *Scrolling*. To stop/restart the scroll, use Ctrl-S.

As an example, when you enter

.DISP ALL   <cr>

you will see the following:

```
Record#  EMP_NUM EMP_NAME      TOWN       ORG EXE DT_OF_HIRE   SALARY NOTE
      1  005     NINA BHARUCHA WEBSTER    BSG .T. 05/24/80  25000.00 Memo
      2  010     PETE JOHNSON  brighton   BSG .T. 02/03/76  27590.00 Memo
      3  015     GLORIA PATEL  FAIRPORT   RMG .T. 07/16/82  27500.00 Memo
      4  020     MAX LEVINSKY  HENRIETTA  RMG .F. 04/13/69  27550.00 Memo
      5  025     KIM BRANDT    FAIRPORT   RMG .F. 04/04/77  36000.00 Memo
      6  030     TIM MONTAL    ROCHESTER  RBG .F. 07/07/81  41900.00 Memo
      7  035     WILLIAM PATEL penfield   GSD .F. 08/17/71  28900.00 Memo
      8  040     JAMES JAMESON ROCHESTER  GSD .T. 10/21/77  29800.00 Memo
      9  045     MORRIS KATZ   webster    BSG .F. 09/14/80  23450.00 Memo
     10  050     PAUL BHARUCHA BRIGHTON   BSG .T. 05/23/73  29100.00 Memo
     11  055     PHIL MARTIN   WEBSTER    RMG .F. 07/19/80  31000.00 Memo
     12  060     JOHN PETERSON BRIGHTON   RBG .T. 04/17/79  31480.00 Memo
     13  065     JOY HARDY     fairport   RBG .F. 01/19/79  34200.00 Memo
     14  070     JAN MOREY     ROCHESTER  GSD .T. 04/23/67  18190.00 Memo
     15  075     JOHN JONES    rochester  GSD .T. 04/04/70  25100.00 Memo
```

Notice that NOTE is a memo field, and so the word *Memo* is displayed, rather than the contents of the memo. This was one reason for my suggestion that if you are not planning long memos, define the field as a character field instead. Later we will see how to DISPLAY the actual contents of the memo field.

Notice also, that for each field displayed, dBASE has provided a column-width to accommodate the wider of the data or the field name, and there is exactly one column of space between the fields being displayed.

RECO n. To display a specific record by record number, you may say:

.DISP RECO 5   <cr>

and you will see:

```
Record#  EMP_NUM EMP_NAME      TOWN       ORG EXE DT_OF_HIRE   SALARY NOTE
      5  025     KIM BRANDT    FAIRPORT   RMG .F. 04/04/77  36000.00 Memo
```

Record #5 is displayed in full. You may, however, recall that the following combination does the same trick, and you won't make typos:

.5	\<cr\>	This moves the pointer to record #5
.DISP	\<cr\>	This displays the record pointed at.

NEXT n. To display a block of records, say five, starting with record #5, you can do the following:

.5	\<cr\>	This moves the pointer to record #5
.DISP NEXT 5	\<cr\>	

and you will see:

```
Record#   EMP_NUM EMP_NAME       TOWN      ORG EXE DT_OF_HIRE  SALARY NOTE
      5   025     KIM BRANDT     FAIRPORT  RMG .F. 04/04/77  36000.00 Memo
      6   030     TIM MONTAL     ROCHESTER RBG .F. 07/07/81  41900.00 Memo
      7   035     WILLIAM PATEL  penfield  GSD .F. 08/17/71  28900.00 Memo
      8   040     JAMES JAMESON  ROCHESTER GSD .T. 10/21/77  29800.00 Memo
      9   045     MORRIS KATZ    webster   BSG .F. 09/14/80  23450.00 Memo
```

Note that the NEXT N option includes the current record as part of the NEXT parameter. Also, the NEXT n option refers to physical records, not logical occurrences!! This point will be clarified later.

If you ask to DISP more than 19 records, only 19 will show up on the screen, and the system will wait for a key press before displaying the next block of 19 records.

REST. The REST parameter will display the rest of the file, starting with the current record.

.10	\<cr\>
.DISP REST	\<cr\>

```
Record#   EMP_NUM EMP_NAME        TOWN      ORG EXE DT_OF_HIRE  SALARY NOTE
     10   050     PAUL BHARUCHA   BRIGHTON  BSG .T. 05/23/73  29100.00 Memo
     11   055     PHIL MARTIN     WEBSTER   RMG .F. 07/19/80  31000.00 Memo
     12   060     JOHN PETERSON   BRIGHTON  RBG .T. 04/17/79  31480.00 Memo
     13   065     JOY HARDY       fairport  RBG .F. 01/19/79  34200.00 Memo
     14   070     JAN MOREY       ROCHESTER GSD .T. 04/23/67  18190.00 Memo
     15   075     JOHN JONES      rochester GSD .T. 04/04/70  25100.00 Memo
```

The above command is identical to a scope of \<a high number\>. For example, the next command has the identical result as the previous one. Keep in mind that only 19 records will be displayed at one time.

.10	\<cr\>
.DISP NEXT 9999	\<cr\>

```
Record#  EMP_NUM  EMP_NAME       TOWN      ORG EXE DT_OF_HIRE   SALARY NOTE
    10   050      PAUL BHARUCHA  BRIGHTON  BSG .T. 05/23/73   29100.00 Memo
    11   055      PHIL MARTIN    WEBSTER   RMG .F. 07/19/80   31000.00 Memo
    12   060      JOHN PETERSON  BRIGHTON  RBG .T. 04/17/79   31480.00 Memo
    13   065      JOY HARDY      fairport  RBG .F. 01/19/79   34200.00 Memo
    14   070      JAN MOREY      ROCHESTER GSD .T. 04/23/67   18190.00 Memo
    15   075      JOHN JONES     rochester GSD .T. 04/04/70   25100.00 Memo
```

You may have noticed that all data from the logical field has been preceded and succeeded by periods, letting you differentiate that data as being from a logical field, rather than from a character field.

The Field-List/Expression-List Parameter

The next parameter is the field-list parameter. This parameter lets you specify which fields you want displayed from those records selected through the scope parameter. In the absence of the field-list parameter, all the fields are selected for display.

> **Note:** The fields will be displayed in the order in which they are named in the command. Note that the commas in the field list are mandatory!

For example, you could enter

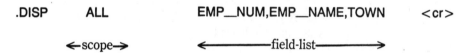

You are asking for a display of data from all records, but only for the fields mentioned in the command. The following listing will be obtained.

```
Record#  EMP_NUM  EMP_NAME       TOWN
     1   005      NINA BHARUCHA  WEBSTER
     2   010      PETE JOHNSON   brighton
     3   015      GLORIA PATEL   FAIRPORT
     4   020      MAX LEVINSKY   HENRIETTA
     5   025      KIM BRANDT     FAIRPORT
     6   030      TIM MONTAL     ROCHESTER
     7   035      WILLIAM PATEL  penfield
     8   040      JAMES JAMESON  ROCHESTER
     9   045      MORRIS KATZ    webster
    10   050      PAUL BHARUCHA  BRIGHTON
    11   055      PHIL MARTIN    WEBSTER
    12   060      JOHN PETERSON  BRIGHTON
    13   065      JOY HARDY      fairport
    14   070      JAN MOREY      ROCHESTER
    15   075      JOHN JONES     rochester
```

If you enter the following:

```
.DISP     ALL          TOWN,ORG,SALARY              <cr>
        ←scope→       ←——field-list——→
```

you will see

```
Record#   TOWN       ORG   SALARY
      1   WEBSTER    BSG   25000.00
      2   brighton   BSG   27590.00
      3   FAIRPORT   RMG   27500.00
      4   HENRIETTA  RMG   27550.00
      5   FAIRPORT   RMG   36000.00
      6   ROCHESTER  RBG   41900.00
      7   penfield   GSD   28900.00
      8   ROCHESTER  GSD   29800.00
      9   webster    BSG   23450.00
     10   BRIGHTON   BSG   29100.00
     11   WEBSTER    RMG   31000.00
     12   BRIGHTON   RBG   31480.00
     13   fairport   RBG   34200.00
     14   ROCHESTER  GSD   18190.00
     15   rochester  GSD   25100.00
```

Try entering:

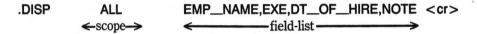

.DISP   ALL   EMP__NAME,EXE,DT__OF__HIRE,NOTE <cr>
        ←scope→   ←————————field-list————————→

In this case, the field NOTE has been specifically mentioned in the field list. So you will see the actual contents of the memos, not just the word *memo*. Note also that depending on how many fields you want to display, the listing of data from a Memo field will not be done as neatly as is shown here; the display of memos is, in fact, a bit cumbersome to control.

You will see the following:

```
Record#   EMP_NAME       EXE DT_OF_HIRE NOTE
      1   NINA BHARUCHA  .T. 05/24/80   To my daughter: Trust you have no
                                        objection to my including your name
                                        in the book.
      2   PETE JOHNSON   .T. 02/03/76   You will be eligible for 3 weeks
                                        vacation as of 12-01-85.
      3   GLORIA PATEL   .T. 07/16/82
      4   MAX LEVINSKY   .F. 04/13/69
      5   KIM BRANDT     .F. 04/04/77   Hope you're enjoying your retirement.
      6   TIM MONTAL     .F. 07/07/81
      7   WILLIAM PATEL  .F. 08/17/71
      8   JAMES JAMESON  .T. 10/21/77
      9   MORRIS KATZ    .F. 09/14/80

     10   PAUL BHARUCHA  .T. 05/23/73   To my son: How could your date of
                                        hire show 1973 when I know you were
                                        born in 1980 ?
     11   PHIL MARTIN    .F. 07/19/80
     12   JOHN PETERSON  .T. 04/17/79   John Peterson, between you and Pete
                                        Johnson, we have managed to make a
                                        successful mess of the payroll.
     13   JOY HARDY      .F. 01/19/79   Any relation to Oliver ?
     14   JAN MOREY      .T. 04/23/67
     15   JOHN JONES     .T. 04/04/70
```

52

If you enter:

```
.DISP     RECO      5      EMP_NAME,TOWN,ORG              <cr>
          ←—scope—→        ←———— field-list ————→
```

```
Record#   EMP_NAME       TOWN       ORG
      5   KIM_BRANDT     FAIRPORT   RMG
```

Note: The field-list parameters could also include expression-lists, if required. You can define your own numerical expressions.

In the next example, we are asking dBASE to display the salaries just as they are, and also to display what the salaries would look like if they were incremented 10 percent. The expression SALARY * 1.1 means salary incremented 10 percent.

```
.DISP     ALL      EMP_NAME, SALARY,SALARY*1.1            <cr>
```

```
Record#   EMP_NAME          SALARY   SALARY*1.1
      1   NINA BHARUCHA   25000.00    27500.000
      2   PETE JOHNSON    27590.00    30349.000
      3   GLORIA PATEL    27500.00    30250.000
      4   MAX LEVINSKY    27550.00    30305.000
      5   KIM BRANDT      36000.00    39600.000
      6   TIM MONTAL      41900.00    46090.000
      7   WILLIAM PATEL   28900.00    31790.000
      8   JAMES JAMESON   29800.00    32780.000
      9   MORRIS KATZ     23450.00    25795.000
     10   PAUL BHARUCHA   29100.00    32010.000
     11   PHIL MARTIN     31000.00    34100.000
     12   JOHN PETERSON   31480.00    34628.000
     13   JOY HARDY       34200.00    37620.000
     14   JAN MOREY       18190.00    20009.000
     15   JOHN JONES      25100.00    27610.000
```

Please note that the above DISPLAY ALL command merely shows what the SALARY would look like, if it were incremented 10 percent. It does not, in any way, change the salary data in the file!!

You can start from a specific position in the database. When you enter:

```
.5    <cr>
.DISP   NEXT 5      EMP_NAME,ORG,DT_OF_HIRE              <cr>
        ←—scope→    ←——————— field-list ———————→
```

you will see:

```
Record#   EMP_NAME        ORG   DT_OF_HIRE
      5   KIM_BRANDT      RMG   04/04/77
      6   TIM MONTAL      RBG   07/07/81
      7   WILLIAM PATEL   GSD   08/17/71
      8   JAMES JAMESON   GSD   10/21/77
      9   MORRIS KATZ     BSG   09/14/80
```

As noted before, commas in the field list in the command line are mandatory!

The FOR Condition

The FOR <condition> parameter is very powerful. It lets you specify simple or complex conditions under which records may be selected for display.

> **Note:** If a scope parameter has not been specified in the command, but a FOR condition has been mentioned, then ALL is the default for scope. That is, all the records that satisfy the condition will be selected for display, unless a specific <scope> has been mentioned. If more than 19 records qualify for the display, the system will display the first 19, then wait for any key entry before it displays the next block of 19 qualifying records, and so on.
>
> **Note:** When you specify values to be satisfied in a condition, then in the case of character fields, the values will have to be supplied in quotes (single quotes or double quotes are both OK). In the case of numeric fields, the values supplied should not be in quotes. For logical fields, no values are necessary, as explained later in this chapter. Date fields would have to be specified either as character or numeric, depending on the context. This will be amply clarified by examples later. Memo fields cannot be used in the FOR expression.
>
> **Note:** When you specify values to be satisfied in a condition, then in the case of character fields, dBASE will take the value that you supply in the literal sense.

Some examples showing the use of the FOR condition follow:

.DISP   FOR   TOWN = 'ROCHESTER'   <cr>

Since a [scope] of operation has not been specified, but a FOR condition has been specified, the default for [scope] is ALL. Note that all those records in which the TOWN field has the literal value ROCHESTER are selected for display.

```
Record#  EMP_NUM EMP_NAME      TOWN      ORG EXE DT_OF_HIRE   SALARY NOTE
     6   030     TIM MONTAL    ROCHESTER RBG .F. 07/07/81  41900.00 Memo
     8   040     JAMES JAMESON ROCHESTER GSD .T. 10/21/77  29800.00 Memo
    14   070     JAN MOREY     ROCHESTER GSD .T. 04/23/67  18190.00 Memo
```

.DISP FOR TOWN = 'rochester'   <cr>

Note that only those records in which the TOWN field has the literal value rochester are selected for display.

```
Record#  EMP_NUM EMP_NAME  TOWN      ORG EXE DT_OF_HIRE   SALARY NOTE
    15   075     JOHN JONES rochester GSD .T. 04/04/70  25100.00 Memo
```

> **Note:** You can provide a generic key. That is, the full key value does not need to be provided. But again, the value you provide must be in quotes since TOWN is a character field.

In the next command, all the records that have an uppercase R O C H in the first four character-positions of the TOWN field will be selected for display.

.DISP FOR TOWN = 'ROCH'   <cr>

Record#	EMP_NUM	EMP_NAME	TOWN	ORG	EXE	DT_OF_HIRE	SALARY	NOTE
6	030	TIM MONTAL	ROCHESTER	RBG	.F.	07/07/81	41900.00	Memo
8	040	JAMES JAMESON	ROCHESTER	GSD	.T.	10/21/77	29800.00	Memo
14	070	JAN MOREY	ROCHESTER	GSD	.T.	04/23/67	18190.00	Memo

.DISP FOR TOWN = 'R'   <cr>

The results are the same as before. All the records that have a town beginning with an uppercase R are selected for display.

Record#	EMP_NUM	EMP_NAME	TOWN	ORG	EXE	DT_OF_HIRE	SALARY	NOTE
6	030	TIM MONTAL	ROCHESTER	RBG	.F.	07/07/81	41900.00	Memo
8	040	JAMES JAMESON	ROCHESTER	GSD	.T.	10/21/77	29800.00	Memo
14	070	JAN MOREY	ROCHESTER	GSD	.T.	04/23/67	18190.00	Memo

The line below also gives the same results.

.DISP   FOR   TOWN =   'R'   <cr>

This example highlights the fact that the commands are essentially *free form*. Spaces before and/or after the parameters and/or logical operators (in this case, the = sign) do not matter.

> **Note:** In all cases, previous and succeeding, you will note that we have compared the *field name* to the *literal*, not the other way around. Always maintain this sequence! If you try to write the statement as .DISP FOR 'ROCH' = TOWN, you find that nothing qualifies!

If you enter the following command:

.DISP   RECO   5   FOR TOWN = 'R'   <cr>

you will see this:

Record#	EMP_NUM	EMP_NAME	TOWN	ORG	EXE	DT_OF_HIRE	SALARY	NOTE

Record 5 may or may not qualify for display, depending on the data in the record. In this case, it does not qualify.

Study the following example carefully:

.USE PERSNL   <cr>
.DISP ALL   <cr>

Record#	EMP_NUM	EMP_NAME	TOWN	ORG	EXE	DT_OF_HIRE	SALARY	NOTE
1	005	NINA BHARUCHA	WEBSTER	BSG	.T.	05/24/80	25000.00	Memo
2	010	PETE JOHNSON	brighton	BSG	.T.	02/03/76	27590.00	Memo
3	015	GLORIA PATEL	FAIRPORT	RMG	.T.	07/16/82	27500.00	Memo
4	020	MAX LEVINSKY	HENRIETTA	RMG	.F.	04/13/69	27550.00	Memo
5	025	KIM BRANDT	FAIRPORT	RMG	.F.	04/04/77	36000.00	Memo
6	030	TIM MONTAL	ROCHESTER	RBG	.F.	07/07/81	41900.00	Memo
7	035	WILLIAM PATEL	penfield	GSD	.F.	08/17/71	28900.00	Memo
8	040	JAMES JAMESON	ROCHESTER	GSD	.T.	10/21/77	29800.00	Memo
9	045	MORRIS KATZ	webster	BSG	.F.	09/14/80	23450.00	Memo
10	050	PAUL BHARUCHA	BRIGHTON	BSG	.T.	05/23/73	29100.00	Memo
11	055	PHIL MARTIN	WEBSTER	RMG	.F.	07/19/80	31000.00	Memo
12	060	JOHN PETERSON	BRIGHTON	RBG	.T.	04/17/79	31480.00	Memo
13	065	JOY HARDY	fairport	RBG	.F.	01/19/79	34200.00	Memo
14	070	JAN MOREY	ROCHESTER	GSD	.T.	04/23/67	18190.00	Memo
15	075	JOHN JONES	rochester	GSD	.T.	04/04/70	25100.00	Memo

Now type the following:

```
.  1          <cr>              This moves the record pointer to record #1.
.DISP NEXT 4    FOR TOWN = 'FAIR'          <cr>
```

Record#	EMP_NUM	EMP_NAME	TOWN	ORG	EXE	DT_OF_HIRE	SALARY	NOTE
3	015	GLORIA PATEL	FAIRPORT	RMG	.T.	07/16/82	27500.00	Memo

Since the NEXT n parameter refers to physical records, not logical occurrences, dBASE will check the NEXT 4 physical records, starting with the current record, and out of those four records, any with TOWN = 'FAIR' will be displayed. dBASE will not look for any four (logical) records anywhere in the file that have a TOWN = 'FAIR'. This is what we mean when we say that the NEXT n parameter refers to physical records, not logical occurrences. That is, we can say that "scope has priority over condition."

The Effect of Sequencing

To the microcomputer, if data were sequenced in normal ascending sequence, then all numbers "come ahead of" (are "logically lower" than) all letters, and within the letter series, the uppercase letters "come ahead of" (are "logically lower" than) the lowercase letters. That is, if you asked for a display sequenced by town, of all the records in our file, you will obtain the following listing. Notice that the record numbers are still the original numbers from the database; the records have only been resequenced to show the result of ascending sequence. The exact processes of sequencing are covered in detail, in a later section.

Record#	EMP_NUM	EMP_NAME	TOWN	ORG	EXE	DT_OF_HIRE	SALARY	NOTE
10	050	PAUL BHARUCHA	BRIGHTON	BSG	.T.	05/23/73	29100.00	Memo
12	060	JOHN PETERSON	BRIGHTON	RBG	.T.	04/17/79	31480.00	Memo
3	015	GLORIA PATEL	FAIRPORT	RMG	.T.	07/16/82	27500.00	Memo
5	025	KIM BRANDT	FAIRPORT	RMG	.F.	04/04/77	36000.00	Memo
4	020	MAX LEVINSKY	HENRIETTA	RMG	.F.	04/13/69	27550.00	Memo
6	030	TIM MONTAL	ROCHESTER	RBG	.F.	07/07/81	41900.00	Memo
8	040	JAMES JAMESON	ROCHESTER	GSD	.T.	10/21/77	29800.00	Memo

```
14   070   JAN MOREY      ROCHESTER GSD .T. 04/23/67  18190.00 Memo
 1   005   NINA BHARUCHA WEBSTER   BSG .T. 05/24/80  25000.00 Memo
11   055   PHIL MARTIN    WEBSTER   RMG .F. 07/19/80  31000.00 Memo
 2   010   PETE JOHNSON   brighton  BSG .T. 02/03/76  27590.00 Memo
13   065   JOY HARDY      fairport  RBG .F. 01/19/79  34200.00 Memo
 7   035   WILLIAM PATEL  penfield  GSD .F. 08/17/71  28900.00 Memo
15   075   JOHN JONES     rochester GSD .T. 04/04/70  25100.00 Memo
 9   045   MORRIS KATZ    webster   BSG .F. 09/14/80  23450.00 Memo
```

The FOR Condition Continued

Keeping the effects of sequencing in mind, let us now try the following experiments, with the original PERSNL file as input:

When you type:

.DISP   FOR   TOWN   <   'R'   <cr>

(< is the less than symbol)

all towns whose data begins with any letter below R in the alphabet series will be selected for display. (Remember the quotes and the rules for UPPER/lowercase sequencing.)

```
Record#  EMP_NUM EMP_NAME      TOWN       ORG EXE DT_OF_HIRE  SALARY NOTE
    3    015   GLORIA PATEL    FAIRPORT   RMG .T. 07/16/82  27500.00 Memo
    4    020   MAX LEVINSKY    HENRIETTA  RMG .F. 04/13/69  27550.00 Memo
    5    025   KIM BRANDT      FAIRPORT   RMG .F. 04/04/77  36000.00 Memo
   10    050   PAUL BHARUCHA   BRIGHTON   BSG .T. 05/23/73  29100.00 Memo
   12    060   JOHN PETERSON   BRIGHTON   RBG .T. 04/17/79  31480.00 Memo
```

When you type:

.DISP   FOR   TOWN   >   "R"   <cr>

(> is the greater than symbol)

all towns whose data begins with any letter above R in the alphabet series will be selected for display. (Remember the quotes and the rules for UPPER/lowercase. Single or double quotes are both OK.)

```
Record#  EMP_NUM EMP_NAME      TOWN       ORG EXE DT_OF_HIRE  SALARY NOTE
    1    005   NINA BHARUCHA  WEBSTER    BSG .T. 05/24/80  25000.00 Memo
    2    010   PETE JOHNSON   brighton   BSG .T. 02/03/76  27590.00 Memo
    7    035   WILLIAM PATEL  penfield   GSD .F. 08/17/71  28900.00 Memo
    9    045   MORRIS KATZ    webster    BSG .F. 09/14/80  23450.00 Memo
   11    055   PHIL MARTIN    WEBSTER    RMG .F. 07/19/80  31000.00 Memo
   13    065   JOY HARDY      fairport   RBG .F. 01/19/79  34200.00 Memo
   15    075   JOHN JONES     rochester  GSD .T. 04/04/70  25100.00 Memo
```

<> is the "not equal to" symbol. Note that you cannot enter this symbol as < >. There cannot be any spaces in between, because the <> sign, although made up of two key strokes, is considered as one symbol.

When you enter:

.DISP FOR TOWN <> 'R' \<cr>

all towns whose name begins with any letter not equal to R in the alphabet series will
be selected for display. (Remember the quotes; single or double quotes are both OK.)

Record#	EMP_NUM	EMP_NAME	TOWN	ORG	EXE	DT_OF_HIRE	SALARY	NOTE
1	005	NINA BHARUCHA	WEBSTER	BSG	.T.	05/24/80	25000.00	Memo
2	010	PETE JOHNSON	brighton	BSG	.T.	02/03/76	27590.00	Memo
3	015	GLORIA PATEL	FAIRPORT	RMG	.T.	07/16/82	27500.00	Memo
4	020	MAX LEVINSKY	HENRIETTA	RMG	.F.	04/13/69	27550.00	Memo
5	025	KIM BRANDT	FAIRPORT	RMG	.F.	04/04/77	36000.00	Memo
7	035	WILLIAM PATEL	penfield	GSD	.F.	08/17/71	28900.00	Memo
9	045	MORRIS KATZ	webster	BSG	.F.	09/14/80	23450.00	Memo
10	050	PAUL BHARUCHA	BRIGHTON	BSG	.T.	05/23/73	29100.00	Memo
11	055	PHIL MARTIN	WEBSTER	RMG	.F.	07/19/80	31000.00	Memo
12	060	JOHN PETERSON	BRIGHTON	RBG	.T.	04/17/79	31480.00	Memo
13	065	JOY HARDY	fairport	RBG	.F.	01/19/79	34200.00	Memo
15	075	JOHN JONES	rochester	GSD	.T.	04/04/70	25100.00	Memo

The # sign can also be used as the "not equal to" symbol. When you type:

.DISP FOR TOWN # 'R' \<cr>

you get the same result as before. This form may be easier to type in.

.DISP FOR TOWN <= 'R' \<cr>

This is the "less than or equal to" combination. Again, you cannot type this in as
< = (no spaces in between!). The <= is considered as one symbol. Note that <=
works, but =< is invalid!

Record#	EMP_NUM	EMP_NAME	TOWN	ORG	EXE	DT_OF_HIRE	SALARY	NOTE
3	015	GLORIA PATEL	FAIRPORT	RMG	.T.	07/16/82	27500.00	Memo
4	020	MAX LEVINSKY	HENRIETTA	RMG	.F.	04/13/69	27550.00	Memo
5	025	KIM BRANDT	FAIRPORT	RMG	.F.	04/04/77	36000.00	Memo
6	030	TIM MONTAL	ROCHESTER	RBG	.F.	07/07/81	41900.00	Memo
8	040	JAMES JAMESON	ROCHESTER	GSD	.T.	10/21/77	29800.00	Memo
10	050	PAUL BHARUCHA	BRIGHTON	BSG	.T.	05/23/73	29100.00	Memo
12	060	JOHN PETERSON	BRIGHTON	RBG	.T.	04/17/79	31480.00	Memo
14	070	JAN MOREY	ROCHESTER	GSD	.T.	04/23/67	18190.00	Memo

.DISP FOR TOWN >= 'R' \<cr>

This is the "greater than or equal to" combination. Again, you cannot type this
in as > = (no spaces in between!) because the >= is considered as one symbol. Note
that >= works, but => is invalid!

Record#	EMP_NUM	EMP_NAME	TOWN	ORG	EXE	DT_OF_HIRE	SALARY	NOTE
1	005	NINA BHARUCHA	WEBSTER	BSG	.T.	05/24/80	25000.00	Memo
2	010	PETE JOHNSON	brighton	BSG	.T.	02/03/76	27590.00	Memo
6	030	TIM MONTAL	ROCHESTER	RBG	.F.	07/07/81	41900.00	Memo

```
 7   035   WILLIAM PATEL  penfield  GSD .F. 08/17/71   28900.00 Memo
 8   040   JAMES JAMESON  ROCHESTER GSD .T. 10/21/77   29800.00 Memo
 9   045   MORRIS KATZ    webster   BSG .F. 09/14/80   23450.00 Memo
11   055   PHIL MARTIN    WEBSTER   RMG .F. 07/19/80   31000.00 Memo
13   065   JOY HARDY      fairport  RBG .F. 01/19/79   34200.00 Memo
14   070   JAN MOREY      ROCHESTER GSD .T. 04/23/67   18190.00 Memo
15   075   JOHN JONES     rochester GSD .T. 04/04/70   25100.00 Memo
```

Now let us play around with numeric fields. Below are some sample commands and their results.

Note: When you specify values to be satisfied in a condition, then in the case of numeric fields, dBASE will take the value that you supply in the algebraic sense. Notice that the value supplied should not be in quotes.

.DISP FOR SALARY < 25000   <cr>

```
Record#  EMP_NUM EMP_NAME     TOWN      ORG EXE DT_OF_HIRE   SALARY NOTE
     9   045     MORRIS KATZ  webster   BSG .F. 09/14/80   23450.00 Memo
    14   070     JAN MOREY    ROCHESTER GSD .T. 04/23/67   18190.00 Memo
```

.DISP FOR SALARY # 25000   <cr>

```
Record#  EMP_NUM EMP_NAME       TOWN      ORG EXE DT_OF_HIRE   SALARY NOTE
     2   010     PETE JOHNSON   brighton  BSG .T. 02/03/76   27590.00 Memo
     3   015     GLORIA PATEL   FAIRPORT  RMG .T. 07/16/82   27500.00 Memo
     4   020     MAX LEVINSKY   HENRIETTA RMG .F. 04/13/69   27550.00 Memo
     5   025     KIM BRANDT     FAIRPORT  RMG .F. 04/04/77   36000.00 Memo
     6   030     TIM MONTAL     ROCHESTER RBG .F. 07/07/81   41900.00 Memo
     7   035     WILLIAM PATEL  penfield  GSD .F. 08/17/71   28900.00 Memo
     8   040     JAMES JAMESON  ROCHESTER GSD .T. 10/21/77   29800.00 Memo
     9   045     MORRIS KATZ    webster   BSG .F. 09/14/80   23450.00 Memo
    10   050     PAUL BHARUCHA  BRIGHTON  BSG .T. 05/23/73   29100.00 Memo
    11   055     PHIL MARTIN    WEBSTER   RMG .F. 07/19/80   31000.00 Memo
    12   060     JOHN PETERSON  BRIGHTON  RBG .T. 04/17/79   31480.00 Memo
    13   065     JOY HARDY      fairport  RBG .F. 01/19/79   34200.00 Memo
    14   070     JAN MOREY      ROCHESTER GSD .T. 04/23/67   18190.00 Memo
    15   075     JOHN JONES     rochester GSD .T. 04/04/70   25100.00 Memo
```

.DISP FOR SALARY> 25000   <cr>

```
Record#  EMP_NUM EMP_NAME       TOWN      ORG EXE DT_OF_HIRE   SALARY NOTE
     2   010     PETE JOHNSON   brighton  BSG .T. 02/03/76   27590.00 Memo
     3   015     GLORIA PATEL   FAIRPORT  RMG .T. 07/16/82   27500.00 Memo
     4   020     MAX LEVINSKY   HENRIETTA RMG .F. 04/13/69   27550.00 Memo
     5   025     KIM BRANDT     FAIRPORT  RMG .F. 04/04/77   36000.00 Memo
     6   030     TIM MONTAL     ROCHESTER RBG .F. 07/07/81   41900.00 Memo
     7   035     WILLIAM PATEL  penfield  GSD .F. 08/17/71   28900.00 Memo
     8   040     JAMES JAMESON  ROCHESTER GSD .T. 10/21/77   29800.00 Memo
     9   045     MORRIS KATZ    webster   BSG .F. 09/14/80   23450.00 Memo
    10   050     PAUL BHARUCHA  BRIGHTON  BSG .T. 05/23/73   29100.00 Memo
    11   055     PHIL MARTIN    WEBSTER   RMG .F. 07/19/80   31000.00 Memo
```

```
12  060    JOHN PETERSON BRIGHTON    RBG .T. 04/17/79    31480.00 Memo
13  065    JOY HARDY     fairport    RBG .F. 01/19/79    34200.00 Memo
15  075    JOHN JONES    rochester   GSD .T. 04/04/70    25100.00 Memo
```

.DISP   FOR   SALARY   >=   25000   <cr>

```
Record#  EMP_NUM EMP_NAME     TOWN      ORG EXE DT_OF_HIRE   SALARY NOTE
      1  005     NINA BHARUCHA WEBSTER   BSG .T. 05/24/80   25000.00 Memo
      2  010     PETE JOHNSON  brighton  BSG .T. 02/03/76   27590.00 Memo
      3  015     GLORIA PATEL  FAIRPORT  RMG .T. 07/16/82   27500.00 Memo
      4  020     MAX LEVINSKY  HENRIETTA RMG .F. 04/13/69   27550.00 Memo
      5  025     KIM BRANDT    FAIRPORT  RMG .F. 04/04/77   36000.00 Memo
      6  030     TIM MONTAL    ROCHESTER RBG .F. 07/07/81   41900.00 Memo
      7  035     WILLIAM PATEL penfield  GSD .F. 08/17/71   28900.00 Memo
      8  040     JAMES JAMESON ROCHESTER GSD .T. 10/21/77   29800.00 Memo
     10  050     PAUL BHARUCHA BRIGHTON  BSG .T. 05/23/73   29100.00 Memo
     11  055     PHIL MARTIN   WEBSTER   RMG .F. 07/19/80   31000.00 Memo
     12  060     JOHN PETERSON BRIGHTON  RBG .T. 04/17/79   31480.00 Memo
     13  065     JOY HARDY     fairport  RBG .F. 01/19/79   34200.00 Memo
     15  075     JOHN JONES    rochester GSD .T. 04/04/70   25100.00 Memo
```

.DISP FOR SALARY <= 25000   <cr>

```
Record#  EMP_NUM EMP_NAME     TOWN      ORG EXE DT_OF_HIRE   SALARY NOTE
      1  005     NINA BHARUCHA WEBSTER   BSG .T. 05/24/80   25000.00 Memo
      9  045     MORRIS KATZ   webster   BSG .F. 09/14/80   23450.00 Memo
```

The WHILE Parameter

In the case of the FOR parameter, all the records that satisfy the FOR condition are selected for display (unless, of course, a specific SCOPE is used).

The WHILE parameter will select records only *while* a condition is true. In other words, even though a record would have normally qualified for a condition, it would not be displayed if it is in the wrong place in the file, and another record has forced the WHILE condition to be <false>.

Look again at the data in the PERSNL file, then study the following example of the difference between the use of the FOR condition and the use of the WHILE condition. First, here is the entire database for you to review.

```
Record#  EMP_NUM EMP_NAME      TOWN      ORG EXE DT_OF_HIRE   SALARY NOTE
      1  005     NINA BHARUCHA  WEBSTER   BSG .T. 05/24/80   25000.00 Memo
      2  010     PETE JOHNSON   brighton  BSG .T. 02/03/76   27590.00 Memo
      3  015     GLORIA PATEL   FAIRPORT  RMG .T. 07/16/82   27500.00 Memo
      4  020     MAX LEVINSKY   HENRIETTA RMG .F. 04/13/69   27550.00 Memo
      5  025     KIM BRANDT     FAIRPORT  RMG .F. 04/04/77   36000.00 Memo
      6  030     TIM MONTAL     ROCHESTER RBG .F. 07/07/81   41900.00 Memo
      7  035     WILLIAM PATEL  penfield  GSD .F. 08/17/71   28900.00 Memo
      8  040     JAMES JAMESON  ROCHESTER GSD .T. 10/21/77   29800.00 Memo
      9  045     MORRIS KATZ    webster   BSG .F. 09/14/80   23450.00 Memo
     10  050     PAUL BHARUCHA  BRIGHTON  BSG .T. 05/23/73   29100.00 Memo
     11  055     PHIL MARTIN    WEBSTER   RMG .F. 07/19/80   31000.00 Memo
     12  060     JOHN PETERSON  BRIGHTON  RBG .T. 04/17/79   31480.00 Memo
     13  065     JOY HARDY      fairport  RBG .F. 01/19/79   34200.00 Memo
     14  070     JAN MOREY      ROCHESTER GSD .T. 04/23/67   18190.00 Memo
     15  075     JOHN JONES     rochester GSD .T. 04/04/70   25100.00 Memo
```

```
         .USE PERSNL                        <cr>
         .6                                 <cr>    This brings the record
                                                    pointer to # 6.

         .DISP WHILE TOWN = 'ROCH'          <cr>
```

```
Record#  EMP_NUM EMP_NAME     TOWN       ORG EXE DT_OF_HIRE   SALARY NOTE
      6  030     TIM MONTAL   ROCHESTER RBG .F. 07/07/81    41900.00 Memo
```

Notice that only record #6 is displayed, since it satisfied the condition, and record #7 broke the condition, so the listing stopped.

```
         .DISP FOR TOWN = 'ROCHESTER'       <cr>
```

```
Record#  EMP_NUM EMP_NAME       TOWN       ORG EXE DT_OF_HIRE   SALARY NOTE
      6  030     TIM MONTAL     ROCHESTER RBG .F. 07/07/81    41900.00 Memo
      8  040     JAMES JAMESON  ROCHESTER GSD .T. 10/21/77    29800.00 Memo
     14  070     JAN MOREY      ROCHESTER GSD .T. 04/23/67    18190.00 Memo
```

Notice above, that all the records that satisfied the FOR condition were selected for display.

The WHILE condition displays records only as long as successive records fulfill the same condition, whereas the FOR condition pulls out all records that satisfy the condition, regardless of their positions in the database. As always, if more than 19 records qualify, the system will wait for a key press between blocks of 19 records.

Look again at the full listing of the PERSNL file (presented just a little earlier), and study the next example, in which the WHILE and the FOR are included in the same statement.

```
         .1
         .DISP NEXT 10    FOR SALARY > 20000    WHILE EXE    <cr>
```

```
Record#  EMP_NUM EMP_NAME     TOWN       ORG EXE DT_OF_HIRE   SALARY NOTE
      1  005     NINA BHARUCHA WEBSTER   BSG .T. 05/24/80    25000.00 Memo
      2  010     PETE JOHNSON  brighton  BSG .T. 02/03/76    27590.00 Memo
      3  015     GLORIA PATEL  FAIRPORT  RMG .T. 07/16/82    27500.00 Memo
```

Notice that although many more than three records qualify for the SALARY condition, the very first nonexempt record (record #4) has forced the listing to end. That is, WHILE takes priority over FOR.

Using Logical Fields with DISPLAY

Note the following command:

```
         .DISPLAY   FOR   EXE          <cr>
```

Notice that we don't need any *logical operators* in this case, since we are dealing with a logical field. The implication is that we are asking for a display of all records in which EXEMPT = <true>

```
Record#   EMP_NUM  EMP_NAME        TOWN       ORG EXE  DT_OF_HIRE   SALARY NOTE
      1   005      NINA BHARUCHA   WEBSTER    BSG .T.  05/24/80   25000.00 Memo
      2   010      PETE JOHNSON    brighton   BSG .T.  02/03/76   27590.00 Memo
      3   015      GLORIA PATEL    FAIRPORT   RMG .T.  07/16/82   27500.00 Memo
      8   040      JAMES JAMESON   ROCHESTER  GSD .T.  10/21/77   29800.00 Memo
     10   050      PAUL BHARUCHA   BRIGHTON   BSG .T.  05/23/73   29100.00 Memo
     12   060      JOHN PETERSON   BRIGHTON   RBG .T.  04/17/79   31480.00 Memo
     14   070      JAN MOREY       ROCHESTER  GSD .T.  04/23/67   18190.00 Memo
     15   075      JOHN JONES      rochester  GSD .T.  04/04/70   25100.00 Memo
```

The following command:

.DISPLAY FOR   .NOT. EXE   <cr>

implies that we are asking for a display of all records in which EXEMPT = <false>

```
Record#   EMP_NUM  EMP_NAME        TOWN       ORG EXE  DT_OF_HIRE   SALARY NOTE
      4   020      MAX LEVINSKY    HENRIETTA  RMG .F.  04/13/69   27550.00 Memo
      5   025      KIM BRANDT      FAIRPORT   RMG .F.  04/04/77   36000.00 Memo
      6   030      TIM MONTAL      ROCHESTER  RBG .F.  07/07/81   41900.00 Memo
      7   035      WILLIAM PATEL   penfield   GSD .F.  08/17/71   28900.00 Memo
      9   045      MORRIS KATZ     webster    BSG .F.  09/14/80   23450.00 Memo
     11   055      PHIL MARTIN     WEBSTER    RMG .F.  07/19/80   31000.00 Memo
     13   065      JOY HARDY       fairport   RBG .F.  01/19/79   34200.00 Memo
```

If the field called EXEMPT had been defined as a regular character field, then to obtain the above listings would have required the following display commands to be entered:

.DISPLAY FOR EXE = 'T'   <cr>

and

.DISPLAY FOR EXE = 'F'   <cr>

Using DATE Fields with DISPLAY

Several examples of the DISPLAY command using Date fields will be provided later, when you study the section concerning functions.

Using MEMO Fields with DISPLAY

To display a memo field, you could enter the following commands:

.1   <cr>   This moves the pointer to record #1
.DISP NEXT 4 EMP_NAME,EXE,DT_OF_HIRE,NOTE   <cr>

        ←scope→ ←————————field list————————→

```
Record#   EMP_NAME       EXE DT_OF_HIRE NOTE
      1   NINA BHARUCHA  .T. 05/24/80   To my daughter: Trust you have no
                                        objection to my including your name
                                        in the book.
```

62

```
 2  PETE JOHNSON   .T. 02/03/76    You will be eligible for 3 weeks
                                   vacation as of 12-01-85.
 3  GLORIA PATEL   .T. 07/16/82
 4  MAX LEVINSKY   .F. 04/13/69
```

As explained earlier, if you don't plan on too many characters in your memos, you would be well-advised to define those fields as character fields. This point will be better appreciated when you have studied the section on functions.

Complex and Multiple Conditions

You can have more than one condition under which records may be selected for display. Below are some examples:

.DISP FOR TOWN = 'ROCH' .AND. SALARY < 25000   <cr>

Note: There are always *periods* preceding and succeeding the *logical operators*. The logical operators are AND, OR, and NOT.

```
Record#  EMP_NUM EMP_NAME      TOWN      ORG EXE DT_OF_HIRE   SALARY NOTE
    14   070     JAN MOREY     ROCHESTER GSD .T. 04/23/67   18190.00 Memo
```

.DISP FOR ORG = 'BSG' .AND. SALARY > = 25000   <cr>

```
Record#  EMP_NUM EMP_NAME      TOWN      ORG EXE DT_OF_HIRE   SALARY NOTE
     1   005     NINA BHARUCHA WEBSTER   BSG .T. 05/24/80   25000.00 Memo
     2   010     PETE JOHNSON  brighton  BSG .T. 02/03/76   27590.00 Memo
    10   050     PAUL BHARUCHA BRIGHTON  BSG .T. 05/23/73   29100.00 Memo
```

.DISP EMP__NUM,EMP__NAME,ORG FOR ORG = 'BSG' .OR. ORG = 'GSD' <cr>

```
     Record#  EMP_NUM EMP_NAME      ORG

         1    005     NINA BHARUCHA BSG
         2    010     PETE JOHNSON  BSG
         7    035     WILLIAM PATEL GSD
         8    040     JAMES JAMESON GSD
         9    045     MORRIS KATZ   BSG
        10    050     PAUL BHARUCHA BSG
        14    070     JAN MOREY     GSD
        15    075     JOHN JONES    GSD
```

You can have any combination of multiple ANDs and ORs.

.DISP FOR TOWN = 'ROCH' .AND. (ORG = 'BSG' .OR. ORG = 'GSD')<cr>

You must use parentheses in order to clarify the intended logic of your command statement. In the absence of parentheses, dBASE will take its own default logic and proceed with an output that you may not have intended at all. In the previous example, we wanted a listing of those records where the TOWN was ROCH and where the ORG was either BSG or GSD.

```
Record#  EMP_NUM EMP_NAME      TOWN      ORG EXE DT OF HIRE    SALARY NOTE
      8  040     JAMES JAMESON ROCHESTER GSD .T. 10/21/77   29800.00 Memo
     14  070     JAN MOREY     ROCHESTER GSD .T. 04/23/67   18190.00 Memo
```

If you enter a command with too many logical operators, you will find that the command line scrolls to the left, as you continue keying in more operators and parameters to the right. This long command will work just as well as any other command, providing that the syntax is correct. You can use the backspace key to make corrections to the long command line or use the ESC (escape) key to escape from this command and start a new one.

The TO PRINT Parameter

As can easily be guessed, all of the above selective displays can be made to go to the printer with the TO PRINT phrase.

The OFF Parameter

The final parameter, for now, is the OFF parameter. This parameter simply removes the record numbers from display. If you have noticed, each of our previous displays had record numbers displayed. (These record numbers were provided by dBASE, as records were appended into the database.) The OFF parameter specifies that you do not want to see the record numbers.

```
.DISP  FOR  TOWN = 'ROCH'   OFF        <cr>

EMP_NUM EMP_NAME      TOWN      ORG EXE DT_OF_HIRE    SALARY NOTE

030     TIM MONTAL    ROCHESTER RBG .F. 07/07/81   41900.00 Memo
040     JAMES JAMESON ROCHESTER GSD .T. 10/21/77   29800.00 Memo
070     JAN MOREY     ROCHESTER GSD .T. 04/23/67   18190.00 Memo
```

THE LIST COMMAND

We had mentioned earlier that the DISP ALL command, regardless of other parameters in the command, will only display up to 19 records at a time on the screen. Even if a FOR <condition> has been mentioned, if more than 19 records qualify for the condition, only 19 records at a time are displayed.

There is another command called the LIST command, which is the same as DISPLAY ALL except that the LIST command has the advantage of not stopping after every 19 records. This is the only difference between DISP ALL and LIST. The parameters of the LIST command are identical to the parameters of the DISPLAY ALL command.

A LIST command will display the entire database on the screen in a rapid *scroll* mode.

> **Note:** On the computer running under either CP/M or MS-DOS, you can temporarily freeze the scroll movement on the screen, during LIST or DISP ALL, via the Ctrl-S option. Another Ctrl-S will restart the scroll movement. That is, Ctrl-S is used as a toggle switch

to stop and restart the scroll movement, during either a DISP ALL or a LIST execution.

.USE PERSNL	\<cr\>	
.LIST	\<cr\>	will list the data on the screen
.LIST TO PRINT	\<cr\>	will send the listing also on the printer.

Note: When sending a LIST (or DISP ALL) to the printer, make sure your printer is in a ready state; otherwise you will be aborted out of dBASE and back to the operating system prompt.

SPECIAL FUNCTIONS

Functions are utility routines built into dBASE that help the user and/or programmer perform specialized tasks. Without these assembly-level routines, these specialized tasks become very difficult, if not impossible, to perform. Using these special built-in functions of dBASE, you can really bolster the power of the DISPLAY (and other) commands. The special functions should be memorized as soon as possible because of the increased capability they provide.

We will be concentrating on those functions most useful in routine tasks and in programs. The complete set of functions is described in the dBASE technical manual.

The TYPE Function

At any time during the processing of a dBASE file, if you want to find out the TYPE definition of any field (character, numeric, logical, date, or memo), you could always enter:

.DISP STRU   \<cr\>

This will display the entire structure, and you could get the information you wanted. If you only wanted to find out the type of any one field, you would enter:

? TYPE('EMP_NUM')   \<cr\>   to verify the type for the EMP_NUM
C   field.

is dBASE's response. The response will always be C, N, L, D, or M (for the various field types). Note that if dBASE responds with a U (for undefined), you have committed some kind of syntax error in the command.

The Substring Function

The substring function applies only to character fields. It is to be used if you want to check for the occurrence of a required string of characters within a character field. For example:

.DISP FOR TOWN = 'ROCH'   <cr>

will select only those records that have an uppercase ROCH in the first four positions of the TOWN field.

If you wanted to select records that had an OCH in the second through the fourth locations of the town field, you would have to specify the following:

.DISP FOR   SUBSTR(TOWN,2,3)   =   'OCH'   <cr>

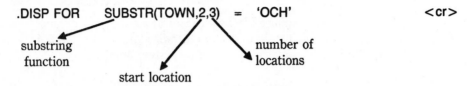

substring
function

start location

number of
locations

You are dividing the town field into substrings, and you must specify the start location (character position 2) and the number of locations (in this case, 3). This command displays all those records that have an uppercase OCH in columns 2, 3, and 4 of the TOWN field. As before, the value you supply, (in this case OCH) should be in quotes, since TOWN is a character field.

Record#	EMP_NUM	EMP_NAME	TOWN	ORG	EXE	DT_OF_HIRE	SALARY	NOTE
6	030	TIM MONTAL	ROCHESTER	RBG	.F.	07/07/81	41900.00	Memo
8	040	JAMES JAMESON	ROCHESTER	GSD	.T.	10/21/77	29800.00	Memo
14	070	JAN MOREY	ROCHESTER	GSD	.T.	04/23/67	18190.00	Memo

Note: If you don't specify the number-of-locations, the default is "through to the end of the string." For example:

.? SUBSTR(TOWN,5)   <cr>   will result in ESTER, for a town with the value 'ROCHESTER'.

dBASE III PLUS also offers a much more powerful form of the substring option that lets you find the character string you want anywhere within a field, instead of in certain locations only.

.DISP FOR 'TER' $(TOWN)   <cr>

This will DISPLAY all records that have an uppercase TER anywhere in the town field.

Record#	EMP_NUM	EMP_NAME	TOWN	ORG	EXE	DT_OF_HIRE	SALARY	NOTE
1	005	NINA BHARUCHA	WEBSTER	BSG	.T.	05/24/80	25000.00	Memo
6	030	TIM MONTAL	ROCHESTER	RBG	.F.	07/07/81	41900.00	Memo
8	040	JAMES JAMESON	ROCHESTER	GSD	.T.	10/21/77	29800.00	Memo
11	055	PHIL MARTIN	WEBSTER	RMG	.F.	07/19/80	31000.00	Memo
14	070	JAN MOREY	ROCHESTER	GSD	.T.	04/23/67	18190.00	Memo

The String Function

Normally the values supplied for numeric fields are considered to be the algebraic values.

66

It is, however, possible to have dBASE view a numeric field as a character field, so that the substring command can be used with that field.

The expression:

STR(SALARY, 8,2)

will make dBASE look upon the SALARY field as a character field.

In general, to have dBASE look upon a numeric field as a character field, you have to specify:

STR(field-name,field-length)

You are said to be *stringing the character*.

If we wanted to obtain a listing of all employees that had the character 2 in the first position of the SALARY field, we can specify the following:

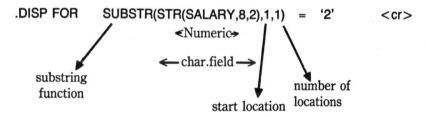

.DISP FOR SUBSTR(STR(SALARY,8,2),1,1) = '2' <cr>

substring function

char.field

Numeric

start location   number of locations

You can read the above as: "Substring the *character* field SALARY, starting at the first location, for one location. If that is equal to the value '2', then display the record."

The value supplied has to be in quotes, since you are now referring to a character field.

```
Record#  EMP_NUM  EMP_NAME        TOWN       ORG  EXE  DT_OF_HIRE   SALARY  NOTE
      1  005      NINA BHARUCHA   WEBSTER    BSG  .T.  05/24/80    25000.00 Memo
     15  075      JOHN JONES      rochester  GSD  .T.  04/04/70    25100.00 Memo

   etc            etc             etc        etc
```

You realize, of course, that if you had wanted the above list of employees who had a 2 in the first location in the SALARY field, that is, all those with salaries equal to or more than 20000 and less than 30000, you could have done it much more easily as follows:

.DISP FOR SALARY > = 20000 .AND. SALARY < 30000   <cr>

The objective here, however, was to show the substring function as it can be used on a numeric field that has been "strung" as a character field. (It's not as confusing as it sounds; it just takes a little doing!)

There are several reasons for wanting to depict numeric fields as character fields, and these will be outlined at the appropriate places in this book. For the moment, let me explain that certain features such as *indexing* and *concatenation* require that numeric fields be "strung" as characters.

The Value Function

The Value function is the opposite of the STRing function, since this function is used to derive numeric data from a character field that contains numeric data. Some examples are provided to clarify the workings of this function. Let us suppose we have some data stored in a character field called COUNTER:

	Contents of the character field called COUNTER	Result of the expression VAL(COUNTER)	
(1)	1234	1234.00	
(2)	12ABC	12.00	
(3)	A212C	0.00	
(4)	(leading spaces) 12ABC	12.00	
(5)	(leading spaces) A123C	0.00	
(6)	123.456 (**character** data !)	123.46	NOTE THIS RESULT
(7)	123.4567(**character** data !)	123.46	NOTE THIS RESULT

The VAL function provides the leading numerical digits out of a character field containing numeric data, and the first nonnumeric stops the process. The function VAL(COUNTER) forces dBASE to recognize COUNTER as a numeric field, but only for the duration of the command using the VAL function. Note also that dBASE provides automatic rounding off to two decimal places by default.

The Uppercase Function

So far we have noticed that in the case of character fields (or numeric fields strung as character fields), dBASE looks for the literal value we have provided in the expression. That is, if your data entry procedure conventions concerning the use of upper- and lowercase characters were not strictly followed, it is possible that your data could end up being a mixture of upper- and lowercase characters. Your DISPLAY commands would end up not finding some or all of the records that actually qualify, but have the wrong type of case for the literal equality.

If you suspect that this might be the case (no pun intended), you can ask dBASE to try and find a match regardless of the case of the characters.

.DISP FOR UPPER(TOWN) = 'ROCH'   <cr>

dBASE will now perform an *internal translation* of all the TOWN field data to uppercase and then make the comparison to 'ROCH'. This will now find all combinations of upper or lowercase of the ROCH characters, in the first four positions of the town field.

Record#	EMP_NUM	EMP_NAME	TOWN	ORG	EXE	DT_OF_HIRE	SALARY	NOTE
6	030	TIM MONTAL	ROCHESTER	RBG	.F.	07/07/81	41900.00	Memo
8	040	JAMES JAMESON	ROCHESTER	GSD	.T.	10/21/77	29800.00	Memo
14	070	JAN MOREY	ROCHESTER	GSD	.T.	04/23/67	18190.00	Memo
15	075	JOHN JONES	rochester	GSD	.T.	04/04/70	25100.00	Memo

The command

.DISP FOR SUBSTR(UPPER(TOWN),2,3) = 'OCH'   <cr>

will find all combinations of upper- or lowercase of the OCH characters in positions 2, 3, and 4 of the TOWN field.

Record#	EMP_NUM	EMP_NAME	TOWN	ORG	EXE	DT_OF_HIRE	SALARY	NOTE
6	030	TIM MONTAL	ROCHESTER	RBG	.F.	07/07/81	41900.00	Memo
8	040	JAMES JAMESON	ROCHESTER	GSD	.T.	10/21/77	29800.00	Memo
14	070	JAN MOREY	ROCHESTER	GSD	.T.	04/23/67	18190.00	Memo
15	075	JOHN JONES	rochester	GSD	.T.	04/04/70	25100.00	Memo

The command

. LIST FOR 'TER' $(UPPER(TOWN))   <cr>

will find all combinations of upper- or lowercase of the TER characters anywhere in the TOWN field.

Record#	EMP_NUM	EMP_NAME	TOWN	ORG	EXE	DT_OF_HIRE	SALARY	NOTE
1	005	NINA BHARUCHA	WEBSTER	BSG	.T.	05/24/80	25000.00	Memo
6	030	TIM MONTAL	ROCHESTER	RBG	.F.	07/07/81	41900.00	Memo
8	040	JAMES JAMESON	ROCHESTER	GSD	.T.	10/21/77	29800.00	Memo
9	045	MORRIS KATZ	webster	BSG	.F.	09/14/80	23450.00	Memo
11	055	PHIL MARTIN	WEBSTER	RMG	.F.	07/19/80	31000.00	Memo
14	070	JAN MOREY	ROCHESTER	GSD	.T.	04/23/67	18190.00	Memo
15	075	JOHN JONES	rochester	GSD	.T.	04/04/70	25100.00	Memo

Permit me to make a suggestion here. I have found it easier to remember these functions if I read the UPPER item as, "regardless of case." Thus, I would read the command above as "List all those items that have a 'TER' anywhere in TOWN regardless of case." The key words are "anywhere" and "regardless of case."

Important Note: The very nature of the uppercase function mandates that the value you supply should all be provided in uppercase only! That is, .DISP FOR UPPER(TOWN) = 'Roch'   <cr> will find nothing! The value you provide must be in UPPER case! dBASE will then search for all combinations of cases, as specified in the command.

The Lowercase Function

If you enter the following commands:

```
.USE PERSNL          <cr>
.LIST FOR LOWER(town) = 'rochester'          <cr>
```

dBASE will perform an *internal translation* of all the TOWN field data to lowercase and then make the comparison to 'rochester'. In effect, this will now find all combinations of upper or lowercase of the rochester characters in the town field.

```
Record#   EMP_NUM EMP_NAME      TOWN      ORG EXE DT_OF_HIRE   SALARY NOTE
     6    030     TIM MONTAL    ROCHESTER RBG .F. 07/07/81   41900.00 Memo
     8    040     JAMES JAMESON ROCHESTER GSD .T. 10/21/77   29800.00 Memo
    14    070     JAN MOREY     ROCHESTER GSD .T. 04/23/67   18190.00 Memo
    15    075     JOHN JONES    rochester GSD .T. 04/04/70   25100.00 Memo
```

Below are some more examples of the use of the LOWER( ) command:

```
.LIST FOR SUBSTR(LOWER(TOWN),2,3) = 'och'          <cr>
```

```
Record#   EMP_NUM EMP_NAME      TOWN      ORG EXE DT_OF_HIRE   SALARY NOTE
     6    030     TIM MONTAL    ROCHESTER RBG .F. 07/07/81   41900.00 Memo
     8    040     JAMES JAMESON ROCHESTER GSD .T. 10/21/77   29800.00 Memo
    14    070     JAN MOREY     ROCHESTER GSD .T. 04/23/67   18190.00 Memo
    15    075     JOHN JONES    rochester GSD .T. 04/04/70   25100.00 Memo
```

```
.DISP FOR 'ter' $(LOWER(TOWN))          <cr>
```

```
Record#   EMP_NUM EMP_NAME      TOWN      ORG EXE DT_OF_HIRE   SALARY NOTE
     1    005     NINA BHARUCHA WEBSTER   BSG .T. 05/24/80   25000.00 Memo
     6    030     TIM MONTAL    ROCHESTER RBG .F. 07/07/81   41900.00 Memo
     8    040     JAMES JAMESON ROCHESTER GSD .T. 10/21/77   29800.00 Memo
     9    045     MORRIS KATZ   webster   BSG .F. 09/14/80   23450.00 Memo
    11    055     PHIL MARTIN   WEBSTER   RMG .F. 07/19/80   31000.00 Memo
    14    070     JAN MOREY     ROCHESTER GSD .T. 04/23/67   18190.00 Memo
    15    075     JOHN JONES    rochester GSD .T. 04/04/70   25100.00 Memo
```

Important Note: The very nature of the lowercase function mandates that the value you supply should all be provided in lowercase only! That is, .DISP FOR LOWER(TOWN) = 'ROCH' <cr> will find nothing! The value you provide must be in lowercase! dBASE will then search for all combinations of cases, as specified in the command.

Note: Memo fields are not accessible through these special functions. It would be very useful if I could list all those records that had the word "overdue" (in upper- or lowercase) in the memo fields of records, so that when I send out bills for services to my clients I could use this clue to insert a polite reminder at the end of the bill. Unfortunately, this is not possible through memo fields. (Needless to say, there are other ways of checking for "overdue." This was merely an example.)

Hence my previous suggestions that if short memos are planned, the fields should be defined as character fields, since "character" fields lend themselves very effectively for such subfield scrutiny.

The + Function

Type in the following commands:

```
.1        <cr>
.DISP NEXT 5  EMP_NUM  EMP_NAME  TOWN       <cr>

Record#   EMP_NUM EMP_NAME        TOWN
      1   005     NINA BHARUCHA   WEBSTER
      2   010     PETE JOHNSON    brighton
      3   015     GLORIA PATEL    FAIRPORT
      4   020     MAX LEVINSKY    HENRIETTA
      5   025     KIM BRANDT      FAIRPORT
```

Now try the following:

```
.1        <cr>
.DISP NEXT 5  EMP_NUM + EMP_NAME + TOWN      <cr>
```

It would help if you interpreted the above + signs as: "EMP_NUM, *immediately followed by* EMP_NAME, *immediately followed by* TOWN." It means "without any spaces between the fields." Now the one blank column between the character fields has been eliminated. This is a *concatenation* (a physical "stringing-together") of *fields*!

```
Record#   EMP_NUM + EMP_NAME + TOWN
      1   005NINA BHARUCHAWEBSTER
      2   010PETE JOHNSON brighton
      3   015GLORIA PATEL FAIRPORT
      4   020MAX LEVINSKY HENRIETTA
      5   025KIM BRANDT   FAIRPORT
```

Note: The + function applies only to character fields, so if you do want to use the same option for numeric fields, you will have to specify the numeric fields as STRings using the STR function, as shown in the example below.

```
.1        <cr>
.LIST NEXT 5 TOWN+STR(SALARY,8,2)      <cr>

Record#   TOWN+STR(SALARY,8,2)
      1   WEBSTER  25000.00
      2   brighton 27590.00
      3   FAIRPORT 27500.00
      4   HENRIETTA27550.00
      5   FAIRPORT 36000.00
```

The – Function

The minus sign is used to remove trailing blanks from a field.

```
.1          <cr>
.DISP NEXT 5  EMP_NUM – EMP_NAME – TOWN        <cr>
```

This command removes all trailing blanks from the EMP_NUM and EMP_NAME fields. It would help if you interpreted the above – signs as "EMP_NUM *minus all trailing blanks*, followed by EMP_NAME *minus all trailing blanks*, followed by TOWN." It means a complete concatenation of the *data* of the named fields.

Note the difference in output between the next two commands:

```
.1          <cr>
.LIST NEXT 5 EMP_NUM, EMP_NAME, TOWN        <cr>
```

```
Record#   EMP NUM  EMP NAME      TOWN
     1    005      NINA BHARUCHA WEBSTER
     2    010      PETE JOHNSON  brighton
     3    015      GLORIA PATEL  FAIRPORT
     4    020      MAX LEVINSKY  HENRIETTA
     5    025      KIM BRANDT    FAIRPORT
```

```
.1          <cr>
.LIST NEXT 5 EMP_NUM – EMP_NAME – TOWN – ORG        <cr>
```

```
Record#   EMP NUM-EMP NAME-TOWN-ORG
     1    005NINA BHARUCHAWEBSTERBSG
     2    010PETE JOHNSONbrightonBSG
     3    015GLORIA PATELFAIRPORTRMG
     4    020MAX LEVINSKYHENRIETTARMG
     5    025KIM BRANDTFAIRPORTRMG
```

> **Note:** The – function applies only to character fields, so if you want to use the same option for numeric fields, you will have to specify the numeric fields as STRings using the STR functions as shown in the example below.

```
.1       <cr>
.DISP NEXT 5    ORG – STR(SALARY,8,2)        <cr>
```

```
Record#  ORG – STR(SALARY,8,2)
     1   BSG25000.00
     2   BSG27590.00
     3   RMG27500.00
     4   RMG27550.00
     5   RMG36000.00
```

Remember that the + function results in a concatenation of the *fields*, while the – function results in a concatenation of the *data* within the fields.

You may also include *literals* in your parameters, as illustrated in the following example:

```
.1        <cr>
.DISP NEXT 5  EMP_NUM + ' ' + EMP_NAME + ' ' + TOWN     <cr>
```

```
Record#   EMP_NUM +' ' + EMP_NAME+' '+TOWN
   1      005 NINA BHARUCHA WEBSTER
   2      010 PETE JOHNSON  brighton
   3      015 GLORIA PATEL  FAIRPORT
   4      020 MAX LEVINSKY  HENRIETTA
   5      025 KIM BRANDT    FAIRPORT
```

The + function concatenates the fields to whatever is contained in the quotes. In this case the literal is a space.

The + and − functions (and the TRIM function, explained next) are very useful in the programming phase, for generating specialized report formats such as mailing labels. The + function is also used for indexing and reporting, both of which are explained in detail later.

The TRIM Function

These commands:

```
.1        <cr>
.DISP NEXT 5      TOWN,ORG       <cr>
```

will result in the familiar output:

```
Record#   TOWN       ORG
   1      WEBSTER    BSG
   2      brighton   BSG
   3      FAIRPORT   RMG
   4      HENRIETTA  RMG
   5      FAIRPORT   RMG
```

Note, however, the results of the following command (assuming that the current record is #1):

```
.DISP NEXT 5     TRIM(TOWN)+ORG        <cr>
```

```
Record#   TRIM(TOWN)+ORG
   1      WEBSTERBSG
   2      brightonBSG
   3      FAIRPORTRMG
   4      HENRIETTARMG
   5      FAIRPORTRMG
```

The TRIM function trims the TOWN field of all trailing blanks, and we have concatenated ORG to the result. Hence the above output. This is identical to the − function, seen earlier. This property of the TRIM function, however, is very useful, as shown in the examples below:

```
.1          <cr>
.LIST NEXT 5 TRIM(TOWN)+' '+ORG          <cr>


Record#   TRIM(TOWN)+' '+ORG
      1   WEBSTER BSG
      2   brighton BSG
      3   FAIRPORT RMG
      4   HENRIETTA RMG
      5   FAIRPORT RMG
```

In the above command, we have asked to TRIM the TOWN field, which removes all trailing blanks from the field(s); to that result we have concatenated one blank space followed by the ORG field.

The above form of the function is useful if data in the next field is required to slide over to the trimmed field. For example, in your file structure, you may have a field called TITLE,C,12 that would contain a salutation such as Mr., Mr. and Mrs., or Ms., etc. In this case, although the length of the TITLE field is fixed at 12 characters, the data in that field could be variable in length, depending on the salutation. In such cases, the name that follows the salutation is required to slide over adjacent to the salutation, regardless of the length of the actual data in the salutation field. The TRIM function accomplishes this task, as shown in the example below:

```
.DISP ALL TRIM(TITLE)+' '+TRIM(LASTNAME)+' '+FIRSTNAME          <cr>
```

Notice that the LASTNAME field was trimmed, so that the FIRSTNAME data could slide over adjacent to the LASTNAME data.

As you may be able to appreciate, this use of the TRIM function has been found particularly useful in mailing-labels types of applications.

> **Note:** The TRIM function only applies to character fields! However, if you want to apply the TRIM option to numeric fields, simply STRing the numeric fields as character fields, and the TRIM function will work with them.

The ISALPHA Function

This function will help to identify the first character of a character string as either alphabetic or numeric.

```
.1          <cr>
.DISP          <cr>


Record#   EMP_NUM EMP_NAME        TOWN      ORG EXE DT OF HIRE   SALARY NOTE
      1   005     NINA BHARUCHA WEBSTER    BSG .T. 05/24/80   25000.00 Memo

    .? ISALPHA(EMP_NUM)          <cr>
    .F.
```

As shown in the above example, although the field is defined as character, the first character of the data is not alphabetic! In contrast, consider the example below:

```
.? ISALPHA('ABC")      <cr>
.T.
```

The ISLOWER Function

This function will help you find out if the first character of a character string is lowercase.

```
.1         <cr>
.DISP         <cr>
```

Record#	EMP_NUM	EMP_NAME	TOWN	ORG	EXE	DT OF HIRE	SALARY	NOTE
1	005	NINA BHARUCHA	WEBSTER	BSG	.T.	05/24/80	25000.00	Memo

```
.? ISLOWER(EMP_NAME)         <cr>
.F.
```

```
.? ISLOWER('hi THERE')         <cr>
.T.
```

The ISUPPER Function

The ISUPPER function will help you find out if the first character of a string is uppercase.

Using the same record for display here are two examples of the use of the ISSUPPER( ) function.

```
.? ISUPPER(ORG)         <cr>
.T.
```

```
.? ISUPPER('hi THERE')         <cr>
.F.
```

The LTRIM Function

The LTRIM( ) function removes all leading blanks from a character string, as shown in the example below:

```
. STORE '      ABC' TO ANY         <cr>
        ABC
```

```
.? LTRIM(ANY)         <cr>
ABC
```

This function is found to have particular use when you output the result of a numeric field or expression in a statement, as shown in the examples below:

```
.STORE 1 TO COUNTER        <cr>
1


.? COUNTER        <cr>
1


.? 'THE VALUE IN COUNTER IS ' + STR(COUNTER,8)        <cr>
THE VALUE IN COUNTER IS        1
```

Notice how far removed the numeric value is from the character literal in the example above, and how the unnecessary spaces have been removed in the example below.

```
.? 'THE VALUE IN COUNTER IS ' + LTRIM(STR(COUNTER,8))        <cr>
THE VALUE IN COUNTER IS 1
```

In the above, the LTRIM function helps you obtain the desired effect. COUNTER was represented in its string form, since the LTRIM function can only operate on a character string.

The RTRIM Function

The RTRIM( ) function will remove all *right-justified (trailing)* blanks from a character field. As the example below indicates, this function is identical to the TRIM( ) function presented earlier.

```
.1        <cr>
.LIST NEXT 5 RTRIM(TOWN)+' '+ORG        <cr>

Record#  TRIM(TOWN)+' '+ORG

     1   WEBSTER BSG
     2   brighton BSG
     3   FAIRPORT RMG
     4   HENRIETTA RMG
     5   FAIRPORT RMG
```

The LEFT Function

The LEFT( ) function returns the leftmost n characters from a string. This would be the same as using SUBSTR( ) with a starting location of 1.

```
.1        <cr>
.DISP        <cr>

Record#  EMP_NUM EMP_NAME        TOWN     ORG EXE DT_OF_HIRE   SALARY NOTE
     1   005     NINA BHARUCHA WEBSTER    BSG .T. 05/24/80    25000.00 Memo

.? LEFT(EMP_NAME,3)        <cr>
NIN
.? LEFT(TOWN,5)        <cr>
WEBST
```

The RIGHT Function

The RIGHT( ) function returns the rightmost n characters from a string. Here is an example using the record shown above.

```
.? RIGHT(TOWN,3)        <cr>
R
```

While at first glance this may seem incorrect, you must remember that the field called TOWN is nine characters wide. Thus the R character is the third character from the right. It is followed by two blanks.

```
.? RIGHT(EMP_NAME,4)        <cr>
UCHA
```

The LEN Function

The LEN( ) function returns the length of a character string, as illustrated in the examples below.

```
Record#  EMP_NUM EMP_NAME      TOWN      ORG EXE DT_OF_HIRE   SALARY NOTE
      1  005     NINA BHARUCHA WEBSTER   BSG .T. 05/24/80   25000.00 Memo
```

```
.? LEN(EMP_NUM)        <cr>
3
```

```
.? LEN(TOWN)        <cr>
7
```

```
.? LEN(RTRIM('ABC      '))        <cr>
3
```

The final statement above can be read as: "What is the LENgth of the Right-TRIMmed string 'ABC   ' ?" Since the right-trimmed string is 'ABC', the length is three.

The REPLICATE Function

The REPLICATE function is very useful in "dolling up" menu screens. For example, if you want to draw a line of asterisks on the screen you could enter:

```
.? REPLICATE('*',50)        <cr>
**************************************************************************
```

You will use this option in the programming phase of this book.

The STUFF Function

The STUFF( ) function helps you overlay existing characters in a character string without your having to reconstruct the entire string, as illustrated in the examples below.

```
.1        <cr>
.DISP         <cr>
```

```
Record#  EMP_NUM EMP_NAME      TOWN      ORG EXE DT_OF_HIRE   SALARY NOTE
     1   005     NINA BHARUCHA WEBSTER   BSG .T. 05/24/80   25000.00 Memo
```

```
.? STUFF(EMP_NAME,5,2,'AL')        <cr>
NINAALHARUCHA
```

In the above example, we have asked something to the effect: "What would the name look like, if the characters starting at the fifth character for two locations (that is, characters five and six) were replaced with 'AL'?"

```
.? STUFF(EMP_NAME,1,3,'ABC')        <cr>
ABCA BHARUCHA
```

In the next two examples, we see a transformation taking place.

```
.? STUFF(EMP_NAME,3,3,'X')       <cr> (Replacing three characters with one)
NIXBHARUCHA
```

```
.? STUFF(EMP_NAME,1,1,'ABC') <cr> (Replacing one character with three)
ABCINA BHARUCHA
```

Notice the transformations. If you replace n characters with a larger or smaller string, the appropriate expansion or contraction takes place in the data.

The INT Function

The INT( ) function provides the integer value of an expression, without the decimal portion involved. Examine the example below.

```
.? 23/3        <cr>                This will provide the answer: 7.67
                                   (automatic rounding to 2 decimals.)
.? INT(23/3)        <cr>           This will provide the answer: 7
```

For example, to round-off a dollar-value to the nearest dollar enter the following:

```
? INT(19.49 + 0.50)        <cr>
19
```

```
? INT(19.51 + 0.50)        <cr>
20
```

To round off the dollar-amount in a field, say, PAY_HIKE, enter the following:

.? INT(PAY__HIKE + 0.50)   <cr>

As will be explained in the programming section, this function can also be used to find out if a number or the result of an expression is odd or even.

The RECNO Function

RECNO( ) is a special function that means *record number.* As a simple example, remember that the dBASE pointer will always be positioned at a record within the file in use. If you quickly wanted to find out the record number of that record, you could always enter:

.DISP   <cr>

and the entire record, including the record number, would be displayed. If you only wanted to access the record number, without the rest of the data, this special function comes in handy. Remember that you had nothing to do with the record numbers (they were provided by dBASE as you were APPENDing data), and so you do not have access to any field in the structure that will provide the record numbers directly: hence this function. To view only the record number of the current record, type the following:

.? RECNO( )   <cr>

In this example we are asking, "What is the record number of the current record?"
    This function is used extensively in computer programming. See the Advanced dBASE section of this book.

The DATE Function

When you first invoke your operating system (DOS), it either provides or asks you to provide today's date. This operating system date is now available through dBASE via the use of the function DATE( ). For example:

.? DATE( )   <cr>

will provide today's date.
    At any point in your processing, if you wish to change an existing system-date, you may type:

.SET DATE TO MM/DD/YY   <cr>   where mm/dd/yy is the new date.

> **Note:** In the next few examples, you are to assume that the pair of parentheses will enclose the field on which the function is to perform. Actual examples will follow soon, but for now these are the generic formats of the date functions, with their meanings.

.? MONTH( )	provides the digits of the month
.? DAY( )	provides the digits of the day
.? YEAR( )	provides the digits of the year
.? CMONTH( )	provides the name of the month as January, February, etc.
.? DOW( )	provides the day of the week as a number, with 1 for Sunday, 2 for Monday, etc.
.? CDOW( )	provides the day of the week as a name, such as Monday, Tuesday, etc.
.? CTOD( )	Read it as "character-to-date" conversion. That is, dBASE will temporarily look upon a character field (which should be in the format MM/DD/YY), as a date field. You can then use this "date-field" for the above-defined functions.
.? DTOC( )	Read it as "date-to-character" conversion. Sometimes you want dBASE to look upon a date field as a character field.

Further explanations of these functions are found in the following examples. Remember that we have the system date (today's date) stored as a function, DATE( ).

.? MONTH(DATE( )) <cr>	provides the month number from the system date.
.? DAY(DATE( )) <cr>	provides the day number from the system date.
.? YEAR(DATE( )) <cr>	provides the four-digit year from the system date.
.USE PERSNL <cr>	brings record #1 in use.
.? DT_OF_HIRE <cr>	displays the date-of-hire of the current record.
05/24/80	
.? MONTH(DT_OF_HIRE) <cr>	gives the month in that date.
5	
.? DAY(DT_OF_HIRE) <cr>	gives the day in that date.
24	
.? YEAR(DT_OF_HIRE) <cr>	gives the year in that date.
1980	
.? DT_OF_HIRE + 35 <cr>	gives a new date exactly 35 days beyond the hire date.

06/28/80
```
.? DATE( ) - DT__OF__HIRE > 365 *5
    <cr>
```
The question being asked is, "Is the difference between today's date and the DT__OF__HIRE greater than five years?" That is, "Has this person been employed for more than five years?"

```
    .T.
.? CMONTH(DT__OF__HIRE)        <cr>  results in the month name of May.
    May
.? DOW(DT__OF__HIRE)           <cr>  results in the number seven since the
                                     date happened to be Saturday.

    7
.? CDOW(DT__OF__HIRE)          <cr>  results in the name Saturday.
    Saturday
```

The CTOD (character-to-date) function can be explained as follows: If you have a field that contains a date but the field was defined as character, whatever the reason, you can either permanently convert the field to a date-type field, or you can let dBASE look upon that field as a date-type field for the duration of specific commands.

For example; suppose we have in USE a file with a field called APPOINTMNT, which was defined as a character field, but has dates in it in the format MM/DD/YY. The command:

```
.? CTOD(APPOINTMENT) - DATE( )        <cr>
```

will provide the number of days that are left before the appointment.

Notice that in this case, the function merely lets dBASE "look upon" the APPOINTMNT field as a date field for the duration of the command, but does not actually alter its format in the file.

The process of physically altering the formats of character fields to date fields will be seen later, when we study the section on EDITING.

As another example, to find the difference in days between the employee's DT__OF__HIRE and the date 06/01/79, you would type the following:

```
? DT__OF__HIRE - CTOD ('06/01/79')        <cr>
358
```

Note that you can only subtract one date field from another date field. Thus the character string '06/01/79' had to be converted into a date field, using the character-to-date function.

Incidentally, a question must have come to your mind at this point. Since there is no way of knowing whether the DT__OF__HIRE is "higher" or "lower" than the date 06/01/79, it is possible for the above subtraction to come out with a negative number! Obviously, if this happens, you should perform the subtraction the other way around.

More Examples of LISTS Involving DATE Fields. Below are a number of examples designed to clarify the use of date fields.

1. List all those hired in the month of April.

```
.LIST FOR MONTH(DT_OF_HIRE) = 4          <cr>
```

Record#	EMP_NUM	EMP_NAME	TOWN	ORG	EXE	DT_OF_HIRE	SALARY	NOTE
4	020	MAX LEVINSKY	HENRIETTA	RMG	.F.	04/13/69	27550.00	Memo
5	025	KIM BRANDT	FAIRPORT	RMG	.F.	04/04/77	36000.00	Memo
12	060	JOHN PETERSON	BRIGHTON	RBG	.T.	04/17/79	31480.00	Memo
14	070	JAN MOREY	ROCHESTER	GSD	.T.	04/23/67	18190.00	Memo
15	075	JOHN JONES	rochester	GSD	.T.	04/04/70	25100.00	Memo

2. List all those hired on a Monday (the second day of the week).

```
.LIST FOR DOW(DT_OF_HIRE) = 2          <cr>
```

Record#	EMP_NUM	EMP_NAME	TOWN	ORG	EXE	DT_OF_HIRE	SALARY	NOTE
5	025	KIM BRANDT	FAIRPORT	RMG	.F.	04/04/77	36000.00	Memo

3. Again, list all those hired on a Monday.

```
.LIST FOR CDOW(DT_OF_HIRE) = 'Monday'          <cr>
```

Record#	EMP_NUM	EMP_NAME	TOWN	ORG	EXE	DT_OF_HIRE	SALARY	NOTE
5	025	KIM BRANDT	FAIRPORT	RMG	.F.	04/04/77	36000.00	Memo

4. String the date fields, for specialized formats.

```
.LIST EMP_NUM + '    ' + EMP_NAME + '    ' + DTOC(DT_OF_HIRE)     <cr>
```

Record#	EMP_NUM + '	' + EMP_NAME + '	' + DTOC(DT_OF_HIRE)
1	005	NINA BHARUCHA	05/24/80
2	010	PETE JOHNSON	02/03/76
3	015	GLORIA PATEL	07/16/82
4	020	MAX LEVINSKY	04/13/69
5	025	KIM BRANDT	04/04/77
6	030	TIM MONTAL	07/07/81
7	035	WILLIAM PATEL	08/17/71
8	040	JAMES JAMESON	10/21/77
9	045	MORRIS KATZ	09/14/80
10	050	PAUL BHARUCHA	05/23/73
11	055	PHIL MARTIN	07/19/80
12	060	JOHN PETERSON	04/17/79
13	065	JOY HARDY	01/19/79
14	070	JAN MOREY	04/23/67
15	075	JOHN JONES	04/04/70

5. List all those who have been on board for more than three months, but for less than six months, assuming 30 days to each month.

```
.LIST FOR DATE( )-DT__OF__HIRE > 90  .AND.  DATE( ) - DT__OF__HIRE
< 180        <cr>
```

will do the trick. (Nobody from our PERSNL file qualifies.)
 6. List all those in the 'GSD' organization who were hired after June 1, 1970.

```
.LIST FOR ORG = 'BSG' .AND. DT__OF__HIRE > CTOD('06/01/70')   <cr>
```

Notice that once again we have asked dBASE to make a character-to-date (CTOD) conversion on the date supplied as '06/01/70'. This conversion is only done for the duration of the command. The following records qualify:

```
Record#  EMP_NUM EMP_NAME        TOWN      ORG EXE DT OF HIRE   SALARY NOTE
      1  005     NINA BHARUCHA  WEBSTER   BSG .T. 05/24/80   25000.00 Memo
      2  010     PETE JOHNSON   brighton  BSG .T. 02/03/76   27590.00 Memo
      9  045     MORRIS KATZ    webster   BSG .F. 09/14/80   23450.00 Memo
     10  050     PAUL BHARUCHA  BRIGHTON  BSG .T. 05/23/73   29100.00 Memo
```

The TIME Function

Typing causes the display of the system time in the format hh:mm:ss. This function can be put to good use in the programming mode of dBASE, where custom screens can be set up with the time showing in one corner. See the Programming section of this book.

```
.? TIME( )
```

The ISCOLOR Function

The ISCOLOR( ) function can be used to find out if the computer is running with a color card, or if it's running a monochrome monitor.

```
.? ISCOLOR ( )        <cr>
.T.
```

This function can serve a very useful purpose if you are writing custom programs for a project, and your users have a mix of color and monochrome monitors. Depending on the outcome of this instruction, you can program to pull in the appropriate codes for either color or inverse video, during the running of the programs. These codes generally help to highlight errors made during data entry and editing. We will explore this concept in detail, in the programming phase of this book.

The OS Function

The operating system function returns the name and version of the operating system in use:

```
.? OS( )        <cr>
MS-DOS 3.00
```

If your programmed system is dependent on the usage of a specific version of the operating system, this function can help to ensure compatibility between the system and your programs.

The DBF Function

The DBF( ) function lets you know which database is in use in the currently selected work area. The concept of the current database in a work area will be explained later.

```
.? DBF( )          <cr>
C:PERSNL.dbf
```

The FIELD Function

The FIELD( ) function returns the name of the field from the structure, if you provide the position of the field in the structure.

```
. ? FIELD(7)        <cr>
SALARY
```

The LUPDATE Function

LUPDATE( ) is the date-of-last-update function. Obviously, this ability to find out when the file was last updated can have an important bearing in programming.

```
.? LUPDATE( )        <cr>
 01/06/86
```

The DISKSPACE Function

The DISKSPACE( ) function obtains the amount of read-write space available on the default drive. It can be either used stand-alone or used as part of a project, in which the computer program prompts the user to change disks if the available space falls below a predetermined value.

```
.? DISKSPACE( )          <cr>
22802432

.? DISKSPACE( ) < 3000          <cr>
.F.
```

The RECCOUNT Function

This is the record-count function.

```
.? RECCOUNT( )        <cr>
15
```

The RECSIZE Function

This is the record-size function.

```
.? RECSIZE( )          <cr>
56
```

Using a combination of DISKSPACE( ) available, the RECSIZE( ) of a master record, and the RECCOUNT( ) of the file, you can determine whether or not you can make a backup copy of the master file on the same disk that contains your master file.

For now, this ends our discussion of special functions. There are some more functions to be covered, but we will take these up at the appropriate places in the book. Mentioning these here will put them out of context and will make comprehension difficult.

THE LOCATE COMMAND

Since we have made ourselves quite familiar with the DISPLAY command, let us introduce an instruction here, which is rather similar to the DISPLAY command, but which has its own niche in the dBASE set of commands.

```
.USE  PERSNL        <cr>
.LOCATE  <scope>     FOR    <condition>       <cr>
```

Here is an example:

```
.LOCATE  FOR  TOWN = 'ROCH'  .AND.  ORG = 'BSG'       <cr>
```

dBASE starts at the top of the database and moves the pointer to the first record that satisfies the condition, but it will not display the record. You may DISPLAY or EDIT (covered later) the record, and when you want dBASE to move on to the next such record (which satisfies the same condition specified before), you may enter:

```
.CONT       <cr>                    [for CONTINUE]
```

This will move the pointer to the next record satisfying the same condition. In this way, you can step through the entire database searching for selected records and you can DISPLAY or EDIT them selectively along the way.

As before, you may use the special functions within your parameters, to enhance the power of the command.

```
.LOCATE  FOR  SUBSTR(TOWN,2,3) = 'OCH'        <cr>
```

If you use the CONT parameter often enough, you will come across an "End of LOCATE scope" message. Further attempts to CONT will produce the same message.

If you use the following format:

```
.LOCATE  <scope>     WHILE    <condition>       <cr>
```

dBASE starts the LOCATE at the position of the current record, not at the top of the file. The interpretation of the WHILE parameter with LOCATE is identical to it's interpretation with DISPLAY.

DISPLAYING DATA FROM MULTIPLE DATABASES

So far, we have studied in detail how data from one database can be displayed in many shapes and forms. We shall now look at an enhancement that enables us to use data from multiple databases simultaneously.

Suppose we have the following files, with their structures as shown:

INVEN1.dbf	PART	COST	DESC
INVEN2.dbf	PART	CGC	(commodity group code)
INVEN3.dbf	PART	ONHAND	
INVEN4.dbf	PART	ONORDER	

Let us also suppose that we have a one-to-one correspondence between the records of the four databases. That is, record number 1 of INVEN1 contains the PART_NUM, DESC and COST of part P1, record number 1 of INVEN2 contains the PART_NUM and CGC of part P1, and record number 1 of INVEN3 contains the PART_NUM and ONHAND for part P1, and so on. It is just as if the second, third and fourth databases were extensions of the first. Given the choice, all the fields would have been placed together in one structure, but for the moment, we have this arrangement.

With this situation, we have to use all four physical files for the display of one logical data file. We start off by informing dBASE that we are going to be working with more than one physical file at the same time.

```
.SELECT 1        <cr>
.USE INVEN1      <cr>
```

These two commands effectively designate INVEN1 as the file that dBASE will open in area-1. dBASE can work with up to 10 data files simultaneously, in 10 different work areas. The word simultaneously simply means that dBASE will maintain separate and independent pointers for the current record in each of the separate work areas.

```
.SELECT 2        <cr>
.USE INVEN2      <cr>
```

These two commands effectively designate INVEN2 as the file kept open in the second work area.

```
.SELECT 3        <cr>
.USE INVEN3      <cr>
```

These two commands effectively designate INVEN3 as the file kept open in the third work area.

```
.SELECT 4        <cr>
.USE INVEN4      <cr>
```

These two commands effectively designate INVEN4 as the file kept open in the fourth work area. In like manner, you could have selected up to 10 files, in 10 different work areas.

You can now set up relationships between the files, two at a time. That is, we connect the first and second files, then connect the second and third files, and then connect the third and fourth files. By connecting them two at a time, we can link all the files to one another. This linking (or relationship) is necessary, since we have presumed that the second, third, and fourth databases were extensions of the first one.

```
.SELECT 1          <cr>
```

This command informs dBASE that, for the moment, you want INVEN1 to be the active file; that is, all commands given should be processed against this file, unless another select is made.

```
.SET RELATION TO RECNO( ) INTO INVEN2          <cr>
```

You have set a relation on record-numbers, between the active file INVEN1.dbf and the linked file INVEN2.dbf. This means that if the record pointer in the active file is moved to record number 5, the record pointer in the INVEN2 file will automatically move to record number 5! You have now successfully established a complete one-to-one correspondence between these two databases.

Since we can only relate two databases at a time, we shall now link INVEN2 with INVEN3, and then link INVEN3 with INVEN4 as follows:

```
.SELE 2          <cr>
.SET RELATION TO RECNO( ) INTO INVEN3          <cr>

.SELE 3          <cr>
.SET RELATION TO RECNO( ) INTO INVEN4          <cr>
```

At this point, all four databases are linked, into one logical file.

```
.SELE 1          <cr>
```

Note the above selection! You must end up on this statement to designate INVEN1 as being the primary or controlling file for the entire linked arrangement!

From now on, having done a .SELE 1, you can move the record pointer to any record in INVEN1, and you can DISPLAY or edit the record. After this you enter .SELE 2 to automatically transfer dBASE control to the same record number in the linked file (INVEN2), and you can DISPLAY or EDIT that record. You can follow this process for any of the linked files.

> **Note:** Having displayed or edited any linked record, ensure that you again designate INVEN1 as your main file (.SELE 1)! In other words, you can only select another record number when you have

selected the main file! Failure to adhere to this rule will result in the record pointers going haywire.

Using a combination of **.SELE 1** and **.SELE 2/3/4**, you can DISPLAY or EDIT data in records with the same record number, from different databases. The process is controlled by the active file.

Here is a complete example of linking 4 files and producing listings from these related files.

```
.SELE 1         <cr>
.USE INVEN1          <cr>
.SELE 2         <cr>
.USE INVEN2          <cr>
.SELE 3         <cr>
.USE INVEN3          <cr>
.SELE 4         <cr>
.USE INVEN4          <cr>
```

The above commands assign four different files to four different work areas. You can designate up to 10 different files in 10 different work areas.

```
.SELE 1          <cr>
.SET RELATION TO RECNO( ) INTO   INVEN2        <cr>
.SELE 2          <cr>
.SET RELATION TO RECNO( ) INTO INVEN3        <cr>
.SELE 3          <cr>
.SET RELATION TO RECNO( ) INTO INVEN4        <cr>
```

The above commands set up the relationships between the files, two at a time, and the relationships are based on *record numbers*.

```
.SELE 1          <cr>                    (Ensure that you end up on this in-
                                         struction!)
```

The above command designates INVEN1 as the controlling file. We will now display the data from all four files.

.LIST PART,INVEN2 – >CGC,INVEN3 – >ONHAND,INVEN4 – >ONORDER <cr>

```
Record#   PART    INVEN2->CGC INVEN3->ONHAND INVEN4->ONORDER
      1   P1      C1                     100             100
      2   P2      C2                     200             200
      3   P3      C3                     300             300
      4   P4      C4                     400             400
      5   P5      C5                     500             500
```

Note the usage of the parameters **INVEN2 – >CGC** and **INVEN3 – >ONHAND**

These only mean the CGC field from the INVEN2 file and the ONHAND field from the INVEN3 file.

The command above requests the display of PART from the active file (INVEN1) and CGC, ONHAND, and ONORDER from the linked files INVEN2, INVEN3, and INVEN4, respectively, for all the records.

It is important to understand that at this point, after the previous listing, INVEN1.dbf is still the *primary*, or controlling, file, since the last SELECT statement referred to work area 1, and we have not changed that selection.

```
.3        <cr>
```

The above statement will move the record pointer to record number 3, in the controlling file!

```
.LIST NEXT 3    PART, INVEN4->ONORDER        <cr>


Record#    PART    INVEN4->ONORDER
      3    P3                  300
      4    P4                  400
      5    P5                  500
```

The command above requests the display of PART from the active file (INVEN1) and ONORDER from INVEN4, but only for record numbers 3, 4, and 5 as controlled by INVEN1.

The INVEN1.dbf file is still the controlling file.

```
.4        <cr>
```

The above statement will move the record pointer to record number 4 in the controlling file!

```
.LIST NEXT 2    PART, INVEN2->CGC, INVEN3->ONHAND        <cr>

Record#    PART    INVEN2->CGC  INVEN3->ONHAND
      4    P4      C4                      400
      5    P5      C5                      500
```

The command above requests the display of PART from the active file (INVEN1), CGC from INVEN2, and ONHAND from INVEN3, but only for record numbers 4 and 5 as controlled by INVEN1.

It is quite possible that you may want to set relationships to a field and not to simple record numbers. For example, you may have an Inventory master file containing PART-NUMBERS, DESCRIPTIONS, UNIT-COSTS and another file containing transaction information for these inventory records. The commonality between these two files is the PART-NUMBER field.

The transaction records may not necessarily follow the same sequence as their master-record counterparts. In this case, too, you can set a similar type of relation, but on the PART-NUMBER field, not on record numbers. The details of this arrangement will be deferred to a later section, since it requires that the linked files be *indexed*. This topic will, therefore, be taken up again in the indexing section of this book.

> **Note:** When you don't have any more need to maintain this kind of relationship between linked files, always *close* the files in the link arrangement, as follows:

```
.CLOSE ALL          <cr>
```

The above command will close all the files involved in the link process, but it will not affect *memory variables* currently available. Memory variables are explained in detail at the appropriate place in the book. For now, please accept the statement that you may want to close files without losing memory variables, and .CLOSE ALL is how you do it.

If you don't close all the files involved in the link process, they remain open, and your attempt to use either INVEN1 or INVEN2 separately, for any other purpose, will fail, since the files are still in USE, in different work areas. So please close the files after the link arrangement has served its purpose.

It is my personal opinion that if you need to have many files linked in different work areas ("many" being a purely subjective number and wide open to debate), then something is radically wrong with your entire systems design!

THE SUM AND AVERAGE COMMANDS

Having obtained the ability to LIST (or DISPLAY) the data in so many ways, I will round off this section with two commands you may find useful. The SUM command provides the sum total of the values in specified fields. The AVERAGE command provides the average value per record.

```
.USE PERSNL         <cr>
.SUM SALARY         <cr>
```

These commands enable you to find the sum of all the salary items in the file.

```
  15 records summed
  SALARY
436760.00
```

```
.SUM SALARY    FOR   ORG = 'BSG'           <cr>
```

This command enables you to find the sum of all salary items for BSG personnel only.

```
  4 records summed
  SALARY
105140.00
```

```
.AVERAGE SALARY          <cr>
```

This command enables you to find the average salary of all personnel in the file.

```
    15 records averaged
    SALARY
29117.33
```

```
.AVERAGE SALARY FOR ORG = 'BSG'        <cr>
```

This command enables you to find the average salary for BSG personnel only.

```
    4 records averaged
    SALARY
26285.00
```

The above commands produced these totals on the screen only. You can, however, specify to dBASE that you want these numbers stored in temporary storage locations in memory for future use. These temporary storage locations are called *memory variables*.

For now, I am going to describe briefly the term *memory variable*. This concept is much more fully explored in the Advanced dBASE Programming section of this book.

If you can set aside a small section of computer memory, and if you have stored some data in that section of memory, you have defined a memory variable. For example, you could type:

```
.STORE '01-01-76' TO D1        <cr>
```

This command stores the literal value 01-01-76 into a section of memory set aside and called D1. Picture it as follows:

| 01-01-76 | ◄─────── the contents of the variable

D1   ◄─────── the name of the variable

Memory variables can be either numeric, character, logical, or date.Once created, you can access the contents of the variable. The SUM and the AVERAGE commands help to create variables that contain, respectively, the sum and the average. Examples follow.

```
.USE PERSNL        <cr>
.SUM SALARY TO    MSAL        <cr>
```

```
    15 records summed
    SALARY
436760.00
```

The above command added up all the SALARY data and stored the result in a memory variable called MSAL.

.4   < cr >
.SUM NEXT 5 SALARY TO MSAL   < cr >

    5 records summed
  SALARY
164150.00

The above command did the same thing, but only for record numbers four through eight in the file.

.SUM SALARY TO MSAL FOR TOWN = 'R'   < cr >

    3 records summed
  SALARY
89890.00

You can find the sum for records satisfying a condition, which could be simple or complex.

The AVERAGE command has an identical format.

.AVERAGE SALARY   < cr >

    15 records averaged
  SALARY
29117.33

. 5   < cr >
.AVERAGE NEXT 5 SALARY TO MSAL   < cr >

    5 records averaged
  SALARY
32010.00

.AVERAGE SALARY TO MSAL   FOR   TOWN = 'R'   < cr >

    3 records averaged
  SALARY
29963.33

Note that if you had multiple numeric fields defined in your file—call them N1, N2, N3, N4—you can, in one statement, sum or average them.

.SUM N1,N2,N3,N4   TO   M1,M2,M3,M4   < cr >

This command would create four memory variables, corresponding to the four numeric fields. That is, the sum of N1 would be in memory variable M1, and the sum of N2 would be in M2, and so on.

An identical format exists for the AVERAGE command.

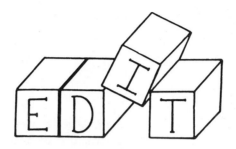

5. Editing Process

W e are now moving into the realm of editing. We shall be studying several ways in which to change the contents of our database records and/or structures. In order to preserve the original data for subsequent reports, please execute the following commands:

```
.USE PERSNL        <cr>
.COPY TO PRESERVE          <cr>      To be explained later
```

The file in use is still PERSNL. Now we can go ahead and practice all we want against the PERSNL file with the editing features to be covered here, and later on we can restore the original PERSNL file.

THE EDIT COMMAND

The EDIT command permits us to make changes to our database, one record at a time. You have to decide which record you want to start editing. The DISPLAY commands will help you obtain the record number of the record to be edited.

```
.USE PERSNL        <cr>
.EDIT 5        <cr>
```

This will bring up record #5 on the screen in full-screen edit mode and subject to the full-screen cursor controls. The data appears in vertical format; hence we can only edit one record at a time.

```
Record No.    5
    -----------------------------------------------
    |                                              |
    |              (CURSOR-CONTROL MENU)           |
    |                                              |
    -----------------------------------------------
EMP_NUM       025
EMP_NAME      KIM BRANDT
TOWN          FAIRPORT
ORG           RMG
EXE           F
DT_OF_HIRE    04/04/77
SALARY        36000.00
NOTE          Memo
```

> **Note:** In the edit mode of operation, even if the cursor is in the first position of the first field in the structure, the use of the <cr> key simply moves the cursor down a field and does not get you out of the EDIT mode.

You can use the F1 key as a toggle switch to see the menu for cursor movement. Remember, the field EXEMPT is a logical field and can only contain T, F, Y, or N for data. The data will reside in the file as entered and will be displayed under edit exactly as it was entered. A subsequent DISPLAY command will display the entry as T or F only.

Use the cursor control keys and make any changes to the record. Having made changes to the record on the screen in front of you, you now have one of four choices of action:

1. You may want to save this record, and present the next one for similar changes. Use Ctrl-C or the PgDn key.

> **Note:** If the current record on the screen is the last record in the database, Ctrl-C or PgDn will save this record and get you out of the edit mode.

2. You may want to save this record and display the previous one for similar changes. Use Ctrl-R or the PgUp key.

> **Note:** If the current record on the screen is the first record in the database, Ctrl-R or PgUp will save this record and get you out of the edit mode.

3. You may want to save this record and get out of the EDIT mode. Use Ctrl-W or the Ctrl-End key.

4. You may want to change your mind about the changes made (to the current record only!) and get out of the EDIT mode. Use Ctrl-Q or ESC.

> **Note:** When you are making the changes to a record, if the last character of the last field is changed OR if the <cr> key is kept depressed beyond the last field, the effect is the same as a Ctrl-C or PgDn. That is, the "next" record is presented for edit. Also, if the record has many fields, and you are unable to see them all when the record is first brought up for edit, the Ctrl-C or PgDn actions will cause the latter portion of the record to be brought into view, and a repeat of the same actions will cause the Ctrl-C effect.
>
> **Note:** Moving the Up-Arrow beyond the first field presents the previous record for edit. Moving the Down-Arrow beyond the last field presents the next record for edit.
>
> **Note:** While in the edit mode, if you enter a Ctrl-U combination, you will be *flagging* the record as deleted! Notice the Del indicator that appears at the top of the screen. Another Ctrl-U will again unflag it. That is, Ctrl-U is a toggle switch for the delete indicator, while in the EDIT mode of operation.

Let us take some combinations of actions and see the results:

Example A:

1. You make changes to record #5, and then type Ctrl-C. All changes to record #5 are saved, and record #6 is presented for edit.
2. Now you enter Ctrl-U, followed by Ctrl-C. Record #6 is flagged as deleted and then saved as such! Record #7 is on the screen.
3. You make changes to record #7 and then enter Ctrl-W.

The net effect is that record #5 is changed, record #6 is flagged as deleted, and record #7 is changed, after which you got out of the edit mode.

Example B:

1. You make changes to record #5 and then enter Ctrl-C. All changes to record #5 are saved, and record #6 is presented for edit.

2. Now you enter:	Ctrl-U,	Ctrl-C,	Ctrl-R	Ctrl-U,	Ctrl-Q.
	deletes record 6.	saves record 6. as deleted and presents record 7.	saves record 7. and presents record 6.	undeletes record 6.	change your mind on the change.

95

As you can see from the sequence of the commands, the net effect is that record #6 is flagged as deleted. To ensure that your changes were typed in correctly, enter the following:

.LIST   < cr >

The deleted record(s) will be displayed with an asterisk in front of the record. We will study more on deleting records later.

> **Note:** If you wish to edit the current record that dBASE happens to be pointing at (say you have just come out of APPEND, to the dot-prompt, and you want to EDIT the last-appended record), then, without knowing the record number, you can get to that record by the command:

.EDIT   < cr >   This will bring up the current record.

Edit Enhancements

While the EDIT command can only edit one record at a time, you can put some muscle behind the editing by preselecting which records you would like to have brought up under control of EDIT.

.EDIT < scope > [FIELD < field-list >] [FOR < condition >] [WHILE < cond. >]

For example:

.EDIT FOR TOWN = 'R'   < cr >

The above command will bring up the first of the qualifying records for edit, and after you have made your changes to the record, PgDn, for forward movement, will bring up the next record qualifying for the same condition! Obviously, PgUp, for reverse movement, will also be restricted to records matching the same condition. The condition can be as simple or as complex as you may want to make it.

.EDIT FIELDS TOWN,ORG   FOR DT__OF__HIRE > CTOD('01/01/79') < cr >

The above command will select only those records in which the date-of-hire is greater than 01/01/79, and from those qualifying records, only the fields TOWN and ORG will be brought to the screen for edit! Note that the fields will be presented to you in the order in which they were defined in the edit command, regardless of their relative positions in the actual database structure.

The meaning of the individual parameters (SCOPE, FIELD, WHILE . . .) is identical to what you have seen in the DISPLAY command discussion.

THE BROWSE COMMAND

Despite what the name of this command may suggest, this command is a very powerful version of the edit command. With this command, you can edit up to 17 records simultaneously on the screen, (11 records, if the cursor-control menu is up), and this time, each record is presented horizontally across the screen. If the record length is longer than screen size, no wrap around occurs, and the rest of the record is beyond the screen. The cursor control menu can be toggled through the use of the F1 key, and a status bar line is always present.

> **Note:** When the BROWSE command is issued, dBASE will bring up to 17 records on the screen, starting with the current record. That is, if you wanted to browse from the top of the database, you would have to move the record pointer to record #1 first.

```
.1          <cr>
.BROWSE        <cr>


EMP_NUM  EMP_NAME-----  TOWN-----  ORG EXE DT_OF_HIRE  SALARY--  NOTE
005      NINA BHARUCHA  WEBSTER    BSG T   05/24/80    25000.00  MEMO
010      PETE JOHNSON   BRIGHTON   BSG T   02/03/76    27590.00  MEMO
015      GLORIA PATEL   FAIRPORT   BSG T   07/16/82    27500.00  MEMO

                        etc   etc   etc   etc

-----------------------------------------------------------------------
| BROWSE      |<C:>| PERSNL      | REC: 1/15          |       | CAPS  |
-----------------------------------------------------------------------
```

The cursor always starts off at the first position of the first field, just as it does in the EDIT mode. The status bar specifies which record you are currently on. The position of the cursor anywhere within a record identifies that record as the current record.

The following additional controls may be used with the BROWSE command.

1. Pressing the <cr> key will make the cursor go forward field-by-field, in the horizontal direction.

2. Within a field, the Ctrl-V option can be used for the Insert feature.

3. Within a field, the Ctrl-G option can be used to delete the character under the cursor.

4. Within a field, the Backspace key can be used to delete the character to the left of of the cursor.

5. Once you have made changes to, say, record #5, entering the Down-Arrow key will move the cursor down vertically into the next record. That has the effect of saving record #5 just as it did in the edit mode.

6. Once you have made changes to, say, record #5, entering the Up-Arrow key will move the cursor up vertically into the previous record. That has the effect of saving record #5 just as it did in the edit mode.

7. While in any record, if you decide to delete the record, you may simply press Ctrl-U to flag the record for delete. Notice the Del indicator appears in the status line. Now when you leave that record, you have saved that record as deleted. Later on, if

your cursor finds itself anywhere in that (deleted) record line again, the Del indicator will again appear in the status line, reminding you that this record has been flagged as deleted. At this point, of course, you can always Ctrl-U again, to undelete the record.

8. Having made the final changes to a record, you may now press Ctrl-W to exit the BROWSE mode with a save of the last record changed, or Ctrl-Q to exit the BROWSE mode without a save of the changes made to the *last* record.

The only items remaining to be covered are those pertaining to fields that are outside of the view of the screen, if the record-length is more than 80 characters. Two new controls for the scrolling process need to be introduced here:

Ctrl-B or Ctrl + Right-arrow   \<cr>   will cause a scroll to the RIGHT, field-by-field.

Ctrl-Z or Ctrl + Left-arrow   \<cr>   will cause a scroll to the LEFT, field-by-field.

Browse Enhancements

As in the case of the edit command, you can put some muscle behind the BROWSE with additional parameters. Some of the parameters you will find most useful at this time include the following:

.BROWSE [FIELDS \<field-list>] [FREEZE \<a field>] [LOCK \<number>]

For example:

.BROWSE FIELDS TOWN,ORG,EMP_NAME   \<cr>

Only the fields TOWN, ORG, and EMP_NAME are brought to the screen for editing in the order listed.

.BROWSE FIELDS TOWN,ORG,EMP_NAME   FREEZE TOWN   \<cr>

This command will bring the fields mentioned to the screen for editing in the order specified, but the actual BROWSE (editing) action will be restricted to the TOWN field! This is useful in case you want to make rapid changes to a specific field, but also want other identifying information on the screen for reference.

The LOCK parameter lets you lock up the leftmost n fields, preventing the scrolling effect from working on these fields. For example, if you want to be able to scroll left and right but would like the EMP_NUM (employee number) field always present as a point of reference, then you may enter the following:

.BROWSE   LOCK 1   \<cr>

This will bring up all the fields for BROWSE, and your scrolling will affect every field except the EMP_NUM field, which happens to the first field in the structure of the file.

.BROWSE FIELDS TOWN,ORG,EMP__NAME,EMP__NAME,....,....,....   LOCK 2

<cr>

This command will present all the fields in the order you requested, but the scrolling will not affect the first two fields, TOWN and ORG. This time the locked fields are the ones you specified in the FIELDS parameter.

> **Note:** The scrolling effect under BROWSE only works if the record length (or the combined field length, if you selected some fields for browse) is greater than the screen width.

Scrolling

Scrolling, in the data processing environment, refers to the apparent movement (vertical or horizontal) of the data on a monitor screen. In scrolling, you have to visualize the data as being stationary, and the screen as moving across the data. If the screen moves to the left, you have scrolled left and if the screen moves up, you have scrolled up, and so on. In reality, of course, the screen does not move anywhere, and when you have scrolled left, that is, when the screen has moved left, the data appears to move to the right! Similarly, a scroll-up occurs when the data moves down, and so on. These left, right, up, and down definitions could be confusing.

If you stick to the convention of the data being stationary and the screen moving across that data, the scroll left or scroll up options will have definite meanings, as outlined before. In this convention, a scroll left means that the data moves right, and vice versa.

THE DELETE COMMAND

The DELETE command is used to flag one or more records as logically deleted. The flag is an asterisk in the extra field that was supplied to us by dBASE (the delete-indicator field), when we first created the structure under dBASE. This logical delete, as opposed to a physical delete, affords us the luxury of a change of mind, in case we decide to re-activate some or all of our deleted records.

.DELETE [scope] [FOR <condition>] [WHILE <condition>]   <cr>

The parameters are optional. In the event of a DELETE command without parameters, the current record is deleted.

> **Note:** In the sets of examples that follow, each group of instructions is independent of any other. That is, we shall presume that a fresh copy of the database records was available for each group of instructions.

Try out the following commands:

.5   < cr >
.DELETE   < cr >

1 record deleted

Notice the * beside record #5. This record is now logically deleted.

. LIST   < cr >

```
Record#   EMP_NUM  EMP_NAME       TOWN       ORG  EXE  DT_OF_HIRE    SALARY  NOTE
      1   005      NINA BHARUCHA  WEBSTER    BSG  .T.  05/24/80    25000.00  Memo
      2   010      PETE JOHNSON   brighton   BSG  .T.  02/03/76    27590.00  Memo
      3   015      GLORIA PATEL   FAIRPORT   RMG  .T.  07/16/82    27500.00  Memo
      4   020      MAX LEVINSKY   HENRIETTA  RMG  .F.  04/13/69    27550.00  Memo
      5  *025      KIM BRANDT     FAIRPORT   RMG  .F.  04/04/77    36000.00  Memo
      6   030      TIM MONTAL     ROCHESTER  RBG  .F.  07/07/81    41900.00  Memo
      7   035      WILLIAM PATEL  penfield   GSD  .F.  08/17/71    28900.00  Memo
      8   040      JAMES JAMESON  ROCHESTER  GSD  .T.  10/21/77    29800.00  Memo
      9   045      MORRIS KATZ    webster    BSG  .F.  09/14/80    23450.00  Memo
     10   050      PAUL BHARUCHA  BRIGHTON   BSG  .T.  05/23/73    29100.00  Memo
     11   055      PHIL MARTIN    WEBSTER    RMG  .F.  07/19/80    31000.00  Memo
     12   060      JOHN PETERSON  BRIGHTON   RBG  .T.  04/17/79    31480.00  Memo
     13   065      JOY HARDY      fairport   RBG  .F.  01/19/79    34200.00  Memo
     14   070      JAN MOREY      ROCHESTER  GSD  .T.  04/23/67    18190.00  Memo
     15   075      JOHN JONES     rochester  GSD  .T.  04/04/70    25100.00  Memo
```

Note: Starting at this point, only the changed or deleted records will be shown in full. Only the employee numbers of the records that have not been affected will be shown.

If you recall, the [scope] parameter could be ALL, RECO n, NEXT n, or REST. Try the following steps:

. 5   < cr >
. DELE NEXT 5   < cr >

5 records deleted

Notice that record numbers 5 through 9 are flagged as deleted.

. LIST   < cr >

```
Record#   EMP_NUM  EMP_NAME       TOWN       ORG  EXE  DT_OF_HIRE    SALARY  NOTE
      1   005.....
      2   010.....
      3   015.....
      4   020.....
      5  *025      KIM BRANDT     FAIRPORT   RMG  .F.  04/04/77    36000.00  Memo
      6  *030      TIM MONTAL     ROCHESTER  RBG  .F.  07/07/81    41900.00  Memo
      7  *035      WILLIAM PATEL  penfield   GSD  .F.  08/17/71    28900.00  Memo
      8  *040      JAMES JAMESON  ROCHESTER  GSD  .T.  10/21/77    29800.00  Memo
```

```
 9 *Ø45      MORRIS KATZ    webster   BSG .F. Ø9/14/8Ø   23450.ØØ Memo
1Ø  Ø5Ø.....
11  Ø55.....
12  Ø6Ø.....
13  Ø65.....
14  Ø7Ø.....
15  Ø75.....
```

      . DELE FOR TOWN = 'ROCH'   < cr >

     3 records deleted

As before, if no [scope] is mentioned but a FOR condition exists, then ALL is the default for the scope.

     . LIST   < cr >

```
Record#  EMP_NUM EMP_NAME       TOWN      ORG EXE DT_OF_HIRE   SALARY NOTE
      1  ØØ5.....
      2  Ø1Ø.....
      3  Ø15.....
      4  Ø2Ø.....
      5  Ø25.....
      6 *Ø3Ø     TIM MONTAL     ROCHESTER RBG .F. Ø7/Ø7/81   41900.ØØ Memo
      7  Ø35.....
      8 *Ø4Ø     JAMES JAMESON ROCHESTER GSD .T. 1Ø/21/77   29800.ØØ Memo
      9  Ø45.....
     1Ø  Ø5Ø.....
     11  Ø55.....
     12  Ø6Ø.....
     13  Ø65.....
     14 *Ø7Ø     JAN MOREY      ROCHESTER GSD .T. Ø4/23/67   18190.ØØ Memo
     15  Ø75.....
```

     . DELE FOR SUBSTR(TOWN,2,3) = 'OCH'   < cr >
     . LIST   < cr >

```
Record#  EMP_NUM EMP_NAME       TOWN      ORG EXE DT_OF_HIRE   SALARY NOTE
      1  ØØ5.....
      2  Ø1Ø.....
      3  Ø15.....
      4  Ø2Ø.....
      5  Ø25.....
      6 *Ø3Ø     TIM MONTAL     ROCHESTER RBG .F. Ø7/Ø7/81   41900.ØØ Memo
      7  Ø35.....
      8 *Ø4Ø     JAMES JAMESON ROCHESTER GSD .T. 1Ø/21/77   29800.ØØ Memo
      9  Ø45.....
     1Ø  Ø5Ø.....
     11  Ø55....
     12  Ø6Ø.....
     13  Ø65.....
     14 *Ø7Ø     JAN MOREY      ROCHESTER GSD .T. Ø4/23/67   18190.ØØ Memo
     15  Ø75.....
```

```
. DELE FOR ORG = 'BSG' .AND. DT__OF__HIRE > = CTOD('01/01/79')<cr>
. LIST          <cr>


Record#   EMP_NUM EMP_NAME         TOWN      ORG EXE DT_OF_HIRE    SALARY NOTE
      1 *005     NINA BHARUCHA WEBSTER     BSG .T. 05/24/80   25000.00 Memo
      2  010.....
      3  015.....
      4  020.....
      5  025.....
      6  030.....
      7  035.....
      8  040....
      9 *045     MORRIS KATZ     webster   BSG .F. 09/14/80   23450.00 Memo
     10  050.....
     11  055.....
     12  060.....
     13  065.....
     14  070.....
     15  075.....
```

As always, the condition can be as simple or as complex as you want to make it.

```
.1          <cr>
.DELE WHILE TOWN = 'WEB'          <cr>
```

The above command deletes only record #1, since record #2 negates the condition. To delete all records, starting with a specific record, enter the following:

```
.11          <cr>
.DELE REST          <cr>
```

This will delete the rest of the file, starting with and including the current record.

Listing Deleted Records

To see the effect of the LIST FOR DELETED( ) command, begin by entering the following commands:

```
. 5      <cr>
. DELE NEXT 5          <cr>
```

5 records deleted

The above command, as we have seen, deletes records 5 through 9. The next command will give you a listing, on the screen, of all the deleted records only. The DELETED( ) function is used here.

```
. LIST FOR DELETED( )      <cr>
```

```
Record#   EMP_NUM  EMP_NAME       TOWN       ORG EXE DT_OF_HIRE  SALARY NOTE
      5   *025     KIM BRANDT      FAIRPORT   RMG .F. 04/04/77  36000.00 Memo
      6   *030     TIM MONTAL      ROCHESTER  RBG .F. 07/07/31  41900.00 Memo
      7   *035     WILLIAM PATEL   penfield   GSD .F. 08/17/71  28900.00 Memo
      8   *040     JAMES JAMESON   ROCHESTER  GSD .T. 10/21/77  29800.00 Memo
      9   *045     MORRIS KATZ     webster    BSG .F. 09/14/80  23450.00 Memo
```

Listing Active Records

This version of the LIST command will list out the valid, active records.

. LIST FOR .NOT. DELETED( )   <cr>

```
Record#   EMP_NUM  EMP_NAME       TOWN       ORG EXE DT_OF_HIRE  SALARY NOTE
      1   005      NINA BHARUCHA   WEBSTER    BSG .T. 05/24/80  25000.00 Memo
      2   010      PETE JOHNSON    brighton   BSG .T. 02/03/76  27590.00 Memo
      3   015      GLORIA PATEL    FAIRPORT   RMG .T. 07/16/82  27500.00 Memo
      4   020      MAX LEVINSKY    HENRIETTA  RMG .F. 04/13/69  27550.00 Memo
     10   050      PAUL BHARUCHA   BRIGHTON   BSG .T. 05/23/73  29100.00 Memo
     11   055      PHIL MARTIN     WEBSTER    RMG .F. 07/19/80  31000.00 Memo
     12   060      JOHN PETERSON   BRIGHTON   RBG .T. 04/17/79  31480.00 Memo
     13   065      JOY HARDY       fairport   RBG .F. 01/19/79  34200.00 Memo
     14   070      JAN MOREY       ROCHESTER  GSD .T. 04/23/67  18190.00 Memo
     15   075      JOHN JONES      rochester  GSD .T. 04/04/70  25100.00 Memo
```

Note: The command .DISP STRU or the function RECCOUNT( ) shows the number of records currently in your file. This count includes the count of the deleted records!

THE RECALL COMMAND

This command is the opposite of the DELETE command, in that it removes the logical indicator of * (the delete-flag) from deleted records. It is identical in format to the DE-LETE command.

.RECALL [scope] [FOR <condition>] [WHILE <condition>]   <cr>

The example that follows illustrates the use of the parameters.

.DELETE ALL   <cr>   deletes all records.
.LIST   <cr>

```
Record#   EMP_NUM  EMP_NAME      TOWN       ORG EXE DT_OF_HIRE   SALARY NOTE
      1   *005.....
      2   *010.....
      3   *015.....
      4   *020.....
      5   *025.....
      6   *030.....
      7   *035 ....
      8   *040.....
      9   *045.....
```

```
10 *050.....
11 *055.....
12 *060.....
13 *065.....
14 *070.....
15 *075.....
```

Now, recall some records:

.RECALL FOR TOWN = 'ROCH' .AND. ORG = 'GSD'   <cr>

All records that satisfy the condition will have their delete flags removed, thus activating them again.

.LIST   <cr>

```
Record#  EMP_NUM EMP_NAME       TOWN       ORG EXE DT_OF_HIRE   SALARY NOTE
      1 *005.....
      2 *010.....
      3 *015.....
      4 *020.....
      5 *025.....
      6 *030.....
      7 *035.....
      8  040     JAMES JAMESON ROCHESTER GSD .T. 10/21/77   29800.00 Memo
      9 *045.....
     10 *050.....
     11 *055.....
     12 *060.....
     13 *065.....
     14  070     JAN MOREY      ROCHESTER GSD .T. 04/23/67   18190.00 Memo
     15 *075.....
```

As always, the condition can be as simple or as complex as you want to make it. The WHILE parameter will only recall records while successive records satisfy the condition.

THE PACK COMMAND

The PACK command is responsible for physically removing records that had, until now, been logically flagged as deleted.

.PACK   <cr>

Note that the PACK command has no parameters. This means that you cannot pick and choose the deleted records to be PACKed. It is an all-or-nothing proposition. All deleted records will be physically zapped out.

Please understand very clearly that once you have packed the database, there is no way that you can ever bring those records back into your control again. So before you use the PACK command, please take a moment to reflect upon the wisdom of your action.

After the PACK operation, your database will be reduced by the number of deleted records that have been removed. The record numbers in your database will have been readjusted to provide for consecutive numbering, starting from 1.

Note that if you use **.DISP STRU** <cr> after a PACK operation, the header you see on the screen may or may not reflect the current, correct number of records in the file. To update the header, you will have to close the file from use. Also, note that the disk space released by the deleted records is reclaimed by the system only when the file is closed. To close the database file, enter the following command:

.USE   <cr>

The USE command without any parameters will close the file currently in use.

Now you can bring the file back into use, and the header will have been updated correctly.

.USE PERSNL   <cr >

.DISP STRU   <cr>   will give the true record count.

Usually before you go ahead and PACK the database, you may want to make a backup copy of your deleted records, so that if you ever decide that you had made an error, you can always have access to the original data.

Later on, after the necessary commands have been covered, I will show you a way of saving your deleted records in another database with the same structure as the master database, prior to issuing the PACK command. In case you ever want to restore those deleted records, it would only take a couple of dBASE commands to do so.

As you can appreciate, the DELETE, RECALL, and PACK commands form a logical sub-set of dBASE commands.

THE ZAP COMMAND

If you wanted to delete all the records from a file, one way of doing it would be:

. DELE ALL   <cr >
. PACK   <cr >

This will retain the file structure, but the structure will now be devoid of all data records. If, however, you had several thousand records in your file, deleting all the records and then packing the file is time-consuming.

An instant delete of all records is possible through the use of the ZAP command:

. ZAP   <cr>

will remove all records instantly.

> **Note:** You only ZAP the file. You do not have to "delete all" the records first. The net effect is identical to a DELE ALL/PACK com-

bination. The file structure is left intact, but devoid of any record.

A word of caution is called for, here. There will be times when your master file will be indexed. (Indexing is explained in great detail, later on.) That means that one or more files called *index files* will be open, along with the master file. In such cases, if you DELE ALL/PACK or ZAP the master file, ensure that you re-build all the index-files associated with this master file!! Don't rely on the DELE ALL/PACK combination or the ZAP command to automatically rebuild the index files. You rebuild the indexes through the use of the INDEX command, explained in detail in a separate section.

THE INSERT COMMAND

The INSERT command, although available, is not of too much direct use in any application. Using this command, you can specify to dBASE that a new record is to be INSERTed exactly between, say, existing records 7 and 8.

Now please understand that there is really no need for you to specify that a new, incoming record should be placed exactly after such-and-such existing record. The new record could be simply APPENDed to the end of the database, and the database could now be either physically sorted or logically indexed to provide you with the desired sequencing effect. The processes of sorting and indexing will be covered in depth, later.

If however, you did want to INSERT a new record at a specific point in the database, you would use the following procedure:

1. Select the record in the database, say, record #7, after which you want to have the new record.

.7   <cr>

2. Then enter the following

.INSERT   <cr>

This opens up a blank structure of the file in use (just like in the APPEND mode). If SET CARRY ON is in effect, the mask contains the contents of record #7.

```
Record No.    8
EMP_NUM    :    :
EMP_NAME   :            :
TOWN       :        :
ORG        :    :
EXE        :?:
DT_OF_HIRE:        :
SALARY     :        :
NOTE       :Memo:
```

This is the mask of the new record to be INSERTed.
Enter the data you want, using cursor controls and full edit features as studied earlier.
Notice that the logical field initially comes up with the ?
Use the F1 key to toggle the cursor control menu, if required.

3. After the data has been entered, you can do only one of two things:

a) Either save the new record and get out of the INSERT mode (either done with a Ctrl-W or a Ctrl-End, or done automatically when you have entered the last character of the last field.)

b) Change your mind on this new record and get out of the INSERT mode (done with a Ctrl-Q or the ESC (escape) key.)

Regardless of the action taken, you will always get out of the INSERT mode. You can only INSERT *one* record at a time except when you are inserting after the last record in the file (In that case it behaves like the APPEND mode, and you can have multiple inserts). In our example, the new record is inserted after the record you are currently on. This new record coming in will now have a record #8, and all succeeding records will have their original record numbers changed!

To try INSERTing records at the end of a file, type the following commands:

```
.GO BOTT        <cr>
.INSERT         <cr>
```

Now the INSERT behaves like APPEND.

You may also INSERT before the current record.

```
.7              <cr>
.INSERT BEFORE          <cr>
```

As always, you are provided with a mask of the structure, and after the new record is saved, record numbers are changed appropriately, to reflect the new record's position in the database. In our example, the new record is now record #7.

Try the following command:

```
.INSERT BLANK    <cr>
```

This will INSERT a blank record after the current record. This blank record may be subsequently edited.

Again, it should be emphasized that you do not have to use the INSERT feature to position records. New records should be APPENDed, and the sorting/indexing features should be used to obtain the sequencing impact you are seeking. As you will see later, you can have dBASE automatically keep your file in sequence, while you append more records.

THE APPEND COMMAND REVISITED

We shall now look at the extended features of this command. The APPEND is very powerful and should be studied in its entirety.

APPEND FROM <file> [FOR <condition>] [SDF] [DELIM <with DELIMITER>]

Essentially what this command enables us to do is take records out of one file and copy them over to another. The FROM file could be either a dBASE file or a file created under a standard text processor, that is a "word processed" file.

The FROM <file> Parameter

Suppose you have a file called MASTER.DBF, with or without records, and another file called TRANS.DBF, with records.

```
.USE  MASTER                <cr>
.APPEND FROM TRANS          <cr>
```

The two above commands will take all the records from the TRANS file and *AP-PEND them (copy them over) to the end of the MASTER file.* The FROM file is not changed in any way, shape or form.

If there were deleted records in the FROM file, these are also copied over, and are reactivated in the destination file!!

If there were memo fields in the from file, the contents of these fields are also copied over!

This implies, obviously, that the structures of the two files should be identical. What if the structures are similar but not identical? For example:

MASTER   **TRANS**

EMP_NUM,C,6   ORG,C,3
TOWN,C,12   DT_OF_HIRE,N,6
ORG,C,3   EMP_NUM,C,6
SALARY,N,8,2   SALARY,N,8,2

Here the structures have some similarity, but are not identical. If we now say:

```
.USE MASTER                 <cr>
.APPEND FROM TRANS          <cr>
```

what would happen?

Only those field names that match are included in the process of APPEND! The other fields are ignored. The matching fields do not have to be in similar positions in both files. A complete reformatting will take place, if necessary! The contents of memo fields will be APPENDed only if the names of the memo fields are identical.

In our example, since the EMP_NUM, ORG, and SALARY field names match, only the data from those fields will be copied over into the structure of the MASTER file, for each of the records. The column identified as the TOWN field in the MAS-TER file will remain blank for each of the new records APPENDed from the TRANS file. None of the data from the DT_OF_HIRE field in the TRANS file is copied over. Obviously, records existing in the master file before the start of the APPEND operation are not affected.

Create another database called STUDENTS containing the following fields:

EMP_NUM,C,3
EMP_NAME,C,13
SALARY,N,8,2

Enter any data you want in this file. Create at least four records of data. Then type the following:

```
.USE PERSNL                        <cr>
.APPEND FROM STUDENTS              <cr>
.LIST                              <cr>
```

You will see gaps in the listing of the file PERSNL for the newly appended records where the field names that could not be matched (between the PERSNL file and the STUDENTS file) were left without any data coming in from the STUDENTS file.

Record#	EMP_NUM	EMP_NAME	TOWN	ORG	EXE	DT_OF_HIRE	SALARY	NOTE
1	005.....							
2	010.....							
3	015.....							
4	020.....							
5	025.....							
6	030.....							
7	035.....							
8	040.....							
9	045.....							
10	050.....							
11	055.....							
12	060.....							
13	065.....							
14	070.....							
15	075.....							
16	001	A. ADAMS			.F.	/ /	15000.00	Memo
17	002	B. BROWN			.F.	/ /	20000.00	Memo
18	003	C. COLBY			.F.	/ /	30000.00	Memo
19	004	D. DAVIDSON			.F.	/ /	40000.00	Memo

The above routine highlights a very important use of the APPEND command. Let us say, for example, that you know of an existing dBASE master file, and you want to use a subset of that information for your own function. All you have to do is to create the structure of the file that you want, ensuring that you use the identical names, types, and sizes of the fields as they have been defined in the structure of the master file.

Suppose the file you have created is called MYFILE, and you enter the following commands:

```
.USE MYFILE                        <cr>
.APPEND FROM MASTER                <cr>
```

All the field names that match will have their data pulled over. *You have now AP-PENDed over (copied over) a subset of information from the MASTER file into your file.*

(Enter .LIST <cr> to find out that this is true.) Later on, in the COPY command, we shall see a much easier way of doing the same thing; that is, of creating a subset of information from a master file.

You might ask the question, "What if the field names match, but the type and/or length is different?" For example: What would happen if you are trying to APPEND data from a field defined EMP_NUM,C,6 to a field defined EMP_NUM,N,5? The answer is that since the field names match, the copying over of data will be attempted, but since the types and/or lengths are different, you will end up with *unexpected results.*

At the end of this section on APPEND, we shall cover these what-if type of questions, since the APPEND command is an important aspect of dBASE, and you need to appreciate the full impact of the results of APPENDing with nonconforming fields. For now we will emphasize the fact that for any data movement to occur during the APPEND process, the field-names *must* match. Ideally, even the type and length should match.

The FOR Condition

You may use a condition thrown in to enhance the utility of the APPEND command. For example:

```
.USE PERSNL        <cr>
.APPEND FROM STUDENTS FOR SALARY > 20000          <cr>
```

Now only those records that satisfy the condition are picked up from the STU-DENTS file, and from those records, only data from the matching field names is copied over. Obviously, the STUDENTS file-structure must contain a field called SALARY.

Please note the following point: Illogical though it may seem, the fields used in the FOR expression must reside in the structure of both databases! Since the SAL-ARY field has been used in the FOR condition, the structures of both "from" and "to" databases must contain the SALARY field. Hopefully, the field definitions will tally exactly.

```
.USE PERSNL        <cr>
.APPEND FROM STUDENTS FOR ORG = 'BSG' .AND. SALARY > 20000<cr>
```

Now both SALARY and ORG must be defined in the structures of both databases. This is true even if you had an *.OR.* as the logical operator!

If you attempt an APPEND of totally dissimilar structures, no records would be appended.

Text/ASCII/SDF Files

dBASE permits you to *import* files that are in *text* format and put them into dBASE format. Before I explain the process of doing this, it is necessary that you clearly understand what text means, since there are various formats to a text file.

A text file is one that has only data, and no structure. A text file is also called an

ASCII file, which is also called a Standard Data Format (SDF) file. One way of creating an ASCII file is by using the nondocument mode of a commercial word-processor. Remember that the terms *text, ASCII,* and *SDF* are synonymous.

An ASCII file can also be defined as one having, in its character set, characters within the range Hexadecimal 00 through Hexadecimal 7F (or decimal 0 through 127). If you did not understand the previous sentence, I suggest you don't lose sleep over it. Loosely translated, an ASCII or text file is one that can be typed on the screen or printed on the printer. If your attempt to TYPE the contents of a file from DOS results in "garbage" going across the screen, that file is not an ASCII file. The same reasoning applies if the printer goes haywire.

If the first-three records from the PERSNL.DBF database were to be created in a regular SDF format, they would appear as follows:

```
005NINA BHARUCHAWEBSTER  BSGT1980052425000.00
010PETE JOHNSON brighton BSGT1976020327590.00
015GLORIA PATEL FAIRPORT RMGT1982071627500.00
```

There is no physical structure to this file, per se, except as may be inferred by the user of the file. Conceptually, you can see the inherent structure of this file, since you can differentiate the employee-number from the employee name, etc. But without some familiarity with the data, you would not know that "BSGT" is actually the organization data (BSG) followed by the exempt/non-exempt data (T), and you could easily take the "BSGT" to be some kind of code.

A regular SDF file is like the one shown above. Other types of SDF files may be *delimited,* that is, these files have quotes and/or commas separating the various fields of information. dBASE provides several facilities to bring in data from any one of the text formats (standard or delimited) into a dBASE format.

Examples of the types of standard (regular and delimited) files are as follows:

```
005NINA BHARUCHAWEBSTER  BSGT1980052425000.00
010PETE JOHNSON BRIGHTON BSGT1976020327590.00
015GLORIA PATEL FAIRPORT RMGT1982071627500.00
```
Regular SDF.

```
"005","NINA BHARUCHA","WEBSTER","BSG",T,19800524,25000.00
"010","PETE JOHNSON","BRIGHTON","BSG",T,19760203,27590.00
"015","GLORIA PATEL","FAIRPORT","RMG",T,19820716,27500.00
```
Delimited with commas and double quotes.

```
'005','NINA BHARUCHA','WEBSTER','BSG',T,19800524,25000.00
'010','PETE JOHNSON','BRIGHTON','BSG',T,19760203,27590.00
'015','GLORIA PATEL','FAIRPORT','RMG',T,19820716,27500.00
```
Delimited with commas and single quotes.

```
,005,,,NINA BHARUCHA,,,WEBSTER,,,BSG,,T,19800524,25000.00
,010,,,PETE JOHNSON,,,BRIGHTON,,,BSG,,T,19760203,27590.00
,015,,,GLORIA PATEL,,,FAIRPORT,,,RMG,,T,19820716,27500.00
```
Delimited with commas only.

```
005 NINA BHARUCHA WEBSTER BSG T 19800524 25000.00
010 PETE JOHNSON BRIGHTON BSG T 19760203 27590.00
015 GLORIA PATEL FAIRPORT RMG T 19820716 27500.00
```
Delimited with blank spaces.

```
$005$,$NINA BHARUCHA$,$WEBSTER$,$BSG$,T,19800524,25000.00
$010$,$PETE JOHNSON$,$BRIGHTON$,$BSG$,T,19760203,27590.00
$015$,$GLORIA PATEL$,$FAIRPORT$,$RMG$,T,19820716,27500.00
```
Delimited with commas and a special character.

dBASE permits the import of any one of these text formats into a dBASE database structure. The processes of doing this is explained next.

The SDF Parameter

This section shows you the formats of the APPEND command that will permit you to transfer data from text files into a dBASE format.

```
.USE PERSNL          <cr>
.APPEND FROM MYFILE SDF          <cr>
```
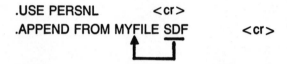

In this command, SDF is a parameter that stands for Standard Data Format, and it is the parameter that tells dBASE that the file called MYFILE is a regular text file, not a dBASE file. That is, the SDF parameter helps to qualify the file named in the command.

dBASE will now look for a file called MYFILE.TXT (as a default for text file), and if it finds it, it will take the records out of that file, character for character, a record at a time, and simply APPEND the data under the database structure of PERSNL. In effect, the structure of the database will define what the newly appended data fields refer to.

Obviously, it stands to reason that if a text file is going to be imported into a dBASE database format, you should ensure that the data in the text file corresponds exactly to the subsequent, expected format of the dBASE file. If you fail to follow this rule, dBASE will not know the difference, and you could end up getting garbage for your result.

For example, suppose the incoming text file had the following record:

My dear so-and-so, How I love you

and you tried to APPEND this record into the structure of the file called PERSNL. dBASE would take this record and plug it under the structure of PERSNL, character for character, so that after this APPEND, the record will appear as follows: (The ^ signifies a "space" character.)

My^   (will be the EMP_NUM, since it was defined as C,3)
dear so-and-s   (will become the EMP_NAME, since it was defined as C,13)
o, How I^   (will become the TOWN, since it was defined as C,9)
etc., etc., etc.

As you can see, dBASE makes a presumption that your regular text file format conforms exactly with the structure of the database that will be receiving the text records, which, of course, is logical enough.

Note: You could have specified:

. USE PERSNL   \<cr>
. APPEND FROM MYFILE.ABC SDF   \<cr>

Now dBASE will look for a text file with the exact name you provide. You do not have to stay with the .TXT qualifier.

The Delimited Parameter

.USE PERSNL   \<cr>
.APPEND FROM MYFILE *DELIM*   \<cr>

The DELIMited parameter shown in the above command is the parameter that tells dBASE that the file called MYFILE is a delimited text file, not a dBASE file or a regular text file. That is, the DELIM parameter helps to qualify the file named in the command. By using the DELIMited parameter by itself, you anticipate the format of the incoming file to be as follows:

"——C——","——C——",——N——,"——C——",—-L—-,—-D—-

The comma and the double quote are the default delimiters. Here you will notice that each character field is enclosed (delimited) in double quotes, and every field is separated (delimited) by a comma. Numeric, logical, and date fields are not enclosed in quotes.

Depending on the expected format of the incoming file, you should specify different delimiters, as follows:

.APPEND FROM MYFILE DELIM WITH '   \<cr>
   '—-C——','——C——',——N——,'——C——',—-L—-,—-D—-

Here the expectation is that in the incoming file, every character field is delimited with the single-quote, and every field is delimited with the comma.

.APPEND FROM MYFILE DELIM WITH "   \<cr>
   "——C——","——C——",——N——,"——C——",—-L—-,—-D—-

This is the same as the first example above.

.APPEND FROM MYFILE DELIM WITH ,   \<cr>
   ,——C——,,,——C——,,——N——,,——C——,,—-L—-,—-D—-

Here the expectation is that the incoming file is delimited with commas only, without quotes of any kind. To explain the apparently random number of commas in between fields, remember that in this case the comma itself is used as a delimiter, the delimiters only enclose character fields, and every field is delimited by a comma.

```
.APPEND FROM MYFILE DELIM WITH BLANK        <cr>
——C——· ——C——· ——N——· ——C——· —-L—· —-D—·
```

You can have the blank character as the delimiter. (Yes, a blank is a character and is as valid as any other character!)

```
.APPEND FROM MYFILE DELIM WITH $        <cr>
$——C——$,$——C——$,——N——·,$——C——$,—-L—·,—-D—·
```

dBASE can even accommodate a special character as the delimiter in the imported file. Any one of the characters found on the top row of the keyboard can be used as the delimiter in the incoming file, and it will be accepted.

The DELIM formats of the APPEND command provide you with the capability of creating a dBASE file out of a standard, *delimited* text file, regardless of the way the file is delimited.

During the process of APPEND from a delimited file, each comma between the fields signals the end of a field. For example, suppose the following text record was appended into the file called PERSNL.

"005","AL ADAMS","","BSG","",19800524,25000.00

This is how the append would work:

005	would enter the field called EMP_NUM
Al Adams	would enter the field called EMP_NAME
The "null-field"	would cause the field called TOWN to be omitted (!!)
BSG	would enter the field called ORG
The "null-field"	would cause the field called EXE to be omitted (!!)
19800524	would enter the field called DT_OF_HIRE
25000.00	would enter the field called SALARY.

At the end of the APPEND process, the commas and the quotes will have been automatically stripped off, each comma would signify the end of a field, and only real data would be APPENDed into the structure of the receiving database.

Notice that if a date has to be appended from a text file into a dBASE format, the data format in the text file should be CCYYMMDD, where CC is the *century*. At the end of the append, the date rests in the dBASE file in the format MMDDYY.

> **Question:** Why do we need to know about the SDF (for standard files) and the DELIM (for delimited files) parameters? After all, if I wanted to create a dBASE file, I would do it directly in dBASE, first by using the CREATE command and then by using the APPEND

command. Why would I create a file through a word processor, create the appropriate structure in dBASE, and then APPEND data from the text file into the dBASE structure?

Answer: The first point to understand is that you would not go out of your way to create a file in the text format (with or without delimiters), just so you can transform it subsequently into a dBASE format. It is much easier to simply CREATE the file in dBASE and then APPEND data into it directly. Thus the question now translates to: Where do these text files, with or without delimiters come from?

These text files are the result of conversion from other commercial software. For example, if you wanted to make use of data files created under the control of MBASIC, SUPERCALC, or LOTUS, these software packages have the ability to create text files out of their own data files. These text files may or may not be delimited, depending on several options. You can now pull these text files into the required dBASE format.

This means that the text format, with or without delimiters, is the common meeting ground between software packages, if data is to be shared.

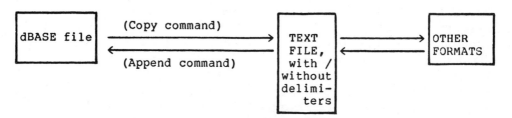

Later, we shall see how we can go in reverse, that is, pull off a standard file, with or without delimiters, from a dBASE file. This will provide the complementary action required for full communication between dBASE and other software, via the SDF format.

Please understand the importance of the delimited parameter in the APPEND commands. What do you suppose would happen if you wanted to APPEND data from a delimited text file, and you informed dBASE that the file was SDF, forgetting to use, the DELIM parameter in the command?

Every comma and quote will be pulled into the structure of your database, as *ordinary data*! dBASE would be unable to differentiate between the comma and quote as data, and the comma and quote as delimiters. If the commas and quotes are meant to be delimiters, inform dBASE of that fact!

The converse mistake would be equally bad. Suppose you had the following non-delimited text file, with only two records shown. This file only contains employee number and employee name data.

001JOHN JONES
002PAUL PONES

I will now append this text file into a dBASE format, but make the mistake of using the DELIM parameter.

. USE PERSNL   <cr>   (For now, this file has only three
                                          records).

.APPE FROM MYFILE DELIM   <cr>
. LIST   <cr>

```
Record#  EMP_NUM EMP_NAME       TOWN      ORG EXE DT_OF_HIRE   SALARY NOTE
      1  005     NINA BHARUCHA  WEBSTER   BSG .T. 05/24/80   25000.00 Memo
      2  010     PETE JOHNSON   brighton  BSG .T. 02/03/76   27590.00 Memo
      3  015     GLORIA PATEL   FAIRPORT  RMG .T. 07/16/82   27500.00 Memo
      4  001                             .F.   /  /                  Memo
      5  002                             .F.   /  /                  Memo
```

Notice that only the employee number was appended, because dBASE was searching for a delimiter in the text file, and finding none, it presumed that the entire record was one field of data! So it appended that one field of data into the first-field of the database structure. Since this first field is only three characters long, only the first three characters got in!

Thus it is crucial to understand that you have to *know* your data well, before you start APPENDing data from one file into another.

Let me reemphasize a point, here. The SDF and the DELIM parameters make it possible for you to import data from a standard text file (regular or delimited) into a dBASE format. You would not, however, go out of your way to create the file in the text format, just so you could change into a dBASE format. These text files are used only because they offer a means of using files produced by other software.

It is advisable to ensure that you have the double quotes and commas as the delimiter in the imported file, since it is possible that the converted data in some of the character fields could have embedded commas. For example, suppose the data you obtained from an external source includes a company named Joseph Armstrong & Sons, Inc. There is a comma embedded in the field. If this text file were delimited with the comma alone, you can imagine that when you attempt to APPEND this data into a dBASE file, the presence of this comma in the name field will lead dBASE to place the Inc. into the next field, thereby giving you garbage for this particular record.

For the same reason, if you have a text file delimited with the BLANK, a subsequent APPEND of this text file into, say, the PERSNL file, will cause every record to go haywire on account of the extra space in the name field between the first and last names! Such data in text format should be delimited with quotes and/or commas.

Obviously, this leads to the logical question: Won't the same kind of problem arise if the data from the text file contained a double quote, and I was using the double-quote as the delimiter?

The answer is NO! This is because a file delimited with double quotes is also automatically delimited with commas, and the comma is the saving grace on this occasion.

For example, suppose the following delimited text record existed. Notice the extra double quote within the name field.

If I were now to specify:

.USE PERSNL   `<cr>`
.APPE FROM TEXTFILE DELIM WITH "   `<cr>`

005   would enter the field called EMP_NUM
NINA   would enter the field called EMP_NAME. The rest of the name would
           be ignored, up through the comma, which signifies the end of the field!
WEBSTER   would enter the field called TOWN, and so on.

If it were not for the comma as the delimiter, every subsequent piece of data after
the name NINA would go haywire, for that record.

If asked to summarize the foregoing discussion, I would emphasize that you should:
(1) know the data you are playing around with, and (2) ensure that your incoming text
files are delimited with double quotes and commas, if the data was meant to be appended under a dBASE structure. This, of course, is only a safety precaution, in case
the actual incoming data contained embedded quotes or commas or blanks.

Incidentally, dBASE readily accepts a special character as the delimiter in the incoming text file. For example, if you had the following data coming in from a delimited
text file called MYFILE.TXT:

```
$005$,$NINA BHARUCHA$,$WEBSTER$,$BSG$,T,19800524,25000.00
$010$,$PETE JOHNSON$,$brighton$,$BSG$,T,19760203,27590.00
$015$,$GLORIA PATEL$,$FAIRPORT$,$RMG$,T,19820716,27500.00
```

and you wanted to pull this data over into the PERSNL database, you would enter:

.APPE FROM MYFILE DELIMITED WITH $ `<cr>`

In place of the $ sign, dBASE permits the use of any of the special characters found
on the upper row of the standard keyboard.

> **Note:** The two files used in the APPEND process need not re-
> side on the same disk. Presuming you have not .SET DEFAULT TO
> B you can always specify:

.USE `<master>`   `<cr>`   (`<master>` is on the logged-in
                                   drive)
.APPEND FROM B:`<trans>` `<cr>`   (`<trans>` is on the B:drive)

> **Note:** dBASE directly supports the import of data from three
> popular spreadsheet software products: VisiCalc, Multiplan and LO-
> TUS 1-2-3. The lines below show the formats that should be used:

.APPE FROM FILEV DIF	\<cr\>	(FILEV is the name of the file from VisiCalc. You can have any name you want for the file.)
.APPE FROM FILEM SYLK	\<cr\>	(The file from Multiplan)
.APPE FROM FILEL WKS	\<cr\>	(The file from LOTUS 1-2-3)

The special parameters DIF, SYLK, and WKS identify the three types of files. In each case, the individual rows convert to .dbf records, and the columns convert to fields under the dBASE format. In each case, the spreadsheet must be stored in *row-major order*, and column headers should be removed. If you leave row names in the files, ensure that your receiving file's dBASE structure was designed with that in mind. Avoid leading blank rows or columns.

Appending a Blank Record

One more form of the APPEND command uses the blank parameter:

.USE PERSNL	\<cr\>
.APPEND BLANK	\<cr\>

This command will append a blank record to the end of an existing database.

.LIST   \<cr\>(Note record #16)

```
Record#  EMP_NUM EMP_NAME      TOWN        ORG EXE DT_OF_HIRE   SALARY NOTE
      1  005.....
      2  010.....
      3  015.....
      4  020......
      5  025.....
      6  030.....
      7  035.....
      8  040.....
      9  045.....
     10  050.....
     11  055.....
     12  060.....
     13  065.....
     14  070.....
     15  075.....
     16                                     .F.  /  /              Memo
```

This form of the APPEND command is not as redundant as it might seem, at first glance. The importance of this form of the command can be highlighted as follows:

Suppose you write a computer program in dBASE (which we will be doing, in the course of this material), which, when invoked, sends up a formatted screen asking the operator to enter a record of information. The format on the screen asks the operator to enter, say, Employee Number, Name, Org, and Salary.

When the required pieces of information have been keyed-in, the program now has to undertake the task of creating a new record of data from the information supplied by the operator. The program will APPEND BLANK to the database in use, creating a blank record of information at the end of the database, and, more important, getting the record pointer to point to the newly appended record. Now the program can replace the appropriate blank fields of the new record with the information that was keyed in by the operator. We shall see examples of this, later, in this book.

Here's a final word about the APPEND command: when appending from a text file (either regular (standard) or delimited), nothing is ever appended into a memo field, if there was one in the receiving file. This is true even if overflow characters are available in the source.

For example: Your database MASTER is structured as follows:

```
NAME        C    10
NOTE        M    10                (this is the memo-field)
```

and your text source file has the following data record:

```
JOHN JONESYOUR ACCOUNT IS PAST DUE. PLEASE PAY NOW.
```

Notice that the name JOHN JONES takes exactly 10 characters. Now if you were to append this text data into your database using the commands:

```
.USE MASTER            <cr>
.APPE FROM MYFILE SDF            <cr>
```

the name JOHN JONES would enter the NAME field, but the message 'YOUR AC-COUNT . . .' would not be recorded in the corresponding .DBT file associated with the dBASE file! This would be true even if your incoming text file was delimited.

Data Movement Outcomes

Now would be an appropriate time to cover the what-if types of questions dealing with data movement. In other words, what is the expected outcome if you were to attempt an APPEND of data between, say, a field defined as EMP_NUM,C,6 and a field defined as EMP_NUM,N,5? I shall attempt to cover all combinations of cases, as outlined on the following page.

One rule of thumb to be followed, for now, is that *the sending field determines justification.* In general, all numeric data is right justified within its field, and all character data is left justified within its field. In conjunction with the rule of thumb specified above, this means that if the sending field is a character field, it implies left justification, and the data is picked up starting at the left from the sending field. Conversely, if the sending field is a numeric field, it implies right justification, and the data is picked up starting at the right from the sending field.

For numeric data movement from either a character or a numeric field, if the receiving field is not wide enough to receive all the numeric characters from the sending field, then garbage in the form of ****** moves over! If numeric data is coming over from a character field, the first nonnumeric stops the data movement. All data entering a numeric field will always be right justified. See the table below, for examples:

Note: The ^ symbol signifies a space character.

FROM field and data   TO field and result

A.	C,6	ABCDEF	C,5	ABCDE
B.	C,6	ABCDEF	C,7	ABCDEF
C.	N,4	1972	C,3	✱✱✱
D.	N,4	1972	C,4	1972
E.	N,4	1972	C,5	^1972
F.	N,4	1972	N,3	✱✱✱
G.	N,4	1972	N,5	^1972

H.	C,3	N,3
	12A	^12
	1A2	^^1
	A21	^^0
	123	123

I.	C,3	N,4
	12A	^^12
	1A2	^^^1
	A21	^^^0
	123	^123

J.	C,3	N,2
	12A	12
	1A2	^1
	A21	^0
	123	✱✱

The moral of the story is: it's better to be safe than sorry. Check out your file structures for compatibility before you start appending.

Suppose you issued an APPEND command, to APPEND data into FILE1, from FILE2. After the APPEND is completed, you should check the condition of the receiving file; if you see ✱✱✱✱✱ in one or more of the receiving fields, you know that this implies data/structure situations as explained above. During the course of the APPEND, however, dBASE does not provide either the names of the fields or the record numbers of the data involved in the process. If you do encounter these messages, *back out* all your APPENDS, modify the appropriate structures and proceed with the APPEND again.

Question: What do we mean by "back out all your Appends?"

Answer: Normally, when the APPEND command has completed its execution, dBASE flashes a message on the screen indicating the number of records that had been appended at the end of existing data into FILE1 from FILE2. These records are the ones that would have to be DELETEd from FILE1, and FILE1 would then be PACKed to physically "back out" all the appended records from FILE1.

In some situations, however, you may have issued a prior command such as .SET TALK OFF (this command will be explained later, in the programming portion of this book). Under the influence of the above SET command, there is no message from dBASE regarding the number of records appended from FILE2. So you should go about getting rid of the appended records as follows. If all the records from FILE2 had been appended, you can type:

```
.USE FILE2      <cr>
.GO BOTT        <cr>
.DISP        <cr>
```

This will display the last record and its record number, so you know exactly how many records should be backed out from FILE1.

If only selected records from FILE2 had been appended into FILE1, you should do the following:

```
.USE FILE2           <cr>
.COUNT FOR <the same condition used for the APPEND>           <cr>
```

Now dBASE will display a number indicating how many records had fulfilled the condition, and hence how many records you should back out of FILE1. Using one of the above methods, you can easily find out how many records from FILE1 need to be backed out.

Now, for the actual process of backing out these records, use the following procedure. Suppose you wanted to back out 100 records. You should enter:

```
.USE FILE1      <cr>
.GO BOTT        <cr>
.DISP        <cr>
```

The record number of the last record provides us with the total number of records in FILE1. Suppose there were 300 records in FILE1. Obviously, if we have to back out the last 100 records out of a total of 300 records, it follows quite logically that we need to back out record-numbers 201 through 300. That is, our starting record number is 201. [(300-100) + 1]. Enter:

.201   <cr>

This will move the record pointer to record number 201. The file in use, of course, is FILE1. Now enter:

.DELE REST   <cr>
.PACK   <cr>

This process will back out all the erroneous appended records.

THE COPY COMMAND

The Copy command is one of the most powerful commands in dBASE. With this command, you can do one or more of the following:

☐ Make a backup copy of any database, including both the structure and the data.
☐ Copy only the structure.
☐ Copy only the data, in the form of a text file.
☐ Copy selected records.
☐ Copy only a limited structure, with or without data.
☐ Create a delimited file for use with other software.

By now, the generic form of the command should tell you all about the capability of the command.

.COPY TO <file> [scope] [FIELD <list>] [FOR <condition>]
                                    [WHILE <condition>]
        [SDF] [DELIM [WITH <delimiter>]]

.COPY FILE <file1> TO <file2>

.COPY TO <file> [STRU] [FIELD <field-list>]

We shall study each one of these parameters. After each command has been executed, you may want to check out the results to satisfy your own curiosity. Use the usual DISP STRU and LIST commands for this purpose.

> **Note:** The COPY command also copies over deleted records!
> If the source file contains memo fields, the associated .DBT source
> file is also copied over. In other words, you will get a good, complete
> copy of the original file.

The To <file> Parameter

The To <file> parameter, as used in the example below, creates another distinct and separate database called BACKUP.DBF, which is identical in structure and data to the file called PERSNL.DBF. This process also creates a file called BACKUP.DBT, which is the supporting memofile for the BACKUP database.

```
.USE PERSNL       <cr>
.COPY TO BACKUP       <cr>
```

Here we have a quick way of making a complete backup copy of any dBASE database master file. In fact, before the start of our EDITING session, we had used this command to preserve our original PERSNL file in the PRESERVE.DBF database.

If a file called BACKUP.DBF had existed before the start of this operation, dBASE will warn you that proceeding with this command will mean overwriting on the existing file. At this point, you may exit gracefully from the situation, if you like.

The Scope Parameter

As you recall, the Scope parameter could be one of the following: ALL, RECORD n, NEXT n, or REST. Below is an example of the use of the Scope parameter in the COPY command:

```
.USE PERSNL       <cr>
.COPY TO BACKUP NEXT 10       <cr>
```

The USE command places dBASE in control over the first record of the PERSNL file. Hence the copy command will copy the entire structure, but only the first ten data records of the file will be copied, to the BACKUP database. The NEXT 10 is, of course, the *scope* of the operation. Deleted records falling within the scope are also copied.

The Field Parameter

The commands below will create a file called BACKUP.DBF, comprising all of the data records from PERSNL, but the record structure of these records will only comprise the fields EMP_NUM, EMP_NAME and ORG, exactly as they have been defined in the structure of the PERSNL file.

```
.USE PERSNL       <cr>
.COPY TO BACKUP FIELD EMP_NUM,EMP_NAME,ORG       <cr>
```

This routine highlights one of the most important uses of the COPY command. It enables you to create a subset of information from a master file. By simply including the FIELDS parameter, you can specify which fields you want copied from the master file, *and in what order!*

The FOR Condition

You can specify a condition under which you want the copy to proceed.

```
.USE PERSNL       <cr>
.COPY TO BACKUP FOR TOWN = 'ROCHESTER'       <cr>
```

Now only records that satisfy the FOR condition will be copied. The fields used in the FOR condition must, of course, be defined in the structure of the from file. In the example above, the BACKUP file will have the same structure as the PERSNL file, but the data records will be limited to records with TOWN = 'ROCHESTER'.

As always, the condition can be as simple or as complex as you want it to be. The special functions mentioned earlier can also be used.

```
.USE PERSNL            <cr>
.COPY TO BACKUP FOR ORG = 'BSG' .AND.
DT__OF__HIRE < CTOD('01/01/77') .OR. DT__OF__HIRE > CTOD('12/31/80')
                                                      <cr>
```

Remember that the DT__OF__HIRE field is defined as a date field, so it can only be compared to another date field. The dates supplied in the quotes are character dates, so they have to be converted to date-fields, with the character-to-date function. The above command will copy all employees in the BSG organization who were hired either prior to 01/01/77 or after 12/31/80. (You will type the entire command on one line at the dot prompt.)

You can, of course, specify more than one parameter in a command. For example:

```
.COPY TO BACKUP FOR TOWN = 'R' FIELDS EMP__NUM,EMP__NAME,ORG
                                                      <cr>
```

This command will create a file called BACKUP.DBF, with only three fields in its structure; the file will contain data copied from the master file, for TOWN = 'R' only.

The WHILE parameter

I have explained before that the behavior of the WHILE parameter is similar to, though not identical to, that of the FOR parameter.

```
.COPY TO BACKUP WHILE TOWN = 'R'          <cr>
```

will copy records for as long as the next record continues to satisfy the condition outlined above. When the next, successive record breaks the condition, the command stops, though there may be other records that satisfy the same condition in other locations in the file.

Saving Deleted Records

At the time we were covering the DELETE, RECALL, and PACK subset of commands, we had mentioned that before you actually PACKed your database, you may want to save all deleted records in another database having the same structure as the master file. This was advisable because you may, after you PACK your database, decide that you did, after all, want to retain some or all of the PACKed records, and that your PACK decision was a hasty one.

```
.USE PERSNL         <cr>
.COPY TO KEEPEM FOR DELETED( )           <cr>
```

This command will copy only the deleted records into a database called KEEPEM.DBF, which is identical in structure to the PERSNL file! The records in the KEEPEM.DBF file will be retained in their deleted status, with the * indicator present in all records.

Subsequently, if you had a change of mind, and wanted these records back again, you would type:

```
. USE PERSNL          <cr>
. APPEND FROM KEEPEM          <cr>
```

This will bring the records back into the PERSNL database, fully activated!

The SDF Parameter

In the command below, I have purposely used the same name, BACKUP, to clarify exactly what the SDF parameter will do.

```
.USE PERSNL         <cr>
.COPY TO BACKUP NEXT 5 SDF          <cr>
```

The SDF parameter informs dBASE that the file called BACKUP is not to be created as a dBASE file, but as a text file (if you remember, SDF stands for Standard Data Format). The creation of a text file by dBASE results in the extension .TXT being given to the file.

You could also have done the following:

```
.COPY TO BACKUP.FIL SDF          <cr>
```

This will create a Text file called BACKUP.FIL. Only in the absence of an extension will a text file be given the qualifier of .TXT by dBASE.

By using the SDF parameter, you can go from a dBASE format to a text format. This is how you can make your dBASE data available for processing under other software! This is complementary to the APPEND command, which lets us create a dBASE file from an SDF file.

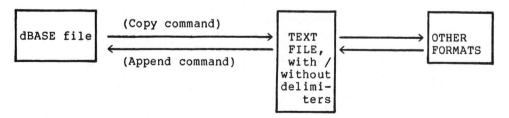

Please remember that a text file has no formalized structure, except as may be inferred by the user of that file. Also, the translation to a text format permits you to include data from a dBASE file as part of a word processed document.

This is what the file called BACKUP.TXT looks like:

```
005NINA BHARUCHAWEBSTER  BSGT1980052425000.00
010PETE JOHNSON brighton BSGT1976020327590.00
015GLORIA PATEL FAIRPORT RMGT1982071627500.00
020MAX LEVINSKY HENRIETTARMGF1969041327550.00
025KIM BRANDT   FAIRPORT RMGF1977040436000.00
```

> **Note:** Memos from the dBASE file are not copied over into the SDF format.

The Delimited [with <delimiter>] Parameter

The last, but by no means the least, of the parameters of the COPY command is the DELIMITED [WITH <delimiter>] parameter. As you can imagine, this parameter can help you create Standard Data Format (text) files that are also delimited.

```
.USE PERSNL          <cr>
.COPY TO MYFILE NEXT 5 DELIM        <cr>
```

As before, this command will produce a file called MYFILE.TXT, which will be a text file, and it will be delimited. This is what the file MYFILE.TXT looks like:

```
"005","NINA BHARUCHA","WEBSTER","BSG",T,19800524,25000.00
"010","PETE JOHNSON","brighton","BSG",T,19760203,27590.00
"015","GLORIA PATEL","FAIRPORT","RMG",T,19820716,27500.00
"020","MAX LEVINSKY","HENRIETTA","RMG",F,19690413,27550.00
"025","KIM BRANDT","FAIRPORT","RMG",F,19770404,36000.00
```

Notice that all fields are separated by commas, and the character fields have been delimited with double quotes (the default).

```
.1        <cr>
.COPY TO MYFILE NEXT 5 DELIM WITH '        <cr>
```

This is what the file MYFILE.TXT now looks like:

```
'005','NINA BHARUCHA','WEBSTER','BSG',T,19800524,25000.00
'010','PETE JOHNSON','brighton','BSG',T,19760203,27590.00
'015','GLORIA PATEL','FAIRPORT','RMG',T,19820716,27500.00
'020','MAX LEVINSKY','HENRIETTA','RMG',F,19690413,27550.00
'025','KIM BRANDT','FAIRPORT','RMG',F,19770404,36000.00
```

```
.1        <cr>
.COPY TO MYFILE SDF DELIM WITH "        <cr>
```

This is what MYFILE.TXT now looks like. (We saw this before.)

```
"005","NINA BHARUCHA","WEBSTER","BSG",T,19800524,25000.00
"010","PETE JOHNSON","brighton","BSG",T,19760203,27590.00
"015","GLORIA PATEL","FAIRPORT","RMG",T,19820716,27500.00
"020","MAX LEVINSKY","HENRIETTA","RMG",F,19690413,27550.00
"025","KIM BRANDT","FAIRPORT","RMG",F,19770404,36000.00
```

.1   <cr>
.COPY TO MYFILE NEXT 5 DELIM WITH ,   <cr>

This is what MYFILE.TXT now looks like:

```
,005,,,NINA BHARUCHA,,,WEBSTER,,,BSG,,T,19800524,25000.00
,010,,,PETE JOHNSON,,,brighton,,,BSG,,T,19760203,27590.00
,015,,,GLORIA PATEL,,,FAIRPORT,,,RMG,,T,19820716,27500.00
,020,,,MAX LEVINSKY,,,HENRIETTA,,,RMG,,F,19690413,27550.00
,025,,,KIM BRANDT,,,FAIRPORT,,,RMG,,F,19770404,36000.00
```

.1   <cr>
.COPY TO MYFILE NEXT 5 DELIMITED WITH BLANK   <cr>

This time around, the delimiter is a blank space. The file MYFILE.TXT looks like this:

```
005 NINA BHARUCHA WEBSTER BSG T 19800524 25000.00
010 PETE JOHNSON brighton BSG T 19760203 27590.00
015 GLORIA PATEL FAIRPORT RMG T 19820716 27500.00
020 MAX LEVINSKY HENRIETTA RMG F 19690413 27550.00
025 KIM BRANDT FAIRPORT RMG F 19770404 36000.00
```

You can provide your own delimiter:

.COPY TO MYFILE NEXT 5 DELIM WITH $ <cr>

```
$005$,$NINA BHARUCHA$,$WEBSTER$,$BSG$,T,19800524,25000.00
$010$,$PETE JOHNSON$,$brighton$,$BSG$,T,19760203,27590.00
$015$,$GLORIA PATEL$,$FAIRPORT$,$RMG$,T,19820716,27500.00
$020$,$MAX LEVINSKY$,$HENRIETTA$,$RMG$,F,19690413,27550.00
$025$,$KIM BRANDT$,$FAIRPORT$,$RMG$,F,19770404,36000.00
```

As you can see the COPY command can provide you with several formats for delimited files.

> **Note:** Memos from the dBASE file are not copied over into the DELIMITED format.
> **Reminder:** A DELIM file is always a text (SDF) file, but a text file may or may not be a DELIM file.
> **Note:** Why would we create a file delimited with quotes? Won't commas alone be good enough as delimiters? Commas alone will not work if your dBASE data itself could contain the comma as part of the data as in "JOHN JONES & SONS, Inc." Such a field must be

enclosed in quotes during the creation of the standard file, or else in a subsequent APPEND phase, the comma in the name field will cause dBASE to make some or all fields go haywire, depending on the location of the comma in the record!

Reminder: The SDF and DELIM parameters help you create text files that can be exported to, and manipulated by, other software products, such as MBASIC, and SUPERCALC.

The COPY FILE Format

The COPY FILE command creates a duplicate of any type of file.

.COPY FILE <filename> TO <filename>   <cr>

Since this format can copy over any kind of file, you must provide the extension.

.COPY FILE PROGRAM1.PRG TO PROGRAM2.PRG   <cr>

If you are using this format to copy a dBASE file that has memo fields, the associated .DBT file must be copied separately!

For copying actual dBASE database files, use the format given earlier:

.USE MASTER   <cr>
.COPY TO BACKUP   <cr>

The Structure Parameter

The STRU parameter, as used in the lines below, informs dBASE that you want to copy only the structure of the file called PERSNL without any of the data. This will create a file called BACKUP.DBF having a structure but no data.

.USE PERSNL   <cr>
.COPY TO BACKUP STRU   <cr>

If the original file had an associated memo file, the shell of the BACKUP.DBT memo file is also created, although, of course, there is no memo data in it yet. This is understandable, since you could be subsequently APPENDing data into the BACKUP.DBF file, along with entries for the memos.

Why would you want to copy over only the structure of any file? It is possible that you want to create another database having a similar, but not exactly identical, structure as that of the PERSNL file. It is so much easier to MODIFY STRU of an existing database for a few changes, than it is to key in a new structure all over again, especially if you have many fields to define in the new structure.

.COPY TO BACKUP STRU FIELDS EMP__NUM,EMP__NAME,ORG,SALARY
          <cr>

This statement will copy the structure of the defined fields only. No data is copied.

THE REPLACE COMMAND

The Replace command is a very powerful *remote edit* feature. That is, with the use of this one command, you can make massive changes to the database. Up until now, you had to enter one or more records (through EDIT or BROWSE), and key in individual changes yourself. The REPLACE command permits you to stand aloof from the database, and order dBASE to make changes to any number of records in the file. That makes the REPLACE command a very powerful command, and, at times, a dangerous one.

By now, the format and the parameters should be self-explanatory:

```
.REPLACE [scope] <field-name> WITH <expression>;
                 <field-name> WITH <expression>;
                 [ FOR <condition> ]
                 [WHILE <condition> ]
```

> **Note:** The REPLACE command only changes the contents of field variables. The REPLACE command will also work on deleted records!

As always, if [scope] is not supplied, the command will act on the current record. If [scope] is not supplied, but a FOR condition exists, the default for scope is ALL. In the examples below, assume that we start off with a fresh copy of the database. Changed records are highlighted.)

```
.USE PERSNL        <cr>
```

The record pointer is at the first record.

```
. REPLACE ORG WITH 'XYZ'
```

1 record replaced

Since no scope of operation was mentioned, the replacement worked only on the current record.

```
. LIST        <cr>
```

```
Record#  EMP_NUM EMP_NAME      TOWN      ORG EXE DT OF HIRE   SALARY NOTE
      1  005     NINA BHARUCHA WEBSTER   XYZ .T. 05/24/80   25000.00 Memo
      2  010.....
      3  015.....
      4  020......
                                   etc    etc    etc
```

```
.REPLACE TOWN WITH 'PERINTON' FOR ORG = 'BSG'        <cr>
```

Since a scope is missing, but a FOR condition exists, all the records that satisfy the condition will be changed.

3 records replaced

. LIST   <cr>

Record#	EMP_NUM	EMP_NAME	TOWN	ORG	EXE	DT_OF_HIRE	SALARY	NOTE
1	005.....							
2	010	PETE JOHNSON	PERINTON	BSG	.T.	02/03/76	27590.00	Memo
3	015.....							
4	020.....							
5	025.....							
6	030.....							
7	035.....							
8	040.....							
9	045	MORRIS KATZ	PERINTON	BSG	.F.	09/14/80	23450.00	Memo
10	050	PAUL BHARUCHA	PERINTON	BSG	.T.	05/23/73	29100.00	Memo
11	055.....							
12	060.....							
13	065.....							
14	070.....							
15	075.....							

. USE PERSNL   <cr>

.REPL EXE WITH .T. ORG WITH 'GSD' FOR SALARY > 25000 <cr>

12 records replaced

. LIST   <cr>

Record#	EMP_NUM	EMP_NAME	TOWN	ORG	EXE	DT_OF_HIRE	SALARY	NOTE
1	005.....							
2	010	PETE JOHNSON	brighton	GSD	.T.	02/03/76	27590.00	Memo
3	015	GLORIA PATEL	FAIRPORT	GSD	.T.	07/16/82	27500.00	Memo
4	020	MAX LEVINSKY	HENRIETTA	GSD	.T.	04/13/69	27550.00	Memo
5	025	KIM BRANDT	FAIRPORT	GSD	.T.	04/04/77	36000.00	Memo
6	030	TIM MONTAL	ROCHESTER	GSD	.T.	07/07/81	41900.00	Memo
7	035	WILLIAM PATEL	penfield	GSD	.T.	08/17/71	28900.00	Memo
8	040	JAMES JAMESON	ROCHESTER	GSD	.T.	10/21/77	29800.00	Memo
9	045.....							
10	050	PAUL BHARUCHA	BRIGHTON	GSD	.T.	05/23/73	29100.00	Memo
11	055	PHIL MARTIN	WEBSTER	GSD	.T.	07/19/80	31000.00	Memo
12	060	JOHN PETERSON	BRIGHTON	GSD	.T.	04/17/79	31480.00	Memo
13	065	JOY HARDY	fairport	GSD	.T.	01/19/79	34200.00	Memo
14	070.....							
15	075	JOHN JONES	rochester	GSD	.T.	04/04/70	25100.00	Memo

Recommendation: Since it is possible for you to alter the contents of your database rather radically through the use of this instruction, you would be well-advised to use the following precaution, before you issue this command.

```
.USE PERSNL        <cr>
.COPY TO BACKUP        <cr>
.REPLACE ALL . . .        <cr>
```

After the REPLACE has been completed, check your replacements, and if they are good, you can delete the BACKUP file.

```
.DELETE FILE BACKUP.DBF        <cr>
```

However, in case a 'typo' caused a mess in your PERSNL database, the BACKUP file would be your way out of the mess.

```
.USE BACKUP        <cr>
.COPY TO PERSNL        <cr>        Existing PERSNL file is deleted.
.USE PERSNL        <cr>
```

Please be sure to take this precaution, and create a backup file, prior to the issue of the REPLACE ALL command.

To further illustrate the power of this command, suppose that you had an INVEN-TRY master file, and you decided it was time to raise unit costs by, say, 10 percent. The following REPLACE command makes this task very simple:

```
.USE INVNTRY        <cr>
.COPY TO BACKUP        <cr>        Keep a backup!
.REPLACE ALL UNIT__COST WITH UNIT:COST * 1.1        <cr>
```

Note: The * symbol signifies multiplication.

All unit-costs are now replaced by amounts that are 10 percent higher. After you have checked out the replacements, you can delete the backup file.

To demonstrate this command using the PERSNL file, assume that you decide to give the employees in a certain organization a raise of say, 10 percent.

```
.USE PERSNL        <cr>
.COPY TO BACKUP        <cr>        A precaution.
.REPLACE ALL SALARY WITH SALARY * 1.1 FOR ORG = 'BSG'        <cr>
```

4 records replaced

```
.LIST        <cr>
```

Only the records with ORG = 'BSG' will have their salary fields changed.

```
Record#   EMP_NUM EMP_NAME        TOWN       ORG EXE DT_OF_HIRE   SALARY NOTE
      1   005     NINA BHARUCHA   WEBSTER    BSG .T. 05/24/80   27500.00 Memo
      2   010     PETE JOHNSON    brighton   BSG .T. 02/03/76   30349.00 Memo
      3   015.....
      4   020.....
      5   025.....
      6   030.....
      7   035.....
      8   040.....
      9   045     MORRIS KATZ     webster    BSG .F. 09/14/80   25795.00 Memo
     10   050     PAUL BHARUCHA   BRIGHTON   BSG .T. 05/23/73   32010.00 Memo
     11   055.....
     12   060.....
     13   065.....
     14   070.....
     15   075.....
```

Check out the changes, then delete the BACKUP file to release space.

Suppose you want to remove all lowercase characters from your file. That is, you want to convert all lowercase characters to uppercase characters throughout the file.

```
.USE PERSNL         <cr>
.REPL ALL TOWN WITH UPPER(TOWN) ORG WITH UPPER(ORG)     <cr>
```

The above command will perform the replacement on the two fields throughout the file!

If you had a field containing dates, but the field had been defined as a character field (whatever the reason), and you wanted to convert this character field to an actual date-field, the easiest process to follow would be to modify the structure of the file and redefine the field as a date field! At the end of the modification, the data in those fields is now considered to be dates and processed accordingly!

THE JOIN COMMAND

Suppose you have an INVENTRY master file with the following structure:

PART_NUM   DESC   UNIT_COST   ONHAND

Suppose, further, that you have another file containing ORDERS for those part numbers, and its structure contains:

PART_NUM   CUST_NAME   ONORDER

PART_NUM, of course, is the common factor in these two structures. We want to use this commonality to produce another file with the following structure:

PART_NUM   CUST_NAME   ONORDER   UNIT_COST

That is, we want to be able to pick up and group together, all individual customer orders for the various part numbers.

The JOIN command is used to add the data from two databases, based on certain selection criteria that you provide, to produce a third database. Both input databases will be kept open at the same time. This only means that dBASE will maintain separate record-pointers for the two files. Further, we will designate one of the files (the INVENTRY file) as the *active* file, with the other file (the ORDERS file) being the *nonactive* file.

Before you provide the actual instructions for the JOIN command, you have to go through the following five commands:

```
.SELECT 1      <cr>
.USE INVENTRY        <cr>
```

> **Note:** The above two instructions effectively identify the INVENTRY file as the file opened in work area #1.

```
.SELECT 2      <cr>
.USE ORDERS        <cr>
```

> **Note:** The above instructions effectively identify the ORDERS file as the file opened in work area #2.

```
.SELECT 1      <cr>     You have to end up on this instruction.
```

Since you ended up on this instruction, you selected 1 as your active file; that is, you designated the INVENTRY file as the active file. This automatically implies that the ORDERS file is the nonactive file. Note that the order of the commands could have been reversed, as follows:

```
.SELE 2      <cr>
.USE ORDERS        <cr>
.SELE 1      <cr>
.USE INVENTRY        <cr>
```

This way you achieve the same result in four instructions. Since you ended up selecting 1, you have made the Inventry file the active file.

Having designated the active and nonactive files, you may now issue the JOIN command.

```
.JOIN WITH ORDERS TO NEWFILE FOR PART_NUM = ORDERS->
PART_NUM                                            <cr>
```

You are specifying to dBASE that you want to JOIN the contents of the active file (INVENTRY) with the contents of the nonactive file (ORDERS), to produce a third file called NEWFILE.DBF.

You have further specified that the condition for joining should be that the PART_NUM from the active file must match the PART_NUM from the nonactive file. The phrase ORDERS->PART_NUM is only a way of saying "the part-number from the ORDERS file."

If NEWFILE.DBF existed before the start of the command, dBASE provides the usual warning message, and you can abort the process if you want.

The way the JOIN command works is as follows: dBASE will latch on to the first record in the active file and compare it, in turn, with each of the records in the other (nonactive) file, trying to find a match based on your selection criteria. Each time it finds a match, it produces an *output* record in the third database, the structure of which is also defined by what is or is not provided in the JOIN command. This process is continued until all records in the nonactive file are compared. Now dBASE latches on to the second record in the active file, and repeats the same comparisons, again with each of the records in the non-active database, trying to find matches based on your criteria. As before, each time it finds a match, you have a record output into the new database. This process is continued until each active record is matched against each of the nonactive records.

The Default Output File Structure

If you are not explicit about what you want as the structure of the new, output file, (which is how we have given the command above), dBASE provides you with a default structure which is the *concatenation* (a stringing together) of the structures of the active and nonactive data bases, in that order. If identical field names exist in both structures, only the fields from the active file are the ones selected for the structure of the output file, with their duplicates in the nonactive file being ignored.

For example, in our previous examples in which the INVENTRY file was the active file and the ORDERS file was nonactive file, since we did not provide explicit parameters for the structure of the new, output file, its structure will be as follows:

PART_NUM DESC   UNIT_COST   ONHAND   CUST_NAME
ONORDER

This structure is a concatenation of the structures of the active file followed by the nonactive file. Notice, therefore, that you will have one field called PART_NUM in the structure of the output file, and this is the one from the active file. However, you do not have to live with this default provided by dBASE. You can pick and choose the structure you want to see in the output file. (The mechanics of this will be covered later.)

> **Note:** If your active and nonactive databases are too large, this process takes a long time, and in the end, it may not be completed. For example, if you have 100 records in your active and 1000 records in your nonactive file, and your joining criteria were so loosely defined that every match was a hit, dBASE will attempt to create 100,000 records in the output database. Your system may not be able to handle this many records, especially if you are running with a floppy-disk system. So apart from taking forever, the process may finally *abend* (abnormal end), if the output file cannot be contained on the diskette.

Note that if the concatenation produces more than 128 fields or more than 4000 characters in the output file, dBASE simply limits the output file to 128 fields or 4000 characters in the structure, with the overflow fields or characters from the nonactive file being ignored.

Specifying Output File Structure

You can, of course, specify the exact format of the output file that you would like to see.

```
.JOIN WITH ORDERS TO NEWFILE FOR PART_NUM = ORDERS->
PART_NUM
    FIELDS PART_NUM,ORDERS->CUST_NAME,ORDERS->ONORDER,UNI-
T_COST       <cr>
```

(The above statement is all on one line.)

We have specified the exact format of the output file called NEWFILE.DBF. We want to see the PART_NUM field from the active file (INVENTRY), the CUST_NAME field from the nonactive file (ORDERS), the ONORDER field from the ORDERS file, and the UNIT_COST field from the INVENTRY file. (Notice that each field you want from the nonactive file has to be preceded with the name of the nonactive file.)

As another example of the use of the JOIN command, let us say we want to keep track of which items of inventory are insufficient to meet pending orders. The following command will do the job.

```
.SELE 1        <cr>          The assumption here is that we have one record
                             for each part number in the ORDERS file.
.USE INVENTRY      <cr >
.SELE 2       <cr>
.USE ORDERS       <cr >
.SELE 1       <cr >

.JOIN WITH ORDERS TO BACKLOG
    FOR PART_NUM  = ORDERS->PART_NUM .AND. ONHAND < OR-
DERS->ONORDER
    FIELDS  PART_NUM,ORDERS->CUST_NAME,ORDERS->ONORDER,
UNIT_COST       <cr>
```

(The above statement is all in one line.)

> **Note:** When you JOIN two files, and one of the files has a memo field, dBASE does not automatically copy the associated memo file in the new name. In our previous example, suppose the INVENTRY file had a memo field in it. In that case, there was a supporting memo file called INVENTRY.DBT. If the concatenation had called for the memo field to be pulled over to the file called BACKLOG (either

through default, or through an explicit reference), dBASE does not make an automatic copy of INVENTRY.DBT and call it BACKLOG.DBT! You would have to make the copy yourself using **.COPY FILE INVENTRY.DBT TO BACKLOG.DBT** <cr>; otherwise the file called BACKLOG would be unusable! Even if you make a copy of the INVENTRY.DBT file in the name BACKLOG.DBT (thus making the database BACKLOG.DBF usable), the memo file would be empty of all memos!

When the JOIN command has served its purpose, you should close the two files involved in the JOIN, as follows:

```
. SELE 1        <cr>
. USE           <cr>
. SELE2         <cr>
. USE           <cr>
```

Failure to close the files will make it impossible for you to invoke the USE command against either file individually, since the files will still be open in their respective work areas. Thus, you really must close the files after the marriage has ended.

SUMMARY

In the last few chapters, we have learned several powerful ways of changing the structures and/or the data of our databases. Since the editing features help you maintain the integrity of your data, it is important that they should be understood well.

We are through with our EDITING features, but before we get out of the EDITING mode completely, our PERSNL file could use some remodelling, as we have been experimenting with it to quite an extent. This is very easily done, since at the start of the EDITING section, we had created a backup copy of PERSNL in the name PRESERVE. We now simply use this file, to restore the PERSNL file:

```
.USE PRESERVE        <cr>
.COPY TO PERSNL      <cr>
```

The existing PERSNL file is copied over. This leaves you, once again, with both the PERSNL and PRESERVE files.

```
.USE PERSNL          <cr>
```

Now you may proceed with the PERSNL file, if need be. You realize, of course, that dBASE is a very powerful software package that requires substantial hands-on experience, if you are to make maximum use of the possibilities offered by dBASE.

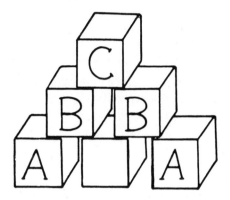

6. Sequencing Process

We will now learn how to prepare our database so that we can pull off reports from it. We are referring to the processes of *physically sorting* or *logically indexing* the database.

SORTing and INDEXing refer to the resequencing of the records of the database, so that these records are presented to any command or program in an expected order. For instance, if you expect to take totals by town on the records of your PERSNL file, the records must be prearranged in the order of the TOWN field. Either the records are physically moved around (the SORT operation) before the start of the command or program, or the records must appear to have been moved around (the INDEX operation) before the start of the command or program. These two processes are discussed at length, below.

> **Note:** For either the SORT or the INDEX process, if two or more records contain the same data in the *key* field(s) being used for the sequencing process, these records will appear in the sorted/indexed versions in the same order as they appear in the original file.

PHYSICAL SORTING

Sorting involves the *physical resequencing* of the records in a database. Perhaps you want the records sequenced so as to be able to produce a report. At the end of the sort process, you will have created another database, identical in structure and size to the original file, but with the records physically rearranged in the required sequence.

The SORT command will also sort deleted records!

Sorting on Any Character Field

You can enter the following commands to use the file called PERSNL and sort it on the TOWN field to produce another database called TSORT.DBF

```
.USE  PERSNL        <cr>
.SORT  ON TOWN  TO TSORT        <cr>
```

Since TSORT.DBF is a file distinct and separate from PERSNL, note that the record numbers in the TSORT file are in order of 1, 2, 3, 4, 5 . . . , etc. TSORT.DBF is the sorted version of the PERSNL file.

```
.USE  TSORT        <cr>
.LIST        <cr>
```

Record#	EMP_NUM	EMP_NAME	TOWN	ORG	EXE	DT_OF_HIRE	SALARY	NOTE
1	060	JOHN PETERSON	BRIGHTON	RBG	.T.	04/17/79	31480.00	Memo
2	050	PAUL BHARUCHA	BRIGHTON	BSG	.T.	05/23/73	29100.00	Memo
3	015	GLORIA PATEL	FAIRPORT	RMG	.T.	07/16/82	27500.00	Memo
4	025	KIM BRANDT	FAIRPORT	RMG	.F.	04/04/77	36000.00	Memo
5	020	MAX LEVINSKY	HENRIETTA	RMG	.F.	04/13/69	27550.00	Memo
6	030	TIM MONTAL	ROCHESTER	RBG	.F.	07/07/81	41900.00	Memo
7	040	JAMES JAMESON	ROCHESTER	GSD	.T.	10/21/77	29800.00	Memo
8	070	JAN MOREY	ROCHESTER	GSD	.T.	04/23/67	18190.00	Memo
9	005	NINA BHARUCHA	WEBSTER	BSG	.T.	05/24/80	25000.00	Memo
10	055	PHIL MARTIN	WEBSTER	RMG	.F.	07/19/80	31000.00	Memo
11	010	PETE JOHNSON	brighton	BSG	.T.	02/03/76	27590.00	Memo
12	065	JOY HARDY	fairport	RBG	.F.	01/19/79	34200.00	Memo
13	035	WILLIAM PATEL	penfield	GSD	.F.	08/17/71	28900.00	Memo
14	075	JOHN JONES	rochester	GSD	.T.	04/04/70	25100.00	Memo
15	045	MORRIS KATZ	webster	BSG	.F.	09/14/80	23450.00	Memo

Notice that the records are sequenced by the TOWN field. Notice the order in which the upper- and lowercase town names were sorted. All uppercase names appeared ahead of all lowercase names in regular ascending order, and within each group of upper- and lowercase names, the ascending sort is also evident.

Obviously, since the sorted version of the PERSNL file is exactly as large as the PERSNL file itself, it stands to reason that you must have at least as much space on the disk to contain the sorted version as is occupied by the PERSNL file. If space is a problem, you will have to produce the sorted file on another disk, by using the following procedure. Suppose you had not .SET DEFAULT TO B:

```
.USE PERSNL        <cr>
```
The PERSNL file is on the logged-in drive.

```
.SORT ON TOWN TO B:TSORT        <cr>
```

This would produce the sorted version on the B: drive.

Sorting on a Character Field in Descending Sequence

You can add /D after the name of the field to sort the database in descending order.

```
.USE PERSNL        <cr>
.SORT ON TOWN /D   TO TSORT        <cr>   The /D signifies
                                          descending.
```

Since our earlier command had already created a TSORT file, dBASE gives the following gentle reminder.

```
TSORT.dbf already exists, overwrite it? (Y/N) Yes
   00% Sorted
  100% Sorted              15 Records sorted .. Copying text file.
```

This message concerns the associated memo file (.DBT file) which is also created.

In future examples, I will not show these messages.

```
.USE TSORT         <cr>
.LIST         <cr>
```

Record#	EMP_NUM	EMP_NAME	TOWN	ORG	EXE	DT_OF_HIRE	SALARY	NOTE
1	045	MORRIS KATZ	webster	BSG	.F.	09/14/80	23450.00	Memo
2	075	JOHN JONES	rochester	GSD	.F.	04/04/70	25100.00	Memo
3	035	WILLIAM PATEL	penfield	GSD	.F.	08/17/71	28900.00	Memo
4	065	JOY HARDY	fairport	RBG	.F.	01/19/79	34200.00	Memo
5	010	PETE JOHNSON	brighton	BSG	.T.	02/03/76	27590.00	Memo
6	055	PHIL MARTIN	WEBSTER	RMG	.F.	07/19/80	31000.00	Memo
7	005	NINA BHARUCHA	WEBSTER	BSG	.T.	05/24/80	25000.00	Memo
8	030	TIM MONTAL	ROCHESTER	RBG	.F.	07/07/81	41900.00	Memo
9	040	JAMES JAMESON	ROCHESTER	GSD	.T.	10/21/77	29800.00	Memo
10	070	JAN MOREY	ROCHESTER	GSD	.T.	04/23/67	18190.00	Memo
11	020	MAX LEVINSKY	HENRIETTA	RMG	.F.	04/13/69	27550.00	Memo
12	025	KIM BRANDT	FAIRPORT	RMG	.F.	04/04/77	36000.00	Memo
13	015	GLORIA PATEL	FAIRPORT	RMG	.T.	07/16/82	27500.00	Memo
14	050	PAUL BHARUCHA	BRIGHTON	BSG	.T.	05/23/73	29100.00	Memo
15	060	JOHN PETERSON	BRIGHTON	RBG	.T.	04/17/79	31480.00	Memo

Now, since the order of the sort is reversed, all uppercase town names appear after all the lowercase names, and within each group, the reverse sort is also evident.

Sorting Regardless of Upper and Lowercase

The /C parameter specifies that dBASE should not differentiate between upper- and lowercase town names for the SORT process.

```
.USE PERSNL        <cr>
.SORT ON TOWN /C   TO TSORT        <cr>
.USE TSORT         <cr>
.LIST         <cr>
```

Record#	EMP_NUM	EMP_NAME	TOWN	ORG	EXE	DT_OF_HIRE	SALARY	NOTE
1	010	PETE JOHNSON	brighton	BSG	.T.	02/03/76	27590.00	Memo
2	060	JOHN PETERSON	BRIGHTON	RBG	.T.	04/17/79	31480.00	Memo
3	050	PAUL BHARUCHA	BRIGHTON	BSG	.T.	05/23/73	29100.00	Memo
4	065	JOY HARDY	fairport	RBG	.F.	01/19/79	34200.00	Memo
5	015	GLORIA PATEL	FAIRPORT	RMG	.T.	07/16/82	27500.00	Memo
6	025	KIM BRANDT	FAIRPORT	RMG	.F.	04/04/77	36000.00	Memo
7	020	MAX LEVINSKY	HENRIETTA	RMG	.F.	04/13/69	27550.00	Memo
8	035	WILLIAM PATEL	penfield	GSD	.F.	08/17/71	28900.00	Memo
9	030	TIM MONTAL	ROCHESTER	RBG	.F.	07/07/81	41900.00	Memo
10	040	JAMES JAMESON	ROCHESTER	GSD	.T.	10/21/77	29800.00	Memo
11	070	JAN MOREY	ROCHESTER	GSD	.T.	04/23/67	18190.00	Memo
12	075	JOHN JONES	rochester	GSD	.T.	04/04/70	25100.00	Memo
13	055	PHIL MARTIN	WEBSTER	RMG	.F.	07/19/80	31000.00	Memo
14	045	MORRIS KATZ	webster	BSG	.F.	09/14/80	23450.00	Memo
15	005	NINA BHARUCHA	WEBSTER	BSG	.T.	05/24/80	25000.00	Memo

Sorting in Descending Sequence Regardless of Case

The /CD parameter specifies that dBASE should not differentiate between upper- and lowercase town names and should sort the database in descending order.

```
.USE PERSNL           <cr>
.SORT ON TOWN /CD   TO TSORT           <cr>
.USE TSORT         <cr>
.LIST           <cr>
```

Record#	EMP_NUM	EMP_NAME	TOWN	ORG	EXE	DT_OF_HIRE	SALARY	NOTE
1	055	PHIL MARTIN	WEBSTER	RMG	.F.	07/19/80	31000.00	Memo
2	045	MORRIS KATZ	webster	BSG	.F.	09/14/80	23450.00	Memo
3	005	NINA BHARUCHA	WEBSTER	BSG	.T.	05/24/80	25000.00	Memo
4	040	JAMES JAMESON	ROCHESTER	GSD	.T.	10/21/77	29800.00	Memo
5	070	JAN MOREY	ROCHESTER	GSD	.T.	04/23/67	18190.00	Memo
6	030	TIM MONTAL	ROCHESTER	RBG	.F.	07/07/81	41900.00	Memo
7	075	JOHN JONES	rochester	GSD	.T.	04/04/70	25100.00	Memo
8	035	WILLIAM PATEL	penfield	GSD	.F.	08/17/71	28900.00	Memo
9	020	MAX LEVINSKY	HENRIETTA	RMG	.F.	04/13/69	27550.00	Memo
10	025	KIM BRANDT	FAIRPORT	RMG	.F.	04/04/77	36000.00	Memo
11	015	GLORIA PATEL	FAIRPORT	RMG	.T.	07/16/82	27500.00	Memo
12	065	JOY HARDY	fairport	RBG	.F.	01/19/79	34200.00	Memo
13	060	JOHN PETERSON	BRIGHTON	RBG	.T.	04/17/79	31480.00	Memo
14	010	PETE JOHNSON	brighton	BSG	.T.	02/03/76	27590.00	Memo
15	050	PAUL BHARUCHA	BRIGHTON	BSG	.T.	05/23/73	29100.00	Memo

Sorting on Multiple Character Fields

You can use the following commands to sort on TOWN, and for records with the same TOWN, to sort on the ORG field.

```
.USE PERSNL         <cr>
.SORT ON TOWN, ORG   TO TSORT          <cr>   Note: The comma is
                                                     mandatory!

.USE TSORT         <cr>
.LIST           <cr>
```

140

Record#	EMP_NUM	EMP_NAME	TOWN	ORG	EXE	DT_OF_HIRE	SALARY	NOTE
1	050	PAUL BHARUCHA	BRIGHTON	BSG	.T.	05/23/73	29100.00	Memo
2	060	JOHN PETERSON	BRIGHTON	RBG	.T.	04/17/79	31480.00	Memo
3	015	GLORIA PATEL	FAIRPORT	RMG	.T.	07/16/82	27500.00	Memo
4	025	KIM BRANDT	FAIRPORT	RMG	.F.	04/04/77	36000.00	Memo
5	020	MAX LEVINSKY	HENRIETTA	RMG	.F.	04/13/69	27550.00	Memo
6	040	JAMES JAMESON	ROCHESTER	GSD	.T.	10/21/77	29800.00	Memo
7	070	JAN MOREY	ROCHESTER	GSD	.T.	04/23/67	18190.00	Memo
8	030	TIM MONTAL	ROCHESTER	RBG	.F.	07/07/81	41900.00	Memo
9	005	NINA BHARUCHA	WEBSTER	BSG	.T.	05/24/80	25000.00	Memo
10	055	PHIL MARTIN	WEBSTER	RMG	.F.	07/19/80	31000.00	Memo
11	010	PETE JOHNSON	brighton	BSG	.T.	02/03/76	27590.00	Memo
12	065	JOY HARDY	fairport	RBG	.F.	01/19/79	34200.00	Memo
13	035	WILLIAM PATEL	penfield	GSD	.F.	08/17/71	28900.00	Memo
14	075	JOHN JONES	rochester	GSD	.T.	04/04/70	25100.00	Memo
15	045	MORRIS KATZ	webster	BSG	.F.	09/14/80	23450.00	Memo

Sorting on Multiple Fields in Ascending/Descending Sequence

As shown below, you can sort on one field in ascending order and on another in descending order.

```
.USE PERSNL          <cr>
.SORT ON TOWN, ORG /D  TO TSORT          <cr>
```

Here again, you are sorting on two fields; the TOWN sort is in the usual ascending sequence, and the records for the same TOWN are sequenced in descending order according to the contents of the ORG field.

```
.USE TSORT          <cr>
.LIST          <cr>
```

Record#	EMP_NUM	EMP_NAME	TOWN	ORG	EXE	DT_OF_HIRE	SALARY	NOTE
1	060	JOHN PETERSON	BRIGHTON	RBG	.T.	04/17/79	31480.00	Memo
2	050	PAUL BHARUCHA	BRIGHTON	BSG	.T.	05/23/73	29100.00	Memo
3	015	GLORIA PATEL	FAIRPORT	RMG	.T.	07/16/82	27500.00	Memo
4	025	KIM BRANDT	FAIRPORT	RMG	.F.	04/04/77	36000.00	Memo
5	020	MAX LEVINSKY	HENRIETTA	RMG	.F.	04/13/69	27550.00	Memo
6	030	TIM MONTAL	ROCHESTER	RBG	.F.	07/07/81	41900.00	Memo
7	040	JAMES JAMESON	ROCHESTER	GSD	.T.	10/21/77	29800.00	Memo
8	070	JAN MOREY	ROCHESTER	GSD	.T.	04/23/67	18190.00	Memo
9	055	PHIL MARTIN	WEBSTER	RMG	.F.	07/19/80	31000.00	Memo
10	005	NINA BHARUCHA	WEBSTER	BSG	.T.	05/24/80	25000.00	Memo
11	010	PETE JOHNSON	brighton	BSG	.T.	02/03/76	27590.00	Memo
12	065	JOY HARDY	fairport	RBG	.F.	01/19/79	34200.00	Memo
13	035	WILLIAM PATEL	penfield	GSD	.F.	08/17/71	28900.00	Memo
14	075	JOHN JONES	rochester	GSD	.T.	04/04/70	25100.00	Memo
15	045	MORRIS KATZ	webster	BSG	.F.	09/14/80	23450.00	Memo

```
.USE PERSNL          <cr>
.SORT ON TOWN /D,  ORG  TO TSORT          <cr>
```

Here we have the TOWN sort in descending sequence, and for the same TOWN, the records are sorted in ascending order according to the contents of the ORG field.

```
.USE TSORT          <cr>
.LIST          <cr>
```

```
Record#   EMP_NUM  EMP_NAME      TOWN       ORG EXE DT_OF_HIRE    SALARY NOTE
      1   045      MORRIS KATZ   webster    BSG .F. 09/14/80   23450.00 Memo
      2   075      JOHN JONES    rochester  GSD .T. 04/04/70   25100.00 Memo
      3   035      WILLIAM PATEL penfield   GSD .F. 08/17/71   28900.00 Memo
      4   065      JOY HARDY     fairport   RBG .F. 01/19/79   34200.00 Memo
      5   010      PETE JOHNSON  brighton   BSG .T. 02/03/76   27590.00 Memo
      6   005      NINA BHARUCHA WEBSTER    BSG .T. 05/24/80   25000.00 Memo
      7   055      PHIL MARTIN   WEBSTER    RMG .F. 07/19/80   31000.00 Memo
      8   040      JAMES JAMESON ROCHESTER  GSD .T. 10/21/77   29800.00 Memo
      9   070      JAN MOREY     ROCHESTER  GSD .T. 04/23/67   18190.00 Memo
     10   030      TIM MONTAL    ROCHESTER  RBG .F. 07/07/81   41900.00 Memo
     11   020      MAX LEVINSKY  HENRIETTA  RMG .F. 04/13/69   27550.00 Memo
     12   025      KIM BRANDT    FAIRPORT   RMG .F. 04/04/77   36000.00 Memo
     13   015      GLORIA PATEL  FAIRPORT   RMG .T. 07/16/82   27500.00 Memo
     14   050      PAUL BHARUCHA BRIGHTON   BSG .T. 05/23/73   29100.00 Memo
     15   060      JOHN PETERSON BRIGHTON   RBG .T. 04/17/79   31480.00 Memo
```

```
.USE PERSNL          <cr>
.SORT TO TOWN /D,  ORG /D  TO TSORT          <cr>
```

Here both the TOWN and the ORG sorts are in descending sequence.

```
.USE TSORT          <cr>
.LIST          <cr>
```

```
Record#   EMP_NUM  EMP_NAME      TOWN       ORG EXE DT_OF_HIRE    SALARY NOTE
      1   045      MORRIS KATZ   webster    BSG .F. 09/14/80   23450.00 Memo
      2   075      JOHN JONES    rochester  GSD .T. 04/04/70   25100.00 Memo
      3   035      WILLIAM PATEL penfield   GSD .F. 08/17/71   28900.00 Memo
      4   065      JOY HARDY     fairport   RBG .F. 01/19/79   34200.00 Memo
      5   010      PETE JOHNSON  brighton   BSG .T. 02/03/76   27590.00 Memo
      6   055      PHIL MARTIN   WEBSTER    RMG .F. 07/19/80   31000.00 Memo
      7   005      NINA BHARUCHA WEBSTER    BSG .T. 05/24/80   25000.00 Memo
      8   030      TIM MONTAL    ROCHESTER  RBG .F. 07/07/81   41900.00 Memo
      9   040      JAMES JAMESON ROCHESTER  GSD .T. 10/21/77   29800.00 Memo
     10   070      JAN MOREY     ROCHESTER  GSD .T. 04/23/67   18190.00 Memo
     11   020      MAX LEVINSKY  HENRIETTA  RMG .F. 04/13/69   27550.00 Memo
     12   025      KIM BRANDT    FAIRPORT   RMG .F. 04/04/77   36000.00 Memo
     13   015      GLORIA PATEL  FAIRPORT   RMG .T. 07/16/82   27500.00 Memo
     14   060      JOHN PETERSON BRIGHTON   RBG .T. 04/17/79   31480.00 Memo
     15   050      PAUL BHARUCHA BRIGHTON   BSG .T. 05/23/73   29100.00 Memo
```

Sorting on Numeric Fields

You can sort on a numeric field as easily as on a character field.

```
.USE PERSNL          <cr>
.SORT ON SALARY  TO SALSORT          <cr>
```

This will produce the usual ascending sort on a numeric field.

```
.USE SALSORT        <cr>
.LIST        <cr>
```

Record#	EMP_NUM	EMP_NAME	TOWN	ORG	EXE	DT_OF_HIRE	SALARY	NOTE
1	070	JAN MOREY	ROCHESTER	GSD	.T.	04/23/67	18190.00	Memo
2	045	MORRIS KATZ	webster	BSG	.F.	09/14/80	23450.00	Memo
3	005	NINA BHARUCHA	WEBSTER	BSG	.T.	05/24/80	25000.00	Memo
4	075	JOHN JONES	rochester	GSD	.T.	04/04/70	25100.00	Memo
5	015	GLORIA PATEL	FAIRPORT	RMG	.T.	07/16/82	27500.00	Memo
6	020	MAX LEVINSKY	HENRIETTA	RMG	.F.	04/13/69	27550.00	Memo
7	010	PETE JOHNSON	brighton	BSG	.T.	02/03/76	27590.00	Memo
8	035	WILLIAM PATEL	penfield	GSD	.F.	08/17/71	28900.00	Memo
9	050	PAUL BHARUCHA	BRIGHTON	BSG	.T.	05/23/73	29100.00	Memo
10	040	JAMES JAMESON	ROCHESTER	GSD	.T.	10/21/77	29800.00	Memo
11	055	PHIL MARTIN	WEBSTER	RMG	.F.	07/19/80	31000.00	Memo
12	060	JOHN PETERSON	BRIGHTON	RBG	.T.	04/17/79	31480.00	Memo
13	065	JOY HARDY	fairport	RBG	.F.	01/19/79	34200.00	Memo
14	025	KIM BRANDT	FAIRPORT	RMG	.F.	04/04/77	36000.00	Memo
15	030	TIM MONTAL	ROCHESTER	RBG	.F.	07/07/81	41900.00	Memo

```
.USE PERSNL        <cr>
.SORT ON SALARY /D  TO SALSORT        <cr>
```

This is a numeric sort in descending sequence.

```
.USE SALSORT        <cr>
.LIST        <cr>
```

Record#	EMP_NUM	EMP_NAME	TOWN	ORG	EXE	DT_OF_HIRE	SALARY	NOTE
1	030	TIM MONTAL	ROCHESTER	RBG	.F.	07/07/81	41900.00	Memo
2	025	KIM BRANDT	FAIRPORT	RMG	.F.	04/04/77	36000.00	Memo
3	065	JOY HARDY	fairport	RBG	.F.	01/19/79	34200.00	Memo
4	060	JOHN PETERSON	BRIGHTON	RBG	.T.	04/17/79	31480.00	Memo
5	055	PHIL MARTIN	WEBSTER	RMG	.F.	07/19/80	31000.00	Memo
6	040	JAMES JAMESON	ROCHESTER	GSD	.T.	10/21/77	29800.00	Memo
7	050	PAUL BHARUCHA	BRIGHTON	BSG	.T.	05/23/73	29100.00	Memo
8	035	WILLIAM PATEL	penfield	GSD	.F.	08/17/71	28900.00	Memo
9	010	PETE JOHNSON	brighton	BSG	.T.	02/03/76	27590.00	Memo
10	020	MAX LEVINSKY	HENRIETTA	RMG	.F.	04/13/69	27550.00	Memo
11	015	GLORIA PATEL	FAIRPORT	RMG	.T.	07/16/82	27500.00	Memo
12	075	JOHN JONES	rochester	GSD	.T.	04/04/70	25100.00	Memo
13	005	NINA BHARUCHA	WEBSTER	BSG	.T.	05/24/80	25000.00	Memo
14	045	MORRIS KATZ	webster	BSG	.F.	09/14/80	23450.00	Memo
15	070	JAN MOREY	ROCHESTER	GSD	.T.	04/23/67	18190.00	Memo

```
.USE PERSNL        <cr>
.SORT ON ORG, SALARY /D  TO OSORT        <cr>
```

This command will sort on ORG in ascending sequence, and for the same ORG, it will sort on SALARY in descending sequence.

```
.USE OSORT        <cr>
.LIST             <cr>
```

Record#	EMP_NUM	EMP_NAME	TOWN	ORG	EXE	DT_OF_HIRE	SALARY	NOTE
1	050	PAUL BHARUCHA	BRIGHTON	BSG	.T.	05/23/73	29100.00	Memo
2	010	PETE JOHNSON	brighton	BSG	.T.	02/03/76	27590.00	Memo
3	005	NINA BHARUCHA	WEBSTER	BSG	.T.	05/24/80	25000.00	Memo
4	045	MORRIS KATZ	webster	BSG	.F.	09/14/80	23450.00	Memo
5	040	JAMES JAMESON	ROCHESTER	GSD	.T.	10/21/77	29800.00	Memo
6	035	WILLIAM PATEL	penfield	GSD	.F.	08/17/71	28900.00	Memo
7	075	JOHN JONES	rochester	GSD	.T.	04/04/70	25100.00	Memo
8	070	JAN MOREY	ROCHESTER	GSD	.T.	04/23/67	18190.00	Memo
9	030	TIM MONTAL	ROCHESTER	RBG	.F.	07/07/81	41900.00	Memo
10	065	JOY HARDY	fairport	RBG	.F.	01/19/79	34200.00	Memo
11	060	JOHN PETERSON	BRIGHTON	RBG	.T.	04/17/79	31480.00	Memo
12	025	KIM BRANDT	FAIRPORT	RMG	.F.	04/04/77	36000.00	Memo
13	055	PHIL MARTIN	WEBSTER	RMG	.F.	07/19/80	31000.00	Memo
14	020	MAX LEVINSKY	HENRIETTA	RMG	.F.	04/13/69	27550.00	Memo
15	015	GLORIA PATEL	FAIRPORT	RMG	.T.	07/16/82	27500.00	Memo

Sorting on a Date Field

Date fields can be sorted in chronological order.

```
.USE PERSNL              <cr>
.SORT ON DT_OF_HIRE  TO DSORT           <cr>
```

The file is sorted on the date-of-hire field in ascending sequence.

```
.USE DSORT        <cr>
.LIST             <cr>
```

Record#	EMP_NUM	EMP_NAME	TOWN	ORG	EXE	DT_OF_HIRE	SALARY	NOTE
1	070	JAN MOREY	ROCHESTER	GSD	.T.	04/23/67	18190.00	Memo
2	020	MAX LEVINSKY	HENRIETTA	RMG	.F.	04/13/69	27550.00	Memo
3	075	JOHN JONES	rochester	GSD	.T.	04/04/70	25100.00	Memo
4	035	WILLIAM PATEL	penfield	GSD	.F.	08/17/71	28900.00	Memo
5	050	PAUL BHARUCHA	BRIGHTON	BSG	.T.	05/23/73	29100.00	Memo
6	010	PETE JOHNSON	brighton	BSG	.T.	02/03/76	27590.00	Memo
7	025	KIM BRANDT	FAIRPORT	RMG	.F.	04/04/77	36000.00	Memo
8	040	JAMES JAMESON	ROCHESTER	GSD	.T.	10/21/77	29800.00	Memo
9	065	JOY HARDY	fairport	RBG	.F.	01/19/79	34200.00	Memo
10	060	JOHN PETERSON	BRIGHTON	RBG	.T.	04/17/79	31480.00	Memo
11	005	NINA BHARUCHA	WEBSTER	BSG	.T.	05/24/80	25000.00	Memo
12	055	PHIL MARTIN	WEBSTER	RMG	.F.	07/19/80	31000.00	Memo
13	045	MORRIS KATZ	webster	BSG	.F.	09/14/80	23450.00	Memo
14	030	TIM MONTAL	ROCHESTER	RBG	.F.	07/07/81	41900.00	Memo
15	015	GLORIA PATEL	FAIRPORT	RMG	.T.	07/16/82	27500.00	Memo

Sorting on a Date Field in Descending Sequence

You can sort the file on the date-of-hire field in descending sequence by using the following commands.

```
.USE PERSNL        <cr>
.SORT ON  DT_OF_HIRE /D  TO DSORT           <cr>
.USE DSORT         <cr>
.LIST         <cr>
```

Record#	EMP_NUM	EMP_NAME	TOWN	ORG	EXE	DT_OF_HIRE	SALARY	NOTE
1	015	GLORIA PATEL	FAIRPORT	RMG	.T.	07/16/82	27500.00	Memo
2	030	TIM MONTAL	ROCHESTER	RBG	.F.	07/07/81	41900.00	Memo
3	045	MORRIS KATZ	webster	BSG	.F.	09/14/80	23450.00	Memo
4	055	PHIL MARTIN	WEBSTER	RMG	.F.	07/19/80	31000.00	Memo
5	005	NINA BHARUCHA	WEBSTER	BSG	.T.	05/24/80	25000.00	Memo
6	060	JOHN PETERSON	BRIGHTON	RBG	.T.	04/17/79	31480.00	Memo
7	065	JOY HARDY	fairport	RBG	.F.	01/19/79	34200.00	Memo
8	040	JAMES JAMESON	ROCHESTER	GSD	.T.	10/21/77	29800.00	Memo
9	025	KIM BRANDT	FAIRPORT	RMG	.F.	04/04/77	36000.00	Memo
10	010	PETE JOHNSON	brighton	BSG	.T.	02/03/76	27590.00	Memo
11	050	PAUL BHARUCHA	BRIGHTON	BSG	.T.	05/23/73	29100.00	Memo
12	035	WILLIAM PATEL	penfield	GSD	.F.	08/17/71	28900.00	Memo
13	075	JOHN JONES	rochester	GSD	.T.	04/04/70	25100.00	Memo
14	020	MAX LEVINSKY	HENRIETTA	RMG	.F.	04/13/69	27550.00	Memo
15	070	JAN MOREY	ROCHESTER	GSD	.T.	04/23/67	18190.00	Memo

```
.USE PERSNL        <cr>
.SORT ON ORG,  DT_OF_HIRE /D  TO OSORT           <cr>
```

The file is sorted on the ORG in ascending sequence, and for the same ORG, the records are sorted in descending order according to the contents of the DT_OF_HIRE field.

```
.USE OSORT        <cr>
.LIST         <cr>
```

Record#	EMP_NUM	EMP_NAME	TOWN	ORG	EXE	DT_OF_HIRE	SALARY	NOTE
1	045	MORRIS KATZ	webster	BSG	.F.	09/14/80	23450.00	Memo
2	005	NINA BHARUCHA	WEBSTER	BSG	.T.	05/24/80	25000.00	Memo
3	010	PETE JOHNSON	brighton	BSG	.T.	02/03/76	27590.00	Memo
4	050	PAUL BHARUCHA	BRIGHTON	BSG	.T.	05/23/73	29100.00	Memo
5	040	JAMES JAMESON	ROCHESTER	GSD	.T.	10/21/77	29800.00	Memo
6	035	WILLIAM PATEL	penfield	GSD	.F.	08/17/71	28900.00	Memo
7	075	JOHN JONES	rochester	GSD	.T.	04/04/70	25100.00	Memo
8	070	JAN MOREY	ROCHESTER	GSD	.T.	04/23/67	18190.00	Memo
9	030	TIM MONTAL	ROCHESTER	RBG	.F.	07/07/81	41900.00	Memo
10	060	JOHN PETERSON	BRIGHTON	RBG	.T.	04/17/79	31480.00	Memo
11	065	JOY HARDY	fairport	RBG	.F.	01/19/79	34200.00	Memo
12	015	GLORIA PATEL	FAIRPORT	RMG	.T.	07/16/82	27500.00	Memo
13	055	PHIL MARTIN	WEBSTER	RMG	.F.	07/19/80	31000.00	Memo
14	025	KIM BRANDT	FAIRPORT	RMG	.F.	04/04/77	36000.00	Memo
15	020	MAX LEVINSKY	HENRIETTA	RMG	.F.	04/13/69	27550.00	Memo

Sorting on Mixed Fields

You can sort on different types of fields in the same command.

```
.USE PERSNL          <cr>
.SORT ON TOWN, ORG, SALARY   TO TSORT          <cr>
```

Here you are sorting by TOWN, and for the same TOWN, by ORG, and for the same TOWN and ORG, by SALARY.

```
.USE TSORT          <cr>
.LIST          <cr>
```

Record#	EMP_NUM	EMP_NAME	TOWN	ORG	EXE	DT_OF_HIRE	SALARY	NOTE
1	050	PAUL BHARUCHA	BRIGHTON	BSG	.T.	05/23/73	29100.00	Memo
2	060	JOHN PETERSON	BRIGHTON	RBG	.T.	04/17/79	31480.00	Memo
3	015	GLORIA PATEL	FAIRPORT	RMG	.T.	07/16/82	27500.00	Memo
4	025	KIM BRANDT	FAIRPORT	RMG	.F.	04/04/77	36000.00	Memo
5	020	MAX LEVINSKY	HENRIETTA	RMG	.F.	04/13/69	27550.00	Memo
6	070	JAN MOREY	ROCHESTER	GSD	.T.	04/23/67	18190.00	Memo
7	040	JAMES JAMESON	ROCHESTER	GSD	.T.	10/21/77	29800.00	Memo
8	030	TIM MONTAL	ROCHESTER	RBG	.F.	07/07/81	41900.00	Memo
9	005	NINA BHARUCHA	WEBSTER	BSG	.T.	05/24/80	25000.00	Memo
10	055	PHIL MARTIN	WEBSTER	RMG	.F.	07/19/80	31000.00	Memo
11	010	PETE JOHNSON	brighton	BSG	.T.	02/03/76	27590.00	Memo
12	065	JOY HARDY	fairport	RBG	.F.	01/19/79	34200.00	Memo
13	035	WILLIAM PATEL	penfield	GSD	.F.	08/17/71	28900.00	Memo
14	075	JOHN JONES	rochester	GSD	.T.	04/04/70	25100.00	Memo
15	045	MORRIS KATZ	webster	BSG	.F.	09/14/80	23450.00	Memo

```
.USE PERSNL          <cr>
.SORT ON TOWN, ORG, SALARY /D   TO TSORT          <cr>
```

Here you are sorting by TOWN, by ORG, and by descending SALARY.

```
.USE TSORT          <cr>
.LIST          <cr>
```

Record#	EMP_NUM	EMP_NAME	TOWN	ORG	EXE	DT_OF_HIRE	SALARY	NOTE
1	050	PAUL BHARUCHA	BRIGHTON	BSG	.T.	05/23/73	29100.00	Memo
2	060	JOHN PETERSON	BRIGHTON	RBG	.T.	04/17/79	31480.00	Memo
3	025	KIM BRANDT	FAIRPORT	RMG	.F.	04/04/77	36000.00	Memo
4	015	GLORIA PATEL	FAIRPORT	RMG	.T.	07/16/82	27500.00	Memo
5	020	MAX LEVINSKY	HENRIETTA	RMG	.F.	04/13/69	27550.00	Memo
6	040	JAMES JAMESON	ROCHESTER	GSD	.T.	10/21/77	29800.00	Memo
7	070	JAN MOREY	ROCHESTER	GSD	.T.	04/23/67	18190.00	Memo
8	030	TIM MONTAL	ROCHESTER	RBG	.F.	07/07/81	41900.00	Memo
9	005	NINA BHARUCHA	WEBSTER	BSG	.T.	05/24/80	25000.00	Memo
10	055	PHIL MARTIN	WEBSTER	RMG	.F.	07/19/80	31000.00	Memo
11	010	PETE JOHNSON	brighton	BSG	.T.	02/03/76	27590.00	Memo
12	065	JOY HARDY	fairport	RBG	.F.	01/19/79	34200.00	Memo
13	035	WILLIAM PATEL	penfield	GSD	.F.	08/17/71	28900.00	Memo
14	075	JOHN JONES	rochester	GSD	.T.	04/04/70	25100.00	Memo
15	045	MORRIS KATZ	webster	BSG	.F.	09/14/80	23450.00	Memo

Note: You cannot sort on the substring of a field. You must use the entire field. For example: .SORT ON SUBSTR(TOWN,2,3) TO

TSORT   <cr> will result in a syntax error.

Note: You cannot sort on either logical fields or memo fields.

Note: Sorting a file that has a memo field in it takes substantially longer than sorting one without any memo fields, since the sort operation has to conclude by copying over the associated memo file (the .DBT file).

Specifying a Scope for the Sort

You can specify the number of records you want included in the sort process. In the following example, we are asking for only the first five records to be sorted to the output file.

```
.USE PERSNL        <cr>
.SORT ON TOWN TO TSORT   NEXT 5        <cr>
.USE TSORT        <cr>
.LIST          <cr>
```

Record#	EMP_NUM	EMP_NAME	TOWN	ORG	EXE	DT_OF_HIRE	SALARY	NOTE
1	015	GLORIA PATEL	FAIRPORT	RMG	.T.	07/16/82	27500.00	Memo
2	025	KIM BRANDT	FAIRPORT	RMG	.F.	04/04/77	36000.00	Memo
3	020	MAX LEVINSKY	HENRIETTA	RMG	.F.	04/13/69	27550.00	Memo
4	005	NINA BHARUCHA	WEBSTER	BSG	.T.	05/24/80	25000.00	Memo
5	010	PETE JOHNSON	brighton	BSG	.T.	02/03/76	27590.00	Memo

Specifying a Condition for the Sort

You can specify which records you want sorted through the use of a condition, as simple or as complex as you want to make it. Only records that fulfill the condition are sent to the output file.

```
.USE PERSNL        <cr>
.SORT ON   TOWN, ORG   TO TSORT   FOR SALARY > 20000        <cr>
```

Here the records with SALARY greater than 25000 are selected, and these selected records are sorted by TOWN and ORG and sent to the output file.

```
.USE TSORT        <cr>
.LIST          <cr>
```

Record#	EMP_NUM	EMP_NAME	TOWN	ORG	EXE	DT_OF_HIRE	SALARY	NOTE
1	050	PAUL BHARUCHA	BRIGHTON	BSG	.T.	05/23/73	29100.00	Memo
2	060	JOHN PETERSON	BRIGHTON	RBG	.T.	04/17/79	31480.00	Memo
3	015	GLORIA PATEL	FAIRPORT	RMG	.T.	07/16/82	27500.00	Memo
4	025	KIM BRANDT	FAIRPORT	RMG	.F.	04/04/77	36000.00	Memo
5	020	MAX LEVINSKY	HENRIETTA	RMG	.F.	04/13/69	27550.00	Memo
6	040	JAMES JAMESON	ROCHESTER	GSD	.T.	10/21/77	29800.00	Memo
7	030	TIM MONTAL	ROCHESTER	RBG	.F.	07/07/81	41900.00	Memo
8	005	NINA BHARUCHA	WEBSTER	BSG	.T.	05/24/80	25000.00	Memo
9	055	PHIL MARTIN	WEBSTER	RMG	.F.	07/19/80	31000.00	Memo

```
10   010   PETE JOHNSON    brighton  BSG .T. 02/03/76   27590.00 Memo
11   065   JOY HARDY       fairport  RBG .F. 01/19/79   34200.00 Memo
12   035   WILLIAM PATEL   penfield  GSD .F. 08/17/71   28900.00 Memo
13   075   JOHN JONES      rochester GSD .T. 04/04/70   25100.00 Memo
14   045   MORRIS KATZ     webster   BSG .F. 09/14/80   23450.00 Memo
```

Sorting Deleted Records

You can specify that you want only the deleted records in a file accepted during the sort process.

```
.USE PERSNL          <cr>
.SORT ON TOWN  TO TSORT  FOR DELETED( )          <cr>
.USE TSORT           <cr>
.LIST           <cr>
```

```
Record#  EMP_NUM EMP_NAME        TOWN      ORG EXE DT_OF_HIRE   SALARY NOTE
      1  *025    KIM BRANDT      FAIRPORT  RMG .F. 04/04/77   36000.00 Memo
      2  *030    TIM MONTAL      ROCHESTER RBG .F. 07/07/81   41900.00 Memo
      3  *040    JAMES JAMESON   ROCHESTER GSD .T. 10/21/77   29800.00 Memo
      4  *035    WILLIAM PATEL   penfield  GSD .F. 08/17/71   28900.00 Memo
      5  *045    MORRIS KATZ     webster   BSG .F. 09/14/80   23450.00 Memo
```

Sorting on Active Records

The reverse is also true! You can remove deleted records from the sorted output file.

```
.USE PERSNL          <cr>
.SORT ON TOWN  TO TSORT  FOR .NOT. DELETED( )          <cr>
.USE TSORT           <cr>
.LIST           <cr>
```

```
Record#  EMP_NUM EMP_NAME        TOWN      ORG EXE DT_OF_HIRE   SALARY NOTE
      1  050     PAUL BHARUCHA   BRIGHTON  BSG .T. 05/23/73   29100.00 Memo
      2  060     JOHN PETERSON   BRIGHTON  RBG .T. 04/17/79   31480.00 Memo
      3  015     GLORIA PATEL    FAIRPORT  RMG .T. 07/16/82   27500.00 Memo
      4  020     MAX LEVINSKY    HENRIETTA RMG .F. 04/13/69   27550.00 Memo
      5  070     JAN MOREY       ROCHESTER GSD .T. 04/23/67   18190.00 Memo
      6  005     NINA BHARUCHA   WEBSTER   BSG .T. 05/24/80   25000.00 Memo
      7  055     PHIL MARTIN     WEBSTER   RMG .F. 07/19/80   31000.00 Memo
      8  010     PETE JOHNSON    brighton  BSG .T. 02/03/76   27590.00 Memo
      9  065     JOY HARDY       fairport  RBG .F. 01/19/79   34200.00 Memo
     10  075     JOHN JONES      rochester GSD .T. 04/04/70   25100.00 Memo
```

A Sort Peculiarity

The SORT command is unable to handle an *empty* file or one with only one record! In either of these cases, dBASE provides an error message "Not enough records to sort," and will not produce the output file. This fact, if not accounted for, could cause a well-programmed application to "bomb out!"

For example, you may have programmed a system that produces a file meant to contain erroneous records. Your daily procedure sorts and prints out the contents of the error file for operator action. On a lucky day, there are no errors detected, but the luck stops there, because your system is bound to bomb out when this error file is to be sorted.

This fact forces you to include another test in the system. Using the RECCOUNT( ) function studied earlier, you will have to ensure that you have at least two records in the error file, before your program attempts to create a sorted output file. If the error file contains no records or only one record, your program will have to *copy* this file over into the sorted file, so the rest of the system can proceed smoothly.

Sorting Speeds

The speed of the sort process depends very much on the hardware on which the sort is performed, since the same sorting algorithm will move much faster on a hard-disk system than on a floppy system.

I conducted the following experiments using a COMPAQ DESKPRO 286 computer, running at 8 MHz (megahertz, referring to the speed of the internal oscillator), with 512K memory.

I used the PERSNL.DBF database we have been using so far, but without the memo field, and through a combination of the COPY and the APPEND commands, with the help of a small program, I forced dBASE to blow up the size of the PERSNL.DBF file to 15,360 records. I also had dBASE provide the time (using the TIME( ) function) at the start and end of the runs, to provide as much accuracy as possible.

15,360 records, 46 characters in length, were put through the sort process as follows:

Test 1:   Sort on the TOWN field
             Key length = 9 characters
             Time: 11 minutes, 37 seconds

Test 2:   Sort on TOWN and ORG, both in ascending sequence
             Key Length = 9 + 3 = 12 characters
             Time: 11 minutes, 59 seconds

Test 3:   Sort on TOWN ascending, ORG descending
             Key length = 9 + 3 = 12 characters
             Time: 12 minutes, 20 seconds

Test 4:   Sort on TOWN and ORG and SALARY all in ascending sequence
             Key length = 20 characters
             Time: 14 minutes, 08 seconds

The above test times would have increased substantially if memo fields were involved.

The Disadvantage of the Sort Process

Possibly the biggest disadvantage with any SORT process, regardless of the speed of execution, is that changes or alterations to the master file are not automatically reflected in the sorted versions of the master, these being distinct and separate databases, and this creates problems of data inconsistency and redundancy! The problem compounds if several users have access to the same set of files.

LOGICAL INDEXING

You will find this segment of our discussion very interesting and informative, and it should be studied closely. Indexing is an inherent part of the dBASE scenario. If your goal is to write sophisticated dBASE systems applications, you cannot do without the indexing feature!

In the process of INDEXing, you inform dBASE of your intention to create an *index file* on one or more of the fields of the master file you are working with (In our case, PERSNL.DBF).

Creating the Index File

Use the following statements to perform logical indexing on PERSNL.

```
.USE PERSNL          <cr>
.INDEX ON  TOWN  TO  TINDX          <cr>
```

This results in the creation of a separate file called an *index file*, whose name is TINDX.NDX. You may provide any primary name you want. dBASE provides the default extension of .NDX.

> **Note:** This index file is just that, an *index* file! It is not a dBASE database. It only contains *pointers* to the actual records in the PERSNL file.

For example, if our database contained the following five records, with only the TOWN data shown, this is what the index would specify.

Master file records	Index file pointers
1 —-PITTSFORD—–-	3 BRIGHTON
2 —-WEBSTER—–—	5 PENFIELD
3 —-BRIGHTON—–—	1 PITTSFORD
4 —-ROCHESTER—–-	4 ROCHESTER
5 —-PENFIELD—–—	2 WEBSTER

Based on the data in the master file, and on the fact that an index on TOWN is created, the index pointers specify that the logical order of the record numbers, based on ascending TOWN sequences, should be 3, 5, 1, 4, 2. That is, dBASE is saying that if you want a sequence by TOWN, record #3 with the town of BRIGHTON comes ahead of record #5 with the town of PENFIELD, and so on. The indexing feature of dBASE provides, by default, an ascending index.

Note: Deleted records *will* be indexed!
Note: You cannot index on either logical fields or memo fields.

The index file is nowhere near the size of the master file, and merely contains key-field values and record-number pointers into the original PERSNL database. The pointers establish the *logical positioning* of the individual records in the master file.

Please note that the original database is untouched! The index pointers merely stipulate what the logical order of the records should be, based on the ascending values currently in the key field you have indexed on.

The index file is not a dBASE database, so don't attempt to USE it as such. It can only be used in conjunction with the database it was created through.

Note: At the time the index is created, it is automatically brought into play with the "master" file. Now any subsequent command will act on the records of the "master" file *in the logical order of the index!*

.LIST   <cr>

Record#	EMP_NUM	EMP_NAME	TOWN	ORG	EXE	DT_OF_HIRE	SALARY	NOTE
10	050	PAUL BHARUCHA	BRIGHTON	BSG	.T.	05/23/73	29100.00	Memo
12	060	JOHN PETERSON	BRIGHTON	RBG	.T.	04/17/79	31480.00	Memo
3	015	GLORIA PATEL	FAIRPORT	RMG	.T.	07/16/82	27500.00	Memo
5	025	KIM BRANDT	FAIRPORT	RMG	.F.	04/04/77	36000.00	Memo
4	020	MAX LEVINSKY	HENRIETTA	RMG	.F.	04/13/69	27550.00	Memo
6	030	TIM MONTAL	ROCHESTER	RBG	.F.	07/07/81	41900.00	Memo
8	040	JAMES JAMESON	ROCHESTER	GSD	.T.	10/21/77	29800.00	Memo
14	070	JAN MOREY	ROCHESTER	GSD	.T.	04/23/67	18190.00	Memo
1	005	NINA BHARUCHA	WEBSTER	BSG	.T.	05/24/80	25000.00	Memo
11	055	PHIL MARTIN	WEBSTER	RMG	.F.	07/19/80	31000.00	Memo
2	010	PETE JOHNSON	brighton	BSG	.T.	02/03/76	27590.00	Memo
13	065	JOY HARDY	fairport	RBG	.F.	01/19/79	34200.00	Memo
7	035	WILLIAM PATEL	penfield	GSD	.F.	08/17/71	28900.00	Memo
15	075	JOHN JONES	rochester	GSD	.T.	04/04/70	25100.00	Memo
9	045	MORRIS KATZ	webster	BSG	.F.	09/14/80	23450.00	Memo

Notice that the records have been listed in the ascending order of the TOWN fields. Notice also, that the record numbers are not in proper sequence (1, 2, 3 . . .), since the record numbers are from the original records in the PERSNL file, and the records have merely been pulled out in the sequence established by the index.

Let me emphasize that the creation of an index does not alter the master file in any way. Once created, however, the index plays a role in subsequent commands, in that the records are processed by the commands *in the logical order of the index*. The index thus influences the master file.

Removing Index File Influence

You can disassociate an existing index from a master file simply by USING the master file.

```
.USE PERSNL        <cr>
.LIST        <cr>
```

Record#	EMP_NUM	EMP_NAME	TOWN	ORG	EXE	DT_OF_HIRE	SALARY	NOTE
1	005	NINA BHARUCHA	WEBSTER	BSG	.T.	05/24/80	25000.00	Memo
2	010	PETE JOHNSON	brighton	BSG	.T.	02/03/76	27590.00	Memo
3	015	GLORIA PATEL	FAIRPORT	RMG	.T.	07/16/82	27500.00	Memo
4	020	MAX LEVINSKY	HENRIETTA	RMG	.F.	04/13/69	27550.00	Memo
5	025	KIM BRANDT	FAIRPORT	RMG	.F.	04/04/77	36000.00	Memo
6	030	TIM MONTAL	ROCHESTER	RBG	.F.	07/07/81	41900.00	Memo
7	035	WILLIAM PATEL	penfield	GSD	.F.	08/17/71	28900.00	Memo
8	040	JAMES JAMESON	ROCHESTER	GSD	.T.	10/21/77	29800.00	Memo
9	045	MORRIS KATZ	webster	BSG	.F.	09/14/80	23450.00	Memo
10	050	PAUL BHARUCHA	BRIGHTON	BSG	.T.	05/23/73	29100.00	Memo
11	055	PHIL MARTIN	WEBSTER	RMG	.F.	07/19/80	31000.00	Memo
12	060	JOHN PETERSON	BRIGHTON	RBG	.T.	04/17/79	31480.00	Memo
13	065	JOY HARDY	fairport	RBG	.F.	01/19/79	34200.00	Memo
14	070	JAN MOREY	ROCHESTER	GSD	.T.	04/23/67	18190.00	Memo
15	075	JOHN JONES	rochester	GSD	.T.	04/04/70	25100.00	Memo

Notice that the original records from the PERSNL file are displayed in their original record number sequence. The USE command effectively removed the influence of the index file.

You can also negate the effects of the index through the command:

```
.CLOSE INDEX        <cr>
```

Understand, also, that the TINDX(.NDX) file created earlier *still exists* on the disk, but we have just negated its influence on the master file.

Reactivating Index File Influence

You may, of course, create an index file today and decide to bring it into play with a master file tomorrow. To reassociate, or reconnect, an *existing* index file with a master file, type the following:

```
.USE PERSNL INDEX TINDX        <cr>
.LIST        <cr>
```

Record#	EMP_NUM	EMP_NAME	TOWN	ORG	EXE	DT_OF_HIRE	SALARY	NOTE
10	050	PAUL BHARUCHA	BRIGHTON	BSG	.T.	05/23/73	29100.00	Memo
12	060	JOHN PETERSON	BRIGHTON	RBG	.T.	04/17/79	31480.00	Memo
3	015	GLORIA PATEL	FAIRPORT	RMG	.T.	07/16/82	27500.00	Memo
5	025	KIM BRANDT	FAIRPORT	RMG	.F.	04/04/77	36000.00	Memo
4	020	MAX LEVINSKY	HENRIETTA	RMG	.F.	04/13/69	27550.00	Memo

```
    6  030     TIM MONTAL     ROCHESTER RBG .F. 07/07/81   41900.00 Memo
    8  040     JAMES JAMESON  ROCHESTER GSD .T. 10/21/77   29800.00 Memo
   14  070     JAN MOREY      ROCHESTER GSD .T. 04/23/67   18190.00 Memo
    1  005     NINA BHARUCHA  WEBSTER   BSG .T. 05/24/80   25000.00 Memo
   11  055     PHIL MARTIN    WEBSTER   RMG .F. 07/19/80   31000.00 Memo
    2  010     PETE JOHNSON   brighton  BSG .T. 02/03/76   27590.00 Memo
   13  065     JOY HARDY      fairport  RBG .F. 01/19/79   34200.00 Memo
    7  035     WILLIAM PATEL  penfield  GSD .F. 08/17/71   28900.00 Memo
   15  075     JOHN JONES     rochester GSD .T. 04/04/70   25100.00 Memo
    9  045     MORRIS KATZ    webster   BSG .F. 09/14/80   23450.00 Memo
```

Notice that the records are once again listed in the order of the index, since we reestablished the index with the PERSNL file.

> **Note:** For the next several pages, I will show you many ways of obtaining different kinds of sequences from your master file. The actual utility value of the indexing feature will be explained later.

Indexing on a Character Field

We have seen one example of how to index on a character field. You can index on any character field simply by mentioning the field name.

```
.USE PERSNL            <cr>
.INDEX ON ORG TO OINDX          <cr>
.LIST         <cr>
```

```
Record#  EMP_NUM EMP_NAME      TOWN      ORG EXE DT_OF_HIRE   SALARY NOTE
      1   005     NINA BHARUCHA WEBSTER   BSG .T. 05/24/80   25000.00 Memo
      2   010     PETE JOHNSON  brighton  BSG .T. 02/03/76   27590.00 Memo
      9   045     MORRIS KATZ   webster   BSG .F. 09/14/80   23450.00 Memo
     10   050     PAUL BHARUCHA BRIGHTON  BSG .T. 05/23/73   29100.00 Memo
      7   035     WILLIAM PATEL penfield  GSD .F. 08/17/71   28900.00 Memo
      8   040     JAMES JAMESON ROCHESTER GSD .T. 10/21/77   29800.00 Memo
     14   070     JAN MOREY     ROCHESTER GSD .T. 04/23/67   18190.00 Memo
     15   075     JOHN JONES    rochester GSD .T. 04/04/70   25100.00 Memo
      6   030     TIM MONTAL    ROCHESTER RBG .F. 07/07/81   41900.00 Memo
     12   060     JOHN PETERSON BRIGHTON  RBG .T. 04/17/79   31480.00 Memo
     13   065     JOY HARDY     fairport  RBG .F. 01/19/79   34200.00 Memo
      3   015     GLORIA PATEL  FAIRPORT  RMG .T. 07/16/82   27500.00 Memo
      4   020     MAX LEVINSKY  HENRIETTA RMG .F. 04/13/69   27550.00 Memo
      5   025     KIM BRANDT    FAIRPORT  RMG .F. 04/04/77   36000.00 Memo
     11   055     PHIL MARTIN   WEBSTER   RMG .F. 07/19/80   31000.00 Memo
```

Notice that the records have been presented in the order of the index. Physically, the order of the records in the original PERSNL file has been untouched.

Indexing Without Regard to Upper- and Lowercase

You can index on a character field without regard to upper- and lowercase characters in the data.

```
.USE PERSNL          <cr>
.INDEX ON UPPER(TOWN)  TO TINDX          <cr>
.LIST          <cr>
```

Record#	EMP_NUM	EMP_NAME	TOWN	ORG	EXE	DT_OF_HIRE	SALARY	NOTE
2	010	PETE JOHNSON	brighton	BSG	.T.	02/03/76	27590.00	Memo
10	050	PAUL BHARUCHA	BRIGHTON	BSG	.T.	05/23/73	29100.00	Memo
12	060	JOHN PETERSON	BRIGHTON	RBG	.T.	04/17/79	31480.00	Memo
3	015	GLORIA PATEL	FAIRPORT	RMG	.T.	07/16/82	27500.00	Memo
5	025	KIM BRANDT	FAIRPORT	RMG	.F.	04/04/77	36000.00	Memo
13	065	JOY HARDY	fairport	RBG	.F.	01/19/79	34200.00	Memo
4	020	MAX LEVINSKY	HENRIETTA	RMG	.F.	04/13/69	27550.00	Memo
7	035	WILLIAM PATEL	penfield	GSD	.F.	08/17/71	28900.00	Memo
6	030	TIM MONTAL	ROCHESTER	RBG	.F.	07/07/81	41900.00	Memo
8	040	JAMES JAMESON	ROCHESTER	GSD	.T.	10/21/77	29800.00	Memo
14	070	JAN MOREY	ROCHESTER	GSD	.T.	04/23/67	18190.00	Memo
15	075	JOHN JONES	rochester	GSD	.T.	04/04/70	25100.00	Memo
1	005	NINA BHARUCHA	WEBSTER	BSG	.T.	05/24/80	25000.00	Memo
9	045	MORRIS KATZ	webster	BSG	.F.	09/14/80	23450.00	Memo
11	055	PHIL MARTIN	WEBSTER	RMG	.F.	07/19/80	31000.00	Memo

You may want to use this feature when you are not too sure of how the data may have been created, and you do not want the records segregated merely on the basis of an upper- and lowercase difference.

Indexing on a Substring of a Character Field

You can index on substrings of a character field! For example:

```
.INDEX ON  SUBSTR(TOWN,1,2)  TO  TINDX          <cr>
```

This command could be used to group together all towns beginning with the same two characters, such as ROCHESTER and ROXY.

```
.USE PERSNL          <cr>
.INDEX ON SUBST(TOWN,2,3) TO TINDX          <cr>
.LIST          <cr>
```

We have indexed on the second, third, and fourth characters of the town field.

Record#	EMP_NUM	EMP_NAME	TOWN	ORG	EXE	DT_OF_HIRE	SALARY	NOTE
3	015	GLORIA PATEL	FAIRPORT	RMG	.T.	07/16/82	27500.00	Memo
5	025	KIM BRANDT	FAIRPORT	RMG	.F.	04/04/77	36000.00	Memo
1	005	NINA BHARUCHA	WEBSTER	BSG	.T.	05/24/80	25000.00	Memo
11	055	PHIL MARTIN	WEBSTER	RMG	.F.	07/19/80	31000.00	Memo
4	020	MAX LEVINSKY	HENRIETTA	RMG	.F.	04/13/69	27550.00	Memo
6	030	TIM MONTAL	ROCHESTER	RBG	.F.	07/07/81	41900.00	Memo
8	040	JAMES JAMESON	ROCHESTER	GSD	.T.	10/21/77	29800.00	Memo
14	070	JAN MOREY	ROCHESTER	GSD	.T.	04/23/67	18190.00	Memo
10	050	PAUL BHARUCHA	BRIGHTON	BSG	.T.	05/23/73	29100.00	Memo

```
12  060   JOHN PETERSON  BRIGHTON   RBG .T. 04/17/79   31480.00 Memo
13  065   JOY HARDY      fairport   RBG .F. 01/19/79   34200.00 Memo
 9  045   MORRIS KATZ    webster    BSG .F. 09/14/80   23450.00 Memo
 7  035   WILLIAM PATEL  penfield   GSD .F. 08/17/71   28900.00 Memo
15  075   JOHN JONES     rochester  GSD .T. 04/04/70   25100.00 Memo
 2  010   PETE JOHNSON   brighton   BSG .T. 02/03/76   27590.00 Memo
```

Indexing on a Substring, Regardless of Case

You can index on a substring using the following commands.

```
.USE PERSNL        <cr>
.INDEX ON SUBSTR(UPPER(TOWN),2,3) TO TINDX        <cr>
.LIST        <cr>
```

Contrast listing below with the previous one. Here we are disregarding the difference in upper- and lowercase, of the second, third, and fourth characters of the TOWN field.

```
Record#  EMP_NUM EMP_NAME      TOWN       ORG EXE DT_OF_HIRE   SALARY NOTE
      3  015     GLORIA PATEL  FAIRPORT   RMG .T. 07/16/82   27500.00 Memo
      5  025     KIM BRANDT    FAIRPORT   RMG .F. 04/04/77   36000.00 Memo
     13  065     JOY HARDY     fairport   RBG .F. 01/19/79   34200.00 Memo
      1  005     NINA BHARUCHA WEBSTER    BSG .T. 05/24/80   25000.00 Memo
      9  045     MORRIS KATZ   webster    BSG .F. 09/14/80   23450.00 Memo
     11  055     PHIL MARTIN   WEBSTER    RMG .F. 07/19/80   31000.00 Memo
      7  035     WILLIAM PATEL penfield   GSD .F. 08/17/71   28900.00 Memo
      4  020     MAX LEVINSKY  HENRIETTA  RMG .F. 04/13/69   27550.00 Memo
      6  030     TIM MONTAL    ROCHESTER  RBG .F. 07/07/81   41900.00 Memo
      8  040     JAMES JAMESON ROCHESTER  GSD .T. 10/21/77   29800.00 Memo
     14  070     JAN MOREY     ROCHESTER  GSD .T. 04/23/67   18190.00 Memo
     15  075     JOHN JONES    rochester  GSD .T. 04/04/70   25100.00 Memo
      2  010     PETE JOHNSON  brighton   BSG .T. 02/03/76   27590.00 Memo
     10  050     PAUL BHARUCHA BRIGHTON   BSG .T. 05/23/73   29100.00 Memo
     12  060     JOHN PETERSON BRIGHTON   RBG .T. 04/17/79   31480.00 Memo
```

Indexing on a Numeric Field

You can index on a numeric field just as you can index on a character field.

```
.USE PERSNL        <cr>
.INDEX ON SALARY TO SALINDX        <cr>
.LIST        <cr>
```

```
Record#  EMP_NUM EMP_NAME      TOWN       ORG EXE DT_OF_HIRE   SALARY NOTE
     14  070     JAN MOREY     ROCHESTER  GSD .T. 04/23/67   18190.00 Memo
      9  045     MORRIS KATZ   webster    BSG .F. 09/14/80   23450.00 Memo
      1  005     NINA BHARUCHA WEBSTER    BSG .T. 05/24/80   25000.00 Memo
     15  075     JOHN JONES    rochester  GSD .T. 04/04/70   25100.00 Memo
      3  015     GLORIA PATEL  FAIRPORT   RMG .T. 07/16/82   27500.00 Memo
      4  020     MAX LEVINSKY  HENRIETTA  RMG .F. 04/13/69   27550.00 Memo
```

```
 2   010    PETE JOHNSON   brighton   BSG  .T.  02/03/76    27590.00 Memo
 7   035    WILLIAM PATEL  penfield   GSD  .F.  08/17/71    28900.00 Memo
10   050    PAUL BHARUCHA  BRIGHTON   BSG  .T.  05/23/73    29100.00 Memo
 8   040    JAMES JAMESON  ROCHESTER  GSD  .T.  10/21/77    29800.00 Memo
11   055    PHIL MARTIN    WEBSTER    RMG  .F.  07/19/80    31000.00 Memo
12   060    JOHN PETERSON  BRIGHTON   RBG  .T.  04/17/79    31480.00 Memo
13   065    JOY HARDY      fairport   RBG  .F.  01/19/79    34200.00 Memo
 5   025    KIM BRANDT     FAIRPORT   RMG  .F.  04/04/77    36000.00 Memo
 6   030    TIM MONTAL     ROCHESTER  RBG  .F.  07/07/81    41900.00 Memo
```

The records are now listed in ascending order of the SALARY field.

Indexing Numeric Fields in Descending Sequence

The indexing feature in dBASE does not support a parameter such as /D, for descending, as the SORT command does. We can, however, fool dBASE into providing us with descending sequences on numeric fields. For this, we will use a bit of common sense arithmetic.

```
.USE PERSNL        <cr>
.INDEX ON    99999.99 - SALARY    TO SALINDX        <cr>
```

That is, you have to substract the numeric field from the highest possible value that can be contained in that field!

```
    .LIST                                              <cr>
```

```
Record#  EMP_NUM  EMP_NAME      TOWN       ORG EXE  DT_OF_HIRE   SALARY NOTE
      6   030     TIM MONTAL    ROCHESTER  RBG .F.  07/07/81    41900.00 Memo
      5   025     KIM BRANDT    FAIRPORT   RMG .F.  04/04/77    36000.00 Memo
     13   065     JOY HARDY     fairport   RBG .F.  01/19/79    34200.00 Memo
     12   060     JOHN PETERSON BRIGHTON   RBG .T.  04/17/79    31480.00 Memo
     11   055     PHIL MARTIN   WEBSTER    RMG .F.  07/19/80    31000.00 Memo
      8   040     JAMES JAMESON ROCHESTER  GSD .T.  10/21/77    29800.00 Memo
     10   050     PAUL BHARUCHA BRIGHTON   BSG .T.  05/23/73    29100.00 Memo
      7   035     WILLIAM PATEL penfield   GSD .F.  08/17/71    28900.00 Memo
      2   010     PETE JOHNSON  brighton   BSG .T.  02/03/76    27590.00 Memo
      4   020     MAX LEVINSKY  HENRIETTA  RMG .F.  04/13/69    27550.00 Memo
      3   015     GLORIA PATEL  FAIRPORT   RMG .T.  07/16/82    27500.00 Memo
     15   075     JOHN JONES    rochester  GSD .T.  04/04/70    25100.00 Memo
      1   005     NINA BHARUCHA WEBSTER    BSG .T.  05/24/80    25000.00 Memo
      9   045     MORRIS KATZ   webster    BSG .F.  09/14/80    23450.00 Memo
     14   070     JAN MOREY     ROCHESTER  GSD .T.  04/23/67    18190.00 Memo
```

Note: It is important to use the correct length of the highest value. That is, the SALARY field was defined in the structure of the file as having the format 99999.99 (a total length of 8, inclusive of 2 decimals). Hence we subtract the SALARY data from 99999.99.

Indexing on the Substring of a Numeric Field

Since the substring function only applies to a character string, to index on a substring of a numeric field, you must use the STRing function with the numeric field.

```
.USE PERSNL          <cr>
.INDEX ON SUBSTR(STR(SALARY,8,2),1,1)  TO YRINDX        <cr>
```

These statements produce an index on the *first* character of the SALARY field.

```
.LIST          <cr>
```

Record#	EMP_NUM	EMP_NAME	TOWN	ORG	EXE	DT_OF_HIRE	SALARY	NOTE
14	070	JAN MOREY	ROCHESTER	GSD	.T.	04/23/67	18190.00	Memo
1	005	NINA BHARUCHA	WEBSTER	BSG	.T.	05/24/80	25000.00	Memo
2	010	PETE JOHNSON	brighton	BSG	.T.	02/03/76	27590.00	Memo
3	015	GLORIA PATEL	FAIRPORT	RMG	.T.	07/16/82	27500.00	Memo
4	020	MAX LEVINSKY	HENRIETTA	RMG	.F.	04/13/69	27550.00	Memo
7	035	WILLIAM PATEL	penfield	GSD	.F.	08/17/71	28900.00	Memo
8	040	JAMES JAMESON	ROCHESTER	GSD	.T.	10/21/77	29800.00	Memo
9	045	MORRIS KATZ	webster	BSG	.F.	09/14/80	23450.00	Memo
10	050	PAUL BHARUCHA	BRIGHTON	BSG	.T.	05/23/73	29100.00	Memo
15	075	JOHN JONES	rochester	GSD	.T.	04/04/70	25100.00	Memo
5	025	KIM BRANDT	FAIRPORT	RMG	.F.	04/04/77	36000.00	Memo
11	055	PHIL MARTIN	WEBSTER	RMG	.F.	07/19/80	31000.00	Memo
12	060	JOHN PETERSON	BRIGHTON	RBG	.T.	04/17/79	31480.00	Memo
13	065	JOY HARDY	fairport	RBG	.F.	01/19/79	34200.00	Memo
6	030	TIM MONTAL	ROCHESTER	RBG	.F.	07/07/81	41900.00	Memo

Indexing on a Date Field

You can also index on a date field.

```
.USE PERSNL          <cr>
.INDEX ON DT__OF__HIRE TO DTINDX        <cr>
.LIST          <cr>
```

Record#	EMP_NUM	EMP_NAME	TOWN	ORG	EXE	DT_OF_HIRE	SALARY	NOTE
14	070	JAN MOREY	ROCHESTER	GSD	.T.	04/23/67	18190.00	Memo
4	020	MAX LEVINSKY	HENRIETTA	RMG	.F.	04/13/69	27550.00	Memo
15	075	JOHN JONES	rochester	GSD	.T.	04/04/70	25100.00	Memo
7	035	WILLIAM PATEL	penfield	GSD	.F.	08/17/71	28900.00	Memo
10	050	PAUL BHARUCHA	BRIGHTON	BSG	.T.	05/23/73	29100.00	Memo
2	010	PETE JOHNSON	brighton	BSG	.T.	02/03/76	27590.00	Memo
5	025	KIM BRANDT	FAIRPORT	RMG	.F.	04/04/77	36000.00	Memo
8	040	JAMES JAMESON	ROCHESTER	GSD	.T.	10/21/77	29800.00	Memo
13	065	JOY HARDY	fairport	RBG	.F.	01/19/79	34200.00	Memo
12	060	JOHN PETERSON	BRIGHTON	RBG	.T.	04/17/79	31480.00	Memo
1	005	NINA BHARUCHA	WEBSTER	BSG	.T.	05/24/80	25000.00	Memo
11	055	PHIL MARTIN	WEBSTER	RMG	.F.	07/19/80	31000.00	Memo
9	045	MORRIS KATZ	webster	BSG	.F.	09/14/80	23450.00	Memo
6	030	TIM MONTAL	ROCHESTER	RBG	.F.	07/07/81	41900.00	Memo
3	015	GLORIA PATEL	FAIRPORT	RMG	.T.	07/16/82	27500.00	Memo

Notice that the records have been sorted in chronological order, by date, from earliest to latest.

Indexing on a Date Field in Reverse Chronological Order

Just as you can use arithmetic to index numerical fields in descending order, you can use it to index date fields in descending order.

```
.USE PERSNL          <cr>
.INDEX ON CTOD('99999999') - DT__OF__HIRE   TO   DTINDX          <cr>
```

> **Note:** If a date field has the value 06/19/47 as data, in the system the date is looked upon as 19470619! We will, therefore, use the same trick we used before for obtaining numeric fields in descending sequences. We will subtract this eight-character date field from the highest date value possible.

The function CTOD('99999999') forces dBASE to convert the character string '99999999' into a date field, for the duration of the command, so we can successfully subtract our date field from the highest value possible in any date field.

```
.LIST          <cr>
```

Record#	EMP_NUM	EMP_NAME	TOWN	ORG	EXE	DT_OF_HIRE	SALARY	NOTE
3	015	GLORIA PATEL	FAIRPORT	RMG	.T.	07/16/82	27500.00	Memo
6	030	TIM MONTAL	ROCHESTER	RBG	.F.	07/07/81	41900.00	Memo
9	045	MORRIS KATZ	webster	BSG	.F.	09/14/80	23450.00	Memo
11	055	PHIL MARTIN	WEBSTER	RMG	.F.	07/19/80	31000.00	Memo
1	005	NINA BHARUCHA	WEBSTER	BSG	.T.	05/24/80	25000.00	Memo
12	060	JOHN PETERSON	BRIGHTON	RBG	.T.	04/17/79	31480.00	Memo
13	065	JOY HARDY	fairport	RBG	.F.	01/19/79	34200.00	Memo
8	040	JAMES JAMESON	ROCHESTER	GSD	.T.	10/21/77	29800.00	Memo
5	025	KIM BRANDT	FAIRPORT	RMG	.F.	04/04/77	36000.00	Memo
2	010	PETE JOHNSON	brighton	BSG	.T.	02/03/76	27590.00	Memo
10	050	PAUL BHARUCHA	BRIGHTON	BSG	.T.	05/23/73	29100.00	Memo
7	035	WILLIAM PATEL	penfield	GSD	.F.	08/17/71	28900.00	Memo
15	075	JOHN JONES	rochester	GSD	.T.	04/04/70	25100.00	Memo
4	020	MAX LEVINSKY	HENRIETTA	RMG	.F.	04/13/69	27550.00	Memo
14	070	JAN MOREY	ROCHESTER	GSD	.T.	04/23/67	18190.00	Memo

We now have the records pulled out in reverse chronological order!

Indexing on Multiple Fields

We will now turn our attention to obtaining an index on multiple fields. These could be any combination of character, numeric, and date fields. In some cases I have provided more than one way of obtaining the same result. These multiple methods are shown where dates are to be indexed in descending sequences.

Suppose we want to index by TOWN, and within that field, by the ORG field. (Notice that both fields are character fields.) The statement would be:

```
.USE PERSNL          <cr>
.INDEX ON TOWN + ORG TO TINDX          <cr>
```

Note that we want to specify a hierarchy. We want to index first on the TOWN field, and for the same TOWN values, we want to index by ORG.

```
.LIST          <cr>
```

Record#	EMP_NUM	EMP_NAME	TOWN	ORG	EXE	DT_OF_HIRE	SALARY	NOTE
10	050	PAUL BHARUCHA	BRIGHTON	BSG	.T.	05/23/73	29100.00	Memo
12	060	JOHN PETERSON	BRIGHTON	RBG	.T.	04/17/79	31480.00	Memo
3	015	GLORIA PATEL	FAIRPORT	RMG	.T.	07/16/82	27500.00	Memo
5	025	KIM BRANDT	FAIRPORT	RMG	.F.	04/04/77	36000.00	Memo
4	020	MAX LEVINSKY	HENRIETTA	RMG	.F.	04/13/69	27550.00	Memo
8	040	JAMES JAMESON	ROCHESTER	GSD	.T.	10/21/77	29800.00	Memo
14	070	JAN MOREY	ROCHESTER	GSD	.T.	04/23/67	18190.00	Memo
6	030	TIM MONTAL	ROCHESTER	RBG	.F.	07/07/81	41900.00	Memo
1	005	NINA BHARUCHA	WEBSTER	BSG	.T.	05/24/80	25000.00	Memo
11	055	PHIL MARTIN	WEBSTER	RMG	.F.	07/19/80	31000.00	Memo
2	010	PETE JOHNSON	brighton	BSG	.T.	02/03/76	27590.00	Memo
13	065	JOY HARDY	fairport	RBG	.F.	01/19/79	34200.00	Memo
7	035	WILLIAM PATEL	penfield	GSD	.F.	08/17/71	28900.00	Memo
15	075	JOHN JONES	rochester	GSD	.T.	04/04/70	25100.00	Memo
9	045	MORRIS KATZ	webster	BSG	.F.	09/14/80	23450.00	Memo

One general observation can be made at this point: the statement is essentially FREE-FORM. The number of spaces before and after the + sign is immaterial. You can even do without the spaces at all.

```
.USE PERSNL          <cr>
.INDEX ON TOWN+ORG+EMP__NUM TO TINDX          <cr>
```

This command establishes a three-level hierarchy.

```
.LIST          <cr>
```

Record#	EMP_NUM	EMP_NAME	TOWN	ORG	EXE	DT_OF_HIRE	SALARY	NOTE
10	050	PAUL BHARUCHA	BRIGHTON	BSG	.T.	05/23/73	29100.00	Memo
12	060	JOHN PETERSON	BRIGHTON	RBG	.T.	04/17/79	31480.00	Memo
3	015	GLORIA PATEL	FAIRPORT	RMG	.T.	07/16/82	27500.00	Memo
5	025	KIM BRANDT	FAIRPORT	RMG	.F.	04/04/77	36000.00	Memo
4	020	MAX LEVINSKY	HENRIETTA	RMG	.F.	04/13/69	27550.00	Memo
8	040	JAMES JAMESON	ROCHESTER	GSD	.T.	10/21/77	29800.00	Memo
14	070	JAN MOREY	ROCHESTER	GSD	.T.	04/23/67	18190.00	Memo
6	030	TIM MONTAL	ROCHESTER	RBG	.F.	07/07/81	41900.00	Memo
1	005	NINA BHARUCHA	WEBSTER	BSG	.T.	05/24/80	25000.00	Memo

```
11   055   PHIL MARTIN     WEBSTER    RMG .F. 07/19/80   31000.00 Memo
 2   010   PETE JOHNSON    brighton   BSG .T. 02/03/76   27590.00 Memo
13   065   JOY HARDY       fairport   RBG .F. 01/19/79   34200.00 Memo
 7   035   WILLIAM PATEL   penfield   GSD .F. 08/17/71   28900.00 Memo
15   075   JOHN JONES      rochester  GSD .T. 04/04/70   25100.00 Memo
 9   045   MORRIS KATZ     webster    BSG .F. 09/14/80   23450.00 Memo
```

Notice record numbers 8 and 14, above. For the same town ROCHESTER and for the same organization GSD within ROCHESTER, employee number 040 has been placed before employee number 070.

Question: How many fields can you string out, for an index on multiple fields?

Answer: When you specify multiple fields, you are specifying the *key length* for the index. The rule is that the total length of the index key should not be more than 100 characters. For example, if the key were specified as: TOWN + ORG + EMP_NAME, the key length as obtained from the structure of the PERSNL file is 9 (for TOWN) + 3 (for ORG) + 13 (for EMP_NAME), or a total of 25. This total cannot exceed 100.

Indexing on Multiple Substrings

```
.USE PERSNL        <cr>
.INDEX ON SUBSTR(TOWN,1,2)+SUBSTR(TOWN,5,6) TO ABC        <cr>
```

The commands below will index on two substrings of the same field. Our data will not produce any meaningful listing, so I shall skip it here. However, an example of a situation in which you may want to use this index feature follows:

Let us say you have a field called PART_NUM, which is 12 characters wide. Within this 12-character structure, characters 1 through 8 form the actual part number, character 9 is the make-or-buy code, and characters 10 through 12 form the part-revision code. It is now necessary to index your file by PART_NUM, and by part revision within part number.

```
.INDEX ON SUBSTR(PART_NUM,1,8) + SUBSTR(PART_NUM,10,3) TO ABC
                                                         <cr>
```

will do the trick.

Indexing on a Combination of Field Types

Creating an index on a single character field, a single numeric field, a single date field, or multiple character fields works well. The problem arises when you are trying to create a *hierarchical index* on multiple fields, *and one or more, or all of the fields are numeric or date.*

In a multiple-field combination for creating a *hierarchical index*, if one or more of the fields to be specified are numeric or date, the numeric and date fields will have to be used with the STRing function! As you recall, to STRing a numeric, you can use STR(field-name,field-length) and to STRing a date you can use DTOC(field-name).

Indexing on a Character Field and a Numeric Field in Ascending Order. Here is an example of indexing on both a character and a numeric field.

```
.USE PERSNL          <cr>
.INDEX ON ORG + STR(SALARY,8,2) TO OINDX          <cr>
```

Remember that the + symbol represents concatenation. We are concatenating the ORG data to the SALARY data of each record, and are pulling off an index on that combination. However, only character fields can be concatenated, so the SALARY field, which is numeric, is represented in its string version.

If you had specified .INDEX ON ORG + SALARY TO ABC, you would have received a syntax error message.

```
.LIST          <cr>
```

Record#	EMP_NUM	EMP_NAME	TOWN	ORG	EXE	DT_OF_HIRE	SALARY	NOTE
9	045	MORRIS KATZ	webster	BSG	.F.	09/14/80	23450.00	Memo
1	005	NINA BHARUCHA	WEBSTER	BSG	.T.	05/24/80	25000.00	Memo
2	010	PETE JOHNSON	brighton	BSG	.T.	02/03/76	27590.00	Memo
10	050	PAUL BHARUCHA	BRIGHTON	BSG	.T.	05/23/73	29100.00	Memo
14	070	JAN MOREY	ROCHESTER	GSD	.T.	04/23/67	18190.00	Memo
15	075	JOHN JONES	rochester	GSD	.T.	04/04/70	25100.00	Memo
7	035	WILLIAM PATEL	penfield	GSD	.F.	08/17/71	28900.00	Memo
8	040	JAMES JAMESON	ROCHESTER	GSD	.T.	10/21/77	29800.00	Memo
12	060	JOHN PETERSON	BRIGHTON	RBG	.T.	04/17/79	31480.00	Memo
13	065	JOY HARDY	fairport	RBG	.F.	01/19/79	34200.00	Memo
6	030	TIM MONTAL	ROCHESTER	RBG	.F.	07/07/81	41900.00	Memo
3	015	GLORIA PATEL	FAIRPORT	RMG	.T.	07/16/82	27500.00	Memo
4	020	MAX LEVINSKY	HENRIETTA	RMG	.F.	04/13/69	27550.00	Memo
11	055	PHIL MARTIN	WEBSTER	RMG	.F.	07/19/80	31000.00	Memo
5	025	KIM BRANDT	FAIRPORT	RMG	.F.	04/04/77	36000.00	Memo

Note that for the same ORG fields, the salaries have been sequenced in ascending sequence. To sequence these salaries in descending order, you could use the following commands.

Indexing on a Character Field and a Numeric Field in Descending Order. Here we are stringing the descending version of the numeric field.

```
.USE PERSNL          <cr>
.INDEX ON ORG + STR(99999.99-SALARY,8,2) TO ABC          <cr>
.LIST          <cr>
```

Record#	EMP_NUM	EMP_NAME	TOWN	ORG	EXE	DT_OF_HIRE	SALARY	NOTE
10	050	PAUL BHARUCHA	BRIGHTON	BSG	.T.	05/23/73	29100.00	Memo
2	010	PETE JOHNSON	brighton	BSG	.T.	02/03/76	27590.00	Memo
1	005	NINA BHARUCHA	WEBSTER	BSG	.T.	05/24/80	25000.00	Memo
9	045	MORRIS KATZ	webster	BSG	.F.	09/14/80	23450.00	Memo

```
 8   040      JAMES JAMESON  ROCHESTER GSD .T. 10/21/77    29800.00 Memo
 7   035      WILLIAM PATEL  penfield  GSD .F. 08/17/71    28900.00 Memo
15   075      JOHN JONES     rochester GSD .T. 04/04/70    25100.00 Memo
14   070      JAN MOREY      ROCHESTER GSD .T. 04/23/67    18190.00 Memo
 6   030      TIM MONTAL     ROCHESTER RBG .F. 07/07/81    41900.00 Memo
13   065      JOY HARDY      fairport  RBG .F. 01/19/79    34200.00 Memo
12   060      JOHN PETERSON  BRIGHTON  RBG .T. 04/17/79    31480.00 Memo
 5   025      KIM BRANDT     FAIRPORT  RMG .F. 04/04/77    36000.00 Memo
11   055      PHIL MARTIN    WEBSTER   RMG .F. 07/19/80    31000.00 Memo
 4   020      MAX LEVINSKY   HENRIETTA RMG .F. 04/13/69    27550.00 Memo
 3   015      GLORIA PATEL   FAIRPORT  RMG .T. 07/16/82    27500.00 Memo
```

Indexing on a Character Field and a Date Field in Ascending Order.

We want to obtain an index on ORG and DATE__OF__HIRE. In a previous example, we indexed on a date field as a stand-alone field. In such cases, dBASE automatically performs an internal conversion, (a logical one, not an actual physical data conversion) such that each date is presented to it in the order YY/MM/DD.

When you are trying to index on multiple fields, however, it is essential to remember that when dates are to be sequenced, you must present them to the system in YY/MM/DD format, not the usual MM/DD/YY format. If this fact is not recognized, and if dates are presented in the erroneous MM/DD/YY format, then a date of 01/02/89 (Jan. 2, 1989) will be positioned ahead of a date of 04/01/86 (April 1, 1986). This, of course, is an error, and it occurs since the month of 01 gets positioned ahead of the month of 04, without regard to the year.

Since the dates must be in the format YY/MM/DD, it is essential that we have dBASE look upon the dates as if they were in the format YY/MM/DD before these dates are actually sequenced. The command SET DATE ANSI will force dBASE to recognize all dates in the format YY/MM/DD, while the command SET DATE AMER will once again produce the normal MM/DD/YY formats.

```
.USE PERSNL        <cr>
.SET DATE ANSI        <cr>
```

The above SET command forces dBASE to perform a *logical conversion* (not an actual physical one) on every date, for any purpose. (SET commands are discussed in detail in another section further along in the book.) Since the dates will now be recognized in the YY/MM/DD format, calling for an index operation is simple enough. (Since the date is to be indexed within the ORG field, remember to convert the date to a character string!)

```
.INDEX ON ORG + DTOC(DT__OF__HIRE) TO ABC        <cr>
.SET DATE AMER        <cr>
```

The above command once again presents all dates in the normal MM/DD/YY formats.

```
.LIST        <cr>
```

Record#	EMP_NUM	EMP_NAME	TOWN	ORG	EXE	DT_OF_HIRE	SALARY	NOTE
5	050	PAUL BHARUCHA	BRIGHTON	BSG	.T.	05/23/73	29100.00	Memo
6	010	PETE JOHNSON	brighton	BSG	.T.	02/03/76	27590.00	Memo
11	005	NINA BHARUCHA	WEBSTER	BSG	.T.	05/24/80	25000.00	Memo
13	045	MORRIS KATZ	webster	BSG	.F.	09/14/80	23450.00	Memo
1	070	JAN MOREY	ROCHESTER	GSD	.T.	04/23/67	18190.00	Memo
3	075	JOHN JONES	rochester	GSD	.T.	04/04/70	25100.00	Memo
4	035	WILLIAM PATEL	penfield	GSD	.F.	08/17/71	28900.00	Memo
8	040	JAMES JAMESON	ROCHESTER	GSD	.T.	10/21/77	29800.00	Memo
9	065	JOY HARDY	fairport	RBG	.F.	01/19/79	34200.00	Memo
10	060	JOHN PETERSON	BRIGHTON	RBG	.T.	04/17/79	31480.00	Memo
14	030	TIM MONTAL	ROCHESTER	RBG	.F.	07/07/81	41900.00	Memo
2	020	MAX LEVINSKY	HENRIETTA	RMG	.F.	04/13/69	27550.00	Memo
7	025	KIM BRANDT	FAIRPORT	RMG	.F.	04/04/77	36000.00	Memo
12	055	PHIL MARTIN	WEBSTER	RMG	.F.	07/19/80	31000.00	Memo
15	015	GLORIA PATEL	FAIRPORT	RMG	.T.	07/16/82	27500.00	Memo

Notice now that for the same ORG 'BSG', the dates are in proper ascending sequence: '73 comes before '76, which comes before '80, and '05/24/80' comes before '09/14/80'.

Remember that if you had not used the SET DATE ANSI command before performing the indexing operation, you would have obtained garbage for the result, since the month would have been indexed first, without regard to the year. Also, after the index operation, remember to SET DATE AMER to produce the normal formats.

Indexing on a Character Field and a Date Field in Descending Order.
We want an index on ORG and the reverse of the DATE_OF_HIRE.

Method 1: Using the same technique as above, we will first obtain a reverse date sequence, copy it over to another file, and then index this file on ORG.

```
.USE PERSNL          <cr>
.INDEX ON CTOD('99999999') - DT_OF_HIRE TO DTINDX          <cr>
```

We have seen the use of the CTOD function before.

```
.COPY TO OTHER          <cr>
```

This creates a file called OTHER.DBF, in reverse date sequence.

```
.USE OTHER          <cr>
.INDEX ON ORG TO OINDX          <cr>
.LIST          <cr>
```

Record#	EMP_NUM	EMP_NAME	TOWN	ORG	EXE	DT_OF_HIRE	SALARY	NOTE
3	045	MORRIS KATZ	webster	BSG	.F.	09/14/80	23450.00	Memo
5	005	NINA BHARUCHA	WEBSTER	BSG	.T.	05/24/80	25000.00	Memo
10	010	PETE JOHNSON	brighton	BSG	.T.	02/03/76	27590.00	Memo

```
11   050   PAUL BHARUCHA  BRIGHTON   BSG  .T.  05/23/73   29100.00  Memo
 8   040   JAMES JAMESON  ROCHESTER  GSD  .T.  10/21/77   29800.00  Memo
12   035   WILLIAM PATEL  penfield   GSD  .F.  08/17/71   28900.00  Memo
13   075   JOHN JONES     rochester  GSD  .T.  04/04/70   25100.00  Memo
15   070   JAN MOREY      ROCHESTER  GSD  .T.  04/23/67   18190.00  Memo
 2   030   TIM MONTAL     ROCHESTER  RBG  .F.  07/07/81   41900.00  Memo
 6   060   JOHN PETERSON  BRIGHTON   RBG  .T.  04/17/79   31480.00  Memo
 7   065   JOY HARDY      fairport   RBG  .F.  01/19/79   34200.00  Memo
 1   015   GLORIA PATEL   FAIRPORT   RMG  .T.  07/16/82   27500.00  Memo
 4   055   PHIL MARTIN    WEBSTER    RMG  .F.  07/19/80   31000.00  Memo
 9   025   KIM BRANDT     FAIRPORT   RMG  .F.  04/04/77   36000.00  Memo
14   020   MAX LEVINSKY   HENRIETTA  RMG  .F.  04/13/69   27550.00  Memo
```

Notice the reverse sequence of the dates, for the same organization field.

Method 2: We will index on the reverse substring of the date field, taking YEAR MONTH DAY as the sequence.

```
.USE PERSNL        <cr>
.INDEX ON ORG + STR(9999-YEAR(DT_OF_HIRE),4) + STR(99-MONTH(DT-
_OF_HIRE),2) + STR(99-DAY(DT_OF_HIRE),2) TO ABC        <cr>
```

We want to extract the YEAR, MONTH and DAY out of each record in reverse sequence and concatenate these to the ORG field. Once again, since concatenation is used, we have to convert the numeric extracts into character strings.

DT_OF_HIRE	is the date field.
YEAR(DT_OF_HIRE)	is the function that extracts the 19xx numeric year from the date field.
9999-YEAR(....)	is the reverse sequence of the year.
STR(9999-(YEAR(...),4)	is the string or character representation of the same 4-digit year in reverse sequence.

```
.LIST        <cr>
```

The result is the same as that obtained using Method 1. The record numbers, however, will be different, because of the combination sort/index used in Method 1.

Indexing on a Date Field and a Numeric Field in Ascending Order. For the duration of this subtopic, I have taken some different values for dates in our PERSNL file to produce a more meaningful result.

We want to index on DT_OF_HIRE (ascending) and SALARY (ascending).

```
.USE PERSNL        <cr>
.SET DATE ANSI        <cr>
```

The reason for using this command has been detailed before.

.INDEX ON DTOC(DT__OF__HIRE) + STR(SALARY,8,2) TO ABC   <cr>

Remember to convert the date to a character string, if it is used with any other field.

.SET DATE AMER   <cr>

The reason for using this command has been detailed before.

.LIST   <cr>

Record#	EMP_NUM	EMP_NAME	TOWN	ORG	EXE	DT_OF_HIRE	SALARY	NOTE
3	005	NINA BHARUCHA	WEBSTER	BSG	.T.	06/19/47	25000.00	Memo
5	015	GLORIA PATEL	FAIRPORT	RMG	.T.	06/19/47	27500.00	Memo
7	010	PETE JOHNSON	brighton	BSG	.T.	06/19/47	27590.00	Memo
1	070	JAN MOREY	ROCHESTER	GSD	.T.	04/23/67	18190.00	Memo
6	020	MAX LEVINSKY	HENRIETTA	RMG	.F.	04/13/69	27550.00	Memo
4	075	JOHN JONES	rochester	GSD	.T.	04/04/70	25100.00	Memo
9	050	PAUL BHARUCHA	BRIGHTON	BSG	.T.	05/23/73	29100.00	Memo
14	025	KIM BRANDT	FAIRPORT	RMG	.F.	04/04/77	36000.00	Memo
13	065	JOY HARDY	fairport	RBG	.F.	01/19/79	34200.00	Memo
12	060	JOHN PETERSON	BRIGHTON	RBG	.T.	04/17/79	31480.00	Memo
2	045	MORRIS KATZ	webster	BSG	.F.	01/01/80	23450.00	Memo
8	035	WILLIAM PATEL	penfield	GSD	.F.	01/01/80	28900.00	Memo
10	040	JAMES JAMESON	ROCHESTER	GSD	.T.	01/01/80	29800.00	Memo
15	030	TIM MONTAL	ROCHESTER	RBG	.F.	01/01/80	41900.00	Memo
11	055	PHIL MARTIN	WEBSTER	RMG	.F.	07/19/80	31000.00	Memo

Notice that for the same year, 06/19/47, the salary of 25000 comes before 27500 which comes before 27590, etc.

Indexing on a Date Field and a Numeric Field in Descending Order.
We want to index on DT__OF-HIRE and descending SALARY.

.USE PERSNL   <cr>
.SET DATE ANSI   <cr>
.INDEX ON DTOC(DT__OF__HIRE) + STR(99999.99-SALARY,8,2) TO ABC
                                                     <cr>
.SET DATE AMER   <cr>
.LIST   <cr>

Record#	EMP_NUM	EMP_NAME	TOWN	ORG	EXE	DT_OF_HIRE	SALARY	NOTE
9	010	PETE JOHNSON	brighton	BSG	.T.	06/19/47	27590.00	Memo
11	015	GLORIA PATEL	FAIRPORT	RMG	.T.	06/19/47	27500.00	Memo
13	005	NINA BHARUCHA	WEBSTER	BSG	.T.	06/19/47	25000.00	Memo
15	070	JAN MOREY	ROCHESTER	GSD	.T.	04/23/67	18190.00	Memo
10	020	MAX LEVINSKY	HENRIETTA	RMG	.F.	04/13/69	27550.00	Memo
12	075	JOHN JONES	rochester	GSD	.T.	04/04/70	25100.00	Memo
7	050	PAUL BHARUCHA	BRIGHTON	BSG	.T.	05/23/73	29100.00	Memo
2	025	KIM BRANDT	FAIRPORT	RMG	.F.	04/04/77	36000.00	Memo

```
 3   065      JOY HARDY      fairport  RBG  .F.  01/19/79   34200.00 Memo
 4   060      JOHN PETERSON  BRIGHTON  RBG  .T.  04/17/79   31480.00 Memo
 1   030      TIM MONTAL     ROCHESTER RBG  .F.  01/01/80   41900.00 Memo
 6   040      JAMES JAMESON  ROCHESTER GSD  .T.  01/01/80   29800.00 Memo
 8   035      WILLIAM PATEL  penfield  GSD  .F.  01/01/80   28900.00 Memo
14   045      MORRIS KATZ    webster   BSG  .F.  01/01/80   23450.00 Memo
 5   055      PHIL MARTIN    WEBSTER   RMG  .F.  07/19/80   31000.00 Memo
```

Indexing on a Date Field in Descending Order and a Numeric Field in Ascending Order.

Method 1:

```
.USE PERSNL           <cr>
.INDEX ON SALARY TO ABC          <cr>
.COPY TO OTHER           <cr>
.USE OTHER          <cr>
.INDEX ON CTOD('99999999') - DT_OF_HIRE  TO ABC           <cr>
.LIST          <cr>
```

```
Record#   EMP_NUM EMP_NAME       TOWN      ORG EXE DT_OF_HIRE   SALARY NOTE
    11   055      PHIL MARTIN    WEBSTER   RMG  .F.  07/19/80  31000.00 Memo
     2   045      MORRIS KATZ    webster   BSG  .F.  01/01/80  23450.00 Memo
     8   035      WILLIAM PATEL  penfield  GSD  .F.  01/01/80  28900.00 Memo
    10   040      JAMES JAMESON  ROCHESTER GSD  .T.  01/01/80  29800.00 Memo
    15   030      TIM MONTAL     ROCHESTER RBG  .F.  01/01/80  41900.00 Memo
    12   060      JOHN PETERSON  BRIGHTON  RBG  .T.  04/17/79  31480.00 Memo
    13   065      JOY HARDY      fairport  RBG  .F.  01/19/79  34200.00 Memo
    14   025      KIM BRANDT     FAIRPORT  RMG  .F.  04/04/77  36000.00 Memo
     9   050      PAUL BHARUCHA  BRIGHTON  BSG  .T.  05/23/73  29100.00 Memo
     4   075      JOHN JONES     rochester GSD  .T.  04/04/70  25100.00 Memo
     6   020      MAX LEVINSKY   HENRIETTA RMG  .F.  04/13/69  27550.00 Memo
     3   005      NINA BHARUCHA  WEBSTER   BSG  .T.  06/19/47  25000.00 Memo
     5   015      GLORIA PATEL   FAIRPORT  RMG  .T.  06/19/47  27500.00 Memo
     7   010      PETE JOHNSON   brighton  BSG  .T.  06/19/47  27590.00 Memo
     1   070      JAN MOREY      ROCHESTER GSD  .T.  04/23/67  18190.00 Memo
```

Method 2:

```
.USE PERSNL          <cr>
.INDEX ON STR(9999-YEAR(DT_OF_HIRE),4)+STR(99-MONTH(DT_OF_
HIRE),2)+STR(99-DAY(DT_OF_HIRE),2) + STR(SALARY,8,2) TO ABC   <cr>
.LIST          <cr>
```

The result is the same as that obtained using Method 1. The record numbers, however, will be different, because of the combination sort/index used in Method 1.

Indexing on a Date Field in Descending Order and a Numeric Field in Descending Order.

Method 1:

```
.USE PERSNL          <cr>
.INDEX ON 99999.99-SALARY TO ABC          <cr>
.COPY TO OTHER          <cr>
.USE OTHER          <cr>
.INDEX ON CTOD('99999999') - DT_OF_HIRE)  TO ABC          <cr>
.LIST          <cr>
```

Record#	EMP_NUM	EMP_NAME	TOWN	ORG	EXE	DT_OF_HIRE	SALARY	NOTE
5	055	PHIL MARTIN	WEBSTER	RMG	.F.	07/19/80	31000.00	Memo
1	030	TIM MONTAL	ROCHESTER	RBG	.F.	01/01/80	41900.00	Memo
6	040	JAMES JAMESON	ROCHESTER	GSD	.T.	01/01/80	29800.00	Memo
8	035	WILLIAM PATEL	penfield	GSD	.F.	01/01/80	28900.00	Memo
14	045	MORRIS KATZ	webster	BSG	.F.	01/01/80	23450.00	Memo
4	060	JOHN PETERSON	BRIGHTON	RBG	.T.	04/17/79	31480.00	Memo
3	065	JOY HARDY	fairport	RBG	.F.	01/19/79	34200.00	Memo
2	025	KIM BRANDT	FAIRPORT	RMG	.F.	04/04/77	36000.00	Memo
7	050	PAUL BHARUCHA	BRIGHTON	BSG	.T.	05/23/73	29100.00	Memo
12	075	JOHN JONES	rochester	GSD	.T.	04/04/70	25100.00	Memo
10	020	MAX LEVINSKY	HENRIETTA	RMG	.F.	04/13/69	27550.00	Memo
15	070	JAN MOREY	ROCHESTER	GSD	.T.	04/23/67	18190.00	Memo
9	010	PETE JOHNSON	brighton	BSG	.T.	06/19/47	27590.00	Memo
11	015	GLORIA PATEL	FAIRPORT	RMG	.T.	06/19/47	27500.00	Memo
13	005	NINA BHARUCHA	WEBSTER	BSG	.T.	06/19/47	25000.00	Memo

Method 2:

```
.USE PERSNL          <cr>
.INDEX ON  STR(9999-YEAR(DT_OF_HIRE),4)+STR(99-MONTH(DT_OF_
HIRE),2)+STR(99-DAY(DT_OF_HIRE),2) + STR(99999.99-SALARY,8,2) TO ABC
                                                                    <cr>
.LIST          <cr>
```

The result is the same as that obtained using Method 1. The record numbers, however, will be different, because of the combination sort/index used in Method 1.

> **Note:** We have seen from previous examples that the date field had to be converted to the string version, if it had to be used along with another field for indexing. What do you suppose would have happened if we had specified the commands without the string functions? That is, if the command had been:

```
.USE PERSNL          <cr>
.INDEX ON DT_OF_HIRE + SALARY  TO ABC          <cr>
.LIST          <cr>
```

Record#	EMP_NUM	EMP_NAME	TOWN	ORG	EXE	DT_OF_HIRE	SALARY	NOTE
1	005	NINA BHARUCHA	WEBSTER	BSG	.T.	06/19/47	25000.00	Memo
14	070	JAN MOREY	ROCHESTER	GSD	.T.	04/23/67	18190.00	Memo
3	015	GLORIA PATEL	FAIRPORT	RMG	.T.	06/19/47	27500.00	Memo
2	010	PETE JOHNSON	brighton	BSG	.T.	06/19/47	27590.00	Memo
15	075	JOHN JONES	rochester	GSD	.T.	04/04/70	25100.00	Memo
9	045	MORRIS KATZ	webster	BSG	.F.	01/01/80	23450.00	Memo
4	020	MAX LEVINSKY	HENRIETTA	RMG	.F.	04/13/69	27550.00	Memo
10	050	PAUL BHARUCHA	BRIGHTON	BSG	.T.	05/23/73	29100.00	Memo
7	035	WILLIAM PATEL	penfield	GSD	.F.	01/01/80	28900.00	Memo
8	040	JAMES JAMESON	ROCHESTER	GSD	.T.	01/01/80	29800.00	Memo
11	055	PHIL MARTIN	WEBSTER	RMG	.F.	07/19/80	31000.00	Memo
12	060	JOHN PETERSON	BRIGHTON	RBG	.T.	04/17/79	31480.00	Memo
13	065	JOY HARDY	fairport	RBG	.F.	01/19/79	34200.00	Memo
5	025	KIM BRANDT	FAIRPORT	RMG	.F.	04/04/77	36000.00	Memo
6	030	TIM MONTAL	ROCHESTER	RBG	.F.	01/01/80	41900.00	Memo

Remember that a date, such as 06/19/47, is maintained internally as 19470619, and so dBASE would have provided an index based on a numerical value created for each record by *adding together* the DT_OF_HIRE and SALARY fields. That is, the record having the *lowest* value as the *sum of the DT_OF_HIRE and SALARY* would be at the top of the list, and the one with the highest such value at the bottom of the list. Such an index, of course, is garbage!

Indexing on a Sum

As an example of a situation in which you may want to use the *sum* (as opposed to a *hierarchy*) of fields to index upon, suppose you had a database of student scores as follows:

NAME,C,20
MATH,N,2   (math. score)
SCIENCE,N,2   (science score)
PHY,N,2   (physics score)
CHEM,N,2   (chemistry score)

If you wanted to index on the sum total of two or more of the numeric fields, you could enter:

.INDEX ON MATH + SCIENCE TO MSINDX   <cr>

This statement would provide you with the lowest through highest scores for the MATH+SCIENCE category.

.INDEX ON   MATH+SCIENCE+PHY+CHEM   TO TOTINDX   <cr>

would provide you with the lowest through highest grand scores.

Note: Please understand that STRinging the numeric expressions implies that you want the index to specify a *hierarchy*, with a major field, some intermediate fields, and a minor field (for example, SALARY within DT__OF__HIRE). Using the numeric field names directly implies that you want to index on only *one* field, which is the sum total of the numeric fields used in the command expression (for example, MATH + SCIENCE).

The precaution of STRinging is to be observed only when you are indexing on combinations of two or more date fields and/or numeric fields, and you want to specify a hierarchy as opposed to a sum. Obviously, if you have even one character field in your index expression, all numerics and/or dates in the expression will have to be represented in STRing version, or you will get a syntax error.

Let us return to our example concerning scores. Suppose we want the following hierarchy: We want to be able to list out all scores in the usual ascending sequence of the grand scores, and for the same grand score, we want to list out records in ascending sequence of the MATH scores. While this may seem complex, you know that you will have to STRing the numerics, since a hierarchy is specified, and you know you also have to add the numeric fields together, since total scores are also involved. The above requirement could be met as follows:

.INDEX ON STR((MATH + SCIENCE + PHY + CHEM),3) + STR(MATH,2) TO GINDX   <cr>

A length 3 was used, since the sum of four 2-digit fields cannot exceed 999.

This time let us suppose we want a slightly different type of hierarchy. We want to be able to display all scores in descending sequence of the grand scores, and for the same grand score, we want to display records in descending sequence of the MATH scores.

While this may seem complex, you know that you will have to STRing the numerics, since a hierarchy is specified, and you know you also have to add the numeric fields together, since total scores are also involved. When you STRing the numerics, don't forget to use the 9999 option, to get descending sequences. The above requirement could be met as follows:

.INDEX ON STR(999-(MATH + SCIENCE + PHY + CHEM),3) + STR(99-MATH,2) TO ABC   <cr>

A length three was used, since the sum of four 2-digit fields cannot exceed 999.

Obtaining the Status of Active Indexes

If at any point in time you wish to find out which index files are currently active against the database in USE, you can do the following:

.DISP STATUS   <cr>

dBASE now comes up with the following:

```
Currently Selected Database:
Select area:  1, Database in Use: C:PERSNL.dbf    Alias: PERSNL
    Master index file:  C:OINDX.ndx   Key: ORG+STR(99999.99-SALARY,8,2)
           Memo file:   C:PERSNL.dbt

Alternate file: C:TEMP1.txt
File search path:
Default disk drive: C:
Print destination:  PRN:
Margin =       Ø
Current work area =     1

Press any key to continue...

ALTERNATE  - ON    DELETED    - OFF   FIXED      - OFF   SAFETY      - ON
BELL       - ON    DELIMITERS - OFF   HEADING    - ON    SCOREBOARD - ON
CARRY      - OFF   DEVICE     - SCRN  HELP       - ON    STATUS     - OFF
CATALOG    - OFF   DOHISTORY  - OFF   HISTORY    - ON    STEP       - OFF
CENTURY    - OFF   ECHO       - OFF   INTENSITY  - ON    TALK       - ON
CONFIRM    - OFF   ESCAPE     - ON    MENU       - ON    TITLE      - ON
CONSOLE    - ON    EXACT      - OFF   PRINT      - OFF   UNIQUE     - OFF
DEBUG      - OFF   FIELDS     - OFF

Programmable function keys:
F2   - assist;
F3   - list;
F4   - dir;
F5   - display structure;
F6   - display status;
F7   - display memory;
F8   - display;
F9   - append;
F1Ø  - edit;
```

This command will provide, first, the name of the database currently in USE and the name(s) of the index-file(s), if any, currently active against this database, with the names of the fields forming the index(es); it will also provide the names of other open files such as *alternate* files (don't worry about alternate files, for now) or memo files. Now the system will WAIT for your response. On entering any key (you would tend to hit the <cr> key), this command then provides a listing of the various SET switches and the Function Key assignments (these will be explained at the appropriate place in the book). In any case, the DISP STAT command could be used to find out which database and which index files are currently active.

Note: If you want to reindex all currently active indexes, simply enter:

.REINDEX   <cr>

Rebuilding index - C:OINDX.ndx
    15 records indexed

You would execute this command if you suspect the index(es) to have somehow gotten out of sync with the master-file.

Advantages of Indexing

Thus far we have seen many ways in which different types of sequences can be obtained. Most of the examples covered an index made up of two fields only, but the same concept can be stretched to a multifield index, as long as the length of the index key does not exceed 100 characters. Apart from providing various sequences to the data, what is the major advantage of indexing over sorting?

Advantage #1. One big advantage of the indexing feature is that indexes that are currently active against a master file are automatically updated if the master file is in any way changed or altered in its key field values; for example:

```
.USE PERSNL          <cr>
.INDEX ON TOWN TO TINDX          <cr>
```

After the above instructions, the index for town is created and is active against the PERSNL file. Now enter:

```
.APPEND          <cr>
```

This, as you know, will open up a blank structure into which you enter the new records. Suppose you appended two records, one with a TOWN value of AAA and the other with a TOWN value of ZZZ. After the APPEND process is ended, if you take a LIST, you will find that the newly appended records are in their proper *logical* positions in the *indexed* file! That is, the record with the town of AAA will be at the top of the indexed list, and the record with the town of ZZZ will be at the bottom of the (uppercase) pile. Physically, of course, the newly appended records are both at the physical bottom of the PERSNL file, since the records were APPENDed to the PERSNL file, but the index has been automatically updated to reflect proper logical sequencing for the new records.

> **Note:** This automatic updating would occur even if you changed an existing record's key field. For example, if you entered the following:
>
> ```
> .EDIT 5          <cr>
> ```
>
> and changed the town field to a value of 'XXXXXXXXX', then after the EDIT operation is completed, this record will be logically repositioned just before the record with the 'ZZZZZZ' key, near the bottom of the (uppercase) pile! Physically, of course, it remains in the PERSNL file exactly where it was before the start of the edit command!

Advantage #2. Another big advantage of the indexing feature is that you can ask dBASE to provide you with a specific record instantly! This is *random access* to data records, and dBASE whips through thousands of records in a couple of seconds to position itself at the record you want! This instant access is done through the use of the FIND command.

The FIND Command

For the duration of this subtopic, let us suppose that the field called TOWN in our PERSNL file is 12 characters wide.

The FIND command is a very powerful feature of dBASE III PLUS, and is used to find a record having a specific value in a key field.

The FIND command can only execute against an INDEXed file, and hence we take it up at this point in our study of dBASE. You can either create an index just before using the FIND command, or you can activate an existing index against the master. For example, let us say that we have indexed a file on the TOWN field. After the index is active, logically all the towns of, say, ROCHESTER will appear together. To "find" the very first occurrence of a town of ROCHESTER, we would enter:

.FIND 'ROCH'   <cr>

The value specified, in this case ROCH, may or may not be in quotes, even though TOWN is a character field!

This command only moves a pointer to the found record, but it will not automatically display the record. To display the record, and of course, all the other ROCH records (which are all logically sequenced together), we can enter:

.DISP NEXT 10   <cr>

This will display 10 records *in the logical order of the index*, starting with the current ROCH record; if there are more ROCH records, they would logically appear together, after the found record.

Each time the FIND command is used, the search begins at the *top* of the *indexed* database.

> **Note.** DELETED RECORDS *WILL* BE FOUND! That seems
> logical enough, since the Index command will accept deleted records
> for Indexing.

Let us go back to the TOWN index. If you enter .FIND 'R', dBASE will find the first record in the indexed file that has an R in the first location of the town field. A command like .FIND 'RO' will find the first record in the indexed file that has an RO in positions one and two of the town field, and so on. That is, the value supplied by you can be generic!

Now let us say that our file has been indexed on TOWN + ORG, and you wanted to find the first record that had a town of 'ROCH' and an organization of 'BSG'.

Understand clearly that dBASE must be provided explicit parameters about the town and organization fields. Since generic values of R, RO, ROC, ROCH, ROCHE, and so on will all find the same record based on the TOWN value, to find a record with the town ROCHESTER *and the organization BSG*, you would have to provide the *primary* key *in full*! In effect, you will have to specify:

```
.FIND 'ROCHESTER  B'        <cr>
```

or

```
.FIND 'ROCHESTER  BS'       <cr>
```

or

```
.FIND 'ROCHESTER  BSG'        <cr>
```

That is, you would have to leave enough spaces after the word ROCHESTER to provide for the 12 characters of the TOWN field!

As a further clarification, if you tried the following:

```
.FIND 'ROCH        BSG'      <cr>
```

it would not work, since there is no TOWN in the database with a full value of ROCH!

Notice that only the *last key-value supplied* can be generic! All preceeding key values should be provided in full, leaving the appropriate number of spaces, if required. As before, the values may or may not be supplied in quotes.

The above discussion is true even if the last key was a *NUMERIC* key! For instance, if your file was indexed on TOWN + STR(SALARY,8,2) and if you entered:

```
.FIND 'ROCHESTER  19'       <cr>
```

This will find the first town of ROCHESTER having a SALARY field that begins with the digits 19. This, of course, ties in with the fact that at the time of creation of the index, the SALARY field was represented as a character string.

> **Note:** The FIND command will accept a generic key value to find character strings, but requires an algebraic key value to find values in numeric fields. For example, if your file was indexed on the SALARY field, and you wanted to FIND the value 25000, you might enter:
>
> ```
> .FIND  25        <cr>
> ```
>
> This will FIND nothing, since we don't have any record in our database with a SALARY value equal to 25!
>
> ```
> .FIND  25000        <cr>
> ```

is what is required.

The above command, however *will NOT work* if the file has been indexed in descending sequence! The indexing feature assumes an ascending sequence, and your fooling around with the '99999' trick in dBASE does not work directly with the FIND command!

Suppose you created a descending index on SALARY, and you now want to find the record with the key value of 25000.

```
.FIND   74999.99          <cr>
```

will find the record with the salary of 25000!

It works this way because when you first created the index, you had specified: 99999.99-SALARY (for the descending index) and so these *complementary values* had been stored in the index file. So while you cannot directly FIND records in a descending-index file, you can always provide the appropriate numerical expression, and thus FIND that record.

Note that the functioning of the LOCATE command for an indexed file is identical to its functioning against an unsequenced file. The only obvious difference is, of course, that in this case, the records are scanned in the order of the index.

Advantage #3. A third advantage to indexing comes about in the ability to SET RELATION TO another file, this time on the indexed key field.

In the section on the DISPLAY command, I highlighted the fact that you could relate multiple databases together on record numbers, such that the record pointers of the linked files moved automatically as the record pointer of the active file moved around. I had emphasized that in such a relationship, there would have to be an exact one-to-one correspondence of the records in all files, exactly as if the linked databases were extensions of the active one. Obviously, not many real-life situations would fall into this category.

Now, we have the ability of being freed from the restraint of an exact one-to-one relationship, in the sense that the linked files do not have to be extensions of the active file. We use indexing to help out here. Everything I explained earlier in the DISPLAY section holds true. The only difference is that now the nonactive files are indexed, and the relationship is on the PART key field.

Using a combination of .SELE 1 and .SELE 2/3/4 you can DISPLAY or edit data in records with the same PART key field, from different databases. The process is controlled by the active file. Keep in mind that you can link multiple files, through the process of linking two files at a time.

A completed example of relating four files on the part number (PART) key field follows. Obviously, this example can be extended to include upto 10 different files.

Step 1. The files to be linked will have to be indexed, since the relationship is to be on the key field.

```
.USE INVEN2         <cr>
.INDEX ON PART TO PINDX2          <cr>
```

```
.USE INVEN3          <cr>
.INDEX ON PART TO PINDX3          <cr>
.USE INVEN4          <cr>
.INDEX ON PART TO PINDX4          <cr>
```

Step 2. Having indexed the files, we will assign the indexed files to the different work areas.

```
.SELE 1          <cr>
.USE INVEN1          <cr>
.SELE 2          <cr>
.USE INVEN2 INDEX PINDX2          <cr>
.SELE 3          <cr>
.USE INVEN3 INDEX PINDX3          <cr>
.SELE 4          <cr>
.USE INVEN4 INDEX PINDX4          <cr>
```

Step 3. Set up the relationships on part number, two files at a time.

```
.SELE 1          <cr>
.SET RELATION TO PART INTO INVEN2          <cr>

.SELE 2          <cr>
.SET RELATION TO PART INTO INVEN3          <cr>

.SELE 3          <cr>
.SET RELATION TO PART INTO INVEN4          <cr>
```

Step 4. Select the controlling file for the linked arrangement.

```
.SELE 1          <cr>
```

Now we can go ahead and pull off the listings. Three examples follow:

Example A

```
.LIST PART,INVEN2->CGC,INVEN3->ONHAND,INVEN4->ONORDER<cr>

Record#    PART    INVEN2->CGC INVEN3->ONHAND INVEN4->ONORDER
      1    P1      C11                    110             115
      2    P2      C22                    220             215
      3    P3      C33                    330             315
      4    P4      C44                    440             415
      5    P5      C55                    550             515
```

The command above requests the display of PART from the active file (INVEN1), and CGC, ONHAND and ONORDER from the linked files INVEN2, INVEN3, and

INVEN4, respectively, for all the records, as controlled by the PART numbers of the controlling file. The INVEN1.dbf file is still the controlling file.

Example B

.3   <cr>

The above statement will move the record pointer to record number 3, in the controlling file!

.LIST NEXT 4 PART,INVEN3->ONHAND,INVEN4->ONORDER   <cr>

```
Record#   PART    INVEN3->ONHAND INVEN4->ONORDER
      3   P3                 330             315
      4   P4                 440             415
      5   P5                 550             515
```

The command above requests the display of PART from the active file (INVEN1), ONHAND from INVEN3, and ONORDER from INVEN4, but only for PART numbers from record numbers 3,4 and 5 as controlled by INVEN1. (Remember that there are only five records in the file.)

The INVEN1.dbf file is still the controlling file.

Example C

.4   <cr>

The above statement will move the record pointer to record number 4, in the controlling file!

.LIST NEXT 2 PART,INVEN2->CGC,INVEN4->ONORDER   <cr>

```
Record#   PART    INVEN2->CGC  INVEN4->ONORDER
      4   P4      C44                      415
      5   P5      C55                      515
```

The command above requests the display of PART from the active file (INVEN1), CGC from INVEN2, and ONORDER from INVEN4, but only for PART numbers from record numbers 4 and 5 as controlled by INVEN1.

.CLOSE ALL   <cr>

Don't forget to close the files involved in the relationship, once the link arrangement has served its purpose. The CLOSE ALL command will close the files, without affecting existing *memory variables*. (Memory variables are covered at appropriate places in the book.)

I have used data in these files that is slightly different from that used in the DIS-

PLAY section, so you can appreciate the different processes.

The General Approach to Indexing

Obviously, you want to take maximum advantage of the fact that dBASE will keep your currently active index files automatically updated, so your FIND commands against the index(es) will work. Your general method of procedure should be as follows: Create a dBASE file, go through all the editing features necessary to ensure its integrity, and then create all the indexes you think you will ever need for this file. Suppose you have built up a PERSNL type of file, and you have now created the following indexes: one on EMP__NUM called EMPINDX, one on SOCNUM called SOCINDX (for Social Security number), one for ORG + EMP__NUM called OINDX. Now, at the start of work each day, you would invoke the master file along with the necessary indexes, as follows:

.USE PERSNL INDEX   EMPINDX,SOCINDX,OINDX   < cr>

In effect, these three indexes are now active against the PERSNL file. Note that the comma between the index names is mandatory.

Now all kinds of updates against the master file (APPEND, EDIT, BROWSE, DELETE-PACK) will automatically update all three indexes.

> **Note:** A delete-pack combination will update all the index files; however, a word of caution is called for. If too many records are deleted, it would be advisable for you to disassociate all indexes from the database before you issued the PACK command. Lack of this precaution may corrupt your index files. After the PACK command, you may proceed to recreate all indexes again.

At any time, up to seven index files can be actively associated with the master file. There may, of course, be any number of index files on the same disk as the master file, but only seven may be actively associated with the master concurrently. If you do have all seven indexes active at one time, the subsequent commands will take much longer to complete (too much system *overhead*), and ideally, you should not have more than three indexes active concurrently.

What would happen in the following LIST command?

.USE PERSNL   INDEX   EMPINDX,SOCINDX,OINDX   < cr>
.LIST   < cr>

Against which index will the LIST command function?

It will function against the first index mentioned. That is, in this case, the records will be listed out in the order of the EMP__NUM field! Should you alter your database, all currently active indexes will be updated, but commands like LIST, EDIT, and BROWSE will *present the records* to you *in the order of the first* index. To repeat, all active indexes will be updated to reflect changes through EDIT, BROWSE, and such commands.

The Disadvantage to Indexing

As you may have come to appreciate, INDEXing, with its automatic index update and its FIND command, is a very useful feature in dBASE, and you should use it to full advantage. There is, however, one drawback to the entire scenario of the indexing feature, which needs to be highlighted here.

Suppose we have created a PERSNL file in which one of the fields is the EMP_NUM field. Suppose further, that the following employee numbers have been loaded through APPEND, one for each record: 01, 10, 65, 35, 55, 656, 45, 56, and 65. Having created our records, suppose we now create our indexes and pull off reports. Even in the small example above, we have already created a problem! The problem is that we have a duplicate employee number 65 for two different records.

The problem occurs since we are building our database first and then creating the index. But by that time, we may have already entered some duplicate data into key fields that should not be allowed to have duplicates! Let me emphasize once again that it is the sequence of steps involved that is creating the problem, not the indexing feature itself. Indexing will help us solve the problem.

If you were now to index this database on the EMP_NUM field, a listing would ensure that all duplicate records would appear together. This would give you a chance to scan the list for duplicates and make corrections. You cannot, however, rely on your sight alone to pick out all duplicates. In order to ensure the integrity of your database, one recourse would be to write a "quick and dirty" computer program in dBASE, which will scan the indexed list of your records and pick out duplicates. Each time the indexed database is updated with new records through APPEND or EDIT commands, you will have to run the program again, since there is no guarantee that the second time around; you had not keyed in any invalid (already existing, or duplicate) data in the key fields.

For those databases in which you cannot afford to have any duplicate values in the key fields (such as employee-master, inventory-master, income-tax file, or customer-list file), you may, perhaps, want to prepare a computer program that will scan an indexed list of the database, and pull out the duplicates for you. This is one way you can ensure the integrity of your database. This program will have to be run as often as records are APPENDed or EDITed into the various master files. By the time you are through with the study of this book, you will know exactly how to write such a computer program.

The computer program referred to above is one way of ensuring the integrity of your database. You may, however, be saying to yourself that all this is after the fact! That is, the computer program merely helps us to clean up the mess after it has been created.

Is there a way of checking for already-existing keys in a file during the APPEND or EDIT process? If we could *flag* duplicate keys as they were being entered or edited, then we would not need to run the quick and dirty program each time, thus streamlining the entire process.

In the Advanced section of this book, we deal exclusively with programming in dBASE, and there you will learn exactly how you can cause the duplicate-check to occur during APPEND or EDIT. Unless, however, you are already advanced in your knowledge of this software and of programming in general, please control the urge to skip ahead. Otherwise you may find yourself in slightly deeper waters than you may prefer at this time.

Periodic Reindexing

We understand now that indexing helps to maintain records in sequence, when changes (additions/deletions, etc.,) are made to the master file. The real use and advantage of indexing, however, will be realized only after you have studied the Programming section of this book. You will learn that any system worth a dime will make great use of the FIND command for rapid access to records. The FIND command, of course, relies on an indexed file.

Since indexing is all-important to the successful, continued running of any system, I would strongly recommend that a routine be established whereby your user periodically updates all index files used in the system. This is merely a precautionary measure, to ensure integrity of the index. A month-end routine would be a good idea. This periodic reindexing can be provided as one more option of the main menu. (Menu-driven systems are discussed in detail in the Programming section.)

Mismatching Files and Indexes

By now, perhaps, this what-if question has come to your mind: suppose you have a master file M1 and an associated index file I1. Suppose the index was on the TOWN field. Can you now bring this I1 index file into play with another master file M2? Let us suppose, for now, that master file M2 also has a field called TOWN defined in its structure.

The answer is both, YES and NO. Physically, it will work, but logically it makes no sense, and in fact, may provide you with erroneous results without any warning messages. Suppose that M1 has the following TOWN values, and so M1 and the index I1 will appear as follows:

```
|   M A S T E R      F I L E   |        |  I N D E X  |
|                              |        |             |
| 1    ------ROCHESTER-----    |        |  3 BRIGHTON |
| 2    ------PERINTON------    |        |  5 FAIRPORT |
| 3    ------BRIGHTON------    |        |  6 GREECE   |
| 4    ------WEBSTER-------    |        |  2 PERINTON |
| 5    ------FAIRPORT------    |        |  1 ROCHESTER|
| 6    ------GREECE--------    |        |  4 WEBSTER  |
|                              |        |             |
```

Now let us suppose that you bring the index I1 in play with another master file M2. Let us also suppose that M2 has only 5 records in the file.

```
.USE M2    INDEX  I1      <cr>
.LIST      <cr>
```

According to the index I1, record #3 from file M2 will be displayed first, followed by record #5, and then the LISTing will stop, since there is no record #6 in the file

M2. You, however, will receive no error or warning messages, and will be led into believing that all is well with the world.

So although physically it can be done, logically it makes no sense to activate the wrong index file against your master file. This only serves to highlight the fact that clear documentation is paramount in the efficient execution of your dBASE systems.

Sorting or Indexing?

Under what situations should you use the SORT command as opposed to the INDEX feature? Based entirely upon experience gained through writing a few sophisticated applications, I know that in most situations, it is imperative to have your master files automatically sequenced in an *on-line mode*, as and when records enter or leave the files. Take, for example, a Dental system written in dBASE. Patients walk in and out of a busy dental office all day, and transactions can pile up very quickly, especially if the clinic is a multi-unit clinic. The transaction file must be updated in an on-line mode and should be written to trap all duplicate-transaction errors, so that, if necessary, the following types of accurate reports can be made available "instantly:"

1. Transactions for any patient, in chronological order. Given the patient-id number, the system can retrieve instantly all the transactions for that patient in date order.

2. Transactions for any doctor, in procedure order. Given the doctor's initials, the system can retrieve instantly all the procedures performed by that individual in a given time frame.

If it is imperative to deal with this kind of situation, then you have no choice but to go with the indexing feature, since the indexes can be updated on-line, when a file is being EDITed or APPENDed.

In the same dental office analogy, the sort command also has its rightful place. Take for instance the daily reports that itemize all financial transactions for the day. This information must be pulled out in a sequence different from that of the transaction file. So the sort command can be used to sort the file just before this report is pulled out. Since the dBASE sort is very fast, this mode of sorting before reporting is quite acceptable.

Most business applications require some kind of master file to be updated in the on-line mode, and you will find that Indexing plays a major role in the successful, user-friendly implementation of the application. I have found it an invaluable tool for business.

> **Note:** As we have seen before, there is one situation wherein you will have to SORT, and that is when you want to sequence your master file in descending sequence on a character field. Here the INDEX feature cannot help you. (I have not yet come across a situation in which it was found necessary to sequence a character field in descending.)

Putting the Pieces Together

Can you use the COPY command in relation to the FIND command in some meaningful, useful way? Suppose you have a file indexed on the TOWN field, and you want to copy all the records with town = 'ROCHESTER' into another file, whatever the reason.

One way of doing this would be to enter the following:

```
.USE <MASTER>          <cr>
.COPY TO KEEPEM    FOR  TOWN = 'ROCH'          <cr>
```

While this method will certainly work, dBASE will have to start at the top of the file and work its way to the bottom, selecting records along the way.

A much faster way would be to use an existing index on the town field, if available:

```
.USE <MASTER>    INDEX  <index-name>          <cr>
.FIND  ROCH        <cr>
.COPY TO  KEEPEM    WHILE TOWN = 'ROCH'          <cr>
```

The above method will be infinitely faster. dBASE will find the very first record with the key value of 'ROCH', and will then copy the records in the order as specified by the index! Since all ROCH records will come together, this copy process will proceed for as long as successive records have the key value of ROCH. (Note the WHILE parameter.) The very first non-ROCH record will stop the copy process.

This is much faster since dBASE does not necessarily have to start at the top of the file, and does not have to work its way to the bottom before wrapping up. Also, a side benefit must have come to mind. If there were no records with town = ROCH, the FIND command itself would have returned a "No find" error message, saving you much valuable time that would have been spent trying to locate nonexistent records!

Indexing Speed

I conducted an Indexing experiment similar to one of the experiments mentioned earlier for the sort process. The parameters, again, were as follows:

The hardware used was a COMPAQ DESKPRO 286 computer, running at 8 MHz (mega-hertz, referring to the speed of the internal oscillator), with 512K memory. I used the PERSNL.DBF database we have been using so far, but without the memo field. Using a combination of the COPY and the APPEND commands, with the help of a small program, I forced dBASE to blow up the size of the PERSNL.DBF file to 15,360 records. I also had dBASE provide the time (using the TIME( ) function) at the start and end of the runs, to provide as much accuracy as possible.

Thus 15,360 records, of record-length 46 characters, were put through the Index process as follows:

Test 1: Index on the TOWN field. Key length nine characters.
Time: 25 minutes, 56 seconds.

Compared to the speed of the sort process under very similar circumstances (11 minutes), the INDEXing proceeded at less than half the speed.

Please note that indexing does not proceed at a consistent rate. By that I mean that it takes significantly longer to index the last 100 records than it takes to index the first 100 records in a file. The larger your database, the larger this time-difference!

THE UPDATE COMMAND

The UPDATE command should logically have been presented in the Editing section; however, I decided to relegate it to this section, since it requires that the files involved be sequenced. Now that you have an understanding of the sorting and indexing processes, here is the explanation of the UPDATE command.

Suppose you have a master file and a transaction file, and you want the records of the transaction file to be used for updating the master file. The transactions usually involve the following: adding new records to the master file, changing existing records of the master file in some of the fields, or deleting existing master records.

Since the APPEND and DELETE commands are two powerful commands that enable you to add and delete records from a master file, the UPDATE command does not handle these features. The UPDATE command only enables you to make changes to existing data records in the master file.

You can ask that the updating proceed in *random* order. If random is selected, the master file has to be indexed, and the transaction file can be in any order. If you decide not to ask for random order of updating, both master and transaction files have to be sequenced (either physically sorted or logically indexed).

To UPDATE sequentially, (not in random order), let us suppose that both files are physically sorted.

```
.SELE 2        <cr>
.USE TRANS        <cr>
.SELE 1        <cr>
.USE MASTER        <cr>
```

After assigning the files to work areas 1 and 2, notice that USE MASTER is the command we have ended up on, prior to the UPDATE command. That is, the master file is the active file.

```
.UPDATE ON PART FROM TRANS
    REPLACE ONHAND WITH ONHAND + TRANS->ONHAND,COST WITH
TRANS->COST        <cr>
```

> **Note:** The comma, between field names for replacement, is mandatory in the UPDATE command. If you recall, the REPLACE command by itself has no such requirement, but in this usage, it is mandatory.

The above UPDATE command asks dBASE to replace the ONHAND field (of the active record) with the sum of: ONHAND (from the active record) + ONHAND (from the nonactive record). The replace also replaces the COST field of the active record with the COST field coming in from the transaction record.

182

From the way the above instruction has been written, it follows that the field called PART__NUM must exist in the structures of both the master and the transaction files. The corresponding TYPEs and LENGTHS should also match. The other fields could have either the same or different names; the syntax of the command clarifies which field is intended.

In the above instructions, if a PART__NUM from the master file is equal to the PART__NUM from the transaction file, then dBASE will ADD the ONHAND in the transaction record to the ONHAND in the master record, thus updating the ONHAND field in the master record. dBASE will also REPLACE the COST field in the master record with the contents of the COST field from the transaction record.

An example of the before and after picture follows:

Master Before	**Transaction**	**Master After**
ONHAND: 500	ONHAND: 50	ONHAND: 550
COST : 50.00	COST : 55.00	COST : 55.00

If you had wanted the transaction record to reduce the ONHAND amount you would have specified the command as:

```
.....REPLACE ONHAND WITH ONHAND - TRANS->ONHAND,COST WITH
TRANS->COST          <cr>
```

You can also ask that the updating proceed in random order. If random order of processing is selected, the master file has to be indexed, and the transaction file can be in any order.

```
.SELE 2          <cr>
.USE TRANS          <cr>
.SELE 1          <cr>
.USE MASTER INDEX <filename>          <cr>


.UPDATE ON PART FROM TRANS     RANDOM
     REPLACE ONHAND WITH ONHAND + TRANS->ONHAND,COST WITH
TRANS->COST          <cr>
```

Notice that the indexed version of the master file is brought into play. Notice also the RANDOM parameter in the command. Once more, I would like to emphasize the necessity of using a comma between the various field names for replacement.

Regardless of the method used for the update, when you are through running this type of command that links two files in separate areas, you should always free up the files in the areas, as follows:

```
.CLOSE ALL          <cr>
```

SUMMARY

Sequencing of records forms an inherent part of any data-processing system, and dBASE provides us with two methods of creating the sequences we want. Of these, INDEXing has two major advantages over SORTing: it allows the immediate update of index files, and it enables you to FIND a specific record instantly.

There are several software products on the market which promise to speed up dBASE's sort and index processes, and your perusal of any magazine on personal computing should provide you with the names of the vendors of these products, if you feel inclined to try them out.

The ability to sort and index our files now leads us to the next logical step in this book, that of attempting to pull off reports from our dBASE files.

7. The Reporting Process

U p until now, our efforts have been concentrated on building up a good, workable database, and we have seen how structures could be built and modified, and how data could be entered and subsequently displayed and edited in a variety of ways. We have also studied the processes of physically sorting and logically indexing our data, so that the records are retrieved in a specifically designed sequence.

Having obtained the skills necessary to be able to guarantee the integrity of our database, we shall now look to the aspect of pulling off reports from the database. After all, the end product of any computerized commercial application is the all-important report that assists management in the decision-making process. In fact, the design of any computerized commercial application starts off with a study of the *outputs* required from the computerized system. And that definitely includes *hard-copy* (printed) outputs.

BUILDING THE REPORT FORMAT FILE

First, we will study the report feature built into dBASE, which will serve us in obtaining fast, accurate reports. However, as is the case with all prepackaged software, the user will have to live within the limitations of the software; that is, the user will have to be content with the format as presented by dBASE. If you want complete freedom in designing your own report formats, you can always write your own computer program to create any report format you want. The study of computer programs in dBASE is presented in a later chapter, where we will learn, among other things, how to write our own reports, in our own formats. For now, however, we shall be studying, in detail, the built-in reporting facility of dBASE.

The Report Format File

Let us suppose that you want a report prepared out of the data you have created, and let us suppose that you are quite clear in your mind about the format of that report. That is, you have visualized the main heading of the report, you know what columns of data are required, and you know the fields on which totals are required, and so on. Now, all you have to do is *translate the requirements of your conceptual report into words and phrases*, telling dBASE exactly what it is that you want!

The process is as follows. You must inform dBASE about your intention to create a report, called, say, RPT1, using a file, say, PERSNL. dBASE will now take you through a cycle of menus, asking you a few questions about the proposed format of the report. In effect, you will be asked questions about the main heading and the page layout specifications, whether or not you want subtotals, and if you do, then on what fields, and what you want as the contents of the various columns in the report, and so on. You will respond to these menus in words and phrases, describing your conceptual report.

Having obtained this information from you, dBASE will now create an internally usable file that describes the report format you had specified. This file is, therefore, appropriately called a *report format file*. In the absence of any secondary qualifier, dBASE will provide a qualifier of .FRM (for report format file). So your request to build a report called RPT1 and your responses to the various menus will result in the creation of a file called RPT1.FRM.

Once a format file is built up, you can ask dBASE to pull off the report. At this point dBASE simply filters your data records from the database, through the descriptive words and phrases of the format file, and pulls off the report you want.

Conceptually, the process could be shown as follows:

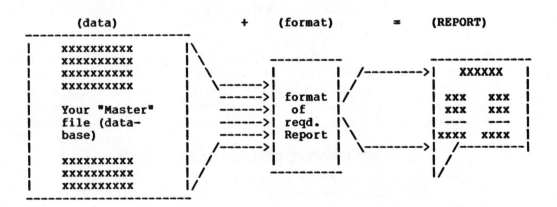

To emphasize, generating any Report simply involves knowing how to produce the report format file (the "words and phrases" file), using dBASE.

As you can imagine, in the study of any report-generating procedure, one can come up with a myriad "What If . . . " types of questions, pertaining to formats, totals, subtotals, and/or "doll-up" of headings, and so on. As a result, one could get quite lost in the various options available, unless one proceeds in some logical manner.

On account of the multitude of options to be covered, (and this book will attempt to anticipate most, if not all, of your "what if . . . " questions), I shall proceed in this section in the following way.

I will first cover all options pertaining to formats alone. That is, I will cover areas relating to main headings, column headings, columns of data on the report, the "doll-up" of the headings and data, extra headings, the spread of the report in a 132-column computer printout, and so on. When we engage in the study of formats, we shall not look at any totals.

After the section concerning formats, there will be a section concerning the generation of totals, at which point we will revert back to a basic format, so as to keep everything in proper perspective. After you are through with the options for totals, you will see how to generate subtotals and sub-subtotals in the report, but again at this point we will keep to a basic format.

Creating Format Files

When you want to start creating a report format file, you have to inform dBASE of that fact, by typing:

.USE PERSNL   <cr>   Some file has to be in use, against which a
                                    report format is required.

.CREATE REPORT RPT1   <cr>

You have specified to dBASE your intention to create a report format file called RPT1.FRM. At this point, dBASE will present to you on the screen the following primary menu.

Note: It is my personal opinion that this screen is quite unnecessarily cluttered up with too much information, and so in order to present a logical explanation of the screen contents, I will map out the screen into three areas, called the A area, the B area, and the C area.

Keep in mind that dBASE is only looking for the following information:

1. What is the general layout of your report?   (OPTIONS)
2. Do you want subtotals and sub-subtotals in your report?   (GROUPS)
3. What information do you want in the report?   (COLUMNS)

On the menu the inverse video, or highlighting, starts off on OPTIONS, so you start off by providing options for the new report. The use of the left and right arrow keys will move the highlighting to the section of an existing report you may want to work on.

```
Options        Groups      Columns       Locate        Exit       <time>
```

```
┌──────────────────────────────────┐
│ Page title                       │
│ Page width (positions)      80   │
│ Left margin                  8   │
│ Right margin                 0   │
│ Lines per page              58   │
│ Double space report         No   │
│ Page eject before printing  Yes  │
│ Page eject after printing   No   │
│ Plain page                  No   │
└──────────────────────────────────┘
```

```
┌──────────────────────────────────────────────────────────────────────────┐
│ CURSOR  <--   --> │Delete char:    Del│Insert column: ^N│Insert:     Ins │
│ Char:   <-    ->  │Delete word:    ^T │Report format: F1│Zoom in:   ^PgDn│
│ Word:   Home  End │Delete column:  ^U │Abandon:       Esc│Zoom out:  ^PgUp│
└──────────────────────────────────────────────────────────────────────────┘
```

```
CREATE REPORT   | <C:> | RPT1.FRM         | Opt: 1/9      |        | Caps
```

The A area is the only portion of the screen you have to concentrate on to build the report format. This is the area of the screen that will lead you into answering the three questions outlined before, about general layout (OPTIONS), subtotals (GROUPS) and columns of information (COLUMNS).

You will notice that an inverse video effect surrounds the word Options, since you first need to answer questions pertaining to the general layout.

The B area serves two purposes, both of which are helpful, but are not absolutely crucial to the building of the report format.

Use 1. Obviously, as it appears, the B area is your guide to the cursor controls. With some practice, you will not need those cursor control hints for much longer.

Use 2. The use of the F1 key changes the appearance of the B-area to the following:

(Alternative B-area)

```
┌─Report Format──────────────────────────────────────────────────────────┐
│                                                                         │
│ >>>>>>>--------------------------------------------------------------   │
│                                                                         │
│ ─────────────────────────────────────────────────────────────────────  │
│                                                                         │
└─────────────────────────────────────────────────────────────────────────┘
```

This alternative format of the B area displays the format of the report as it is being built up. At the moment, of course, there is no report format built-up, so this area is blank.

Regardless of the mode you are working in (Options, Groups, Columns, etc.), the F1 key will toggle the B area between the view of the cursor controls and the view of the report format.

The C area is the status area; it provides information on the name of the report file being worked on and the number of options you have to either fill-in or take defaults on. For example, in the A area, you will notice that there are nine options to be responded to, and the "Page title" with the highlighting is the first of nine options. Hence "Opt: 1/9" is shown in the status line. The status line also tells you if you are working in CAPS mode, and will provide messages on any errors you make.

Please understand that the B and C areas remain constant, regardless of whether you are working with OPTIONS, GROUPS, or COLUMNS. Use the F1 key to see either the cursor controls or the report format, in the B area.

So we understand now that we are in the OPTIONS mode, and the highlighting is at "Page title." Use the Up-and-Down arrow keys to move the highlighting to any portion of the OPTIONS menu.

> **Note:** The following description is the way you make any entry, whether it is for a title, margins, lines per page, a column of data, or any other type of entry.

1. First you touch the return key. For yes/no type responses, the use of the <cr> is all that is needed to toggle the response from yes to no, and vice versa. If your entry needs more than a yes/no response, go on to step 2.

2. Now you make your entry at the specified location on the screen. In some cases, the specified location is a special box that opens up, and in some other cases, it is just where the cursor is located when you did the <cr>.

3. Having made your entry, touch <cr> for the entry to be accepted. In some cases, you will find it easier to press PgDn to have the entry accepted, rather than touch <cr> multiple times.

4. Having made your entry, you can always use the backspace key to negate your entry, if you change your mind.

At this point, to enter the page title, please follow the instructions above, and touch <cr>. The following box opens up.

(A-area)

Options	Groups	Columns	Locate	Exit	<time>

```
Page title
Page width (positions)      80
Left margin                  8
Right margin                 0
Lines per page              58
Double space report         No
Page eject before printing  Yes
Page eject after printing   No
Plain page                  No
```

In the special box, please enter the heading "REPORT 1 - BASIC REPORT" (without the quotes). You may enter this in any one of the four main heading lines.

Having entered the heading, either touch <cr> four times, or touch PgDn to have dBASE accept the header and remove the box. The highlighting remains on the "Page title" line, so touch the down-arrow key to move to the next item. Remember, we are specifying OPTIONS for the general format of the report.

Initially, I will take the defaults for the page-format options, since they provide a workable format. For example, I find that a left-margin of 8 columns is good enough to allow for three-hole punching of the report, if necessary, and also makes for a good appearance on the report. Usually, too, I have no need to double space my reports, and for now, we will bring our reports to the screen, and hence a width of 80 columns is sufficient. You are, of course, at liberty to make changes by moving the cursor to the appropriate field.

Please note the "Page eject before printing . . . " line. Move the highlighting to this line, touch <cr>, and notice that the response changes to "No." We want to ensure that the printer does not eject to a new page each time you ask for a report to be printed out.

The "Page width" entry controls the width of the report. As you build up the report format, dBASE keeps track of the number of columns taken up by the format, and will force you to keep the format within the width specified. Since the main heading lines are automatically centered across the width, you should always specify the exact intended width of the report for proper centering of the heading.

> **Note:** The left-margin specification is included in the width of the report! That is, in an 80-column report (from column 1 through column 80), the report will begin at column 8.

Having entered the main heading (up to four lines, of 60 characters each), and having made any page-format changes required, you can use the right-arrow key to proceed to the GROUPS menu. The A area now displays the GROUPS menu.

(A area)

Options	Groups	Columns	Locate	Exit	<time>

```
Group on expression
Group heading
Summary report only          No
Page eject after group
Sub-group on expression
Sub-group heading
```

This menu wants information about any proposed subtotals and sub-subtotals you may want to take. Since I will first concentrate on formats only, we will skip this menu, for now.

Use the right-arrow key, to move the highlighting to the COLUMNS submenu, which appears as follows, in the A area:

```
Options        Groups        Columns        Locate        Exit        <time>
```

```
┌──────────────────────────────────────────────────────────────────────┐
│ Contents                                                               │
│ Heading                                                                │
│ Width                          Ø                                       │
│ Decimal places                                                         │
│ Total this column                                                      │
└──────────────────────────────────────────────────────────────────────┘
```

Notice that the highlighting is on the "Contents" line. For this first column of data, we want to show employee numbers.

Touch the <cr> key. At this point, you need to enter the field name EMP_NUM. If you have forgotten the name of the field, touch F10, and another box opens up, giving you the field names from the file in USE. At this point, you can use the up and down arrow keys to move the highlighting to the appropriate field, and touch <cr>, or just type in the field name you want and touch <cr>. One way or another, you now have the field name EMP_NUM where the cursor is located. Now touch <cr> again, so this entry is accepted. Notice that the width automatically jumps to three, which is the width of the EMP_NUM field. Touch the down-arrow key to move to the "Heading" line. This heading , obviously, refers to the column heading that will appear above the data you may want in the report. Touch <cr>, and a special box opens up. In this box, please enter the literals as shown:

```
Options        Groups        Columns        Locate        Exit        <time>
```

```
┌──────────────────────────────────────────────────────────────────────┐
│ Contents             EMP NUM                                           │
│ Heading                                                                │
│ Width                   8                                              │
│ Decimal places                                                         │
│ Total this column                                                      │
│                                                                        │
        ┌───────────────────────────────────────────────────────┐
        │ EMPLOYEE                                                │
        │ NUMBERS                                                 │
        │                                                         │
        └───────────────────────────────────────────────────────┘
```

Having entered the column-header literals, either touch <cr> two times, or touch PgDn, to have these entries accepted. Notice that the width number jumps to 8, which is the length of the longer of the literals. dBASE automatically provides for a column width that is the larger of the column data or column header. Notice also, that the "Heading" line now contains the literal "EMPLOYEE;NUMBERS."

When your column-header literal has been accepted, you can touch the down-arrow key to move to the width, if you like, and change it to, say, 10. To change it, of course, touch <cr>, make the change, and then touch <cr> again.

If you were describing a numeric field, the default for "Total this column" is "Yes." Obviously, if you let it remain as is, this column will be totalled in the actual report. You may, if required, move the cursor down to that line and touch <cr> to toggle the "Yes" to "No" or vice versa.

At this point, you will have described the contents of the first column of information.

Touch PgDn again, to get to the (identical) blank screen for the next column of information. Using the sequence described above, please describe three more fields, one each for EMP_NAME, TOWN, and ORG. Their column definitions are shown below:

```
| Contents           EMP_NAME                        |
| Heading                                            |
| Width              13                              |
| Decimal places                                     |
| Total this column                                  |
|_____|
```

```
            | EMPLOYEE                               |
            | NAMES                                  |
            |                                        |
            |_____|
```

```
| Contents           TOWN                            |
| Heading                                            |
| Width              9                               |
| Decimal places                                     |
| Total this column                                  |
|_____|
```

```
            | TOWN                                   |
            | ----                                   |
            |                                        |
            |_____|
```

```
| Contents           ORG                             |
| Heading                                            |
| Width              3                               |
| Decimal places                                     |
| Total this column                                  |
|_____|
```

```
            | ORG                                    |
            | ---                                    |
            |                                        |
            |_____|
```

If you want to move back and forth between column descriptions (to either verify something or to make changes), use PgUp and PgDn.

To quickly locate an existing field definition for changes, scroll (using the left/right arrows) to the Locate menu, and notice that it is a vertical string of the columns of information requested in the report format. Use the up and down arrow keys to go to the field definition you want to pull up on the screen, and touch <cr>. This may make it easier to find a specific field definition quickly, instead of using PgUp and PgDn in the Columns mode to find the specific field.

If you decide to add a new column definition in place of an existing one, use Ctrl-N. For example, if you have defined ORG as the fourth field (column) of the report, and you want to enter another field name as the fourth field, go up to the ORG definition menu, then touch Ctrl-N. Now the ORG field becomes the fifth field, and a new menu opens up, asking you for the definition of the new fourth field. If you want to insert multiple fields in place of an existing one, use Ctrl-N multiple times.

If your attempt to add more fields results in a beep and an error message "Exceeded report print width . . .," this obviously implies that you need to increase the report width in the OPTIONS menu. Keep in mind, again, that the left-margin position is also included in the width of the report.

If you want to remove a field definition from the report format, bring up the appropriate field definition on the screen, and then type Ctrl–U, to delete that field.

If you decide to make a change either at the OPTIONS or GROUPS level, use the left and right arrow keys to move to the appropriate menu.

Having entered your field definitions, use the right-arrow key to move to the "Exit" option. You will have one of two options: "Save" or "Abandon," with the highlighting on Save. If you now touch <cr>, this report format will be saved. You could, of course, move the highlighting to "Abandon," and then touch <cr>, if necessary.

To make changes to an existing report format, you can enter: .MODI REPO RPT1 <cr>. dBASE will now present you with the primary screen of this existing format file, so you can scroll (using left and right arrows) through the various screens, and make any changes you want. As always, use the Exit option to either "Save" or "Abandon" your changes to the report format.

Please note that you can also "Abandon" at any time, regardless of the menu you are in, through the use of the Escape key. dBASE will ask you to verify your intent to escape, to which you respond with Y (for yes).

Having created your report format file, you can now pull off the report as follows:

```
.REPO FORM RPT1          <cr>


Page No.      1
02/07/86
                        REPORT 1 - BASIC REPORT

EMPLOYEE  EMPLOYEE       TOWN        ORG
NUMBERS   NAMES          ----        ---


005       NINA BHARUCHA WEBSTER      BSG
010       PETE JOHNSON  brighton     BSG
015       GLORIA PATEL  FAIRPORT     RMG
020       MAX LEVINSKY  HENRIETTA    RMG
025       KIM BRANDT    FAIRPORT     RMG
030       TIM MONTAL    ROCHESTER    RBG
```

```
EMPLOYEE  EMPLOYEE        TOWN       ORG
NUMBERS   NAMES           ----       ---

035       WILLIAM PATEL   penfield   GSD
040       JAMES JAMESON   ROCHESTER  GSD
045       MORRIS KATZ     webster    BSG
050       PAUL BHARUCHA   BRIGHTON   BSG
055       PHIL MARTIN     WEBSTER    RMG
060       JOHN PETERSON   BRIGHTON   RBG
065       JOY HARDY       fairport   RBG
070       JAN MOREY       ROCHESTER  GSD
075       JOHN JONES      rochester  GSD
```

Observations on Report Formats

1. The main heading is automatically centered across the width we had asked for.

2. The column headings and the column data are automatically justified within the requested column width: information is left justified for character fields, and right justified for numeric fields.

3. The words *Page No.*, the actual page number, and the date have been provided by dBASE.

4. Between columns of data, regardless of whether they are character or numeric fields, dBASE automatically provides us with one column of space.

5. When you are defining a column of data for the report, dBASE automatically provides a column width that is the larger of the column data or the column header. You have the option of overriding this default and asking for a larger width. If, however, by mistake you ask for a smaller width, both the column header literal and the data coming in would qualify for a *wrap around*, within the confines of the column-width.

6. To send this report to the printer, simply enter:

.REPORT FORM RPT1   TO PRINT   <cr>

The report format now goes to both, screen and printer.

> **Note:** When you invoke the TO PRINT option, depending on what you specified on the Options menu, dBASE may or may not issue a primary eject to a new page, before starting to print the report. If your primary option specified "Yes" for "Page eject before printing," you have the option of causing a temporary override, through entering:

.REPORT FORM RPT1   NOEJECT   TO PRINT   <cr>

> **Note:** This is only a temporary override for the duration of the command; it does not affect the permanent definition of the report format. Also, it affects only the primary eject at the start of the report printout. Subsequent page ejects, for a report longer than one page, will take place automatically.

7. The report format merely specifies the format (or design) of the report. It does not specify which data records should enter the report format! To use this same report format, but restrict the output of the report to selected records, you can specify a condition, in the report command:

```
.REPORT FORM RPT1   [NOEJECT]     [TO PRINT]   FOR <condition>
```

Now only records that satisfy the condition will appear in the report. They will be in the format as designed in the format file. As always, the condition can be as simple or as complex as you want to make it. We have seen many examples of the FOR condition earlier.

8. To use this same report format, but restrict the output of the report to selected records, you can specify a scope, in the report command:

```
.REPORT FORM RPT1   [NEXT n]    [TO PRINT]
```

Now only the next N records will appear in the report, starting with the current record. They will be in the format as designed in the format file.

```
9. .REPORT FORM RPT1    TO    TEMP        <cr>
```

This will send the report output into a file called TEMP.TXT, which is a text file. This file can now be word-processed, if necessary.

```
10. .REPORT FORM RPT1   PLAIN        <cr>
```

This will cause the printing of a no frills report in which the page literal and number, and date do not appear on the report. Also, the main heading will be printed only on the first page of the report. If your primary option specified "No" for "Plain page," (that is, you want complete titles on every page of the report), then you have the option of causing a temporary override, for the duration of a specific report, through the use of the PLAIN parameter.

11. On subsequent occasions, to pull off this report again, we simply have to enter: .REPORT FORM RPT1   [TO PRINT], and dBASE will pull off the report again, provided that the correct database has been brought into USE.

12. If you want a special heading placed above the entire report, you can use this command line:

```
.REPORT FORM RPT1 FOR TOWN = 'R'   HEADING   'REPORT THROUGH
JAN. 31, 1986.'        <cr>
```

```
                    REPORT 1 - BASIC REPORT.

EMPLOYEE EMPLOYEE       TOWN       ORG
NUMBERS  NAMES          ----       ---

030      TIM MONTAL     ROCHESTER RBG
040      JAMES JAMESON ROCHESTER GSD
070      JAN MOREY      ROCHESTER GSD
```

This implies that although the report was pulled off "today" (02/14/86), the data in the report is valid only up through JAN. 31, 1986. It is quite common to see such special headings in reports.

13. The commands CREATE and MODIFY can be used interchangeably. That is, you can ask to CREATE an existing report format file, or you can ask to MODIFY a new report format file.

Obtaining a Good Spread of the Report

Now we shall look at methods of obtaining more than just the one column of space that dBASE provides as default between columns of data in the report. We want to be able to specify our own *spread* for the various columns, and to be able to come out with the exact format we want for a report. Suppose for now, that we want five columns of spread between our columns of data.

We will define the EMP_NUM field, then ask for five columns of spread, then define the EMP_NAME field, then ask for five columns of spread, and so on. For now, copy RPT1.FRM into RPT2.FRM as follows:

.COPY FILE   RPT1.FRM   TO RPT2.FRM   <cr>

Now you are ready to make changes to RPT2.FRM to create the spread between columns. Change the page heading in the OPTIONS menu to whatever you like. Using Ctrl-N at the appropriate places, create new columns #2, #4, and #6, each of them to have the following definitions:

```
| Contents              ' '                             |
| Heading                                               |
| Width                  5                              |
| Decimal places                                        |
| Total this column                                     |
|_____|
```

Notice the quote-blank-quote, for the field contents. You are specifying that across a span of five columns, you want the literal *BLANK*; that is, you are specifying that you want five blanks as the second column of information. There is, of course, no heading over that blank space, so you simply bypass the Heading. (Note that instead of the quote-blank-quote for the field-contents above, you could have entered quote-quote and obtained identical results). Make similar entries for the new columns #4 and #6. Now pull off the report format RPT2.

.REPO FORM RPT2 FOR TOWN = 'R'   <cr>

```
Page No.     1
02/07/86
             REPORT 2 - OBTAINING A BETTER SPREAD OF THE DATA.

EMPLOYEE              EMPLOYEE                 TOWN              ORG
NUMBERS              NAMES                    ----              ---


030                  TIM MONTAL               ROCHESTER         RBG
040                  JAMES JAMESON            ROCHESTER         GSD
070                  JAN MOREY                ROCHESTER         GSD
```

In the above example, did we really manage to obtain five columns of spaces between our columns of data? As you may have noticed, dBASE treats the column of spaces you asked for as any other column of information. Now since dBASE always provides us with one column of space between columns of data, if you ask for a column of five spaces between FIELD A and FIELD B, you will end up with seven spaces for that spread. (one column after FIELD A, the column of five blanks, and one column after the column of 5 blanks.) So you will always end up with two more spaces between fields, than you had bargained for. Keeping this in mind, if you really want 10 spaces between columns of real data fields, you should ask for eight, and so on. Through this process, you can obtain the exact spacing you want between columns of real data in a report.

> **Note:** dBASE also maintains an extra column of space after the left-margin! In our case, since the left-margin specification is eight, the first column of data begins in column 10. Keep this in mind when computing spreads.

The 132-Column Spread

Systems analysts and users generally prepare layouts of expected reports on specially prepared paper called the *printer spacing chart*, which is like graph paper; each column and line on that paper reflects a physical column and line that the printer can assume on regular paper. Using this printer spacing chart to prepare an exact format of an expected report facilitates the creation of the report format file in dBASE, since the exact number of columns of space can now be readily counted.

Using the formatting features studied so far, you can now prepare a report format, spread out to your exact specifications. Ensure that in the primary menu, when asked for the "Page width," you specify 132, so the literals of the main heading are centered correctly.

If your report format file specifies a width greater than that which your printer can handle, then during the report printout, all the overflow characters either are crunched into the last position on the printer, or wrap around onto the next line, depending on the printer setting. If that happens, you can either pare down the width of your report format, or alter the pitch setting on your printer, to more than 10 characters per linear inch. Try a 12-pitch setting or a 15-pitch setting, if your printer allows it. Please understand, however, that the appropriate print-wheel is recommended for the different pitch-settings. Otherwise your report will have a highly compressed appearance.

Displaying Record Numbers

As we have seen earlier, you can specify that the report format be generated only for records satisfying a specific condition. Now it would be necessary, in many situations, to be able to come up with the record numbers of those records that satisfied the condition for the report. To bring the record numbers into play, use the RECNO( ) function.

Make a copy of RPT2.FRM into RPT3.FRM in the same manner as you copied RPT1.FRM into RPT2.FRM. Now use Ctrl-N to open up a new field as field #1 and ask for the record number as the very first field of information.

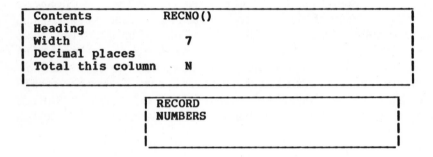

```
Contents          RECNO()
Heading
Width                7
Decimal places
Total this column    N
```

```
          RECORD
          NUMBERS
```

Make sure that you specify that you do not want totals for this field. If you don't observe this, dBASE will provide a running total of the sum of all the record numbers of the qualifying records. This total, of course, is garbage. This is because RECNO( ) is considered numeric. Notice that the width of the field automatically jumps to 10, but you can bring it down to, say, 7—just enough to accommodate the column header.

Enter field #1 as the RECNO( ) field, and enter another field #2 to present five spaces, as you have done before:

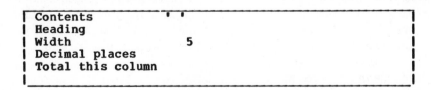

```
Contents          ' '
Heading
Width                5
Decimal places
Total this column
```

Now pull of the new report, with record numbers of records selected for the condition:

```
Page No.      1
02/07/86
                REPORT 3 - PRINT RECORD NUMBERS OF SELECTED RECORDS.

    RECORD        EMPLOYEE       EMPLOYEE          TOWN          ORG
    NUMBERS       NUMBERS        NAMES             ----          ---


        6          030          TIM MONTAL        ROCHESTER     RBG
        8          040          JAMES JAMESON     ROCHESTER     GSD
       14          070          JAN MOREY         ROCHESTER     GSD
```

Obtaining a Record Count

We will make a small, but meaningful, enhancement to the above report format. If you had several pages of the above report printing out, it would be beneficial to have not only the record numbers of those records that qualified for the condition, but also a total specifying how many such records qualified for the condition. You should be able to go right to the bottom of the report and find out exactly how many records qualified for the condition.

For this enhancement, we will define another field in the report format. This field will be physically removed from the other fields so as to differentiate it as a kind of a *dummy* field.

Make a copy of RPT3.FRM into RPT4.FRM, as you have done before. (I will remove the spaces between the fields to conserve space on the screen.) After the ORG field, ask for a field of 10 spaces (we have seen before how to do this), then ask for a field as follows:

```
┌─────────────────────────────────────────────────────────────┐
│ Contents            1                                        │
│ Heading                                                      │
│ Width               4                                        │
│ Decimal places      0                                        │
│ Total this column   Yes                                      │
│                                                              │
└─────────────────────────────────────────────────────────────┘
```

Notice that we have asked for a *numeric value of 1* for the content of the last field. This is a dummy field, so there is no header. The width of this field is four (explained later), and we have asked for a total on this field!

In effect, we have asked dBASE to provide to us, at the end of every qualifying record of data printed out, the numeric value 1, and we have asked that totals be taken on this value 1. In effect, if 25 records qualify, then each line on the report will have the numeric literal 1, at the end of the line, and the sum total of these 1s will be the value 25, which is printed at the end of the report! We have successfully fooled dBASE into providing us with the record count of the number of records that qualify.

Note that we asked for a width of four digits for this field. In other words, we are sure that the sum total of all the ones (that is, the number of qualifying records) will not go higher than 9999 records. If more records qualified than the field-width would have permitted, you will have ******* in the field, not the total count of the qualifying records. Enter:

```
.REPO FORM RPT4 FOR TOWN = 'R'          <cr>
```

to produce the report that shows the record count.

```
Page No.      1
02/07/86
              REPORT 4 - OBTAIN RECORD COUNTS OF SELECTED RECORDS.

 RECORD EMPLOYEE EMPLOYEE        TOWN       ORG
 NUMBERS NUMBERS NAMES           ----       ---


      6 030      TIM MONTAL      ROCHESTER RBG
      8 040      JAMES JAMESON   ROCHESTER GSD
     14 070      JAN MOREY       ROCHESTER GSD
*** Total ***
```

We know, at one glance, that only three records qualified for the condition in the report statement. In the case of a long report, the last page will provide the exact number of qualifying records. Notice that the field with the numeric value 1 was spaced away from the main body of the report, so as to identify it as being some kind of a dummy field.

What do you suppose would have happened if you had defined the value 1 with quotes, in effect making it a character literal 1 instead of the numeric literal 1? dBASE would have treated it like a character literal, and your attempt to ask for a total against this field would have failed! During the report-generation stage, the literals would have been printed beside each record, but there would have been no final total at the end, and your purpose would have been defeated.

Expressions in Report Formats

In mentioning which fields you want listed out in a report, you are not restricted only to the fields defined in the structure of the file in use. You could even invent some fields of your own!

For example, if you want a listing that provides SALARY, and you also want to show the salary field again, but this time with an increase of 10 percent in the amount, you could define the "increment" field as follows:

```
| Contents          SALARY * 1.1                    |
| Heading                                           |
| Width             10                              |
| Decimal places    2                               |
| Total this column Yes                             |
|_____|


              | INCREASED                           |
              | SALARY                              |
              |                                     |
              |_____|
```

200

You are specifying, for the "increment" column of data, that across a span of 10 columns, you want the expression SALARY * 1.1. That is, you are specifying that you want to see what the salary increased by 10 percent, would look like in that column. The reason for asking for 10 columns is to ensure that the total of the increased salaries fits in the column span. Obviously, this expression is valid only for the duration of the report and does nothing to the original salary data in the file under USE. To produce the report, enter:

```
.REPO FORM RPT5 FOR TOWN = 'R'          <cr>

Page No.      1
02/07/86
                    REPORT 5 - EXPRESSIONS IN REPORT FORMATS.

EMPLOYEE  EMPLOYEE            SALARY   INCREASED
NUMBERS   NAMES              ------     SALARY


030        TIM MONTAL      41900.00   46090.00
040        JAMES JAMESON   29800.00   32780.00
070        JAN MOREY       18190.00   20009.00
*** Total ***
                           89890.00   98879.00
```

At this point you may note that the column of information used on a report can be any of the following:

- □ a field name from the file under use (like TOWN)
- □ a numeric literal (like the number 1)
- □ a character literal (like the spaces)
- □ an expression (like SALARY * 1.1)

Further examples of situations in which you may use the power of the expression are as follows:

Suppose you are working with an inventory file, and you have defined in the structure of the file, the following fields (among others):

QTY__ON__HAND . . . . . . UNIT__COST . . . . . .

Now in the body of the report, if you want to show the dollar amount of inventory carried in each item, you could specify, in the appropriate menu:

```
| Contents          QTY_ON_HAND * UNIT_COST        |
| Heading                                          |
| Width              9                             |
| Decimal places     2                             |
| Total this column  . Yes                         |
|_____|


        | DOLLAR                              |
        | INVENTORY                           |
        |                                     |
        |_____|
```

Here is one more example of the use of an expression. Suppose you had a mailing file of names and addresses, and you had separate fields for the LASTNAME and FIRSTNAME. You want to pull off a report, but would like to show the format as follows:

NAME	STREET	CITY	TOWN	STATE	ZIP
ARMSTRONG, ADAM	....				
BAKER, BILL	....				
CHARLES, LARRY	....				
DAYTON, PETE	....				

Note that we want the lastname and firstname separated by just a comma and a space, regardless of the lengths of the actual lastnames.

The following definition will do the trick:

```
| Contents          TRIM(LASTNAME)+', '+FIRSTNAME    |
| Heading                                            |
| Width             25                               |
| Decimal places                                     |
| Total this column                                  |
|_____|
```

```
| NAME                                               |
|                                                    |
|                                                    |
|_____|
```

In this example, we used the functions of TRIM and concatenation. TRIM(LAST-NAME) removed all trailing blanks from each lastname, and to this result we concatenated a comma and blank, and to this we concatenate the FIRSTNAME.

Obtaining Ratios

For this next report, I will make use of another small file called SHOES.DBF, containing the fields SHOE_ITEM, SHOE_SIZE, and YTD_SALES. Suppose I now want a report to show each shoe item and size, and I want to show what the *average monthly sales* have been for each item, up through the current month; that is, I will provide an expression in the report format; the expression will be YTD_SALES divided by current month.

You know, of course, how to define field 1 and field 2 for the SHOE_ITEM and the SHOE_SIZE. Field 3, which is the one for the average monthly sales to date, should be defined as follows:

```
| Contents           YTD_SALES / MONTH(DATE())    |
| Heading                                          |
| Width              8                             |
| Decimal places     2                             |
| Total this column  No                            |
|_____|
```

```
| AVG.                                             |
| SALES                                            |
|                                                  |
|_____|
```

As always, the field width should be large enough to provide for the data or the column header.

Notice that our field contents have been defined as a ratio. We are dividing the YTD_SALES figure for each shoe item by the current month number, as obtained from the system date! So regardless of the time of the year this report is run, you will obtain the average monthly sales up through the current month.

```
.USE SHOES          <cr>
.REPO FORM RPT6          <cr>
```

```
Page No.     1
03/15/86
             REPORT 6 - OBTAINING RATIOS. (Using SHOES.dbf).

ITEM         ITEM                      YTD              AVG.
NUMBER       SIZE                      SALES            SALES

SHOE1        S-1                       200              66.67
SHOE1        S-2                       300             100.00
SHOE2        S-4                       150              50.00
SHOE2        S-5                       250              83.33
SHOE3        S-1                       100              33.33
SHOE3        S-4                       200              66.67
*** Total ***
                                      1200
```

Reporting From Multiple Databases Simultaneously

So far we have seen how we can format a good report, using one database. Now let us enhance the formatting to include multiple databases, simultaneously. In our study of the DISPLAY command, we have seen how we may activate multiple databases, through the use of the .SELECT commands along with the SET RELATION TO command. We shall follow the same procedure here.

I will use the same four files used earlier, INVEN1, INVEN2, INVEN3, and INVEN4, to show the relationships. As before, we will produce two reports with different data—one to show the relationships on record numbers and the other to show the relationships based on the PART number key field.

Using Relationships Based on Record Numbers

Remember that the relationship based on record numbers assumes that the files to be linked have an exact one-to-one correspondence (which is not often valid in real-life situations). I have explained in detail what this means in the earlier sections.

```
.SELE 1          <cr>
.USE INVEN1          <cr>
.SELE 2          <cr>
.USE INVEN2          <cr>
.SELE 3          <cr>
.USE INVEN3          <cr>
.SELE 4          <cr>
.USE INVEN4          <cr>
```

The above commands assign the files to the different work areas. You can have up to 10 such assignments, if necessary.

```
.SELE 1          <cr>
.SET RELATION TO RECNO () INTO INVEN2          <cr>
.SELE 2          <cr>
.SET RELATION TO RECNO () INTO INVEN3          <cr>
.SELE 3          <cr>
.SET RELATION TO RECNO () INTO INVEN4          <cr>
```

The above commands set up the relationships between the files to be linked, two files at a time. Note that the relationship is based on record numbers.

```
.SELE 1          <cr>
```

The above command selects the primary or controlling file. Now the other record numbers will move in conjunction with the record pointer movement in this controlling file.

To build the report format, establish the following field definitions:

```
Contents          PART
Heading
Width             8
Decimal places
Total this column
```

```
PART
NUMS.
```

```
Contents          INVEN2->CGC
Heading
Width             10
Decimal places
Total this column
```

```
|  CGC FROM                                                            |
|  INVEN2.DBF                                                          |
|                                                                      |
|_____|
```

```
|  Contents            INVEN3->ONHAND                                  |
|  Heading                                                             |
|  Width                      11                                       |
|  Decimal places                                                      |
|  Total this column                                                   |
|_____|
```

```
|  ONHAND FROM                                                         |
|  INVEN3.DBF                                                          |
|                                                                      |
|_____|
```

```
|  Contents            INVEN4->ONORDER                                 |
|  Heading                                                             |
|  Width                      12                                       |
|  Decimal places                                                      |
|  Total this column                                                   |
|_____|
```

```
|  ONORDER FROM                                                        |
|  INVEN4.DBF                                                          |
|                                                                      |
|_____|
```

To run the report, enter:

.REPO FORM RPT7A   <cr>

```
Page No.      1
03/10/86
                REPORT 7A - REPORT FROM MULTIPLE DATA-BASES.
                       (RELATION ON RECORD-NUMBERS)

PART          CGC FROM        ONHAND FROM        ONORDER FROM
NUMS.         INVEN2.DBF      INVEN3.DBF         INVEN4.DBF


P1            C1                     100                100
P2            C2                     200                200
P3            C3                     300                300
P4            C4                     400                400
P5            C5                     500                500
*** Total ***
                                    1500               1500
```

Once the report has been obtained you must negate the relationship by entering:

.CLOSE ALL   <cr>

Using Relationships Based on Key Fields

The key-field method presumes that there is some connecting field among the various files. The PART number field is the key field for connecting the files together. The INVEN1 file is in the order in which you want the records to be listed in the report. (It could be sorted, or indexed.) The other files *must be indexed* on the key field that connects the files together.

Here are the steps for preparing the files:

```
.USE INVEN2          <cr>
.INDEX ON PART TO PINDX2          <cr>

.

.USE INVEN3          <cr>
.INDEX ON PART TO PINDX3          <cr>

.

.USE INVEN4          <cr>
.INDEX ON PART TO PINDX4          <cr>
```

The above statements index the files that are going to be linked to the primary or controlling file (INVEN1).

```
.SELE 1          <cr>
.USE INVEN1          <cr>
.SELE 2          <cr>
.USE INVEN2 INDEX PINDX2          <cr>
.SELE 3          <cr>
.USE INVEN3 INDEX PINDX3          <cr>
.SELE 4          <cr>
.USE INVEN4 INDEX PINDX4          <cr>
```

The above statements assign the files to the different work areas. You can have up to 10 such assignments.

```
.SELE 1          <cr>
.SET RELATION TO PART INTO INVEN2          <cr>

.

.SELE 2          <cr>
.SET RELATION TO PART INTO INVEN3          <cr>

.

.SELE 3          <cr>
.SET RELATION TO PART INTO INVEN4          <cr>
```

The above commands set up the relationships among the files on the basis of the PART number key fields.

```
.SELE 1          <cr>
```

The above command selects the INVEN1 file as the primary or controlling file. Now the record-pointer movement for the linked files will be dependent on the value of the PART number key field found for each record in the controlling file.

The process of defining the report format file is identical to what we have done in method 1. The only difference in these two methods lies in the way the relationship is set. Now the report can be pulled off.

.REPO FORM RPT7B　　　　<cr>

. REPO FORM RPT7B

Page No.　　1
03/10/86

REPORT 7B - REPORT FROM MULTIPLE DATA-BASES.
(RELATION ON PART-NUMBERS)

PART NUMS.	CGC FROM INVEN2.DBF	ONHAND FROM INVEN3.DBF	ONORDER FROM INVEN4.DBF
P1	C11	110	115
P2	C22	220	215
P3	C33	330	315
P4	C44	440	415
P5	C55	550	515
*** Total ***		1650	1575

After the link arrangement has served its purpose, enter:

.CLOSE ALL　　　<cr>

In these two methods we used the built-in REPORT command to pull off the report from multiple, related files, with each file opened in its own work area. In the advanced (programming) section of the book, I have shown you how you can write a computer program to *link* any number of files, using just two work areas, and pull off your required report in any format you want.

Vertical Formats

The built-in REPORT command can be used to provide us with *vertical* formats in our reports. For example, let us suppose that we want the following format to be generated:

(REPORT TITLE)

EMPLOYEE-NUMBER EMPLOYEE-NAME	TOWN ORG	DT_OF-HIRE SALARY
070707 NINA BHARUCHA	WEBSTER BSG	1980 36300.00
-------- --------	--------	-------- --------

207

We can use the special functions of concatenation of character strings to generate such a format. The fields should be defined as follows:

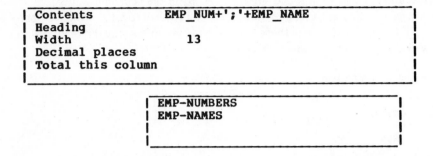

```
| Contents              EMP_NUM+';'+EMP_NAME      |
| Heading                                         |
| Width                 13                        |
| Decimal places                                 |
| Total this column                              |
|_____|

        | EMP-NUMBERS                      |
        | EMP-NAMES                        |
        |                                  |
        |_____|
```

For the first column of information, we have specified that we want to see a concatenated string consisting of EMP_NUM immediately followed by—though on the next line—EMP_NAME. When you first ask for this concatenation of fields, the width automatically increases to the combined lengths of the concatenated fields. Since you only need the width to be wide enough to accommodate the widest of the fields in the vertical concatenation or the column-literals, you can go with the EMP_NAME width of 13.

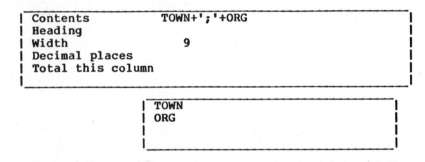

```
| Contents              TOWN+';'+ORG              |
| Heading                                         |
| Width                 9                         |
| Decimal places                                 |
| Total this column                              |
|_____|

        | TOWN                             |
        | ORG                              |
        |                                  |
        |_____|
```

For the second column of information, let us suppose that we have asked for five blanks. For the third column of information, we have specified that we want to see a concatenated string consisting of TOWN immediately followed by—though on the next line—ORG. The field width for this combination need not exceed the TOWN field width of nine characters.

```
| Contents              DTOC(DT_OF_HIRE)+';'+STR(SALARY,8,2)+';;;' |
| Heading                                                          |
| Width                 9                                          |
| Decimal places                                                  |
| Total this column                                              |
|_____|

        | DATE/HIRE                        |
        | SALARY                           |
        |                                  |
        |_____|
```

For the fourth column of information, we have asked for five blanks again. For the fifth column of information, we have specified that we want to see a concatenated string consisting of DT_OF_HIRE immediately followed by—though on the next line—SALARY. The width of the field is wide enough to accommodate the column heading.

When you specify a long string for the column data, you will notice that an automatic scroll takes place, within the confines of the line where you specify the column requirement.

Notice also, that concatenation applies only to string variables, and so the date-to-character function had to be used with the DT_OF_HIRE field and the string function had to be used with the SALARY field.

After the SALARY field has been specified as the last of the items of information from any record, the ';;;' symbol appears. This symbol has been used to inform dBASE that we want to keep two spaces after each SALARY field has been printed out. That is, we have asked for two spaces between records printed out. Please note that three semicolons will produce two spaces, four semicolons will produce three spaces, and so on.

In this case, since each column comprises two fields, the definition of the ';;;' for spacing between records could have gone with any one of the column definitions. If you had columns with unequal numbers of fields to be listed vertically, the ';;;' spacing requirement should, obviously, be defined with the longest of the column definitions.

> **Important:** Since the SALARY field had to be specified as a string function, we would not have been able to ask for any totals on the salary field, even if we had wanted to.

We can now pull off this vertical-format report.

```
.REPO FORM RPT8 FOR TOWN = 'R'          <cr>
```

```
Page No.     1
02/07/86
                       REPORT 8 - VERTICAL FORMATS.

EMP-NUMBER              TOWN                DATE/HIRE
EMP-NAMES              ORG                 SALARY


030                    ROCHESTER           07/07/81
TIM MONTAL             RBG                 41900.00


040                    ROCHESTER           10/21/77
JAMES JAMESON          GSD                 29800.00


070                    ROCHESTER           04/23/67
JAN MOREY              GSD                 18190.00
```

Extra Spacing Lines

If we wanted to generate a few extra blank lines between the main heading lines and the body of the report, this too could be done with semicolons after the main heading definitions. For example:

Options	Groups	Columns	Locate	Exit	<time>

```
| Page title                     |
| Page width (positions)      80 |
| Left margin                  8 |          _____
| Right margin                 0 |  |MAIN HEADER, WITH SEMI-COLONS !;;;;      |
| Lines per page              58 |  |                                         |
| Double space report         No |  |                                         |
| Page eject before printing  No |  |_____|
| Page eject after printing   No |
| Plain page                  No |
```

The result in the report format is the generation of extra spacing lines between the heading and the body of the report.

Multiple Main and Column Heading Lines

Here is a quick report to show the four heading lines you can have in either the main header or the column headers in the report. You would build up the primary menu screen as usual. Simply enter the four heading lines you would like to see in the report.

. REPO FORM RPT9 FOR TOWN = 'R'   <cr>

```
02/07/86
                              REPORT 9.
                    TO SHOW MULTIPLE HEADING LINES.
                    REPORT TO BE SENT TO THE CEO.
                    LIST SALARY INCREMENTS OF 10%

EMPLOYEE        EMPLOYEE           SALARY        INCREASED
NUMBERS         NAMES              ------         SALARY


030             TIM MONTAL        41900.00       46090.00
040             JAMES JAMESON     29800.00       32780.00
070             JAN MOREY         18190.00       20009.00
*** Total ***
                                  89890.00       98879.00
```

All four lines of the header are automatically centered across the width of the report you asked for. You can do the same thing, for column headings.

Using Variables in the Auxiliary Header

As you recall, the auxiliary header comes into play if you mention it in the report command itself.

. REPO FORM RPTXX   HEADING 'XXXXX XXXXX XXXXX XXXXX XXXXX'

The above format of the REPORT command provides the extra heading line over and above the normal four heading lines defined in the report format itself. I will now show you an enhancement you can make to the auxiliary header.

For now, I am going to describe, briefly, the term *memory variable*. This concept is much more fully explored in the advanced dBASE (programming) section of the book.

If you set aside a small section of computer memory and store some data in that section of memory, you have defined a *memory variable*. For example you could enter:

.STORE '01-01-76' TO D1   <cr>

This command has stored the literal value 01-01-76 into a section of memory set aside called D1. Picture it as follows:

```
  ┌─────────────┐
  │  Ø1-Ø1-76   │   ◄────────── the contents of the variable
  └─────────────┘
    Dl              ◄────────── the name of the variable
```

Suppose I had used a similar STORE command to set aside the date 12-31-79 in a variable called D2.

```
  ┌─────────────┐
  │  12-31-79   │   ◄────────── the contents of the variable
  └─────────────┘
    D2              ◄────────── the name of the variable
```

If I now pull off an existing report called RPT10 as follows:

. REPO FORM RPT10   HEADING 'For hire-dates between &D1 AND &D2'
FOR DT__OF__HIRE > = CTOD('&D1') .AND. DT__OF__HIRE < = CTOD('&D2')
        <cr>

I will get the following result:

```
Page No.      1   For hire-dates between Ø1-Ø1-76 and
                                         12-31-79
Ø2/Ø7/86

          REPORT 1Ø - TO CHECK OUT VARIABLES IN AUXILIARY HEADER.

EMPLOYEE        EMPLOYEE            DATE OF
NUMBERS         NAMES               HIRE

Ø1Ø             PETE JOHNSON        Ø2/Ø3/76
Ø25             KIM BRANDT          Ø4/Ø4/77
Ø4Ø             JAMES JAMESON       1Ø/21/77
Ø6Ø             JOHN PETERSON       Ø4/17/79
Ø65             JOY HARDY           Ø1/19/79
```

This works because the above command translates to:

.REPO FORM RPT10 HEADING 'For hire-dates between 01-01-76 AND 12-31-79'
FOR DT__OF__HIRE > = CTOD('01-01-76') .AND. DT__OF__HIRE < =
CTOD('12-31-79')   <cr>

That is, in place of the &D1 or the &D2, dBASE simply enters the values contained in the memory variables D1 and D2, and executes the resulting, expanded version of the command!

Obviously, if your auxiliary heading states that the report is for such-and-such dates of hire, there must be an appropriate FOR condition in the command statement to extract the qualifying records.

We had to use the CTOD (character-to-date) function since the DT__OF__HIRE field in the file is defined as a date field, and the '01-01-76' and the '12-31-79' are character variables.

Note that the &D1 and the &D2 are called *macros* (again, this will be fully explained in the programming section of the book). The use of the macro makes it possible to place, in the auxiliary header, variables such as the one shown above. Each time this report runs it will pick up the current dates in the memory variables D1 and D2, and produce the correct auxiliary header and the resulting report.

Unfortunately, dBASE-III PLUS version 1.0 does not (as yet) support the use of macro variables in either the main heading or the column headings of the report format. Hopefully, this enhancement will appear in later versions.

The Immediate If Function

I would like to wrap up the formatting section by showing you an interesting innovation. This involves the use of the Immediate If function, and the explanation of the function is taken up here. Study the following statement:

IIF(EXE,'YES','NO')

The *IIF* identifies the immediate if function. The statement should be read by you as: "If EXEMPT (is true), give me a 'yes'; otherwise give me a 'no'." It's as simple as that.

Take another example:

IIF(TOWN = 'R','*','?')

This line means: "If TOWN = 'R' (is true), give me an asterisk; otherwise give me a question mark."

Here is another example:

IIF(TOWN = 'R','*',' ')

This line means "If TOWN = 'R' (is true), give me an asterisk; otherwise give me a blank space! Note the blank space between the quotes. The last expression above could also have been entered with two single quotes without the blank space in between. The interpretation would be the same.

Suppose I want to pull off a report showing EMP_NUM, EMP_NAME, and the EXEMPT/non-EXEMPT status of the employee. If I keep our current definition of the EXEMPT field, I will get the .T. or .F. response from dBASE, and that is ordinarily good enough. This time, however, I want dBASE to specify "yes" and "no" for EXEMPT and non-EXEMPT, respectively. Therefore I define the EXEMPT field in the report format as follows:

```
| Contents            IIF(EXE,'YES','NO')              |
| Heading                                              |
| Width                6                               |
| Decimal places                                       |
| Total this column                                    |
|_____|
```

```
| E/NE                                 |
| STATUS                               |
| ------                               |
|_____|
```

Note that the width asked for is large enough to accommodate the column-header literal.

. REPO FORM RPT11   <cr>

Page No.   1
02/07/86
            REPORT 11 - TRY OUT THE IIF INSTRUCTION.

EMPLOYEE NUMBER	EMPLOYEE NAME	TOWN	E/NE STATUS
005	NINA BHARUCHA	WEBSTER	YES
010	PETE JOHNSON	brighton	YES
015	GLORIA PATEL	FAIRPORT	YES
020	MAX LEVINSKY	HENRIETTA	NO
025	KIM BRANDT	FAIRPORT	NO
030	TIM MONTAL	ROCHESTER	NO
035	WILLIAM PATEL	penfield	NO
040	JAMES JAMESON	ROCHESTER	YES
045	MORRIS KATZ	webster	NO
050	PAUL BHARUCHA	BRIGHTON	YES
055	PHIL MARTIN	WEBSTER	NO
060	JOHN PETERSON	BRIGHTON	YES
065	JOY HARDY	fairport	NO
070	JAN MOREY	ROCHESTER	YES
075	JOHN JONES	rochester	YES

As another example, this time I want a report showing EMP_NUM, EMP_NAME, and TOWN, and I want to flag records with the TOWN of Rochester, so as to highlight them in the report. This last (flag) column of the report can be specified as follows:

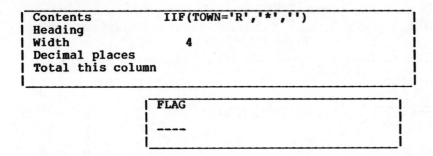

```
| Contents            IIF(TOWN='R','*','')    |
| Heading                                     |
| Width                  4                     |
| Decimal places                              |
| Total this column                           |
|_____|


| FLAG                                        |
|                                             |
| ----                                        |
|_____|
```

Again, the width is large enough for the column-header literal.

. REPO FORM RPT12A   <cr>

```
Page No.      1
02/07/86
                  REPORT 12A - TRY OUT THE IIF INSTRUCTION.

EMPLOYEE         EMPLOYEE           TOWN             FLAG
NUMBER           NAME
------           ----               ----             ----

005              NINA BHARUCHA      WEBSTER
010              PETE JOHNSON       brighton
015              GLORIA PATEL       FAIRPORT
020              MAX LEVINSKY       HENRIETTA
025              KIM BRANDT         FAIRPORT
030              TIM MONTAL         ROCHESTER          *
035              WILLIAM PATEL      penfield
040              JAMES JAMESON      ROCHESTER          *
045              MORRIS KATZ        webster
050              PAUL BHARUCHA      BRIGHTON
055              PHIL MARTIN        WEBSTER
060              JOHN PETERSON      BRIGHTON
065              JOY HARDY          fairport
070              JAN MOREY          ROCHESTER          *
075              JOHN JONES         rochester
```

For the next report, we shall put aside our PERSNL file, and take up an inventory file. I want to produce a report from this file that will serve to highlight all inventory records in danger of a stock run-out.

Obviously, it can be appreciated that such timely reports are crucial to the successful management of any manufacturing or marketing enterprise. I will take the following simple formula for highlighting items in danger of a stock run-out.

If ONHAND is less than or equal to DAILY-USAGE * (LEAD-TIME + leeway), this item is in danger of a run-out. For example, if I have 50 units of an item ONHAND, and my average daily consumption is 5 units, then I know that I have, at most, 10 days worth of stock on hand. Now, if it takes 14 days for new stocks to come in, I am already in trouble. Hence the "leeway" placed in the formula. I increase the LEAD-TIME by, say, 10, and this becomes my internal processing time.

If I run a report with such a formula, and an item is not highlighted on the report on Monday, but it is highlighted on Tuesday, I know that I now have 10 days in which to initiate orders for more supplies for this item.

I will use an immediate IF instruction to produce the flag for items meeting the above condition. (Assume that ONHAND, USAGE and LEAD are fields in the file structure.)

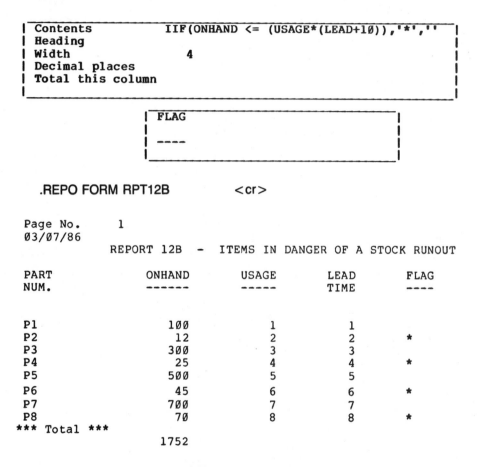

```
| Contents            IIF(ONHAND <= (USAGE*(LEAD+10))),'*',''  |
| Heading                                                      |
| Width                    4                                   |
| Decimal places                                              |
| Total this column                                           |
```

```
| FLAG                                         |
|                                              |
| ----                                         |
```

.REPO FORM RPT12B   <cr>

```
Page No.     1
03/07/86
             REPORT 12B  -  ITEMS IN DANGER OF A STOCK RUNOUT

PART            ONHAND       USAGE       LEAD       FLAG
NUM.            ------       -----       TIME       ----


P1               100           1           1
P2                12           2           2          *
P3               300           3           3
P4                25           4           4          *
P5               500           5           5
P6                45           6           6          *
P7               700           7           7
P8                70           8           8          *
*** Total ***
               1752
```

Taking Totals in Reports

When identifying the data columns you want to see in a report, you can ask for a numeric field just as easily as you can a character field, and dBASE defaults to a Yes for totals for that column. You can, of course, override the default. (Reminder: To make a change, just touch <cr>.)

Please ensure that the width of the numeric field you ask for is large enough to hold the largest of the field width, the column header, or the grand total of the column. If the cumulative total is unable to fit into the width of the field as defined, the report will show ******* in place of the total! Below is a report that shows the total of the

215

SALARY fields from the selected records in the PERSNL database.

```
. REPO FORM RPT13 FOR TOWN = 'R'        <cr>
```

```
Page No.     1
02/07/86
                    REPORT 13 - TAKING TOTALS

EMPLOYEE        EMPLOYEE            SALARY
NUMBERS         NAMES               ------


030             TIM MONTAL          41900.00
040             JAMES JAMESON       29800.00
070             JAN MOREY           18190.00
*** Total ***
                                    89890.00
```

Totals in Vertical Formats

Can we take totals in our report, if we have specified vertical formats? The answer is NO, at least for those numeric fields that form a part of a vertical format. The reason, as we have seen before, is that such numeric fields have to be specified as character strings in order to format them vertically, and dBASE will not permit you to specify totals on character fields. You may, however, have a mixture of columns in your report, where column 1 may be in a vertical format, and column 2 may be a stand-alone numeric field. During the report file generation, since each field definition is asked for separately, there is nothing to prevent you from requesting totals on the stand-alone numeric field. An example follows:

```
. REPO FORM RPT14 FOR TOWN = 'R'        <cr>
```

```
Page No.     1
02/07/86
             REPORT 14 - TAKING TOTALS IN VERTICAL FORMATS.

EMP-NUMBER        TOWN          DATE/HIRE        SALARY
EMP-NAMES         ORG           SALARY           ------


030               ROCHESTER     07/07/81         41900.00
TIM MONTAL        RBG           41900.00


040               ROCHESTER     10/21/77         29800.00
JAMES JAMESON     GSD           29800.00


070               ROCHESTER     04/23/67         18190.00
JAN MOREY         GSD           18190.00


*** Total ***
                                                 89890.00
```

Subtotals in Reports

We will now move on into the realm of providing subtotals within our report format. To obtain more meaningful results, I will convert all the lowercase data in the PERSNL file to uppercase.

```
. USE PERSNL          <cr>
. REPL ALL TOWN WITH UPPER(TOWN) ORG WITH UPPER(ORG)       <cr>
```

> **Note:** If you want to take subtotals on, say, the TOWN field, it stands to reason that the file will have to be either physically sorted or logically indexed on the TOWN field. Obviously, records with the same towns must appear together for correct subtotals. Also, if you want to take subtotals at two levels of control (say, on TOWN and, for the same TOWN, on ORG), then the file will have to be sequenced by TOWN and ORG.

```
. USE PERSNL          <cr>
. INDEX ON TOWN + ORG TO TINDX          <cr>
```

Now to build the report format file, you should respond to the primary menu as usual. I will use the Groups menu to provide four reports that do the following:

1. Produce subtotals on the TOWN level only
2. Produce subtotals on the TOWN and ORG levels
3. Group the records on the TOWN level only
4. Group the records on the TOWN and ORG levels.

Report 1: Subtotals by TOWN.

```
| Group on expression       TOWN                            |
| Group heading             SUBTOTALS FOR TOWN OF           |
| Summary report only       No                             |
| Page eject after group    No                             |
| Sub-group on expression                                  |
| Sub-group heading                                        |
|_____|
```

We want to take subtotals at the TOWN level; that is, the TOWN data is the first level of control. If you asked for a summary report only, you would not obtain all the detailed records in the report. If you ask for a page eject on each subtotal break, you will be using up much unnecessary paper in the report.

Note the group heading. dBASE wants to know if you would like to "doll up" the report at the place it prints out the subtotals. If you leave this entry blank, it will print out only the subtotal values. You only have to specify the literal such as SUBTOTALS FOR TOWN OF. dBASE will plug in the appropriate TOWN name at the time it prints the report.

It is important to remember that when you subsequently define, in another menu, the numeric data fields to be printed in the report, you must specify Yes for totals to be printed. This will also generate the subtotals in the report.

```
. REPO FORM RPT15          <cr>


Page No.      1
02/07/86
                  REPORT 15 - SUBTOTALS AT THE TOWN LEVEL.

EMPLOYEE         EMPLOYEE                  SALARY
NUMBERS          NAMES                     ------


** SUBTOTALS FOR TOWN OF BRIGHTON
   010           PETE JOHNSON             27590.00
   050           PAUL BHARUCHA            29100.00
   060           JOHN PETERSON            31480.00
** Subtotal **
                                          88170.00

** SUBTOTALS FOR TOWN OF FAIRPORT
   065           JOY HARDY                34200.00
   015           GLORIA PATEL             27500.00
   025           KIM BRANDT               36000.00
** Subtotal **
                                          97700.00

              etc etc etc etc etc
```

At the end of the report you will be provided the grand total.

Report 2: Subtotals by TOWN and ORG.

```
| Group on expression       TOWN                                      |
| Group heading             *******************   SUBTOTALS FOR |
| Summary report only       No                                       |
| Page eject after group    No                                       |
| Sub-group on expression   ORG                                      |
| Sub-group heading         *********   SUBTOTALS FOR                |
```

Now I have specified two levels of controls, a higher control TOWN and a lower control ORG. I have placed a special comment with leading asterisks so as to highlight this line on the report.

Remember to specify that you want totals for some or all numeric fields to be included in the report, when you fill out the appropriate menus.

```
. REPO FORM RPT16          <cr>
```

REPORT 16 - SUBTOTALS AT TOWN AND ORG LEVELS.

```
EMPLOYEE          EMPLOYEE                    SALARY
NUMBERS           NAMES                       ------

** ******************       SUBTOTALS FOR BRIGHTON

* ********** SUBTOTALS FOR BSG
  010             PETE JOHNSON                27590.00
  050             PAUL BHARUCHA               29100.00
* Subsubtotal *

                                              56690.00

* ********** SUBTOTALS FOR RBG
  060             JOHN PETERSON               31480.00
* Subsubtotal *

                                              31480.00

** Subtotal **

                                              88170.00

** ******************        SUBTOTALS FOR FAIRPORT

* ********** SUBTOTALS FOR RBG
  065             JOY HARDY                   34200.00
* Subsubtotal *

                                              34200.00

* ********** SUBTOTALS FOR RMG
  015             GLORIA PATEL                27500.00
  025             KIM BRANDT                  36000.00
* Subsubtotal *

                                              63500.00

** Subtotal **

                                              97700.00
                     etc etc etc.
```

The grand total follows at the end.

Report 3: Grouping Records at the TOWN Level. The grouping of records provides a compact printout of records sharing similar conditions.

```
| Group on expression      TOWN
| Group heading            ********************  RECORDS FOR
| Summary report only      No
| Page eject after group   No
| Sub-group on expression
| Sub-group heading
```

We only want to *group* records at the TOWN level. Since we do not want any totals now, make sure, when you fill out the subsequent menus, that you specify No when asked if you want totals on any numeric fields:

. REPO FORM RPT17   <cr>

Page No.   1
02/07/86
             REPORT 17 - GROUPING RECORDS AT THE TOWN LEVEL.

EMPLOYEE   EMPLOYEE   SALARY
NUMBERS   NAMES   ------

** ******************** RECORDS FOR BRIGHTON
  010   PETE JOHNSON   27590.00
  050   PAUL BHARUCHA   29100.00
  060   JOHN PETERSON   31480.00

** ******************** RECORDS FOR FAIRPORT
  065   JOY HARDY   34200.00
  015   GLORIA PATEL   27500.00
  025   KIM BRANDT   36000.00

                    etc etc etc etc.

Report 4: Grouping Records at the TOWN and ORG Levels.

Group on expression	TOWN
Group heading	******************** RECORDS FOR
Summary report only	No
Page eject after group	No
Sub-group on expression	ORG
Sub-group heading	********* RECORDS FOR

We now want to *group* records at the TOWN and ORG levels. Since we do not want any totals now, make sure, when you fill out the subsequent menus, that you specify No when asked if you want totals on any numeric fields.

. REPO FORM RPT18   <cr>

Page No.   1
03/07/86
           REPORT 18 - GROUPING RECORDS AT THE TOWN AND ORG LEVELS.

EMPLOYEE   EMPLOYEE   SALARY
NUMBERS   NAMES   ------

** ******************** RECORDS FOR BRIGHTON

* ********** RECORDS FOR BSG
  010   PETE JOHNSON   27590.00
  050   PAUL BHARUCHA   29100.00

* ********** RECORDS FOR RBG
  060   JOHN PETERSON   31480.00

```
EMPLOYEE         EMPLOYEE                    SALARY
NUMBERS          NAMES                       ------

** ******************   RECORDS FOR FAIRPORT

* **********     RECORDS FOR RBG
065              JOY HARDY                  34200.00

* **********     RECORDS FOR RMG
015              GLORIA PATEL               27500.00
025              KIM BRANDT                 36000.00

                      etc    etc    etc
```

The WHILE Parameter for Report Formats

Note: If we are using an indexed file to pull off a report, the records are obtained in the order of the index. Now, if for some reason the same report format is to be used for only one category of records (say for records for the TOWN of ROCHESTER), then one method of producing such a report would be:

.USE PERSNL INDEX TINDX   <cr>   (the TOWN index is active)
.REPORT FORM XXXXX FOR TOWN = 'ROCHESTER'   <cr>

These commands, however, will force the system to go through an appreciable amount of overhead, since every record in the master file will have to be accessed via the index. The record will then have to be checked for TOWN = 'ROCHESTER' and either accepted or rejected; the cycle will have to be repeated for each record in the entire file.

A far better approach is to make use of the fact that in the indexed file, all ROCHESTER records appear together, and we need to have dBASE pull off the records only as long as the key of the index is equal to the value ROCHESTER.

.FIND   ROCH   <cr>

This command will place the record pointer on the very first record in the indexed file that has a TOWN = 'ROCHESTER'. Now enter the following statement:

.REPORT FORM XXXX *WHILE TOWN =   'ROCHESTER'*   <cr>

This will pull off only those indexed records with the key value equal to ROCHESTER, and as soon as another key is sensed, the report process will cease. This method will save valuable time, since it will not necessarily start at the top of the indexed file and does not have to go all the way through to the end of the indexed file.

Incidentally, a side benefit of this method may have come to your mind. If your file had no records with TOWN = 'ROCHESTER', the FIND command itself would have returned a "No find" message, saving you much valuable time that would otherwise have been spent trying to produce a report on nonexistent records!

Enhancing Your Reports

Perhaps by now, as you were reading this or working out some examples, the thought has come to mind that you would like to see some more creativity in your reports, such as the use of boldface print, underscores, elongated print, headers, compressed print, your own form length, and your own line density. Unfortunately, the dBASE report generator falls short in this area. To compensate, you can do one of two things. You can send your report into a text file, and then word process the file and add all the enhancements you want—or better yet, you can wait till you have studied the advanced (programming) section of the book. In that section, I have provided detailed instructions on how you can obtain any kind of report you want, with all of the above-mentioned fancy footwork thrown in.

Generating Mailing Labels

I will round off this section on reporting by describing the process of generating mailing labels, using the LABEL command. By now you will have gained familiarity with the types of screens obtained in the reporting phase, and while the LABEL generation screens are not identical to the report screens, there is much similarity between them.

Let us assume you have a name and address file called NAMES, and you want to produce mailing labels out of this file. The scenario here is identical to the reporting process. Once again, you have to produce a special format file, called a *label format* file. After this dBASE merely filters the data from the NAMES file through the label format file and produces the labels.

Conceptually, the process could be shown as follows:

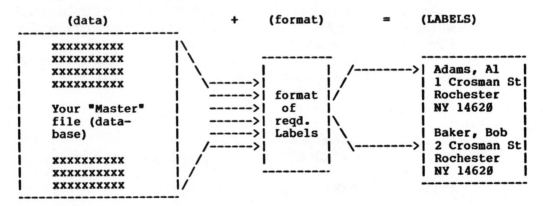

To inform dBASE that you want to generate a label format file, you start off with the following commands:

```
.USE NAMES        <cr>
.CREATE LABEL  ZIPS        <cr>
```

> **Note:** As is the case with reporting, you can use the words CRE-ATE or MODIFY interchangeably.

The above command informs dBASE that you want to create a label format file called ZIPS.LBL (the default secondary name is LBL).

Now dBASE presents the following primary screen.

```
Options                     Contents                Exit            (time)

Predefined Size:      3 1/2 x 15/16 by 1

Label width:                35
Label height:               5
Left margin:                Ø
Lines between labels:       1
Spaces between labels:      Ø
Labels across page:         1
```

The predefined option provides a few popular label formats. Toggle the "Predefined Size" line with the <cr> key to go through the various options. You will find that the other options for "width" and "spaces" also automatically change. You can, if required, provide any width or number of spaces you want for a format different from the predefined formats. Use the down-arrow key to select any of the other options you want to change, touch <cr>, make the change and then touch <cr> again.

In effect, you can choose a specific label format through this screen. In the middle of the screen, you have your usual cursor control menu, which can be toggled on and off through the use of the F1 key. At the bottom of the screen you have the usual status bar line.

Once you have chosen the overall label format, you can specify the contents of the labels. Use the right-arrow key to move the highlighting to "Contents." You now have up to five lines of label information to fill in. The highlighting is on the first line of the label. Touch the <cr> key, and enter the name of the field you would like to see on the first line of the label.

> **Note:** If you forget the names and widths of the fields in the structure of the NAMES file, you can do the following: first make sure you have pressed the <cr> key, then toggle F1 so that the cursor-control menu is OFF, and then touch F10. dBASE provides the structure boxes at the left and at the bottom of the screen, as shown:

```
Options                       Contents

----------------              --------------------------------------------
| LASTNAME     |              | Label contents   1:                      |
| FIRSTNAME    |              |                  2:                      |
| STREET       |              |                  3:                      |
| CITY         |              |                  4:                      |
| STATE        |              |                  5:                      |
| ZIP          |              |-----------------------------------------|
----------------

                              --------------------------------------------
                              | Field Name       Type     Width   Decimal|
                              |-----------------------------------------|
                              |NAMES->LASTNAME   Character  2Ø            |
                              |-----------------------------------------|
```

Now plug in the field name you want on the first line of the label. Suppose you want LASTNAME, FIRSTNAME on this line. That is, you want the lastname, followed by a comma, a space, and the firstname. You can use the TRIM function here. You would specify the format of the first label line in the following manner:

```
------------------------------------------------------------
| Label contents    1:TRIM(LASTNAME)+', '+FIRSTNAME  |
|                   2:                                |
|                   3:                                |
|                   4:                                |
|                   5:                                |
|------------------------------------------------------------
```

Use the above sequence of actions to define the other required lines of the label format.

Next use the right-arrow key to move the highlighting to "Exit," and exit with a save of the label format file. At this point, you have defined a label format file called ZIPS.LBL.

To test the spacing and widths, I would suggest that you use regular paper instead of actual labels. Obtain your test pattern on this regular paper, and then hold up the test pattern over a page of blank labels against a source of light, and see how well the printout masks itself over the actual labels! This way you will save yourself valuable labels.

To obtain a test pattern on regular printer paper, you can do the following (assuming that the file NAMES.dbf is already in USE):

.LABEL FORM ZIPS   SAMPLE TO PRINT   <cr>

To change the format spacing or width, you can always enter the following:

.MODI LABEL ZIPS   <cr>

and make changes to the spacing and/or width options, in the primary "Options" screen.

When your test pattern, compared to the actual label page, is satisfactory, you can print the labels on the actual labels. Remember to have your master file either physically sorted or logically indexed, if labels are required in some definite sequence, such as zip-code sequence.

The format of the label-print command is:

.LABEL FORM ZIPS [TO PRINT] [FOR <condition>] [WHILE <condition>]
    [SCOPE] [TO <filename>]

You have seen all these parameters before.

SUMMARY

In this section we learned to produce reports in varied formats. We are now able to obtain any report spread you want, doll-up column headings and main headings substantially, provide for record counts, totals, and subtotals, and even produce vertical formats for our reports.

While the built-in reporting feature of dBASE provides great flexibility in creating your own report formats, it is not, as you have observed, without its own set of restrictions. For instance, you have to live with the fact that the date and page number will always be provided at the top left of the page, not the top right. In those situations where you must have a radically different format for a report and the built-in reporting facility cannot be of much help, you still have the freedom of writing your own report programs. That is, you can write a computer program in dBASE, and this program will generate any report format you may have in mind.

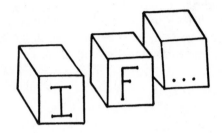

8. Configuring dBASE

I n an earlier chapter of the book I had mentioned that dBASE can be specially tailored to your needs. This means that the software can be either made to go through a series of commands the moment it is invoked or internally altered so that some commands now perform differently than they would have done in an unaltered version of the software.

THE SET COMMANDS

Basically you alter the workings of the software through the use of SET commands. The complete repertory of the SET commands will be found in the technical manual. For the purposes of this book, I will explain the workings of several of the SET commands, limiting this explanation for now to those SET commands that relate to the topics we have covered so far. Other SET commands that are typically used in the programming scene will be explained in the programming section. At the end of this explanation I will show you exactly how these SET commands could be automatically invoked when dBASE is loaded.

SET BELL

We have seen this SET BELL before, in the Append mode. In all the APPEND, EDIT, and MODIFY commands you have seen so far, you noticed that each time your cursor went to the end of a field, it automatically dropped down to the next field with a beep. If you entered invalid data into any field, you again got the beep. There are times when this beep can be very annoying, and you can always turn it off by using the SET BELL OFF command. The default is ON.

SET CARRY

We have seen the SET CARRY command before, in the Append mode. If you have many records to append into your file, and you find that much common data is to be entered across records, then issue the SET CARRY ON command before issuing the APPEND command. This command will ensure that the next record comes up with a mask of the data of the previous record. Now you can skip the fields with the common information, and hence there will be a faster overall throughput of data. The default is OFF.

SET COLOR

The SET COLOR command can be used with either monochrome monitors or color monitors. This command is used for controlling screen attributes such as regular display, inverse display, blinking display, and border display. For color monitors, these displays are shown in color.

.SET COLOR TO   <standard> [,<enhanced>] [,<border>] [,<background>]
                   F/B   F/B   L5   L6

Standard display refers to light letters on a dark background, the kind obtained when you type in commands at the dot prompt or the kind of instructional display you get when you ask to Create or Append.

Enhanced display refers to dark letters on a light background, the kind obtained at the data-entry positions on the screen (that is, at positions where you may enter data in full-screen Edit, Append, or Modify modes). Enhanced display is also known as *inverse-video* display.

Border display refers to the presentation of a border around the edge of the screen. (Background will be explained later.)

F stands for Foreground; B stands for Background, and L5 and L6 represent specific letters as described below.

The format of the above command now translates to:

.SET COLOR TO   L1/L2,L3/L4,L5,L6 where L1 . . . 6 are specific letters.

The L1/L2 letters produce the foreground/background combination for the standard display mode. The L3/L4 letters produce the foreground/background combination for the enhanced (inverse-video) display mode. L5 produces the border display.

Using specific letters for color codes (shown later), try out various SET COLOR commands. For monochrome monitors, you will find that different combinations of letters produce varying shades of foreground and/or background and/or border.

The color-codes are as follows:

BLACK - N   BLANK - X   BLUE - B   BROWN - GR   CYAN - BG
GREEN - G   MAGENTA - RB   RED - R   WHITE - W   YELLOW - GR+

A plus sign after the code implies high-intensity, and an * after the code indicates blinking. The YELLOW color is obtained as high-intensity brown—that is, with the code GR+. Note that the + (high-intensity) and the * (blinking) codes apply to the foreground only. For example, to set color to red on white for standard display and black on cyan for enhanced display, with a blue border, you would set the color codes as follows:

    .SET COLOR TO R/W,N/BG,B   <cr>

Having set this color combination, try the effect of entering the following commands:

    .USE PERSNL   <cr>
    .APPE   <cr>

You will see the color combinations you requested for the standard, enhanced (inverse-video) and border displays.

> **Note:** These color codes are *positional parameters*! That is, if for some reason you only want a border display, leaving the standard and enhanced displays intact, you would have to provide two commas in the command, to bypass the first two parameters. That is, entering
>
>   .SET COLOR TO ,,BG   <cr>
>
> will provide only a border display in color! Note the two commas that inform dBASE that you are bypassing the first two parameters for standard and enhanced displays respectively.
>
> **Note:** .SET COLOR TO without any number parameters will produce the normal video effect—that of having light characters on a dark background. This will kill all color effects.

The L6 color attribute applies only to systems that cannot handle the setting of background colors individually for normal and enhanced displays. On such systems, L6 represents the common background color.

SET CONFIRM

Normally, when your cursor reaches the end of a field, it drops down to the next field. When you enter .SET CONFIRM ON, you are specifying to dBASE that unless you touch <cr>, the cursor should not be made to automatically go to the next field. In essence, you want to confirm what you have keyed in before moving ahead. The default is OFF.

SET CONSOLE

The SET CONSOLE command turns the screen display on or off from within a program only. Entering .SET CONSOLE ON or .SET CONSOLE OFF at the dot prompt has no effect on the system. For example, I can write a program to ask the operator for a password, then use .SET CONSOLE OFF so the operator's response cannot be read by someone in the vicinity, and then use .SET CONSOLE ON again.

> **Note:** Even with CONSOLE OFF, error messages produced from within the program will appear on the screen. The default is, of course, ON.

SET DECIMALS

For any math that does not involve multiplication, the number of decimals in the result will always be the same as the number of decimal places found in the number with the highest number of decimal places. For math involving multiplication, the number of decimal places in the result will always be the sum of the number of decimal places involved in the multiplication process.

SET DECIMALS TO only affects the functions of division, SQRT( ), LOG( ), and EXP( ). The normal default for these functions is a minimum of two decimal places, rounded, but you can .SET DECIMALS TO three or any other number to obtain the result to n number of decimal places. Please note that the result is rounded off to the specified number of decimal places.

SET DEFAULT

We have seen the SET DEFAULT option before. It lets you choose the default drive on which dBASE can hope to find all your files (data, program, report, etc.) For example, if all your files are on the B drive, you can enter .SET DEFAULT TO B so you don't have to enter B:<filename> for each filename reference. The default is the drive from which you loaded dBASE.

SET DELETED

The SET DELETED command is an interesting feature and applies to deleted records. If you enter .SET DELETED ON, then most commands of dBASE act as if the deleted record was not in the file. With this feature ON, you cannot FIND, LOCATE, or LIST deleted records. It acts as a sort of filter, and filters out the deleted records.

This feature finds good use in any application. Let us suppose you are working on the development of a menu system (details in the programming section), and you provide one option to find specific records and another option to delete specific records. Using your menu system, suppose you delete a specific record. The record is flagged as deleted, with the * character. Now, if you were to use the option to find that same record, logically it should not be found. If you had entered the command .SET DELETED ON as one of your housekeeping commands in the beginning of the menu, then your attempt to find this deleted record would fail, which is how it should be! Without the use of the .SET DELETED ON command you would be able to use one option of the menu to delete a specific record, and then use the other option of the menu to find that same record! This, of course, is illogical and an error in the system. The default for this option is OFF.

This action, however, is not universal to all commands. For example, with SET DELE ON, you can still INDEX and REINDEX deleted records; you can DISPLAY <the current deleted record>; you can DISPLAY RECO N (a deleted record); and you can GOTO n (a deleted record). The most important use of the .SET DELE ON command is in the fact that the FIND command will not find deleted records. The default is OFF.

SET EXACT

You know how the following command works:

```
.USE PERSNL          <cr>
.LIST FOR TOWN = 'ROCH'          <cr>
```

This command will list all those records that have an uppercase R O C H in the first four positions of the TOWN field.

With SET EXACT ON, you can guess as to what would happen. The above command would not display any record, since you have now stipulated that you want an exact match on all character string evaluations. The default is OFF.

SET FILTER

If you SET FILTER TO <any condition, simple or complex>, dBASE will now behave as if the entire database is only comprised of records that meet that condition.

If you have multiple files open at one time, you can have a different filter condition for each of the open files.

```
.SELE 1          <cr>
.USE PERSNL          <cr>
.SET FILTER TO   <condition>          <cr>
.SELE 2          <cr>
.USE PAYROLL          <cr>
.SET FILTER TO   <condition>          <cr>
```

Note: To deactivate the filter, don't provide any condition.

```
.SET FILTER TO          <cr>
```

will negate the effect of the filter in the current work area.

Does the .SET FILTER TO .NOT. DELE( ) command perform better than the .SET DELE ON command for filtering out deleted records? No: experiments suggest that .SET DELE ON provides the same result as .SET FILTER TO .NOT. DELE( ) for this function.

SET FIXED

As you recall, the SET DECIMALS TO n affects the functioning of the DIVISION operator, the SQRT( ) function, the LOG( ) function, and the EXP( ) function. The minimum is two decimal places, rounded. If you have entered .SET DECIMALS TO 3, numeric outputs from these operations will be limited to three decimal places, rounded, and so on.

If you now have entered SET FIXED ON, you are specifying to dBASE that the numeric output of any computation should be processed to the number of decimal places as provided in the .SET DECIMALS TO command.

If you have used neither SET DECIMALS TO n nor SET FIXED ON, the default is a minimum of two decimal places, rounded, which is probably what you would like to live with for commercial applications. The default is OFF.

SET FUNCTION

By using the SET FUNCTION feature, you can write miniprograms that can be executed with the touch of the function keys on your keyboard. For example, if you want to program the F2 key to CLEAR the screen, USE the file called PERSNL, and LIST the data, you could enter:

```
.SET FUNCTION 2 TO 'CLEAR;USE PERSNL;LIST;'        <cr>
```

Note that each semicolon is interpreted as, "I have hit the <cr> key." That is, the above statement can be interpreted to mean:

```
.SET FUNCTION 2 TO 'CLEAR        <cr>
        USE PERSNL        <cr>
        LIST        <cr>'
```

This results in a series of commands, in effect creating a mini program. The length of the character string depicting the commands is a maximum of 30 characters.

To set function key 2 back to its default value, enter:

```
.SET FUNCTION 2 TO   <cr>
```

The default settings of the function keys are provided in the manual. They are as follows:

```
HELP/ASSIST/LIST/DIR/DISP STRU/DISP STAT/DISP MEMO/DISP/APPEND/EDIT
 1      2     3    4     5        6          7        8     9     10
```

Note that the F1 key cannot be reprogrammed.

SET HEADING

When you enter the LIST or DISP command, regardless of parameters, you always obtain the titles of the fields across the top of the data. This is, of course, very useful, because it lets you know exactly what you are looking at. If, for any reason, you want to do away with the field headings, you may enter SET HEADING OFF. The default is ON. I suggest you leave it ON.

SET INDEX

The SET INDEX command permits you to specify the name of the controlling index file. For example, I have a PERSNL file, and I produce the following three indexes:

```
.USE PERSNL          <cr>
.INDEX ON TOWN TO TINDX          <cr>
.INDEX ON ORG TO OINDX          <cr>
.INDEX ON SALARY TO SINDX          <cr>
```

If I were to enter .USE PERSNL INDEX TINDX,OINDX,SINDX, then all three index files are active against the PERSNL file, and all three indexes will be updated for any changes made to the PERSNL file. However, the TINDX.NDX file, because it is mentioned first in the list, is the *controlling* index file, or the primary index file, in the sense that all commands will process the records in the order of the town index. That is, the LIST (or DISP) command will list records in the order of TOWN, the FIND command will try to find the value provided against the TOWN index, and so on.

If I want to list the records in the order of another field and yet keep all three indexes active, I could specify:

.SET INDEX TO OINDX,TINDX,SINDX   <cr> Now the ORG index is primary.
.SET INDEX TO SINDX,OINDX,TINDX   <cr> Now the SALARY index is primary.

As another example, suppose you design a telemarketing type of application in which your user maintains a database of active and prospective clients, and you want the ability to call a client record to the screen via either the company name or the telephone number. You would keep two indexes active against the master file, one for the company name and one for the phone number. Depending on the option chosen from the menu, your program will either SET INDEX TO PHONENDX,COMPNDX to make the phone index the major index, or SET INDEX TO COMPNDX,PHONENDX to make the company name index active. Now the FIND command will find values provided against the appropriate active index, and both indexes will be updated with changes made to the master file.

We mentioned before that you can disassociate all active indexes from a master file by USING the master file:

.USE PERSNL   <cr> This will disassociate (close) all index files from this master.

You could also specify CLOSE INDEX or SET INDEX TO to obtain the same result.

SET INTENSITY

The SET INTENSITY command affects either monochrome or color monitors. When you are in the Edit, Append, or Modify modes, ordinarily you would see data-input items in inverse video. .SET INTENSITY OFF removes the inverse video effect. The default is ON, and you may prefer to leave it as such. This effect exists regardless of the setting of the color codes.

SET MEMOWIDTH

During DISPLAY or LIST commands, if you mention the memo field by name, you will see the contents of the field on the screen. Depending on how many other fields you display at the same time, the display of the memo contents may cause the screen to go haywire, cluttering up the display. You can SET MEMOWIDTH TO <some number>, so the display of the memo contents is restricted to this column-spread. This helps in the overall visual display of the data. The default is 50 columns. For example, you could enter:

```
.USE PERSNL        <cr>
.SET MEMOWIDTH TO 25      <cr>
.LIST EMP_NUM,EMP_NAME,NOTE        <cr>
```

```
Record#   EMP_NUM EMP_NAME       NOTE
      1   005     NINA BHARUCHA  To my daughter: Trust you
                                 have no objection to my
                                 including your name in
                                 the book.
      2   010     PETE JOHNSON   You will be eligible for
                                 3 weeks vacation as of
                                 12-01-85.

      3   015     GLORIA PATEL
      4   020     MAX LEVINSKY   You will be eligible for
                                 5 weeks vacation as of
                                 12-01-85

                      etc   etc   etc
```

SET MENU

In the fullscreen Create, Edit or Appendt modes, by default you will see a mini menu across the top of the screen, providing hints for cursor control movement. You may enter SET MENU OFF, if you don't require this help; however, the use of the F1 key toggles this miniscreen on and off anyway, regardless of the setting of this option, so you don't really need to specify this option. The default is ON.

SET ORDER

When you enter the following:

```
.USE PERSNL INDEX   TINDX,OINDX,EINDX        <cr>
```

TINDX becomes the controlling index. If you now want the OINDX file as the controlling index-file, one way would be to type:

    .USE PERSNL INDEX OINDX,TINDX,EINDX   <cr>

While this will work, it will force a closing of the index files and then a reopening of the files in the new order in the current work area. This is time-consuming.

Since the first command (.USE PERSNL INDEX TINDX,OINDX,EINDX) opened up the OINDX as the second index file, to make it the leading index file without closing and reopening files, you would specify:

    .SET ORDER TO 2   <cr>

Now the OINDX file is the leading file; that is, further commands against the indexed file will proceed in the order of the organization index. Note that all three index files are still active, and updates to the master file will be reflected across these indexes, but the order of precedence has been changed.

To make the Employee-number index the predominant index, you would enter:

    .SET ORDER TO 3   <cr>

To make the town index the active index again, you would enter .SET ORDER TO 1 <cr>

The master file can be made to appear in the normal, unindexed order through the use of the command:

    .SET ORDER TO 0   <cr>

Now commands like DISP and LIST will show the records from the file in their normal, unindexed sequence. Please note that *any updates to the files at this point will not update the indexes!* For the indexes to be updated during changes to the master file, the indexes must be active, regardless of the setting of the order of the indexes. That is, you must .SET ORDER TO <number greater than 0> for all indexes to be actively updated with changes to the master file.

SET PATH

The meaning of the DOS subdirectory structure and the word PATH have been explained in Appendix A.

If, for any reason, you have the dBASE system programs installed on one directory and you want to work with datafiles in another directory, you will have to inform dBASE of that fact either through the use of a path call or through the directory name supplied directly in the command itself. For example:

    .SET PATH TO   \;\DENTAL;\MEDICAL   <cr>

This is a series of *paths*, separated by semicolons (or commas), and is known as a *path call*. After entering this line, if you .USE <filename>, dBASE will first search the current directory for the <file>, and failing to find it, will check to see if a PATH has been established. Our path definition above says: "Search the root directory; then if the <file> is not found, search the path ROOT- - ->DENTAL; then if the <file> is not found, search the path ROOT- - ->MEDICAL; then if the <file> is not found, return an error message." dBASE will now search for the file in this order. Note that the current directory is always checked first, followed by any other directories defined in a path call.

If you specified the command as:

.USE \ PROJECTS \ MEDICAL \ PERSNL   <cr>

dBASE will search for the PERSNL.DBF file in the specific subdirectory PROJECTS- - - - ->MEDICAL. If dBASE cannot find the file in this subdirectory, it will come up with an error message. Note that the above command has not provided a path call. The command has supplied an exact subdirectory, not a list of possible subdirectories!

> **Note:** You provide a path call only if you want dBASE to search for *existing files* in other directories, besides the current directory. Commands that can create files (such as CREATE, COPY, JOIN, and SORT) can, if necessary, allow you to provide the other subdirectory name in the command itself, for example:

.CREATE \ PROJECTS \ MEDICAL \ PERSNL   <cr>

> **Note:** .SET PATH TO   <cr> will negate any current path call, and return the default to the current directory.

SET RELATION

The SET RELATION command helps to link two databases together, so that you can LIST or REPORT data from both files. This setting of the relationship has been fully explained in earlier pages.

SET SAFETY

You have noticed that each time you try to create any kind of file that already exists on the disk, dBASE provides you with a warning message, giving you the opportunity to back out. This is because SAFETY is ON. If you enter SET SAFETY OFF, there is no warning when you are about to CREATE a file over an existing one, or destroy an existing index file, which may have taken some time to build. The SAFETY ON provides a buffer of protection that you would be wise to leave on. The default is ON.

SET SCORE

In fullscreen Edit or Append modes, you may have noticed a "Caps" message, either at the top of the screen or in the special status line at the bottom of the screen. If you don't want this message displayed, you may enter SET SCORE OFF. The default is ON.

SET STATUS

The SET STATUS ON command provides us with the status line at the bottom of the screen. The default is OFF when you start up with dBASE at the dot prompt phase. Regardless of its setting, however, STATUS always defaults to ON in the Assistant mode of operation, in the CREATE/MODIFY (<file> or <report> or <label>) mode of operation, and in the BROWSE mode of operation.

SET TALK

When dBASE executes commands, it usually sends out confirmation messages to you. For example, if you ask to index a file, it tells you how many records were indexed. There are times when you want dBASE to "stop talking" to you. These instances will be seen in the programming section of the book. You can SET TALK OFF to get this effect. The default is ON.

SET UNIQUE

We have seen many instances in which we indexed a file on TOWN, and all the towns of ROCHESTER appeared together. The same is true for any other value of the key field (town). However, if you wanted the indexing operation to produce only one of the ROCHESTER records, one of the WEBSTER records, and one of each unique key value record to be indexed, in effect removing the duplicate entries from the index file (they will remain on the master file, of course), then you have to SET UNIQUE ON.

```
.USE PERSNL          <cr>
.SET UNIQUE ON       <cr>
.INDEX ON TOWN TO TINDX       <cr>
```

With this setting, dBASE will accept only the first record of many duplicates in the master file, into the indexing process, ignoring the others. Now any command against the indexed file will process only these records, not the duplicates.

This option could be used, for example, in a mailing-list type of application, so that duplicate records inadvertently placed in the file are not printed out more than once. It can also be used to validate the uniqueness of a file. Say, you have an inventory file, containing PART_NUM as the key field. To validate uniqueness, you can enter:

```
.? RECCOUNT( )       <cr>
```

This will tell you how many records you have in your file. Now enter the following commands:

```
.SET TALK ON         <cr>
.SET UNIQUE ON       <cr>
.USE INVENTRY        <cr>
.INDEX ON PART_NUM   TO   ABC       <cr>
```

At the end of the indexing process, dBASE will inform you of the number of records that were indexed. This number should be the same as the record count obtained before. Obviously, a discrepancy will mean that you have duplicates in your file.

While these uses, at first glance, seem good, you may or may not want to go that route, depending on your requirements. For instance, in the mailing list example, if I have duplicate records, I would prefer to see them listed out on paper instead of just being ignored, so I can make corrections. Perhaps the duplicate errors occurred on account of a simple data entry error, and a code 1234 was entered as code 2134. Using SET UNIQUE ON will eliminate one of the 2134 entries, and it may not be the one in error, depending on its position in the file! Besides, it means that one valid party would not get a mailing, simply because an entry was ignored during the processing.

The same argument would hold true for the inventory file example, with even greater impact on business. "Losing" a whole record of inventory is far worse than a customer not receiving a mailing sample of your product. Besides, simply knowing that you have some duplicates in your file is not as useful as knowing which records are showing duplicate keys.

There are ways of ensuring a more effective process, in which your data entry routines would be as watertight as possible, trapping duplicate errors at the time of data entry. In the programming section of the book, we shall study, in detail, methods for setting up custom screens for data entry, and for validating operator input for uniqueness. The default for UNIQUE is OFF.

AUTOMATIC PRESET

So much for the various SET commands for now: I have yet to cover some more of these commands, but for the most part, the other SET commands are most often used when you are writing computer programs, so I will explain these later at the appropriate places in the book. For now, I want to show you exactly how you can automatically preset these SET statements, so dBASE will turn things ON and OFF exactly as you want, before presenting you with the dot prompt on the screen.

In Appendix A, I explain the workings of the MS-DOS hierarchical directory structure and also explain how MS-DOS loads itself. To summarize, MS-DOS first searches the ROOT directory for a file called CONFIG.SYS and executes any commands there, and then searches the ROOT directory for a file called AUTOEXEC.BAT and executes any commands there. One of the commands in the AUTOEXEC.BAT file could be DBASE. That is, as soon as MS-DOS has loaded itself, it will load dBASE!

dBASE also searches for a special file called CONFIG.DB (configure dBASE) in the same directory that dBASE is loaded from, and as you may have guessed, it will execute any commands stored there! So all you have to do is to set up a file called CONFIG.DB in the same directory that contains your dBASE system files and place all the SET statements in that file.

Use the built-in dBASE word-processor to create the CONFIG.DB file:

.MODI COMM   CONFIG.DB   <cr>

When the dBASE word processor comes into play, you enter your settings as follows: (Pick and choose the ones that you want to be different from the defaults, and *please* don't type the comments in parenthesis! These are only there for your guidance.)

BELL = OFF	(I don't want the 'beeps' on data-entry/edit.)
MENU = OFF	(I don't want the cursor-control menu on every full-screen command invoked.)
SCORE = OFF	(I don't want the CAPS message appearing on the top line of the screen, in full-screen mode.)
COLOR = R/GR,	
N/BG,G	(I have outdone myself this time!)
DELE = ON	(I want deleted records ignored in listings and in FIND commands.)
F2 = CLEAR;LIST	(I want to set up my function keys.)
F3 = EDIT	
etc	
etc	

Having entered the settings you would like to see, touch Ctrl-W to save the contents of the file CONFIG.DB. This in itself does nothing, but the next time you load the system, MS-DOS will load itself and then automatically load dBASE, and dBASE will automatically go through the predefined settings, before presenting you with the dot prompt on the screen!

A pictorial representation of the directory structure, with the CONFIG.SYS, AUTOEXEC.BAT, and CONFIG.DB files would be as follows:

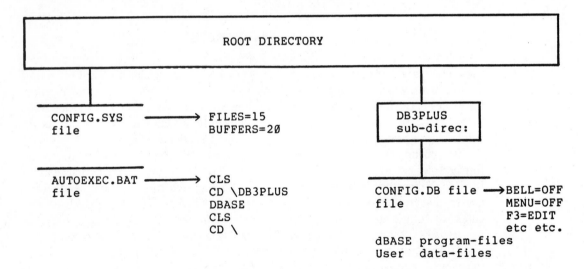

SUMMARY

In this section we learned about the effects of the various SET switches on the internal execution of dBASE. Of interest to color-monitor users are the various color codes that can be set from within the software.

We also learned how these SET switches could be predefined, so that at the time of loading dBASE, the switch settings are automatically brought into effect before you are presented with the dot prompt.

Part 3

ADVANCED FEATURES

9. PROGRAMMING IN dBASE-III PLUS

So far we have studied, in depth, several dBASE commands that can be executed as stand-alone instructions, and that really tend to make an instant programmer out of the user. Commands such as COPY and APPEND, and functions such as STR(ing) and SUBSTR(ing) are so powerful that even an experienced programmer would have to put in considerable effort to be able to do what you, the user, can do through the use of these instructions and functions alone.

The scope of dBASE, however, extends far beyond the provision of stand-alone instructions for execution. dBASE provides you with the capability of combining the very same instructions we have studied all along into *modules* of instructions. These *modules* can then be initiated for execution, providing you with the ability to execute a number of instructions without any further actions on your part. This is what forms the basis of *programming* in any computer language.

This portion of the book is designed to show you how you can write your own computer programs in dBASE and really bolster up the capability and efficiency of your computerized applications. Out of necessity, of course, we will have to study some more commands and concepts in addition to the ones we have seen so far, to be truly effective in writing computer programs in dBASE.

I want to emphasize that programming is an art, not a science. Any number of programmers may come up with any number of variations in the programming solution to a problem, all of them converging on the identical end result. But there are such things as good programs and bad programs, depending on how they are written and documented, and on how well they lend themselves to comprehension and modification by other programmers.

Note: If you look up some books on computer programming, they invariably provide several pages of explanation on concepts such as flowcharting, pseudocoding, and the like. This book is not geared towards providing detailed philosophical explanations of these concepts, many of which I personally don't believe in. I have written countless programs, but have never drawn a flowchart or written pseudocode. I don't wish to imply that these are unnecessary, only that I have not found the need for flowcharting or pseudocoding. In this section, I will follow what I believe is a very logical path towards teaching you how to program in dBASE.

We will start off with the simplest of computer programs and increase the complexity gradually, until we find ourselves generating our own screen formats in support of sophisticated, highly versatile, *menu-driven* systems. Upon completion of this portion of the book, you may realistically expect to be able to write and understand complex dBASE programs. At this point in time, you should be fairly conversant with the basics of dBASE.

AN OVERVIEW OF THE PROGRAMMING SCENARIO

A computer program is nothing more than a *set of instructions* to a computer, causing the computer to perform a series of functions. The instructions are, for the most part, sequential in nature. If you can group together a string of computer instructions (in any language), give the group a name, and store the group on a disk, you have created a computer program. A computer program is also referred to as a *module*.

In dBASE, when you are at the dot prompt, you are being prompted with a "what next" type of situation. That is, dBASE expects you to enter a command. At this stage, if you were to try to create a *group* of dBASE instructions, as soon as you enter the first instruction, dBASE would take off and execute it. This means, of course, that you cannot hope to build your computer program at the dot prompt.

To start the process of creating a program, you have to inform dBASE of your intention to build a set of instructions with the following command:

.CREATE COMMAND   Pgm1   <cr>

(Note that Pgm1 is merely the name of the program. You may come up with any name you want.)

This command informs dBASE of your intention to create a *command file* (program) called Pgm1.PRG. The screen is now erased; the dBASE word processor takes over; there is no dot-prompt; and whatever you key in will remain on the screen, under your control, until you either SAVE your creation (Ctrl-W), or decide you don't want it after all (Ctrl-Q). Use the F1 key to check out the cursor controls.

To invoke the *execution* of an existing program, you simply request dBASE to:

.DO   PGM1   <cr>

We will start off with examples of programs and add to the complexity of these programs as we proceed.

A Sequential Command File

As the name suggests, our first program will be nothing more than a pure *sequential series* of instructions to the machine. That is, there will be no logic involved. Suppose we enter the following command:

.CREATE COMM   PGM1   < cr >

When the screen goes blank, you can key in your program instructions, or code. Please note that you may have *comment lines* dispersed among your program lines of code. These comment lines begin with the * character and are ignored by dBASE during execution. Comment lines are strongly encouraged for use as headings and explanations.

Throughout this book, I will follow this convention. All explanations of program lines will be provided in the program itself, using the *-comment lines. One or more lines of code will be followed by an explanation of that code.

```
* PGM1A.PRG
* ---------
CLEAR
*      The CLEAR command clears up the screen. It only clears up the screen,
*      so don't hesitate to use it.
USE PERSNL
*      Bring the PERSNL file into use and take control of the first record
INDEX ON TOWN TO TINDX
*      Create an index on the TOWN field
LIST
*      Provide a listing in the order of the index (via TOWN)
WAIT
*      Wait for the operator to see the listing
CLEAR
*      Clean up the screen again
INDEX ON ORG TO OINDX
*      Create an index on the ORG field
LIST
*      Provide a listing in the order of the index (via ORG)
WAIT
*      Wait for the operator to see the listing
*                         END  OF  PGM1A
```

Having entered the command statements, you will have to enter a Ctrl-W, to save your program. (A Ctrl-Q is used to change your mind about saving the program.) At this stage, dBASE slips back to the dot-prompt.

Now that your program, has been saved, execute it with the DO command:

```
.DO   PGM1          <cr>
```

As you may appreciate, when the program executes, it will proceed to execute the instructions exactly as they had been specified in the program, and so we can expect the following string of events to take place:

The screen goes blank; the PERSNL file is USEd; dBASE gives you an INDEX on the TOWN field; dBASE then gives you a LISTing of the indexed file; and then dBASE WAITs, for you!

The WAIT command is important and is widely used in programming with dBASE. The effect of this command is that the literal "Press any key to continue . . ." appears on the screen, providing you with the opportunity to study the LISTing that preceded the WAIT. Please note that if at this stage you don't do anything, dBASE will wait for you indefinitely! In reality, dBASE is waiting for you to enter any key (you would tend to press <cr>), and it will then take off to execute the next group of instructions after the wait.

In our example, if you do a <cr> in response to the "Press any key . . ." statement, dBASE will proceed to clean up the screen again; INDEX the same file, this time on the ORG field; provide an indexed LISTing by organization; and again WAIT for your response.

At this stage, if you press <cr>, dBASE simply slips back to the dot prompt, asking you "What Next?", because there are no more instructions in the program.

And that, basically, is an overview of creating and running any dBASE program. Obviously, our example was one of a very trivial program, which had no logic embedded in it. We will increase the complexity of our programs gradually.

Making Changes to a Program

Let's make a slight modification to our previous program. We can display any literal we want at the WAIT, or we can have the literal suppressed! To make changes to an existing program, use the following command:

```
.MODIFY COMM  Pgm1          <cr>
```

and if Pgm1.PRG exists, the screen will show the contents of the program. To scroll back and forth in the body of an existing program, use PgUp and PgDn. Enter Ctrl-W to save all your changes or Ctrl-Q to negate all the changes.

```
*  PGM1B.PRG
*  ----------
CLEAR
USE PERSNL
INDEX ON TOWN TO TINDX
LIST
WAIT ''
*      Note the two single quotes following the WAIT command. There may or
*      may not be any spaces between the single quotes. By placing these
*      quotes, you are preventing any message line from appearing at the
```

```
*       WAIT command. By contrast, you can specify any literal between quotes
*       after the WAIT, and that literal will appear on the screen.
CLEAR
INDEX ON ORG TO OINDX
LIST
WAIT ''
*
                              END   OF   PGM1B
```

Using the mechanics outlined above, let us suppose we have keyed in the following sequential program:

```
* PGM2.PRG      (An example only.)
* --------
CLEAR
USE PERSNL
SORT ON TOWN TO TSORT
SORT ON ORG TO OSORT
SORT ON EMP_NUM TO ESORT

USE TSORT
REPORT FORM RPT1 TO PRINT
USE OSORT
REPORT FORM RPT2 TO PRINT
USE ESORT
REPORT FORM RPT3 TO PRINT
USE
*       Note that the USE command, without any parameters, will close the
*       file last in use.
DELETE FILE TSORT.DBF
DELETE FILE OSORT.DBF
DELETE FILE ESORT.DBF
*
                              END   OF   PGM2
```

When this program is executed, we can see from the commands provided that the following events will take place:

The PERSNL file will be USEd; then three sorted files will be created out of that file, one each for a TOWN sort, an ORG sort, and an EMP_NUM sort. Now the program will proceed to use the TOWN sort file and produce a report out of that file; it will then do the same with the other two sorted files. After producing the three reports, the program will proceed to close the file last in use and then delete the sorted files to release space. After that, of course, it will drop back to the dot prompt.

General Comments on dBASE Programs

1. A program may be entered in uppercase or lowercase or a combination of upper and lowercase.

2. If a program line extends to more than one line on the screen (you may have plenty of FORs and .AND.s and .OR.s in the statement), then you have to provide a semicolon as the *continuation character*, to inform dBASE that the statement is not yet

complete. Since you will be breaking the line between full words, ensure that you have a space character before the semicolon.

3. You can have only one command statement on one physical line.

4. An asterisk (*) at the start of a line indicates to dBASE that the line is to be treated as a comment, not as a command. Comments can be used to provide the name of the program, the objective of the program, and can also provide an explanation of what the next few or preceding few lines of code do in the program. I would strongly encourage the use of comment-lines, freely interspersed within your programs.

5. You can also provide comments on the same line as the line of code. Simply start off the comment with the && (double ampersands) and then place your comments on that line. Note, however, that in the case of a command statement extending to more than one line, the && comment cannot be placed after a semicolon (for continuation). It must be at the end of the entire command, regardless of how many lines the command spans. A suggestion would be to provide brief programming notes in && comments, and lengthier statements using the * comment-lines.

6. Notice that both the programs start off with the CLEAR command, which clears the screen of any previous data. This is a good practice, and I would encourage you to start all programs with the CLEAR command.

7. After you have typed in your program instructions, you can either Ctrl-W to save your program, or Ctrl-Q to change your mind on saving the creation. If you use Ctrl-Q, you will have a second chance to confirm your intention.

8. If you have to make changes to an existing program, use the same command as you did to create the program:

```
.MODI COMM    Pgm1           <cr>
```

If Pgm1.PRG exists, the first screen will show the contents of the program. To scroll back and forth in the body of an existing program, use PgUp and PgDn. As before, Ctrl-W will save all your changes, and Ctrl-Q will negate the changes.

9. Note that the command file (program file) is a *text* file, and if you feel more comfortable using a text editor or a word-processor program to build and change your program files, feel free to do so. Of course, to subsequently execute these program-files, you will have to go back into dBASE.

10. The converse is also true. Having created your program file in dBASE, you may print out the entire program itself, using any word processor program.

11. To print out any program from within dBASE, turn the printer on, then enter .TYPE xxxxx.PRG TO PRINT <cr>. In this printout, however, you will not obtain any page breaks such as are provided with word processor printouts.

12. There are times when you want to create a program (PGM2) which is similar to an existing program (PGM1). Obviously it would make life much easier if you could make a copy of the existing program under the new program name, rather than having to key in the new program from scratch.

Use the dBASE copy command to make this copy as follows:

```
.COPY FILE PGM1.PRG TO   PGM2.PRG          <cr>
```

Now you can proceed to make changes to PGM2.PRG.

13. The words CREATE and MODIFY can be used interchangeably.

A Decision Command File

Let me now introduce an elementary piece of *logic* to our computer program, so that instead of just following commands sequentially, the program can make minor or major decisions during execution. We shall proceed with minor decisions first.

The purpose of this program is to do the following:

1. Ask the operator for a town name, and wait for a response.
2. Accept the response entered by the operator.
3. Read the first record out of our PERSNL file. (Note that this program will read only the first record!)
4. Check to see if the town name (from that record) matches the response of the operator.
5. Indicate the outcome of the comparison with either a "Good Match" or "Too Bad, Try Again" message on the screen.

In order to be able to create this program, we shall have to study a new command, called ACCEPT:

.ACCEPT "Please enter a town name   " TO MTOWN   <cr>

On execution, this instruction will cause the literal following the ACCEPT command to appear on the screen, and wait for the operator's response. The literal can be defined either with single quotes or with double quotes. Now when the operator keys in a response and uses the Return key, the response entered will be accepted and placed into a *character memory variable* called MTOWN. If no response is made, but the operator enters <cr>, the character *null* is generated into the memory variable. (A *null* means literally nothing! It is not the same as a *blank*! A blank is a *character* having the same status as any other character in computer memory.)

> **Note:** A *memory variable* is a piece of memory set aside, containing some data. You may name the variable whatever you like. The size of the memory variable created through the ACCEPT command will vary, depending on the contents of the variable. The maximum length of a memory variable name is 10 characters. If you define a name of more than 10 characters, only the first 10 are accepted.

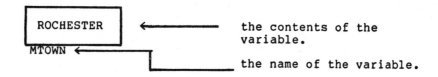

ROCHESTER ← ———— the contents of the variable.
MTOWN ← the name of the variable.

Note: You must differentiate between the name of the memory variable and the contents of that memory variable.

Note: Since the ACCEPT command is used, the memory variable created is automatically of the character type. That is, if *quotes* are used in entering the response, the *quotes* will be accepted as *part of data*! If digits are entered, these numbers will be stored as character data!

Note: In the ACCEPT command, I have left blank spaces at the end of the literal. If you don't leave the spaces, at the time of execution the cursor comes to rest just after the literal, and your response merges with the literal on the screen. From an aesthetic point of view, you want your literals to always end with some spaces.

Now let's write the program described above.

```
* PGM3A.PRG - A decision command-file
* ---------
CLEAR
ACCEPT "Please enter a town name       "  TO   MTOWN
*       This will cause the literal to appear on the screen; the system
*       will automatically wait for the operator's response, which, on <cr>,
*       will be accepted and stored in the character memory variable called
*       MTOWN.
USE PERSNL
IF UPPER(TOWN) = UPPER(MTOWN)
*       If the content of the TOWN field from the record in use is equal to
*       the content of the MTOWN memory variable (both items compared in
*       upper case).....
    @ 15,10 say "Good"
*       This will display the "Good" comment starting at line 16 column 11
*       on the screen.
ELSE
*       That is, in case the above condition is not true.....that is, if
*       TOWN is not equal to the contents of MTOWN.....
    @ 15,10 say "Too Bad, Try Again"
ENDIF
*       Normally, every IF...ELSE logical combination must end with a match-
*       ing ENDIF statement. In this special case, since there are no more
*       program statements following, we could have done without the ENDIF
*       here. However, to enforce a necessary habit, I have shown the ENDIF
*       statement here.
*                                END  OF  PGM3A
```

An IF statement identifies the start of a fork in the logic of any program. Program control can only follow instructions in one of the two branches of the fork. Which branch is selected (or, in other words, "the outcome of a logical decision") during execution depends entirely on the incoming data and on the results of data comparisons. The IF statement in this program compares the data in the TOWN field to the data in the MTOWN memory variable. The data are either equal or not equal. The program has specified different actions to be taken, depending on whether the items are equal or not equal.

> **Note:** The screen configuration is 24 lines by 80 columns. The lines, however, are numbered from 0 through 23, and the columns are numbered from 0 through 79.

The @ 15,10 command identifies the screen coordinates as the 16th line and the 11th column on the screen. This is the position where a literal has to start, or the contents of memory variable have to be displayed. Avoid the use of 0,0 since this line and column are required by dBASE for its internal use.

The use of the UPPERCASE function suggests that you may not be too sure of how the data was created in the master file (upper- or lowercase) and you cannot, of course, rely on the operator's responses being all in uppercase, either. The use of the upper case function is very strongly recommended in all areas where variable operator inputs are accepted.

Variations of the Decision Program

The following variation provides some more information to the operator instead of just "Too bad, Try again". It informs the operator of what the actual value was.

```
* PGM3B.PRG - A decision command-file
* ----------
CLEAR
ACCEPT  "Please enter a town name      "  TO    MTOWN
USE PERSNL
IF  UPPER(TOWN) = UPPER(MTOWN)
    @ 10,15 SAY "GOOD MATCH"
ELSE
    @ 10,15 SAY "THE TOWN WAS NOT"
    @ 10,35 SAY MTOWN
*     MTOWN is where the operator's response was saved.
    @ 12,15 SAY "IT WAS"
    @ 12,35 SAY TOWN
*     TOWN is the field from the record in use.
ENDIF
*                   END  OF  PGM3B
```

> **Note:** This point is very important. In the above examples, we were comparing the contents of a field name (TOWN) to the contents of a memory variable (MTOWN). You must always follow this sequence. Always compare the field name to the memory variable, never the other way around. For example, in the above programs, if the statement had been:

IF UPPER(MTOWN) = UPPER(TOWN)   (here you are comparing the memory variable to the field name)

the result will always be a logical false, even though the contents match!

For now, we will use the standard form of the @—Say command, and the various other possibilities will be introduced later.

A Repetition Command File

We will now enhance the complexity of the logic of this program. We want to increase the scope of this program to do the following:

1. Put out the message, as usual.
2. Accept the response.
3. Compare the response with the appropriate field from the first record.
4. Repeat the comparison for each record of the file and provide "Good" or "Bad" messages for each comparison.

Here is one way of writing the program:

```
* PGM4.PRG. A Repetition program - Logical Loop
* ---------
CLEAR
ACCEPT "Please enter a town name        " TO    MTOWN
*      This will cause the literal to appear on the screen, the system
*      will automatically wait for the operator's response, which, on <cr>,
*      will be accepted and stored in the character memory variable called
*      MTOWN.
CLEAR
USE PERSNL
DO WHILE .NOT. EOF()
*      Start a logical loop. "For as long as it is not the end-of-file,
*      continue doing all the commands that follow, up through an ENDDO
*      ("end of DO") statement. That is, keep looping within the DO loop
*      for as long as it is not the end-of-file."
   IF UPPER(TOWN)=UPPER(MTOWN)
*      If the content of the TOWN field from the record in use is equal to
*      the content of the MTOWN memory variable
      @ 15,10 say "Good"
*      This will put out the "Good" comment starting at line 16 column 11
   ELSE
*      That is, if the content of the TOWN field does not match the content
*      of the memory-variable MTOWN.....
      @ 15,10 say "Too Bad, Try Again"
   ENDIF
*      This ENDIF is very crucial !  This is the end of the IF statement.
*      That is, this statement tells dBASE "regardless of the outcome of the
*      IF statement, go to the next instruction !"
   WAIT ''
*      The system will WAIT for you to touch any key, before continuing with
*      the program. This WAIT permits the operator to see the outcome of the
*      previous comparison, the "Good" or the "Bad" message.
      @ 15,10
*      Specifying nothing means that you want to clear the line starting at
*      the position of the cursor  and proceeding to the end of the line. In
*      effect, you are clearing the previous "Good" or "Bad" literal.
```

```
    SKIP
*       dBASE will take control of the next record in the file.
ENDDO
*       The ENDDO statement informs program control to go back into the
*       DO WHILE... loop. That is, check the condition controlling the loop,
*       and if the condition remains satisfied (if it is still not the end
*       of the file), continue executing the instructions in the loop.
*
*       Only after the last record is processed will the SKIP command force
*       the end-of-file condition to be true. Since the looping effect is
*       dependent on the end-of-file to stop looping, dBASE will now transfer
*       program control to the next instruction, out of the loop.
CLEAR
@ 15,1Ø SAY "How's that, folks ?"
*       Note that in this literal, double quotes are mandatory, since the
*       literal itself contains a single quote within the string.
*                           END  OF  PGM4
```

Below are some explanations concerning this program.

1. After the program has accepted all the required operator inputs, it would be good practice to have it CLEAR the screen, before proceeding to pull off any type of display or report.

2. You have to inititate the start of a logical *loop* through the command DO WHILE .NOT. EOF( ). (There are other ways to start loops, and we shall see these later.) Each DO WHILE is accompanied by an ENDDO statement. The DO WHILE statement says that as long as the condition in the DO WHILE is satisfied, all the statements following the DO WHILE, through the statement just before the ENDDO, should be continuously executed. This is one way of pumping several records (one record at a time) through the same logic of several instructions. Thus, for as long as it is not the end of the file, the statements within the DO WHILE/ENDDO combination will continue being executed.

3. The statement after the DO WHILE is the IF statement. Since the previous USE command has passed control to record #1 of the PERSNL file, the first time the IF statement is executed, it will check the operator's response against the TOWN field from record #1, and come out with a "good" or "bad" message. As a reminder, always compare the field name to the memory variable, not the other way around. Also, use the UPPER function, to avoid any inaccuracy based on case. The result of execution of the IF statement would be a message on the screen, either "Good" or "Too bad . . ."

4. The ENDIF statement is very important. It breaks the logic of the IF statement. The ENDIF statement says something to the effect, "This is it!" Regardless of the outcome of the IF statement, control should pass to the instruction after the ENDIF. If you forget to place ENDIF statements, or if you misplace them in the logic of your program, the output results of such a program will not be worth a dime.

5. After the comparison resulting in either "good" or "bad," (regardless of the outcome) we want the program to pause and wait for us to see the outcome of the comparison with record #1. This is the function of the WAIT statement. Having checked out the result, we now press <cr> to go ahead with the next instruction in the pro-

gram. (Basically, we want to repeat the comparison for the second record.) Before we pass control to the next record, we want to erase the "good" or "bad" literal from the screen; otherwise, for example, a "GOOD" followed by a "BAD" will result in "BADD" appearing on the screen, since both literals are sent to the same location on the screen.

6. Having seen the outcome of the comparison for the first record, we now <cr> to clean up the literal; then control passes to the next record through the SKIP command.

7. We want to send this next record through the same logic of the instructions: Go through the comparison, come up with "good" or "bad," let the operator check the result, erase the literal, pass control to the next record, and so on. That is where the ENDDO statement plays a role. I said before that a DO WHILE and an ENDDO are always in pairs, and that program control will continuously execute all instructions that lie between these two instructions, for as long as the condition in the DO WHILE is satisfied. If you forget to place an ENDDO statement to complement the DO WHILE, there is nothing to inform dBASE as to when you want to loop back, and in that case only record #1 would be processed through your entire program.

8. After the last data-record from the PERSNL file has been processed (that is, at end-of-file), the condition specified in the DO WHILE statement is no longer true, and control breaks out of the loop and passes to the instruction after the ENDDO statement. At that point, you can provide any clean-up instructions you may want.

9. It is crucial to understand that the USE statement should be outside of the DO WHILE loop. If your USE statement is within the loop itself, then although the SKIP statement passes control to record #2, as soon as the ENDDO statement sends control back to repeat the loop, the USE statement would place the record pointer back to record #1. This means that record #1 will be processed repeatedly, and you will never encounter the end-of-file. Since the looping effect is dependent on the end-of-file to stop looping, you will have landed yourself in an *infinite loop*, with record #1 being sent through the mill each time.

On reading the above paragraph, was there something that apparently seemed a bit illogical? I mentioned what would happen if the USE statement was placed after the DO WHILE .NOT. EOF( ) statement. What may seem illogical is that if we have not yet brought any file into USE, will the DO WHILE .NOT. EOF( ) statement, which is executed first, have any meaning to dBASE? Will this cause a problem at this point? The answer is that even when you start off with a clean slate, there is a built-in dBASE function called EOF( ), which is set to a logical FALSE. Try it, the next time you enter dBASE. At the dot prompt entering .? EOF( ) will result in .F. So if your USE statement is wrongly placed as discussed, dBASE will not *abend* (abnormal end), but will definitely go into a loop.

10. To cancel (interrupt) the execution of any program, use the ESC key.

11. The statements within the DO WHILE-ENDDO combination have been indented only for ease of readability. With indentation, you can identify the start and end of the looping instructions very quickly. The instructions within the IF-ENDIF combination have also been indented for ease of comprehension of logic, and as we shall see later, for helping to ensure that each IF is matched up with an ENDIF statement. Without the indentation, execution will proceed correctly, but the programmer is more likely to mismatch the IFs and the ENDIFs, or the DO WHILEs and the ENDDOs.

A Practical Program

From here on, our programs will begin to have a more practical appearance. Let's write a program to do the following:

    1. Ask the operator for an ORG name.

    2. Accept the response.

    3. Read the file called PERSNL.

    4. For those records that match the operator's response, display EMP_NUM, EMP_NAME, and SALARY.

There are a couple of ways of writing this program. The first method is the one that is easier to use. I have also provided the second method, to continue emphasizing the concept and usage of loops.

Method 1.

```
* PGM5A.PRG - A Practical Program
* ----------
CLEAR
ACCEPT "Please enter an ORGANIZATION name      " TO MORG
CLEAR
USE PERSNL
DISP    EMP_NUM,EMP_NAME,SALARY   FOR  UPPER(ORG) = UPPER(MORG)
*       The above statement will display all the records that satisfy the
*       condition. This is the easiest way of writing this program. If more
*       than 19 lines qualified for the display, dBASE would automatically
*       wait for you to enter any key, before proceeding with the listing.
WAIT ''
*       Note:  We needed to have a WAIT command after the end-of-file was
*       encountered, so as to be able to view the records that were selected
*       for display by the program. Without this WAIT command, the screen
*       would have been CLEARed by the next command, without providing the
*       operator a chance to study the output.
CLEAR
@ 15,10 SAY "HOW'S THAT, FOLKS !"
*                         END  OF  PGM5A
```

The second method emphasizes the use of the DO WHILE . . . ENDDO loop.

Method 2.

```
* PGM5B.PRG - A Practical Program
* ----------
CLEAR
ACCEPT "Please enter an ORGANIZATION name      " TO MORG
CLEAR
USE PERSNL
*     Bring up the first record, under control of dBASE.
DO WHILE .NOT. EOF()
   IF UPPER(ORG) = UPPER(MORG)
      DISP EMP_NUM,EMP_NAME,SALARY
   ENDIF
```

```
*       If the first ("current") record qualified for display, display the
*       selected fields to the screen
*       Regardless of the outcome of the IF statement, go to the next
*       instruction.
   SKIP
*       Now the "next" record is the "current" record.
ENDDO
WAIT ''
*       Note the WAIT command.
CLEAR
@ 15,10 SAY "HOW'S THAT, FOLKS !"
*                               END   OF   PGM5B
```

When you execute the above program, you will notice that dBASE clutters up the output with record numbers of those records that did not match. (dBASE's way of being helpful.) To get dBASE to stop being so helpful in displaying the additional comments (in effect, to stop talking to you), you have to use the instruction SET TALK OFF. This is one of the many housekeeping instructions available.

```
* PGM5C.PRG - A PRACTICAL PROGRAM
* ----------
SET TALK OFF
CLEAR
ACCEPT 'PLEASE ENTER AN ORGANIZATION NAME       ' TO MORG
CLEAR
USE PERSNL
DO WHILE .NOT. EOF()
   IF UPPER(ORG) = UPPER(MORG)
      DISP EMP_NUM,EMP_NAME,SALARY
   ENDIF
   SKIP
ENDDO
WAIT ''
CLEAR
@ 15,10 SAY "HOW'S THAT, FOLKS !"
```

In the previous program, PGM5C.PRG, you noticed that dBASE puts out a heading line for each record that qualifies for display. This is, obviously, not too desirable, so you could try the following version:

```
* PGM5D.PRG - A PRACTICAL PROGRAM
* ----------
SET TALK OFF
CLEAR
ACCEPT 'PLEASE ENTER AN ORGANIZATION NAME       ' TO MORG
CLEAR
USE PERSNL
DO WHILE .NOT. EOF()
   IF UPPER(ORG) = UPPER(MORG)
      DISP EMP_NUM,EMP_NAME,SALARY
      SET HEADING OFF
*       The first record that qualifies for display will have the heading
*       line displayed. Now if you SET HEADING OFF, the subsequent records
*       will be displayed, without the heading line.
```

254

```
    ENDIF
    SKIP
ENDDO
WAIT ''
CLEAR
@ 15,10 SAY "HOW'S THAT, FOLKS !"
SET HEADING ON
*                          END  OF  PGM5D
```

PGM5D.PRG works, but because the first record is displayed with the header line, you will find that it does not quite line up with the other records that are displayed without the header. In effect, you will see something like this, in the output listing:

```
Record#  EMP_NUM EMP_NAME        SALARY
      1  005     NINA BHARUCHA 25000.00
      2  010 PETE JOHNSON   27590.00
      9  045 MORRIS KATZ    23450.00
     10  050 PAUL BHARUCHA 29100.00
```

This spacing is a result of the spacing in the header literal. You could have specified SET HEADING OFF right at the start (along with SET TALK OFF), and then you would not have this problem. But in that case, you would not have any heading either.

You would conclude, very correctly, that Method 1 is not only easier to key in, but is also effective. My objective here, however, is to emphasize the usage of the DO WHILE . . . ENDDO loop, which will prove to be one of the most valuable options available in the dBASE programming language. So don't give up on the above anomaly. There are many ways of correcting the above result, and we shall be outlining these along the way.

> **Note:** These preliminary programs are meant to give you an understanding of programming concepts, such as decisions and loops, and are not meant to be watertight programs. For example, in the previous program, if too many records qualified for the condition, the resultant listing will force some of the records off the screen. Obviously, in this program we need to include a check for the number of records being displayed. Also, all programs must provide for an escape mechanism for the operator, in case the operator starts an option but then decides to back out of it. We will build upon the complexity of the programs gradually.
>
> **Note:** One important rule of programming is that if you set a switch on or off in the body of your program, remember to set the switch off or on, respectively, at the end of the program. If you forget this, the switch setting remains in its changed status across other programs and systems. Therefore we SET HEADING ON before we exit from the program.

To send the output of these programs to the printer, try using SET PRINT ON in the housekeeping section. Remember to have another SET PRINT OFF as the last instruction in your program; otherwise the printer will remain active.

> **Note:** SET PRINT ON has no effect on @- - - - SAY commands.
> It only affects DISPLAY commands, in that the output of the DIS-
> PLAYs would then go to the printer.

The types of programs you have seen so far are quite useful in that they are totally generic. Nothing is hard-coded, and depending on the responses provided by the operator, different outputs can be obtained.

In a previous section of the book, I have covered several of the SET commands. In this section we will study some of the other SET commands, which pertain to the programming aspect of dBASE. SET TALK OFF and SET PRINT ON are examples.

> **Note:** Normally when you index a file, dBASE informs you about
> the number of records indexed, provided that TALK (is) ON. If you
> have .SET TALK OFF, then you will not get any message at the end
> of the indexing.

Extending the Logic with More Variables

You can extend the logic of this program to include more variables. The program can be written to request the operator to respond with a town name and an organization name. Now only those records meeting both criteria will be selected for display.

```
* PGM6.PRG - Extending the Logic with More Variables
* --------
SET TALK OFF
CLEAR
ACCEPT "Please enter a town-name      "    TO    MTOWN
CLEAR
ACCEPT "Now please enter an organisation-name    "    TO    MORG
*      Notice the second ACCEPT command, to ask for another variable.
CLEAR
USE PERSNL
DO WHILE .NOT. EOF()
   IF  UPPER(TOWN)  =  UPPER(MTOWN)  .AND.  UPPER(ORG) = UPPER(MORG)
*      Notice the extra comparison, now, for the second variable. Only if
*      the record qualifies on both TOWN and ORG will the record DISPLAY.
      DISP EMP_NUM,EMP_NAME,SALARY
       SET HEADING OFF
   ENDIF
   SKIP
ENDDO
WAIT ''
CLEAR
@ 10,15 SAY "HOW'S THAT, FOLKS ?"
SET HEADING ON
*                              END  OF  PGM6
```

The program above is an example of an *interactive* program; that is, it is a program that interacts with the operator in its execution. Such programs request low-volume operator inputs at various times during execution, and the logic of such programs is designed to produce specific outputs during execution, depending on the response from the operator.

From another perspective, the word *interactive* merely means *in dialogue mode*; that is, a dialogue is maintained between the program and the user, with the program intermittently asking for operator inputs, and the operator providing parameters and/or yes/no type responses, to which the program reacts as per the logic of its instructions.

Accepting Numeric Input

Write a program that will do the following:

1. Use the file called PERSNL.
2. Accept two responses from the operator concerning TOWN and SALARY. Caution: SALARY is defined as a numeric field. (See the note below.)
3. Read through PERSNL, and from those records that match on TOWN but whose SALARY is less than the operator's response, display EMP_NAME, ORG, and DT_OF_HIRE.
4. Use the SET PRINT ON/OFF feature.

Note: Instead of using the ACCEPT command, which always stores an entry as a character variable, you may try the INPUT command, which can store an entry as either a numeric or a character variable; for example,

INPUT "Please enter any character/s you wish" to MCHAR

During the execution of this command, the memory variable created could be of either character or numeric type. The type of the memory variable created depends on the response entered by the operator; for example, if the operator enters 1234 or 12.34 the memory variable is automatically of the numeric type and will contain the value keyed in by the operator. If the operator enters a numeric value with leading spaces, the spaces are ignored, and the numeric value will be retained. If the operator enters something like 2 5, the value 2 will be retained, and everything after the first space will be ignored. If the operator enters 2AB, only the 2 will be retained as the input. If the data is entered as 2A3B then again only the 2 is retained as the input. The entry AB23C will result in a syntax error because the INPUT statement anticipates *numeric* data (unless the entry is enclosed in quotes).

If the operator enters "ABCD" or "1234" or '12.34', the memory variable is automatically of the character type and will contain exactly what the operator has keyed in, but without the quotes. Obviously, the quote (single or double) makes the difference between the character and the numeric variable.

If the operator enters   ABCD   or   AB23C   dBASE will flag this entry as an error and will request the operator to reenter the data.

The program specified earlier could be coded as follows:

```
* PGM7.PRG - Accepting Numeric Input
* --------
SET TALK OFF
CLEAR
ACCEPT "Please enter a town-name      "    TO    MTOWN
CLEAR
INPUT "Now please enter the SALARY     "    TO    MSAL
*      Notice the usage, now, of the INPUT command. We want the operator's
*      entry to be stored as a numeric variable, not as a character
*      variable.
CLEAR
USE PERSNL
DO WHILE .NOT. EOF()
   IF  UPPER(TOWN)  =  UPPER(MTOWN)  .AND.  SALARY < MSAL
       DISP EMP_NAME,ORG,DT_OF_HIRE
       SET HEADING OFF
   ENDIF
   SKIP
ENDDO
WAIT ''
CLEAR
@ 10,15 SAY "HOW'S THAT, FOLKS ?"
SET HEADING ON
*                              END  OF  PGM7
```

Providing a Record Count

The above program can be extended to provide a count of the number of records that actually meet the selection criteria. Look at the following instruction.

```
STORE   COUNTER + 1   TO COUNTER
```

This is dBASE's way of saying "Add 1 to COUNTER." (COUNTER would be set up as a numeric memory variable.)

> **Note:** You will first have to *define* the memory variable, before you can place values into it. In the housekeeping section, you need to provide another instruction: STORE 0 TO COUNTER. This instruction will define a numeric memory variable called COUNTER, giving it an initial value of zero. The following is the shell of the program:

258

```
[    SET TALK OFF
     STORE Ø TO COUNTER
     ------
     ------
     ------
     IF <the required condition is satisfied>
         DISP .............
         STORE  COUNTER+1  TO  COUNTER
         ------
         ------      ]
     ENDIF
```

At the end of this program, provide instructions to display the contents of the memory variable, as follows:

NUMBER OF MATCHING RECORDS: 999

The actual program follows:

```
* PGM8.PRG - Providing a Record-Count
* ---------
SET TALK OFF
STORE Ø TO COUNTER
*     Note the STORE statement. This defines a memory variable called
*     COUNTER, and gives it an initial value of zero. Note that if the
*     above command had been: STORE 'Ø' TO COUNTER, then this would have
*     created a character variable called COUNTER, with an initial value
*     of a (character) zero.
CLEAR
ACCEPT "Please enter a town-name      "    TO    MTOWN
CLEAR
INPUT "Now please enter the SALARY      "    TO    MSAL
CLEAR
USE PERSNL
DO WHILE .NOT. EOF()
   IF  UPPER(TOWN)  =  UPPER(MTOWN)   .AND.  SALARY < MSAL
        DISP EMP_NAME,ORG,DT_OF_HIRE
        SET HEADING OFF
        STORE COUNTER+1  TO  COUNTER
*     If the record qualifies, display it, and add 1 to the variable
*     called COUNTER
   ENDIF
   SKIP
ENDDO
WAIT ''
CLEAR
@ 1Ø,15 SAY "NUMBER OF MATCHING RECORDS"
@ 1Ø,45 SAY COUNTER
SET HEADING ON
*                              END  OF  PGM8
```

In the last two statements, we are displaying a literal starting at line 10 column 15 (actually, line 11 column 16 because the count starts at zero, but we won't split hairs here). We also want to display the contents of a memory variable on the same line, but obviously farther to the right. The column location selected must be such that it does not overlap the character literal, so all you need to do is to count the length of your character literal and have the memory variable placed anywhere after the end of the literal.

When you actually run the program, you will find that the contents of the memory location called COUNTER appear much further removed from the literal than what your calculation implied. We must remember that numeric fields are accepted up to 15 digits of accuracy, and so the memory variable called COUNTER is at least nine digits wide. Hence the actual salary data appearing in the report will appear rather far removed from the literal, since it will be right justified in the 9-digit wide memory variable. At a later stage I will show you how to position the contents of a memory variable exactly where you want it to appear. See "Positioning and the use of Masks" in a later section.

Providing a Timing Loop

As you recall, program four asks for an operator entry for the TOWN name and then checks each record in the PERSNL file for the TOWN entered by the operator. The program gives "Good" or "Bad" messages and then waits for the operator to see the outcome. The operator then has to press <cr>, to process the next record.

The WAIT statement causes an indefinite wait; that is, if the operator does not touch any key to continue, the system will wait forever! You can, however, provide a bit of an exotic touch by having the system go into a small *timing loop*, so that the operator will see the message for a few seconds, after which the system breaks the loop and takes off to process the next record automatically. Such timing loops, while not crucial to any system, are more useful than a dead wait in situations where messages are to be passed to the operator, but no specific operator action (other than pressing <cr>) is required.

I have provided program four again, this time with the timing loop segregated and highlighted. Note that these few statements replace the one WAIT command that causes processing to halt indefinitely.

```
* PGM4A.PRG - A REPETITION COMMAND FILE, WITH TIMING LOOP.
* ---------
CLEAR
SET TALK OFF
ACCEPT 'PLEASE ENTER A TOWN NAME    ' TO MTOWN
CLEAR
USE PERSNL
DO WHILE .NOT. EOF()
    IF UPPER(TOWN) = UPPER(MTOWN)
        @ 15,10 SAY 'GOOD'
    ELSE
        @ 15,10 SAY 'TOO BAD, TRY AGAIN'
    ENDIF
    STORE 0 TO COUNTER
    DO WHILE COUNTER < 100
        STORE COUNTER+1 TO COUNTER
    ENDDO
*       The above instructions force the system to initialize a counter to
*       zero, then keep adding the number 1 into the counter till the counter
```

```
*          value equals 100. In effect, the system "waits" only for the few
*          seconds it takes for dBASE to count to 100 ! This is a "temporary"
*          wait, as opposed to a "dead-halt" wait.
*
*          Since the program uses a counter to count to 100, I have also
*          included the "SET TALK OFF" command (which is not in the original
*          program-4), else numbers will flash by on the screen, each time the
*          program starts counting to 100.
     @ 15,10
     SKIP
ENDDO
CLEAR
@ 15,10 SAY "HOW'S THAT, FOLKS !"
```

Providing Averages

The previous program can be extended to provide *averages*. We want to obtain the average salary of a few, selected records. The shell of the program is as follows:

```
IF   <the required condition is satisfied>

     STORE   RECCNT + 1   TO   RECCNT

     STORE   TOTSAL + SALARY    TO    TOTSAL

     ................
     ................
ENDIF
```

At the end, to display the average, we display the results of the expression:

TOTSAL / RECCNT

The complete program could be written as follows:

```
* PGM9A.PRG - Providing Averages
* ----------
SET TALK OFF
STORE 0 TO RECCNT,TOTSAL
*          This command defines two numeric variables, and initializes them
*          to zero.
CLEAR
ACCEPT "Please enter a town-name      "    TO     MTOWN
CLEAR
INPUT "Now please enter the SALARY      "    TO    MSAL
CLEAR
USE PERSNL
DO WHILE .NOT. EOF()
     IF   UPPER(TOWN)   =   UPPER(MTOWN)   .AND.   SALARY < MSAL
          DISP EMP_NAME,DT_OF_HIRE,SALARY
          SET HEADING OFF
          STORE RECCNT+1   TO   RECCNT
          STORE TOTSAL + SALARY   TO TOTSAL
*          The above store commands will add 1 to counter, and add the salary
*          from the current, qualifying record into TOTSAL.
```

261

```
      ENDIF
      SKIP
ENDDO
WAIT ''
CLEAR
@ 10,15 SAY "NUMBER OF MATCHING RECORDS"
@ 10,45 SAY RECCNT
@ 12,15 SAY "TOTAL SALARY"
@ 12,45 SAY TOTSAL
@ 14,15 SAY "AVERAGE SALARY"
@ 14,45 SAY TOTSAL / RECCNT
SET HEADING ON
*       The above 2 statements provide the actual average.
*                          END    OF   PGM9A
```

An Enhancement

In the preceding program, we made one important presumption, and that is that at least one record would match the condition in the IF statement. What would happen if none of the records met the specified condition? The record count would remain at its initialized value of zero, and in an attempt to find the average, we would be dividing by zero, which is a mathematical impossibility. This will cause dBASE to provide a string of asterisks in place of the average result. Regardless of programming language, the rule of thumb is that you should always check for and avoid the likelihood of dividing by zero.

In the above program, the final lines of code should be:

```
IF RECCNT > 0
*
*       Only if the record count is greater than zero.....
*
*
   @ 14,15 SAY "AVERAGE SALARY"
   @ 14,45 SAY TOTSAL / RECCNT
ENDIF
```

Now the average will be computed provided at least one record qualified for the condition. If nothing qualified, there would be no output on line 14 of the screen.

The Transfer of Control From One Program to Another

Just as you invoke the execution of a program by asking dBASE to DO <program name>, you can invoke the execution of another program from within the first one in the same way.

```
* PGM10.PRG - CALLING PROGRAM          * ACCEPTS.PRG - CALLED PROGRAM
* ─────────                            * ─────────
*
*
PUBLIC MTOWN,MORG
SET TALK OFF
CLEAR
```

```
DO Accepts ────→──────→──────→──────→          ACCEPT "Please enter a ;
                (transfer of control)          town name"
                                               TO MTOWN

                (transfer of control)
CLEAR          ←──────←──────←──────←──────
USE PERSNL
DO WHILE .NOT. EOF()                           CLEAR
   IF UPPER(TOWN)=UPPER(MTOWN) ;               ACCEPT "Now please ;
      .AND.  UPPER(ORG)=UPPER(MORG)                     enter an org. ;
      DISP                                             name" TO MORG
      SET HEADING OFF
   ENDIF                                       ←──RETURN
   SKIP
ENDDO
SET HEADING ON
```

PGM10.PRG is our *calling* program; that is, at some logical point in its execution, it transfers control to the program called ACCEPTS(.PRG). This *subprogram* (or submodule, or just plain *module*) will now be responsible for obtaining all the inputs required from the operator and creating the memory variables called MTOWN and MORG. At the end of the execution of the submodule, control is automatically transferred to the instruction after the DO instruction that passed control to the submodule. At that point, we want to erase the screen of all entries and inputs from the operator and start pulling off records that match the operator's requirement. Obviously, both PGM10.PRG and ACCEPTS.PRG must be ready before this little system will function, and PGM10 will have to be invoked (DO PGM10) to get the ball rolling.

This concept of transferring control to subprograms and then receiving control back at the main program is very important to the programmer, since it permits the breakdown of a large complicated system into subsets of logically connected, more manageable subprograms. This makes the system much more comprehensible not only to other programmers but also to the creator of the system. It is very easy to forget the detailed workings of a specific system, if you have been working on several systems.

> **Note:** Please remember the following very important point. The memory variables called MTOWN and MORG were created at the *called program* level, that is, at the subprogram, or *lower*, level in the system hierarchy. Such memory variables are normally released at the end of execution of the subprogram, and are, therefore, not available to any *higher* or calling program! To ensure that the memory variables called MTOWN and MORG are available to the calling program when the subprogram has finished executing, we had to define these variables as being *public* or *global!* Without this PUBLIC declaration, the calling program will abend when control returns to it, for lack of the variables MTOWN and MORG.

The declaration of PUBLIC could have been done at the subprogram level; that is, the ACCEPTS.PRG program could have had the PUBLIC statement in it, and the system would have worked. The rule to be satisfied is that the variables have to be declared PUBLIC before they are created.

Apart from permitting the sharing of PUBLIC variables, the PUBLIC declaration ensures that memory variables remain in memory at the end of the execution of the program(s). This fact serves as an excellent *debugging* tool that can be used to resolve programming errors. (I discuss several debugging options, as a separate topic later on.)

> **Note:** Memory variables created at a higher level in the hierarchy are automatically available to the lower programs, without the necessity of defining these as public! However, when the higher program is through executing, these variables are not available in memory any more. To make these remain behind in memory for debugging purposes, they have to be defined as PUBLIC! A public declaration is the only way of ensuring that memory variables are *global*, that is, available to any program called for execution and remaining in memory for the programmer's inspection.
>
> **Note:** The RETURN statement at the end of the called module is not mandatory. Program control is transferred back to the main module even in the absence of the RETURN statement.

At this point, you may want to review the section on Accepting Numeric Input, to clearly understand the difference in behavior between the ACCEPT and the INPUT commands.

Displaying the Contents of Memory Variables

Let us assume you have run a program with the PUBLIC declaration made for one or more memory variables. The program has ended, and you want to inspect the contents of the variables.

.DISP MEMO   < cr >

The above command will display, on the screen, the name, the type (private or public), and the content of each of the variables currently available in memory. You can define up to 256 memory variables, but within this limitation, there is a further limitation. The total number of bytes (characters) defined for all the variables cannot be more than 6000.

If you want to check the contents of a specific variable, enter:

.? MTOWN   < cr >

The contents of the variable MTOWN will be displayed.

Nested IF Statements

You can have an IF statement *nested* within another IF statement. In this program example, the nesting is highlighted.

```
*  PGM11.PRG - NESTED IF STATEMENTS
*  ----------
SET TALK OFF
CLEAR
USE PERSNL
DO WHILE .NOT. EOF()
    IF UPPER(TOWN) = 'ROCH'
        @ 10,15 SAY 'ROCHESTER'
    ELSE
        IF UPPER(TOWN) = 'WEB'
            @ 10,15 SAY 'WEBSTER'
        ELSE
            IF UPPER(TOWN) = 'FAIR'
                @ 10,15 SAY 'FAIRPORT'
            ELSE
                @ 10,15 SAY 'NEITHER: ROCH/WEB/FAIR'
            ENDIF
        ENDIF
    ENDIF
*     Note that on account of the ENDIF statements, control will pass to
*     the next statement regardless of the outcome of the IF statements.
    WAIT ''
*     As explained in PGM4A, you could have a timing loop here, as opposed
*     to the "permanent wait" command.
    @ 10,15
    SKIP
ENDDO
*                        END  OF  PGM11
```

In the above example, we are checking each record for the town of ROCHESTER, WEBSTER, or FAIRPORT, and are displaying the appropriate literal for the town name. In the event that the TOWN is not ROCHESTER, WEBSTER, or FAIRPORT, we display a message to that effect.

I had emphasized in the past that you must always compare the field name to the memory variable, not the other way around. The same caution holds good here too: always compare a field name to a literal, not the other way around! If you fail to observe this, the outcome will always be a logical FALSE, regardless of the data compared.

You must always have a matching ENDIF statement for any IF statement. To be sure that you do not miss out on this crucial requirement for the successful nesting of IF statements, you would be well-advised to indent your nested IF statements, as shown in the example above. *Indentation* refers to the practice of starting a line of code away from the leftmost column, so that you are able to match the IF . . . ELSE . . . ENDIF statements. (The matching refers to the logical matching of these statements, not to their physical alignment in one straight line.)

There is nothing to prevent you from starting every line of code in your program at the first column. The program will execute correctly, provided you have been able to complement each IF with its matching ENDIF. The indentation approach makes this matching much easier.

The CASE Approach

Instead of using the nested IF approach, you may use the CASE approach in creating the logic of your program.

```
-----
-----
DO CASE
            CASE     UPPER(TOWN) = 'ROCH'  .AND.  UPPER(ORG) = 'BSG'
            -----
*    Now you can write any dBASE commands you want executed  for records
*    satisfying the above condition.
            -----
            -----
            CASE     UPPER(TOWN) = 'ROCH'  .AND.  UPPER(ORG) = 'GSD'
            -----
            -----
*    Now you can write any dBASE commands you want executed  for records
*    satisfying the above condition.
            -----
            -----
ENDCASE
```

During execution, if any of the CASEs is true, the appropriate set of instructions is executed, and then control is passed to the instruction after the ENDCASE statement. This means that if a record qualifies for more than one CASE, only the commands for the *first* CASE that is satisfied are executed; then control drops out of the CASE construction.

You can use the CASE approach, instead of nested IFs, to obtain the same end result as you would with the nested-IF statements.

```
* PGM12.PRG - THE "CASE" APPROACH
* ----------
SET TALK OFF
CLEAR
USE PERSNL
DO WHILE .NOT. EOF()
    DO CASE
        CASE   UPPER(TOWN) = 'ROCH'
               @ 10,15 SAY 'ROCHESTER'
        CASE   UPPER(TOWN) = 'WEB'
               @ 10,15 SAY 'WEBSTER'
        CASE   UPPER(TOWN) = 'FAIR'
               @ 10,15 SAY 'FAIRPORT'
        OTHERWISE
               @ 10,15 SAY 'NEITHER: ROCH/WEB/FAIR'
    ENDCASE
*    Regardless of the outcome of the above "case-studies", control will
*    pass to the next instruction.
    WAIT ''
*    As explained in PGM4A, you could have a timing loop here, as opposed
*    to the "permanent wait" command.
    @ 10,15
    SKIP
 ENDDO
*                        END  OF  PGM12
```

Note the use of the OTHERWISE statement to include all other possibilities. Some folks find it much easier to grasp this method, as opposed to the indented-IF approach. The end result is identical.

Writing Your Own Report Program

If you have understood the preceding topics, we can now go ahead and attempt to write a report. This time, we shall write our own program to generate the report instead of using the built-in reporting feature.

It is interesting to note that while the ability to write your own report programs in dBASE frees you from the built-in REPORT command restraints, you may come to realize, after you have read the next few paragraphs, that the built-in REPORT command is not bad at all, and makes reporting far easier than attempting to write your own report programs.

In any case, the following paragraphs will demonstrate how you could manipulate report formats to obtain just about any format you have in mind. You could then extend this logic to more complex reports.

The program will do the following:

    1. Obtain operator inputs for town and organization.
    2. Display column headings on the screen.
    3. Read every record out of PERSNL. If records match the required town and organization, it will do the following:

        A. Keep count of the number of records that qualify.
        B. Display EMP_NUM, EMP_NAME, DT_OF_HIRE, SALARY.
        C. Ensure that each line follows the previous one (no overlap).
        D. Keep track of salary total.

    4. Print out the total obtained for the salary and the average at the end of the program.

```
* PGM13.PRG - A Report Program
* ---------
SET TALK OFF
CLEAR
PUBLIC MTOWN,MORG,LINECNT
DO ACCEPTS
*      This subprogram will accept operator inputs for TOWN and ORG. Since
*      MTOWN and MORG are defined at the subprogram level, and since they
*      will be subsequently addressed by the calling program, they were
*      defined as PUBLIC in the calling program.
CLEAR
SET DEVICE TO PRINT
*      The above command ensures that the output of all @---SAY commands
*      get sent to the printer.
*      The statement SET PRINT ON (which is the same as a ctrl+P option in
*      dBASE) will only send the output of DISPLAY statements onto the
*      printer. In this report program, we will be responsible for format-
*      ting every requirement of this report on paper, through the @---SAY
*      commands, and so we need the instruction SET DEVICE TO PRINT. Now the
*      output of the @---SAY commands will be sent to the printer.
DO HDR
*      This subprogam will put out main headings and column headings on
*      the printer, and will also initialize a memory variable called
*      LINECNT. In order, therefore, to make LINECNT available to the
```

```
*        calling program, it is defined as PUBLIC in the calling program.
STORE Ø TO TOTSALARY,RECORDCNT
USE PERSNL
DO WHILE .NOT. EOF()
    IF UPPER(TOWN) = UPPER(MTOWN)  .AND.  UPPER(ORG) = UPPER(MORG)
        @ LINECNT,10 SAY EMP_NUM
        @ LINECNT,25 SAY EMP_NAME
        @ LINECNT,43 SAY DT_OF_HIRE
        @ LINECNT,58 SAY SALARY
```

* The **line-number** at which each qualifying record from the file should
* print out must, of course, be made a **variable**, since it has to be
* incremented for each record to be printed out. Hence the use of the
* variable LINECNT. This variable has been initialized in the sub-
* program called "HDR."

* In the subprogram called HDR, the 'EMP-NAME' column header
* has been specified as starting in column 25. The EMP_NAME **data** should
* be made to go in **left-justified** under that column, that is, it should
* also be made to start in column 10. Similar reasoning applies to the
* other character fields defined in the display. For the SALARY field,
* please note that the SALARY heading literal extends from column 60
* through column 65. The SALARY data field, therefore, which is 8
* locations wide, should be made to start in column 58, so as to appear
* **right-justified** under the column heading. Such calculations would
* have to be made, for all numeric data displays.

```
        STORE RECORDCNT+1  TO RECORDCNT
        STORE TOTSALARY + SALARY    TO  TOTSALARY
        STORE LINECNT+1 TO LINECNT
```

* You want to add 1 to record count, keep a running total of salary,
* and increment the line count by 1 (for the next record) **only** if the
* current record under scrutiny meets the conditions specified
* in the IF statement. So these statements are all **within** the
* IF statement.

* At this point, the program has scanned the first record; if it meets
* the condition, this record data has been displayed, and the program
* has incremented the LINECNT field, so the next qualifying record goes
* to the next line on the screen, and the program has added 1 to the
* RECORDCNT field, and has added the SALARY of the qualify-
* ing record to the appropriate memory variable. Now the program has to
* check to see if the linecount on the paper calls for going onto a
* new page.

```
        IF  LINECNT > 55
            DO HDR
```

* If the LINECNT variable has reached the number 56, we will force
* the HDR program to execute, in effect, bringing up a new page, put-
* tout the heading literals again, and initializing the LINECNT variable
* to a fresh value.

```
        ENDIF
    ENDIF
    SKIP
```

* Regardless of whether or not the record qualifies, skip to the next
* record

```
ENDDO
```

* Note the correct pairing off, of the IF-----ENDIF statements.
* At EOF, program control passes to the next statement and prints out
* totals and the average.

```
STORE LINECNT+3 TO LINENT
```

* The above statement ensures that regardless of where the last line

```
*       has printed out, we will leave at least 3 spaces before printing out
*       the summary.
@ LINECNT,10 SAY "SALARY TOTAL:"
@ LINECNT,25 SAY TOTSALARY
STORE LINECNT+1 TO LINECNT
@ LINECNT,10 SAY "TOTAL RECORDS"
@ LINECNT,25 SAY RECORDCNT
STORE LINECNT+1 TO LINECNT
IF RECORDCNT > 0
    @ LINECNT,10 SAY "AVG: SALARY:"
    @ LINECNT,25 SAY (TOTSALARY/RECORDCNT)
ENDIF
*       Note the following point. Some printers will not print out the last
*       line unless another line is sent "to print." So if you leave the
*       program to execute as is, the "average salary" line may not print
*       out. To ensure that the last line prints out, send a blank character
*       to the printer.
@ LINECNT+3,10 SAY ' '
*       We have sent a dummy character to LINECNT+3 (this is called relative
*       addressing). That is, if LINECNT had reached a value of 15 before
*       this instruction was executed, then we are sending the blank charac-
*       ter to line 18, column 10. This will ensure that the required last
*       line will print out.
SET DEVICE TO SCREEN
*       At the end of all report programs where the output is sent to the
*       printer, do not forget to reset the "device" to a screen default,
*       else even after the program ends execution, subsequent @---SAY outputs
*       will continue to go to the printer.
*                           END  OF  PGM13
```

Note: TOTSALARY was initially defined as a memory variable without decimals. However, we have subsequently been adding the SALARY fields into TOTSALARY, and SALARY is defined with two decimals. Now TOTSALARY also has the two decimals defined in its structure.

Note: The memory variable LINECNT should be incremented only if the record matches the required condition, and hence the increment has to be *within* the logic of the IF statement.

The Accepts Program

Note that this is one of the called programs in our three-program system.

```
* ACCEPTS.PRG - CALLED FROM PGM13.PRG
* -----------
ACCEPT "Please enter a town name       "  to   MTOWN
CLEAR
ACCEPT "Now please enter an organisation name   "  to   MORG
RETURN
*                           END  OF  ACCEPTS
```

The HDR Program

Note that this is the second called program in our three-program system.

```
* HDR.PRG - CALLED FROM PGM13.PRG
* -------
EJECT
*      The EJECT statement positions the printer to a new page.
@ 1,01 SAY DATE()
@ 1,28 SAY "REPORT AS OF MARCH 30, 1986."
@ 2,01 SAY TIME()
*      If, for some reason, you find that you have the wrong system date in
*      your computer, you can always run the MS-DOS "DATE" (and/or TIME)
*      command right from the dot-prompt.
*      .RUN   DATE     <CR>
*      The RUN command of dBASE provides the interface with the operating
*      system directly. It is as if you had entered the date command at the
*      C> (MS-DOS prompt) directly. This RUN command can be used for running
*      any other MS-DOS command at the operating system level.
@ 2,28 SAY "----------------------------"
@ 5,10 SAY "EMP-NUMBER"
@ 5,25 SAY "EMP-NAME"
@ 5,43 SAY "DT/HIRE"
@ 5,60 SAY "SALARY"
STORE 8 TO LINECNT
RETURN
*                              END   OF   HDR
```

You may have noticed that while you have the flexibility of writing a report using any format you want, even a simple report program can get to be quite a task. The complexity of such programs increases rapidly if subtotals at more than one level are involved, or vertical formats are required. You would conclude, very correctly, that the built-in report generator feature of dBASE is, after all, quite handy.

Cautions on Printed Reports

For screen displays, you can SAY something at line 10 before you SAY something at line 5. When you are sending the outputs to the printer, however, your lines must be specified in perfect sequence; that is, you must send something to line 3 before you send something to line 5. Also, column positions within lines must be in perfect sequence, without any overlap of columns; that is, you must send something to line 3 column 10 before you send something to line 3 column 20, making sure that the output sent to column 10 is not overwritten with output sent to column 20. Failure to adhere to this rule will cause your printer to play tricks on you.

Perhaps the thought has crossed your mind that you would like to enhance your printer outputs with effects such as boldface type, underscores, compressed print, elongated characters, emphasized print, or customized form length. In the final section of the book, I have provided detailed instructions on exactly how you can obtain these effects and controls.

Positioning and the Use of Masks

Suppose you entered the following lines of code in a program:

```
@ 10,15 SAY 'TOTAL DOLLAR-AMOUNT = '
@ 10,38 SAY DOLLARS
```

The literal 'TOTAL DOLLAR-AMOUNT = ' itself spans the columns 15 through 36, so of course the memory variable called DOLLARS should begin beyond column 36; in this case we have chosen column 38. If the actual data in DOLLARS was the value 100, would this value appear starting in column 38? The answer is NO, since the memory variable itself could be as much as 15-digits wide, depending on how it was created, and the value 100 is right justified within that width. So while the variable would begin in column 38, the number 100 would appear much further away from column 38!

For various reasons, you may prefer to have the actual amount (however small or large it may be) start exactly at the column you had specified in your code; in this case, we want the 100 to appear starting in column 38. You can accomplish this through the use of *masks*.

A mask can be looked upon as a shell that specifies how your data (in this case, numeric data) should be presented as output. Suppose you had modified the two lines of code above slightly, as follows:

```
@ 10,15 SAY 'TOTAL DOLLAR-AMOUNT = '
@ 10,38 SAY DOLLARS PICTURE '999.99'
```

(PICTURE can be abbreviated to PICT).

The mask of '999.99' specifies that digits out of DOLLARS would replace the 9's in the mask. Thus if DOLLARS contained the value 100, then since the mask starts in column 38, the output starting in column 38 would appear as 100.00. Now your literal and numeric data are in close proximity, as intended. The following table summarizes the results obtained using different combinations of data and masks:

Input Data	PICT <mask>	Output Result
1	999.99	1.00
12	999.99	12.00
1	.99	.00
12.34	99999	12
12.34	9,999.99	12.34
12.34	***9.99	**12.34
12.34	*,**9.99	***12.34
12.34	**,*99.99	****12.34
12.34	***99.99	***12.34
12.34	$999.99	$ 12.34
12.34	***.**	*12.34
12.34	$$$.$$	$12.34
12.34	*,***.**	***12.34
-123.45	9999.99	-123.45
-123.45	999.99	123.45
-123.45	$999.99	-123.45
-123.45	$$999.99	$-123.45
123.45	-999.99	-123.45

You should be aware of the following information about the use of masks:

```
```

1. The mask should be at least as large as the expected number of digits to be accommodated.

2. The system aligns the decimal point in the data (actual or implied) with the decimal point provided in the mask, if any.

3. The mask will start at the column location specified by you; it should not, of course, overlay any columns containing literals or other data masks.

4. The minus sign in a data field behaves just like any other digit.

5. The above table also portrays the handling of numeric results obtained through computation, rather than from an existing field or memory variable. That is, the command:

@ 10,38 say (TOT_DOLLAR / REC_COUNT) PICT '999.99'

would produce results similar to those shown in the table above.

6. You can even specify special functions when defining masks. These mask functions are recognized by dBASE if you start off the mask with the @ character. I have shown examples with a column-definition line, so you can appreciate the differences in the outputs.

Input Data		PICT <mask>	Output Result
			1----+----2----+----3----+----4----+
A.	-123.45	@(	(123.45)
B.	123.45	@(	123.45
C.	-123.45	@X	123.45 DB
D.	123.45	@X	123.45
E.	-123.45	@C	-123.45
F.	-123.45	@B	-123.45
G.	-123.45	@BX	123.45 DB
H.	-123.45	@BX(	(123.45)
I.	-123.45	@B(X	123.45 DB
J.	-123.45	@XC	123.45 DB
K.	123.45	@XC	123.45 CR

In the above table, the @ symbol specifies the beginning of a function. The (symbol will place a negative number in parentheses, leaving a positive number unchanged. The X symbol will produce a DB (debit) symbol after a negative number, but will leave the positive numbers unchanged. The C symbol will produce a CR (credit) symbol after positive numbers only. The B symbol will left justify the number. The BX combination will left justify and produce the DB symbol.

Take note of example H. I have specified left justification, the DB symbol, and the parenthesis, in that order. Since DB and parenthesis both apply to negative values, the parentheses, mentioned last, have overridden the request for the DB symbol. In example I, I have asked for left justification, parentheses, and the DB symbol, in that order. Therefore I got the left justification and the DB symbol.

Note examples J and K. The XC combination automatically produces a DB symbol for negative values and a CR symbol for positive values.

The use of masks will help you enhance your outputs, both in your report programs and in your screen layouts designs (to be covered later).

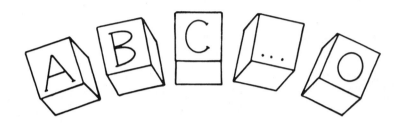

10. Writing Menu-Driven Systems

S o far we have written stand-alone programs that are not part of a system. We can now go to program a more functional *menu-driven* system. The concepts presented so far have paved the way for this end result, the all-important menu system, which provides for the user-friendliness mandated in all application systems. Let me explain the way a menu system works.

When the menu program is invoked, it first displays a *menu* on the screen, providing the operator with several functional alternatives, from which the operator chooses one function to perform. That choice results in the execution of a program *called* by the menu program. At the end of the chosen function, the menu screen comes up again, asking the operator for another choice of function. This process goes on until the operator chooses the option that will cause dBASE to exit from the menu loop.

In our pursuit of menu-driven systems, we shall make use of another database, called the INVENTRY database. The format of our fictional inventory file will be as follows, for the duration of the menu-system description:

PART,C,6   COST,N,8,2   SELLPRICE,N,8,2

ONHAND,N,3   ONORDER,N,3   USAGE,N,2   LEAD,N,2

Most of the fields are self-explanatory; USAGE refers to the estimated daily usage or consumption of the item, and LEAD refers to the lead time in days required between ordering new supplies and receiving them in stock.

THE MENU SHELL

Throughout this menu system, I have used comment statements to explain the working of groups of instructions. The same sequence used earlier will be followed here. First you are given a few lines of code, then you are provided an explanation of those lines of code. This sequence has been followed for all the programs that make up the menu system.

```
* MENU.PRG - INVENTORY CONTROL MENU.
* ---------
CLEAR ALL
SET TALK OFF
SET BELL OFF
SET DELE ON
*       "CLEAR ALL" will close all files, clear out all memory variables,
*       etc. That is, you start out with a clean slate. "SET TALK OFF" will
*       ensure that no extraneous verbiage comes out of dBASE during
*       the execution of programs. "SET BELL OFF" ensures that we will
*       not hear the 'beep' on each field entry/edit operation. "SET DELE
*       ON" ensures that deleted records will be ignored by the all-
*       important FIND command against any indexed file in this system.
*       By placing these "housekeeping" instructions in the menu shell,
*       we ensure that these don't need to be specified in any of the
*       sub programs of the system.
*       Please understand clearly that if there are any PUBLIC declarations
*       to be made, these should be made after any CLEAR ALL statements.
STORE ' ' TO ERRMSG
*       Define a memory variable to hold error messages, in case the operator
*       enters an option that is not in the menu. Note that the length of
*       the variable defined is one character.
DO WHILE .T.
*       Please note this instruction. It attempts to DO <something> WHILE
*       "TRUE". Since .T. (logical TRUE) will always be "TRUE", this type of
*       DO WHILE specifies the beginning of an infinite loop !
    CLEAR
    ?? DATE()
    ?? "                    INVENTORY CONTROL MENU"
    ? "                    -----------------------"
*       "CLEAR" will clear the screen, since each time the menu program
*       receives control back from a subprogram, it should send the
*       menu onto a clean screen.
*       The way the ? command executes is as follows: First, the cursor moves
*       to the next line on the screen, and then whatever follows the ? shows
*       up on the screen. (This is provided you have not SET PRINT ON.  With
*       SET PRINT ON, first the carriage-mechanism of the printer moves to
*       the next line, and then whatever follows the ? gets sent to the
*       printer.) The output of the ? command could be literals, field-
*       names, memory variables, or expressions.  The ? can be read as:
*       "What is......".
*       The ?? command works the same way, but without a carriage-return-
*       line-feed sequence to trigger if off !  That means, that whatever
*       follows the ?? gets sent up on the screen or the printer at the cur-
*       rent position of the cursor or printer carriage.
*       So the above commands will work as follows: The screen gets cleared,
*       the date and the main heading appear on the "first" line of the
*       screen, and the underscores come up below the main header.
```

274

TEXT

* The TEXT command identifies the start of text that has to be shown
* on the screen **as is** ! This means that you can now define the menu-
* screen layout exactly as you would want it to appear when invoked.

```
A  -  LIST     items of inventory below a stated level
B  -  LIST     items of inventory in danger of run-out
C  -  FULL     inventory report
D  -  ADD      more records into the inventory file
E  -  ADD      more records - with duplicates-check
F  -  EDIT     sequentially - no changes to key-field
G  -  EDIT     sequentially - with duplicates check
H  -  EDIT     randomly on record-numbers - with duplicates check
I  -  EDIT     randomly on part-numbers - with duplicates check
J  -  DELETE   randomly on record-numbers
K  -  DELETE   randomly on part-numbers
L  -  SCAN     sequentially on record-numbers
M  -  SCAN     sequentially on part-numbers
N  -  REMOVE   (delete) duplicate records from inventory file
O  -  EXIT     from this menu
```

ENDTEXT

* The ENDTEXT command identifies the end of the text. That is, we
* are informing dBASE that what follows once again are normal commands.

```
?
?
?  '                    '+ERRMSG
?
```

* After the menu text, the program leaves a couple of blank lines,
* then puts out the contents of the variable called ERRMSG. Obviously,
* the first time around, this variable is "blank," so the operator will
* see nothing on the screen, but should an error have been committed,
* the subsequent appearance of the menu will contain the error message.
* Note the concatenation of a few blanks, before the ERRMSG memory
* variable, to position the error message to the center of the screen.

WAIT '   Option ? ' TO ACTION

* This will cause the program to go into a wait state, with the
* "Option ? " message on the screen. Now the **single character** that the
* operator enters in response to the request automatically releases the
* wait. This character is then placed into a **character** memory vari-
* able called ACTION. The program should now go ahead and check the
* entry made by the operator, that is, check the contents of ACTION.
* Note that the leading spaces before the word "Option ?" only serve
* to move that literal towards the center of the screen, under the
* body of the menu.
* It should be noted that you may name the memory variable anything you
* like. You could have said   **WAIT TO ETERNITY**   and then a character
* memory variable called ETERNITY would have been created. The program
* would then have to check the contents of the variable called
* ETERNITY.

STORE ' ' TO ERRMSG

* As a good programming guideline, whenever an operator entry has been
* accepted, you must always initialize all error messages, so that, if
* an error is repeated, the subsequent lines of code will detect the
* error(s) and reactivate the error message(s). If you don't clean up
* the error-message variable, then in the event the operator makes an
* error the first time around, then makes a valid choice the second
* time around, when the menu comes back up to the screen the third
* time, the error message, which is still hanging around in the memory
* variable, will show up on the screen !

* Our program will now check the entry placed in the mem-var called
* ACTION. In essence, we have to check to see if any entry between the
* letters A through O has been made, and if so, either transfer control
* to the appropriate program, or cancel the execution of the menu
* program, as the case may be.

* Since we cannot presume that the operator will always enter UPPER
* case letters in response to the menu, we will have to accept either
* upper or lowercase letters. Hence the use of the UPPERcase
* function, in the next few statements.
* **Checking the results of operator action - lengthy process.**
* We will first look at the lengthy, but easier to understand, approach
* to testing the contents of ACTION, and at a later, more appropriate
* place in the book, we shall study **one** IF-statement that can produce
* the same result.

```
IF UPPER(ACTION) = 'A'
    DO PGMA
ENDIF
```

* PGMA is a sub program (module) that has been programmed to do what
* option "A" in the menu suggests. Similar programming will be required
* of the other sub modules, to come up with a fully working system.

```
IF UPPER(ACTION) = 'B'
    DO PGMB
ENDIF
IF UPPER(ACTION) = 'C'
    DO PGMC
ENDIF
IF UPPER(ACTION) = 'D'
    DO PGMD
ENDIF
IF UPPER(ACTION) = 'E'
    DO PGME
ENDIF
IF UPPER(ACTION) = 'F'
    DO PGMF
ENDIF
IF UPPER(ACTION) = 'G'
    DO PGMG
ENDIF
IF UPPER(ACTION) = 'H'
    DO PGMH
ENDIF
IF UPPER(ACTION) = 'I'
    DO PGMI
ENDIF
IF UPPER(ACTION) = 'J'
    DO PGMJ
ENDIF
IF UPPER(ACTION) = 'K'
    DO PGMK
ENDIF
IF UPPER(ACTION) = 'L'
    DO PGML
ENDIF
IF UPPER(ACTION) = 'M'
    DO PGMM
ENDIF
IF UPPER(ACTION) = 'N'
```

```
          DO PGMN
     ENDIF
     IF UPPER(ACTION) = 'O'
          RETURN
     ENDIF
     IF ACTION < 'A'    .OR.   UPPER(ACTION) > 'O'
          STORE 'INVALID !!      RE-ENTER, OR EXIT !' TO ERRMSG
          ? CHR(7)
     ENDIF
ENDDO
*     The ENDDO statement signifies the end of the DO WHILE .T. infinite
*     loop.
*     Note once again that the syntax of  IF .... ENDIF  has been
*     maintained.
*               E N D   O F   M E N U   P R O G R A M
```

Let us suppose that the operator chooses option A, so PGMA is to be executed. At the end of its execution, program control transfers back to the menu program, to the very next instruction. Now, of course, if the ACTION was A, it was not B or C or D . . . or O, and it wasn't either less than A (numbers would qualify) or greater than O, so once again control passes through to the end of the loop, and the menu comes up, asking for the next operator action.

If the operator selected option O, the RETURN command would return program control back to the native dBASE mode; that is, to the dot prompt.

Note also that if the operator makes a choice other than what has been requested in the menu screen (which is quite likely), then the only IF statement that will be true is the one in which we check for an operator entry less than the letter A (numbers would qualify) or for an entry greater than the letter O. In this case an error message is placed into the memory variable called ERRMSG (as you know, the menu provides for displaying ERRMSG on the screen), there is a beep, and once again the menu screen comes up, this time with the error message displayed. The statement ? (CHR(7) produces the 'beep' at the console.

Since the loop has been set up as an infinite loop, the set of commands within the loop will execute indefinitely. That is, after the execution of any function chosen by the operator, program control will again force the screen to be CLEARed and the menu screen to come up. The only way out of this loop is for the operator to enter an O to exit from the menu back to the dot prompt.

You may have noticed that in our menu program we are providing for a lengthy error message, and yet in the same program, we use only one blank to blank out the ERRMSG memory variable. If we use memory variables to store different types of messages, we don't have to define it with an exact length. When our memory variable has to be blanked out, it hardly matters to us whether it is a one-character blank or a hundred-character blank; hence we can use only one blank to clean up the ERRMSG memory variable. You may, subsequently, store a lengthy message into the same memory variable that had been initialized with just one space. In effect, you keep redefining the same memory variable to different lengths.

Memory variables need to have exact predefined lengths only when they will be

277

used for replacing values in data fields of any file in use. In that case their lengths must tally with those of the data fields they will be replacing (more on this, later).

> **Note:** When the menu program is initiated, it first CLEARs ALL memory variables, to start with a clean slate. Since memory variables defined in the higher level (calling) program are accessible across lower level (called) programs, it is essential that none of the submodules should contain the CLEAR ALL command; otherwise the memory variable called ACTION would no longer exist after the execution of the very first submodule, and as soon as program control was transferred back to the next IF statement in the menu program, your system would *crash*, for lack of the memory variable called ACTION. This is true only because of the way we have written the IF statements in our program. We have several individual IF statements checking the result of ACTION. If we had written a nested IF statement, or had taken the CASE approach in checking out the results in ACTION, the above paragraph would not hold true.

The CASE Approach

We will see a slightly different way of writing our menu program using the CASE approach. As I said before, programming is an art, not a science, and there are many ways of achieving the same end result.

When any valid option is selected, control passes to the appropriate subprogram.

```
. . . . . . . . . . . . . . .
. . . . . . . . . . . . . . .
*       The leading statements are the same as we have seen before, up
*       through the WAIT statement.
*       The following DO CASE.....ENDCASE combination replaces the many
*       strings of IF.....ELSE.....ENDIF combinations seen earlier.
    STORE ' ' TO ERRMSG
    DO CASE
        CASE      UPPER(ACTION) = 'A'
                  DO PGMA
        CASE      UPPER(ACTION) = 'B'
                  DO PGMB
        CASE      UPPER(ACTION) = 'C'
                  DO PGMC
*   Repeat the identical format of commands, for all the other options
*   D through N.
        CASE      UPPER(ACTION) = 'O'
                  RETURN
        OTHERWISE
                  STORE 'INVALID !!      RE-ENTER, OR EXIT !' TO ERRMSG
                  ? CHR(7)
    ENDCASE
ENDDO
*                       END  OF  CASE  APPROACH
```

When the subprogram has completed execution, control is transferred back, at which point it drops out of the case study and back into the loop. That is, the menu program comes up again, asking the operator for another selection.

> **Note:** This menu example is obviously an overkill, since in any real-world situation, you would not have such an extravagant combination of functions for any system. You would pick and choose the options you want to provide for your user. However, since my objective here is to highlight the power of programming in dBASE, I have elected to present all of the above programs.

As promised earlier, I would now like to show you the one IF statement that can check the operator's entry, as opposed to several IF statements, one for each option in the menu. However, before I can do this, we have to ensure that you have a good understanding of *macros*.

Understanding Macros

A macro is a shorthand notation for specifying an entire instruction, a command out of an instruction, or a parameter of the instruction. For example, at the dBASE dot prompt, you could enter the following instruction:

.STORE "REPLACE ALL TOWN WITH 'ROCH' FOR ORG = 'BSG' " TO REPL

<cr>

> **Note:** Double quotes were required, since the literal itself has single quotes embedded in it.

The above instruction will place a long literal into a character memory variable called REPL. This long literal also happens to resemble a dBASE command! Now at the dot prompt, suppose you type in the following:

.&REPL   <cr>

dBASE will recognize the &REPL as being a macro instruction, and will interpret this to be our lazy way of saying, "Please execute the long instruction in the REPL memory variable." The effect of the &REPL command would be as though you had typed, at the dot prompt, the entire REPLACE command.

This means you can STORE a command once and have it executed several times simply by using the macro version of the command.

> **Note:** All macros are *character* memory variables only!

The macros can be used for parameters, too, and are not limited to entire commands; for example:

.STORE "FOR ORG = 'BSG' .OR. ORG = 'GSD' " TO COND <cr>

stores the literal in the character memory variable called COND. If you now enter:

.REPLACE ALL TOWN WITH 'ROCH' *&COND*   <cr>

This has the same effect as if you have typed out:

.REPLACE ALL TOWN WITH 'ROCH' FOR ORG = 'BSG' .OR. ORG = 'GSD'
                                                          <cr>

The important point to understand is that, depending on where in a statement the macro has been specified, it will be interpreted as being either an entire command or merely a parameter of a command. During execution, dBASE simply expands the statement containing the macro with the contents of the variable and tries to execute the resultant command. This feature is very handy, since it lets you make use of variables entered by an operator during the execution of a program. For example, in a program, we have the following instructions:

CLEAR

ACCEPT "Which master-file do you want to use?" TO F

USE &F

During execution of the program, the operator's response for the filename enters the character memory variable called F, and the program will then use the contents of F, to bring the appropriate file into USE. In this case again, the &F has been used as a macro, this time as a parameter, rather than as an entire command.

To highlight the use of a macro, let us take this extreme example:

.STORE 'USE' TO M1   <cr>
.STORE 'PERSNL' TO M2   <cr>
.STORE 'DISP' TO M3   <cr>
.STORE 'FOR' TO M4   <cr>
.STORE "TOWN = 'ROCH' " TO M5   <cr>

Now you can use the macros alone, as follows:

.&M1 &M2   <cr> (Use PERSNL)

.&M3 &M4 &M5   <cr> (DISP FOR TOWN = 'ROCH')

You may recall that in the section on reporting, we made use of macros to place variable dates in the auxiliary heading of reports.

Using Macros: The Menu Program Revisited

We will now attempt to use the shorthand method of checking for operator action. Note that the leading statements are the same as before, up through the WAIT statement.

```
        . . . . . . . . . . . . .
        . . . . . . . . . . . . .
        . . . . . . . . . . . . .
    STORE ' ' TO ERRMSG
    IF UPPER(ACTION) = 'O'
       RETURN
    ENDIF
*       The check for exiting from the menu should be made as usual.
    IF UPPER(ACTION)   $('ABCDEFGHIJKLMN')           . . . . . . . . .(A)
          STORE 'PGM' + UPPER(ACTION)   TO   CHOICE . . . . . . . . .(B)
          DO  &CHOICE                                 . . . . . . . .(C)
    ELSE
          STORE 'INVALID !!       REENTER, OR EXIT !' TO ERRMSG
          ? CHR(7)
    ENDIF
ENDDO
```

The statement at (A) says, "If the uppercase version of the value in ACTION is to be found anywhere in the string ABCDEFGHIJKLMN" . . .

The statement at (B) says, "Store the literal PGM immediately followed by the uppercase version of the result of ACTION, to a memory variable called CHOICE." Thus, if the operator chooses the option A, "PGMA" would be stored in the memory variable CHOICE. If the operator chooses the option G, "PGMG" would be stored in CHOICE, and so on.

The statement at (C) is, of course, our *macro*! As you can see, if the operator option is A, the statement at (C) becomes DO PGMA, and if the option made was H, the statement at (C) becomes DO PGMH, and so on. This is much more effective than typing out the multiple IF statements or the multiple CASE statements.

We will now go ahead and complete the rest of the programs for the system.

PROGRAM A

Program A produces a report of items with an on-hand balance below a stated level. This module has to identify items of inventory with an ONHAND balance below the level specified by the operator. Since the menu itself should not be cluttered up with these subsequent types of operator inputs, the A module itself should be made to display a miniscreen that asks the operator to identify the level of inventory below which items should be included in a report. Hence PgmA.PRG should be created as follows:

```
* PGMA.PRG - REPORT ITEMS WITH ONHAND BELOW STATED LEVEL
* --------
CLEAR
@ 01,01 SAY DATE()
```

```
@ 01,21 SAY 'REPORT OF INVENTORY BELOW A STATED LEVEL'
@ 07,01 SAY "Enter inventory level for which status is required"
@ 10,20 SAY 'Touch  <CR>, to exit......'
*        The above statements will clear the screen, put out the date
*        and the heading literal, and ask the operator to enter the
*        inventory level for which a status is required.
*        The statement at line 10 provides an escape route from this
*        option, in case the operator decides not to go ahead with the
*        report. Note that all subprograms should provide some kind of
*        escape mechanism permitting the operator to discontinue.
STORE 0 TO LEVEL
@ 18,20 SAY 'Your entry:  ' GET LEVEL PICT '999'
READ
IF LEVEL = 0
    RETURN
ENDIF
*        The program initializes a memory variable called LEVEL.
*        The @---SAY---GET---READ combination of commands has been explained
*        at great length just a little further along in the book. For now, let
*        me explain that the literal "Your entry:   " at line 18 comes up to
*        the screen, and dBASE waits for you to make an entry. Your entry will
*        now be accepted into the memory variable called LEVEL.
*        Notice that the PICT clause limits the operator's data entry to
*        numbers only. The first item the program has to check is whether the
*        operator took the escape route. So we check if the value in
*        the variable is still set at zero. If so, we return to the
*        calling program (the main menu). If the operator did not escape,
*        then program control will continue as follows:
CLEAR
USE INVENTRY INDEX PARTINDX
REPORT FORM RPTA FOR ONHAND < LEVEL     [TO PRINT]
WAIT
RETURN
*        The program will again clear the screen (you should always clear
*        the screen after obtaining operator inputs), and use the inventory
*        file to pull off the appropriate report for the condition that
*        ONHAND is less than the LEVEL requested by the operator.
*                          END OF PGMA
```

The INVENTORY file may or may not be indexed, depending on the required report format. Note that after the report has been generated on the screen, you want to say WAIT; otherwise the end of the report will be followed immediately by the menu screen's being displayed again, as soon as control is transferred back to the menu program. Of course, if the report is being sent TO PRINT, then you should not have the WAIT statement.

You have to generate the appropriate *report format* file, before this section of the system has been completed. Report formats have been covered in great detail earlier, I refer you to Chapter 7 for review, if necessary. The format and content of the report depend entirely on the requirements of the user of the system.

The Concept of a NULL Variable

I want to introduce the concept of a *null* variable, so I will present a different way of writing program A.

```
* PGMA.PRG  -   ANOTHER METHOD.
* --------
CLEAR
?? DATE()
?? '                   REPORT OF INVENTORY BELOW A STATED LEVEL'
?
?
?
? 'What is the minimum inventory level for the status report '
?
? '                      Touch  <CR>,  to  exit.....'
?
?
*       Put out the date and the heading literal on the first line of the
*       screen, leave a few more blank lines for visual effect, and ask
*       the operator for the minimum inventory level. Provide instructions
*       for an escape. The extra spacing is only for visual impact. You could
*       have used the @---SAY statements up to this point.
ACCEPT '                        Your entry  ? '  TO LEVEL
*       The ACCEPT statement will put out the question on the screen and
*       wait for the operator's response, which will be placed in the
*       character memory variable called LEVEL. However, if the operator
*       decides to touch <CR> and escape from this option, the length
*       of the variable generated will be zero (a null variable).
IF LEN(LEVEL) = Ø
   RETURN
ENDIF
*       Note the use of the LEN function. If the operator touches <CR> to
*       escape, then program control will return to the main menu, else
*       program control will reach the next statement.
IF LEVEL < 'Ø' .OR. LEVEL > '9'
   RETURN
ENDIF
*       Since the ACCEPT command will also accept character input, we have
*       to ensure that the operator did not enter any characters other than
*       the numbers in the range of Ø through 9. Only if a valid number is
*       entered will program control proceed with the next instruction.
*       Notice that the numbers 'Ø' and '9' are actually treated as
*       character data,  since the ACCEPT command only creates a character
*       variable.
CLEAR
USE INVENTRY INDEX PARTINDX
REPORT FORM RPTA FOR ONHAND < VAL(LEVEL)       [TO PRINT]
WAIT
*       Note the VAL function, since LEVEL is a character variable.
*       The WAIT is not necessary if you are printing the report.
RETURN
*                       END OF PGMA
```

Using Macros: Program A Revisited

In this enhancement, we use our knowledge of macros, to enter a special header in the report.

```
* PGMA.PRG  -  Enhanced with special header
* --------
```

283

```
CLEAR
@ 01,01 SAY DATE()
@ 01,21 SAY 'REPORT OF INVENTORY BELOW A STATED LEVEL'
@ 07,01 SAY "Enter inventory-level for which status is required"
@ 10,20 SAY 'Touch  <CR>, to exit......'
STORE 0 TO LEVEL
@ 18,20 SAY 'Your entry:  ' GET LEVEL PICT '999'
READ
IF LEVEL = 0
   RETURN
ENDIF
STORE STR(LEVEL,3) TO LEVEL
CLEAR
USE INVENTRY INDEX PARTINDX
REPORT FORM RPTA FOR ONHAND < VAL(LEVEL) ;
       HEADING "REPORT FOR ONHAND LESS THAN &LEVEL"   [TO PRINT]
WAIT
RETURN
```

The above program is identical to what we have seen before, with one exception. We have converted the numeric memory variable LEVEL into a character memory variable. The STR(LEVEL,3) corresponds to the fact that the operator cannot enter more than a three-digit number for the level. When the report is requested, we have provided for a special header line that reports on the level requested by the operator! Note the use of the macro &LEVEL in the special header line. Note also the use of the VAL function, since LEVEL is now a character variable.

PROGRAM B

Program B produces a report of items in danger of a stock run-out. In this option, the PGMB program must pull off, in another report format, all those items of inventory for which a stock run-out is imminent. As you may appreciate, such timely reports are absolutely crucial for successful management of any business enterprise. Examine the following formula:

ONHAND is less than DAILY__USAGE   * LEAD__TIME

(50)   (5)   (14)

If you had 50 pieces of an item in stock, and your average daily usage is 5 pieces, you know that at most you have 10 days worth of stock on hand. Now if it takes 14 days, from when you request new supplies to when you get them in stock, then you know that you are already in trouble for that item.

Obviously, management needs to be informed of the potential for this kind of unwelcome situation before it presents itself. We need to be able to come up with a formula that will flag an item for action, providing us with enough days of leeway during which an order for fresh supplies could be placed with the supplier, and also providing us with enough days for the item to be received in stock. Let us check out the following formula:

ONHAND is equal to or less than

$$DAILY\_USAGE \quad * \quad (LEAD\text{-}TIME \quad + \quad (Internal\ Processing))$$

$$\longleftarrow\text{leeway}\longrightarrow$$

Let us suppose, for now, that for any particular item, the DAILY__USAGE quantity fluctuates very slightly from day to day (or month to month), and can be considered to be constant. Suppose we had the following situation, for an item:

DAILY__USAGE = 10 units,   LEAD-TIME = 20 days,   IP = 10 days

From the above formula it follows that if the ONHAND value for this item falls to a level equal to, or below, 300, our program (to be provided later) will flag this item for action. For this particular item, we now have 10 days of *leeway*, during which an order for fresh supplies should be initiated.

Out presumption is that a report request containing the above formula is run daily. Now if an item is not flagged today, but the item is flagged on the report tomorrow, you now have 10 days in hand, during which to initiate orders for more supplies.

Please understand clearly that it is not my intention to provide a complete formula for this type of inventory control. Indeed, I am not qualified to provide such a formula. Even at first glance you realize that the quantity-on-order will have to be taken into account in this formula. The intent here, however, is to show you how you could use dBASE to provide for inventory control, presuming that you have access to some foolproof formula.

Obviously, different items would require different amounts of leeway days for internal processing, and the inventory master file could contain this factor as one more field of information for each item in inventory.

Program B should have the following lines of code:

```
* PGMB.PRG - REPORT INVENTORY ITEMS IN DANGER OF STOCK RUN-OUT
* --------
CLEAR
USE INVNTRY       [INDEX.....]
REPORT FORM RPTB FOR ONHAND <= USAGE * (LEAD+(IP))    [TO PRINT]
*       IP stands for "internal processing" days, and could be one more field
*       in the structure of the file. In place of the variable value IP, you
*       could go with a fixed value, say 10 or 15.
WAIT
RETURN
*                         END  OF  PGMB
```

Again, report form RPTB(.FRM) should be prepared before this section of the system can be complete. The report format should be designed to provide, among other things, the maximum amount of leeway days provided for the item, so the user can expedite processing accordingly. You may, of course, also send this report TO PRINT, in which case you don't need the WAIT statement in the program.

PROGRAM C

Program C produces a full inventory report. The only code lines you need to use are shown below:

```
* PGMC.PRG  -  PROVIDE FULL INVENTORY REPORT
* --------
CLEAR
USE INVNTRY     [INDEX.....]
REPORT FORM RPTC    [TO PRINT]
WAIT
RETURN
```

RPTC.FRM must be prepared, for this section of the system to execute successfully.

The other options D through N defined in our menu system (D through N) will be covered a little later, after we learn to generate our own screen formats.

GENERATING SCREEN FORMATS

Learning the use of the ACCEPT and INPUT commands helped in obtaining low-volume input from the operator during execution of a program. Menu-driven systems will go a long way towards establishing a complete dBASE system. But we will now enhance our programming capability by learning to write our own full-screen layouts. These full-screen layouts help in obtaining high-volume inputs from the operator, and these inputs can be edited and verified for accuracy, before they are accepted as parts of new or changed records of information.

As an example of where we may want to use our own formats, recall the way the APPEND command displays the blank structure of any file in use and allows you to enter data. Each record is then automatically added into the database.

If you want to display only a restricted structure, instead of the entire structure, you would have to design your own screen format, accept the data entered by the operator, and then proceed to produce a new record of information in the master file. If you want to display your own format and then edit the data keyed in by the operator (which the APPEND command, as it stands, does not let you do), then, again, you would have to design your own format and logic to edit the data. An example of a formatted screen is as follows:

```
03-10-86        INVENTORY SYSTEM DATA-ENTRY SCREEN.
                ------------------------------------

ENTER THE FOLLOWING PIECES OF REQUIRED INFORMATION:
--------------------------------------------------------

PART-NUMBER:         :
COST        :        :
SELLPRICE   :    :
ONHAND      :    :
ONORDER     :    :
USAGE       :  :
LEAD        :  :

             Leave part-number field blank, and ctrl-W, to exit.
```

The screen layout has to be described and then saved in a file called a screen-format file. This is just like the report-format description, which has to be saved in a report format file. The name of the screen-format file will end in .FMT. The screen format file is to be built using the @ . . . SAY . . . GET group of commands. Before we proceed with the generation of screen formats, a complete understanding of this group of commands is essential.

Understanding the @- - - SAY- - - GET Command

The general format of the @- - - SAY- - - GET command is:

```
@     <coords>     SAY           field-name from a file in use    or
                                 memory-variable                  or
                                 literal                          or
                                 expression                       or
                                 function

                   PICT          <output edit-mask>

                                 (to the screen or the printer)
```

and/or

```
                   GET           field-name                       or
                                 memory-variable

                   PICT          <output/input    edit-mask>

                                 (to    /from     the screen.)

                   RANGE         <exp.>, <exp.> [CLEAR]
```

The coordinates refer either to screen coordinates (default) or to printer coordinates and are always in the format line,column. That is, @ 10,15 refers to the 11th line and the 16th column on the screen or on the printer. When you first invoke dBASE, the default of one of the SET commands is SET DEVICE TO SCREEN. So by default, the coordinates refer to screen coordinates, and all the outputs of the @ • • • say commands are displayed on the screen.

Example 1.

```
@ 10,15 SAY 'TOTAL SALARY = '
@ 10,30 SAY TOTSAL PICT '99999.99'
```

Assume that you have kept .SET DEVICE TO SCREEN intact and that you have a memory variable called TOTSAL. The two statements above will display the literal 'TOTAL SALARY = ' at line 11 column 16 and then display the contents of the memory variable TOTSAL next to the literal. The mask, as we have seen before, helps to establish the proper positioning of the numeric value. (See "Positioning and the Use of Masks" in Chapter 9 if necessary.)

Example 2.

```
USE PERSNL
@ 10,10 SAY 'The employee name from the first record is'
@ 10,53 SAY EMP_NAME
```

In this example, we have used the SAY command to display a literal and a field name from the record in use.

Example 3.

```
USE PERSNL
@ 10,10 SAY 'THE CURRENT SALARY IS $'
@ 10,41 SAY SALARY PICT '99999.99'
@ 12,10 SAY 'THE INCREMENTED SALARY WILL BE '
@ 12,41 SAY SALARY * 1.1 PICT '99999.99'
```

In this example, we have used the SAY to display literals, a field name, and an expression.

Example 4.

The two examples above could be handled slightly better, as follows:

```
USE PERSNL
@ 10,10 SAY 'The employee name from the first record is ' + EMP_NAME
```

In this case, we have displayed a concatenation of two character strings, one a literal and the other a character field from the record in use.

```
@ 10,10 SAY 'The current salary is          $' + STR(SALARY,8,2)
@ 12,10 SAY 'The incremented salary will be  $  + STR(SALARY*1.1,8,2)
```

In these examples, we have displayed a concatenation of character strings (literals) and numerics, with the numerics strung as characters. If you recall, only character strings can be concatenated.

Example 5.

```
@ 01,01 SAY DATE ( )
@ 02,01 SAY TIME ( )
```

In every system I write, I make it a point to display the current date on every screen, so the user is always aware of the date that the application is using. Many applications are date dependent for many functions, such as the creation of an aged accounts-receivable report.

As you can appreciate, there are quite a few ways of SAYing different items to the screen (or printer). It is important to understand that outputs to the screen can be displayed in any order. For example, you may SAY something at line 15 before you SAY something at line 10. Outputs to the printer, however, must be sent in order; otherwise a page eject will take place between your SAY commands. For example, if you have SET DEVICE TO PRINT and you SAY something at line 10, and then you SAY something at line 5, dBASE will presume that you want line 5 on a new page, since the printer is already positioned beyond line 5 on the current page. The same caution applies to column specifications when you have SET DEVICE TO PRINT. In other words, you should SAY something at line 10 column 15 before you say something at line 10 column 50. Also, the output at column 50 must not overlap whatever has been put out at column 15! Failure to adhere to this caution will cause your printer carriage mechanism to play some tricks on you.

Example 6.

```
STORE '               ' TO MNAME
```

An easier way to writing the above statement is:

```
STORE SPACE(20) TO MNAME
```

Either of the above statements will define a memory variable called MNAME that is 20 characters in length.

```
@  10,15  SAY  'ENTER  YOUR  NAME  '  GET  MNAME  PICT
'XXXXXXXXXXXXXXXXXXXX'
READ
```

The two statements above will SAY, to the screen, the literal as specified, and will GET, to the screen, the contents of the memory variable called MNAME. This variable, of course, contains blanks, so the operator will see only blanks after the literal. Now the READ command causes the system to wait for the operator's response, and whatever the response, the system will now GET (READ it) again from the screen and place it into the memory variable.

Conceptually, you can understand the workings of the GET and READ statements as follows:

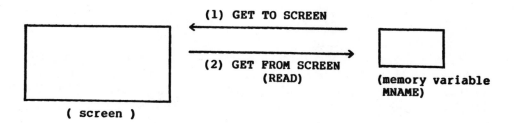

First a GET to the screen takes place. Then, when the operator has made an entry on the screen, a GET from the screen takes place. Please understand that the GET statement, by itself, only gets the memory variable to the screen. The READ statement causes a wait, so the system will wait for your entry and then get (or read) your entry from the screen back into the memory variable.

In summary, GET will *get to the screen*, the contents of the specified item (in this case, the memory variable). GET/READ will *get your response from the screen* into the same item (the memory variable).

If the item in question had been a field name from a file in use, and not a memory variable, the GET/READ combination would GET the contents of the field to the screen, and READ the operator's entry back into the same field. This is the basis of editing existing data.

Please understand the importance of the READ statement. If you only had the GET statement without the READ, dBASE will do step (1) but not step (2) in the conceptual diagram above. That is, it will GET the contents of the memory variable to the screen, but will not wait at the appropriate spot on the screen to GET your input from the screen and store it in the memory variable; instead it will proceed to execute the next instruction in your program.

Example 7.

```
USE INVENTORY
@ 10,01 SAY 'PART-NUMBER'
@ 10,15 SAY PART
@ 12,01 SAY 'COST          ' GET COST PICT '99999.99'
READ
```

The above code brings the INVENTRY file into use, displays the literal followed by the value of the part number from the first record on line 10, and then displays out the literal, followed by the value of the cost from the first record on line 12. Now the READ statement asks dBASE to GET some values input by the operator. Since the PART field has a SAY and not a GET, the cursor will ignore line 10 on the screen, and stop on line 12 at the COST field, which is the first field eligible for GETting data. At this point, the PART field is out of the reach of the operator. If you want to ensure that the cursor skips certain fields during the data-entry process, in effect ensuring that no changes are made in that field, *you must not provide any GET clauses* for these fields in the format-file definition. Only SAY clauses should be provided for such fields.

Since you could SAY or GET either a field name from a file in use or a memory variable existing at the time, please note that if you have a memory variable with the same name as one of the fields of the file in use, dBASE will always pick up, by default, the field name and not the name of the memory variable.

To avoid this situation, it is a good idea to start all your memory variable names with the letter M, so as to distinguish them from field names from the file in use. For example, the memory variable designed to hold ITEM information could be called MITEM, to differentiate it from the ITEM field from the Inventory file.

Example 8.

```
STORE 0 TO MCOST
@ 10,10 SAY 'ENTER UNIT-COST     ' GET MCOST PICT '999.99' RANGE 15,35
READ
```

In these lines, the literal comes up, and dBASE waits for your response. Your response is limited to digits and is edited to ensure that it is within the two limits, both inclusive. Any erroneous entry results in an error message with the usual beep. The numbers in the RANGE are the lower and upper limit, respectively. The RANGE can also specify a range of dates, as we shall see later.

If you want to specify only the lower limit, specify the range as RANGE 15, (*Note the comma!*). If your want to specify only an upper limit, specify RANGE ,35. (*Note the comma!*).

Example 9.

```
STORE CTOD('01/01/86') TO LOWER
STORE CTOD('06/30/86') TO UPPER
```

These two commands have stored two dates in memory.

```
STORE CTOD('        ') TO MDATE
```

The above command has stored a blank date variable of eight blanks to MDATE.

```
@ 10,10 SAY 'ENTER A DATE     ' GET MDATE PICT '99/99/99' RANGE
LOWER,UPPER
READ
```

The two statements above will put out the literal asking for a date to be entered and then wait for the operator's response. The PICT mask ensures that only numerics are accepted, so a correctly formatted date is read. dBASE will assume that your entry for the date is in MM/DD/YY format and will edit to ensure that the date entry is now within the LOWER and UPPER limits specified, both inclusive. Any error is flagged with a beep.

It is important to understand that this example is identical to Example 8. As long as similar items are compared, dBASE does not care whether it is comparing two numbers or two dates. Just ensure that all your dates are stored as date variables in memory.

> **Note:** In the previous examples, the 'XXXXXX' and the '99999.99' are input masks, specifying the type of data that will be expected to be entered in the field by the operator when the format file is activated. When the format is displayed during execution, an inverse video outline will signify the maximum length of the data ex-

pected in each field. The X in the picture mask of any field implies that a character (either alpha or numeric) will be accepted in place of each X. The picture mask for the MDATE field obviously implies that only numeric data will be accepted as input for this field. Also, the operator will be forced to input data in the specified format.

Note: If you wish to ensure that the operator enters all upper-case characters for a character field, the mask should be defined as PICTURE '!!!!!!'. Now, any letter keyed in will be accepted in upper-case only. If numeric data is keyed in, it will, of course, be accepted. Also, if a field is to contain alphabetic data only in certain positions of the field, the edit mask should be something like PICTURE 'AX-XAXA' or some such combination of the X and the A. Any character will be accepted in the X positions, and only alphabetic input will be accepted in the A positions. You may have masks made up of required combinations of X and A. For example, !!XX!!XX!! implies uppercase alphas in specified locations of the field.

Other symbols that can be used in the input mask include the following: L (for logical data only), # (for digits, blanks, and + or − signs), and N (for letters and digits). Personally, I have found the use of the 9 (for numeric and + and − signs), the X (for any character), and the ! for uppercase input to be more than adequate for most applications. In the section on "Positioning and the Use of Masks" in Chapter 9, I have detailed how the output mask can be specified to obtain different numeric output displays.

Characters other than the acceptable *template* symbols have no special meaning and will be displayed as part of the variable or expression. For example, slashes were used in the template for displaying the date in Example 9 above.

Example 10.

@ 10,10

This line will clear a line on the screen, beginning at the column location, and going through to the end of the line.

@ 10,10 CLEAR

This line will clear the rest of the screen, starting from the coordinate position provided and going forward and down to the end of the screen.

> **Note:** You can use a GET against a memo field, provided that this GET is invoked from within a format file. Individual @- - - SAY - - - GET statements within a program will not permit GETs on a memo field. You *cannot SAY* the contents of any memo field. The above phase, "invoked from within a format file," will be explained a little further along in the book.

Building the Screen-Format File

Having understood the workings of the @- - - SAY- - - GET command, we can use the built-in dBASE word processor to define our screen-format file. Since this screen-format file is to be used with Program D (adding more records into the inventory file), I suggest that we name this file LAYOUTD. I find that this method of naming files is quite convenient and leaves nothing to guesswork. For example, all my menus have options A, B, C, and so on, and all the corresponding subprograms have names PGMA, PGMB, PGMC, and so on. The screen-format files used by the various programs are LAYOUTA, LAYOUTB, LAYOUTC, and so on. If PGMA used multiple layouts, I would name the layout files LAYOUTA1, LAYOUTA2, and so on.

To start the process of building the screen-format file called LAYOUTD.FMT, enter the following command at the dot prompt:

.MODI COMM LAYOUTD.FMT   <cr>

> **Note:** You must provide the extension .FMT. Without this, dBASE will presume you want to create a computer program called LAYOUTD.PRG.

When you enter the above command, the dBASE word processor comes into effect. Key in the following @- - - SAY- - - GET commands for this screen layout file. Please note that a screen-format file can only have the @- - - SAY- - - GET commands in it! You may have asterisks to start off comments, and you can have blank lines in the format file, for visual-aid/esthetic reasons, but no other commands, per se, are permitted in such a file. Use the F1 key to toggle the cursor controls menu.

```
*  LAYOUTD.FMT - CALLED FROM PGMD.PRG
*  -----------
@ 02,01 SAY DATE()
@ 2,25  SAY 'INVENTORY SYSTEM DATA-ENTRY SCREEN'
@ 3,25  SAY '----------------------------------'
@ 4,25  SAY 'Adding more records into inventory:'
@ 6,26  SAY 'PgUp/PgDn for Forward/Backward'
@ 08,5  SAY 'PART-NUM ' GET PART      PICTURE 'XXXXXX'
@ 10,5  SAY 'COST     ' GET COST      PICTURE '99999.99'
@ 12,5  SAY 'SELLPRICE' GET SELLPRICE PICTURE '99999.99'
@ 14,5  SAY 'ONHAND   ' GET ONHAND  PICTURE '999'
@ 16,5  SAY 'ONORDER  ' GET ONORDER PICTURE '999'
@ 18,5  SAY 'USAGE    ' GET USAGE   PICTURE '99'
@ 20,5  SAY 'LEAD     ' GET LEAD    PICTURE '99'
@ 23,15 SAY 'Leave the screen blank, and <CR>, to exit.....'
```

After you have typed in the above statements, enter Ctrl-W, to save the format file.

Notice the DATE( ) function in the header line. I ensure that the operator always sees a date on every screen brought up, so that the operator is aware of the date the system is working with. Many system functions such as the creation of an aged-accounts receivable report, are date-dependent. If you like, you can always show the time just below the date through the use of the TIME( ) function.

Notice that all the literals have been provided the same length. While this is not at all necessary for the successful execution of the program, if all literals have the same length, then all variables will start at the same relative columns on the screen, and this creates a much more appealing screen, from an esthetic point of view.

> **Note:** It is up to you to ensure that your mask size corresponds to the size of the individual fields in your master file. After all, each complete screen entry by the operator will be used for the creation of a new record of data, in the master file.

A program (in this case, PGMD.PRG) will control this screen layout file. During execution, the program will invoke the format file, so that the literals specified in the layout come up on the screen.

Making Changes to Screen-Format Files

To make any changes to an existing screen-format file, start off with the same syntax you used for creating a new format file:

   .MODI COMM LAYOUTD.FMT   <cr>

If LAYOUTD.FMT exists, the screen comes up with the contents of the format file, and you can make changes at will, using the usual cursor controls. Use the F1 key for showing the cursor controls.

PROGRAM D

Now that we have our layout file ready, we will write Program D to fulfill the promise of the menu—namely, to help us add more records to the master inventory file.

```
* PGMD.PRG - ADD RECORDS TO INVENTORY MASTER FILE
* --------
CLEAR
USE INVENTRY INDEX PARTINDX
SET FORMAT TO LAYOUTD
*     This command will activate the screen-format file.
  APPEND
*     Since the format file has been activated, instead of the usual append
*     screen you have been used to seeing, dBASE will present the custom
*     format as specified in the layout file!  In effect, the operator
*     will see the exact structure of the format as specified with the @--
*     SAY---GET commands. The combination of the SET FORMAT TO LAYOUTD
*     statement and the APPEND statement has "invoked the format file from
*     within the program."
*     Note that the APPEND has a built-in read command associated with it,
*     so in this case we don't need to supply the "read" statement.
*     This is identical to the usual APPEND, except for the appearance of
*     the screen. During data entry, the cursor will skip from one GET
*     field to the next, as the operator keys in the required entries, and
*     the GET statements will "get" the entries from the screen (input
*     operation) into the appropriate field names as defined by the GET
```

294

```
*        statement of the format file!  Cursor controls are identical to
*        those we have studied  for the APPEND mode, in case you want to move
*        the cursor around to make changes.
*        If you should want program control to accept a partially filled-in
*        record without having to enter data into all fields, enter ctrl-W.
*        Notice that the screen also provides instructions on paging
*        forward or backward through the records.
*        When you are through entering more data, leave the screen blank,
*        like the instructions specify, and touch <cr>, to exit.
*        A word of explanation on the action of the CTRL-W is called for,
*        here. A ctrl-W is, in effect, a shorthand notation for entering the
*        <CR> key as many times as there are fields on the screen.  In
*        effect, the ctrl-W says to dBASE: "Go ahead, my data entry is done."
*        In place of the ctrl-W, a PgUp,or PgDn,or Ctrl±C has the same effect.
SET FORMAT TO
*        Note:  The "SET FORMAT TO" command will deactivate the format file.
*        Without this deactivation, evan a stand-alone command such as APPEND
*        will cause the format-file format to appear on the screen, not the
*        normal full-screen APPEND format you have seen so often. Also, you
*        cannot make changes to the format-file layout, if need be, unless
*        the format file is closed.   So you really want to deactivate the
*        format file before exiting.
RETURN
*        This statement is not mandatory. Control will return to the main
*        menu, with/without this statement.
*                             END  OF  PGMD
```

Note: You could have also specified SAY CARRY ON, just ahead of the APPEND command in the program. This would be used if you had much common information to be keyed in over several records.

Please note the following point about the use of the indexed file in the previous program. Since the index was active against the master file, the index would automatically be updated as records were APPENDed into the master file. At this stage, however, if duplicate keys were entered into a few records, there is no way for these to be filtered out, and they would be accepted.

THE ADVANTAGES OF USING A FORMAT FILE

The next two paragraphs do *not* apply to the previous program, because of the AP-PEND command used in the program, but they will apply to the rest of the programs in the system.

It is not mandatory that you have a separate and distinct file called a format file, which will be invoked by a calling program. You can have all the @- - - SAY- - - GET statements for your format file right in the middle of your calling program itself, *in place of the statement* SET FORMAT TO LAYOUTD. (Ensure that the @- - - SAY- - - GETs are preceded by the CLEAR command, which clears the screen.)

The advantages, however, of having a format file distinct and separate from your calling program are many. For example, you save time because a change made to the screen-layout necessitates a change and a save of only the format file, instead of the entire program. More important, some programs could be quite complex, and may require the invoking of the screen format from different sections of the program. In such cases, if you had one gigantic module, you would end up repeating the @- - - SAY- - - GET collection of statements at several places in your program. To say the least, this could result in "terminal" illness for the programmer. Also, a screen format invoked through the SET FORMAT TO < filename > command physically executes much faster than the same screen format would execute using individual @- - - SAY- - - GET statements preceded by the CLEAR command.

Now that you have obtained the skills required to create a custom-designed screen and program for data entry, let's try an enhanced program that will accept our entries for new records and check them to ensure that we are not placing any duplicate records in the master file.

PROGRAM E

Program E enables you to add more records and checks them for duplicate keys. The guts of this enhancement is the creation and use of an index built on the key field you want to check on. The operator will key in new data for each new record to be appended, but before the program actually does the APPEND, the program will use the FIND command to scan the indexed file, to check for an already-existing key with the same value as the key that the operator has entered for the new record key.

If the FIND command is successful in locating such an existing record, the FOUND( ) function will be a logical TRUE. If the FIND command could not find an already-existing record with the key entered by the operator, the FOUND( ) function will be a logical FALSE. This will be our basis for checking for duplicate keys.

If the key is found, the record pointer will be positioned at the found record, and the RECNO( ) function will contain the record number of that record. These two facts are very important to remember, when you are writing your own programs in dBASE.

We will first build-up our screen-format file for this program. We will call it LAYOUTE.FMT.

Note: The following command:

.COPY FILE LAYOUTD.FMT TO LAYOUTE.FMT   < cr >

will give you a working copy, to start making changes on. Now you enter the command:

.MODI COMM LAYOUTE.FMT   < cr >

and make the necessary changes.

```
* LAYOUTE.FMT - CALLED FROM PGME.PRG
* ------------
@ 02,01 SAY DATE()
@ 2,28  SAY 'INVENTORY DATA-ENTRY SCREEN'
@ 3,28  SAY '---------------------------'
@ 4,20  SAY 'Adding new records, with duplicates-check'
@ 6,1   SAY 'Enter the following items of information:'
@ 08,1  SAY 'PARTNUM  ' GET MPART PICTURE '!!!!!!'
```

296

```
@ 10,1  SAY 'COST     ' GET MCOST PICTURE '99999.99'
@ 12,1  SAY 'SELLPRICE' GET MSELL PICTURE '99999.99'
@ 14,1  SAY 'ONHAND   ' GET MONHAND PICTURE '999'
@ 16,1  SAY 'ONORDER  ' GET MONORDER PICTURE '999'
@ 18,1  SAY 'USAGE    ' GET MUSAGE PICTURE '999'
@ 20,1  SAY 'LEAD     ' GET MLEAD PICTURE '99'
@ 22,10 SAY 'LEAVE PART-NUMBER FIELD BLANK, AND  ctrl-W,  TO EXIT.'
@ 08,50 SAY MWARN
```

Notice that the screen format above refers to memory variables, not to field names from the file in use. Note also the introduction of one more memory variable, which will hold a warning message to be displayed, in case the operator enters the wrong key value.

The logical flow of our program will be as follows: Send up a formatted screen, asking for the data to be entered. Start a loop that says that as long as there is an error in the operator's entry for the part number field, the formatted screen will keep bouncing up on the screen. If a valid new part number is entered, it will be accepted along with the rest of the information, and the program will create a new record of data. The formatted screen will then come up again, and the cycle will be repeated.

```
* PGME.PRG - ADD MORE RECORDS, WITH DUPLICATES-CHECK
CLEAR
USE INVENTRY INDEX PARTINDX
*      Note:  The use of the index feature has been explained above. The
*      actual index file must already have been created, prior to the exe-
*      cution of the program. The index should be created on UPPER(PART), to
*      ensure that upper and lowercases are not differentiated.
DO WHILE .T.
    STORE '      ' TO MPART
    STORE 0 TO MCOST,MSELL,MONHAND,MONORDER,MUSAGE,MLEAD
    STORE ' ' TO MWARN
*      Start an infinite loop. Define all memory variables required by
*      the format file. These memory variables must pre-exist at the time
*      the format is activated, else the format will abend. Also, the
*      "calling" program must initialise the memory variables to the exact
*      length of the corresponding fields in the structure of the master
*      file. Hence the variable called MPART is defined as 6 characters,
*      since that variable will be used to replace the field called PART
*      in the structure of inventory file. Note that all numeric variables
*      can be initialized with one statement. Character variables having the
*      same lengths can also be initialized with one statement.
    STORE .T. TO NOGOOD
    DO WHILE NOGOOD
*      We are defining a logical variable, NOGOOD, as TRUE. The DO WHILE
*      NOGOOD statement now permits us to enter this loop for the first
*      time. Our objective here is that for as long as the operator's entry
*      into the part number field results in a duplicate find, that is, for
*      as long as the operator's entry is "no good", we want the formatted
*      screen to keep coming up.
*      Please note that the above combination of:   STORE .T. TO NOGOOD
*                                            and     DO WHILE NOGOOD
*                                                    . . . . . . .
*                                                    . . . . . . .
*                                                    ENDDO
```

297

```
*       is very useful in forcing a "loop-until-a-condition-is-satisfied"
*       type of situation, and I use this simple technique extensively.
        SET FORMAT TO LAYOUTE
        READ
*       Within the loop, send up the formatted screen, and wait to read the
*       operator's entries.
*       The operation of the GET statement has been described in detail
*       in earlier sections. Cursor controls are identical to those found
*       in the regular APPEND mode.
        STORE ' ' TO MWARN
*       As soon as the read operation has been completed, we want to blank
*       out the variable called MWARN. The reason is that if the operator
*       makes an error the first time, the error message will flash on the
*       screen, and if you don't clear up the message, then a subsequent good
*       entry will be accepted, and the third time around the screen will
*       come up with the error-message still in place!  As a general rule of
*       thumb, all messages to the screen must be erased immediately after
*       a READ command. After all, another error will cause the error message
*       to be recreated, if the situation calls for it.
        IF MPART = '        '
           SET FORMAT TO
           RETURN
        ENDIF
*       Since the screen tells the operator to leave part-number blank as
*       a sign that the operator wants to go home, you must check for this
*       entry right away. If part-number is blank, program control will
*       close the format file and return to the main menu program.
*       If part-number is not blank, the program control will come to the
*       next statement. We now have to check what the operator entered for
*       the part-number field.
        FIND &MPART
        IF FOUND()
           STORE 'DUPLICATE KEY !' TO MWARN
           ? CHR(7)
        ELSE
           STORE .F. TO NOGOOD
        ENDIF
     ENDDO
*       Notice the macro in the FIND command. If the operator entered P1 for
*       the part-number, then the above statement becomes  FIND P1, and if
*       the operator entered P2, the command becomes  FIND P2, etc.
*       CAUTION: IF THE FIND MACRO ENDS IN A SPACE, IT WILL NOT WORK !
*       If the FIND command was successful in finding a record with the same
*       key, we now have a duplicate-key condition, so we store the appro-
*       priate error message,  beep the console, and loop back through the
*       ENDDO statement, leaving the NOGOOD condition intact.

*       If the FIND was not successful, then we know we have a unique key,
*       so we should negate the NOGOOD condition and go back into the loop.
*       Depending on whether or not the NOGOOD condition still exists, the
*       program will either send up the formatted screen again with an error
*       message, or break the loop and go ahead to execute the next command.
     APPEND BLANK
*       If an acceptable PART-NUMBER value is entered, the program will go
*       ahead and APPEND BLANK to the INVENTRY file.  This will create a
*       blank record at the end of the inventory file, and more important,
*       the record pointer will be positioned at the new, blank record. The
*       program will now proceed to REPLACE all the appropriate fields of the
```

```
*       blank record with the data that had been captured in the memory
*       variables, thus creating a new record of data, appended into the
*       inventory file. Notice the semicolons in the REPLACE commands,
*       for continuation.
     REPLACE PART WITH MPART;
             COST WITH MCOST;
             SELLPRICE WITH MSELL
     REPLACE ONHAND WITH MONHAND;
             ONORDER WITH MONORDER;
             USAGE WITH MUSAGE;
             LEAD WITH MLEAD
ENDDO
*       When one record has been successfully appended, the last ENDDO will
*       take control back into the "infinite" loop, which sends up another
*       blank, formatted screen, and the cycle repeats.
*       The only way out is when the operator follows the directions to exit
*       from a screen.
*                          END  OF  PGME
```

Note that the STORE statements are within the DO WHILE .T. loop, since the memory variables must be initialized to blanks or zero for each new record to be appended. To have your own SET CARRY ON type of effect for the above program, all you need to do is to have the STORE commands outside of the DO WHILE .T. loop. If this were done, the memory variables would not be cleared between records, and you would be automatically carrying data from one record to the next. Notice, however, that if this were done, the operator would have to blank out the part number field in order to exit!

Note: If you decide to interrupt program execution using the ESCape key, or if the program abends for any reason, it is possible that the SET FORMAT TO instruction may not have executed. That is, the format file may still be open. If you were now to say MODI COMM LAYOUTE.FMT, in an attempt to make some changes to the format file, dBASE will tell you that the file is still open, and you will have to execute a .SET FORMAT TO <cr> instruction before proceeding.

Note: Since we are using our own logic to add records to the file, without using the built-in APPEND command, we would have to provide our own logic to move forward or backward through the file, if such an option was needed. We will be covering examples of this later.

An Enhancement for Program E

At this point, I want to introduce an enhancement in the previous program. This enhancement will let us ensure that valid numeric data is entered into the COST and SELLPRICE fields.

One possible method would be to use the RANGE option of the GET command, to ensure data within a specified range. For example, in the layout file LAYOUTE.FMT, you could have specified:

```
* LAYOUTE.FMT - CALLED FROM PGME.PRG
* -----------
@ 02,01 SAY DATE()
@ 2,28  SAY 'INVENTORY DATA-ENTRY SCREEN'
@ 3,28  SAY '---------------------------'
@ 4,20  SAY 'Adding new records, with duplicates-check'
@ 6,1   SAY 'Enter the following items of information:'
@ 08,1  SAY 'PARTNUM  ' GET MPART PICTURE '!!!!!!!'
@ 10,1  SAY 'COST     ' GET MCOST PICTURE '99999.99' RANGE 10,15
@ 12,1  SAY 'SELLPRICE' GET MSELL PICTURE '99999.99' RANGE 20,25
```

(The rest of the statements remain the same as before.)

Notice the addition of the range clauses, for the COST and SELLPRICE memory variables. Now when the program invokes the format screen, dBASE will make an automatic check of the data entered for these two items and will provide an error message if required.

There may, however, be circumstances when this range check may not be suitable. Suppose you had a situation in which the cost of the item could be either between 10 and 15 dollars, between 20 and 25 dollars, or between 30 and 35 dollars. That is, you have multiple valid ranges of dollar amounts, depending on the item being entered. The range check cannot help you, since it can only accept one range of numbers. Second, even if you had only one range, dBASE provides the error message in the upper right-hand corner of the screen, and since the menu program had specified SET BELL OFF, you will not hear the beep. If the operator enters some data in error, the message comes up silently in the upper right-hand corner, and the operator is left guessing, even if only for a few seconds, why the data entry won't be accepted. So I suggest that you should program for these edit-checks yourself. In the following complete listing of PGME, I have shown the edit-check enhancements in bold.

```
* PGME.PRG - ADD MORE RECORDS, WITH DUPLICATES-CHECK
CLEAR
USE INVENTRY INDEX PARTINDX
DO WHILE .T.
    STORE '       ' TO MPART
    STORE 0 TO MCOST,MSELL,MONHAND,MONORDER,MUSAGE,MLEAD
    STORE ' ' TO MWARN
    STORE .T. TO NOGOOD
    DO WHILE NOGOOD
        SET FORMAT TO LAYOUTE
        READ
        STORE ' ' TO MWARN
        IF MPART = '       '
            SET FORMAT TO
            RETURN
        ENDIF
        FIND &MPART
        IF FOUND()
            STORE 'DUPLICATE KEY !' TO MWARN
            ? CHR(7)
            LOOP
        ENDIF
        IF MCOST < 10 .OR. MCOST > 15
            STORE 'INVALID COST !' TO MWARN
```

```
          ? CHR(7)
          LOOP
      ENDIF
   IF MSELL < 20 .OR. MSELL > 25
          STORE 'INVALID SELL-PRICE !' TO MWARN
          ? CHR(7)
          LOOP
      ENDIF
      STORE .F. TO NOGOOD
ENDDO
*       The above lines of code check for a duplicate key, and if a duplicate
*       is found, then the code stores the appropriate error message and
*       loops out, so the format screen comes up again, with the error
*       message. If the key entry is valid, the code checks for the cost
*       entry, and if invalid, stores an error message and loops out, so the
*       formatted screen comes up again. If the cost is valid, the code now
*       checks out the sell price entry, and if in error, stores an error
*       message and loops out.
*       "Loops out" simply means that program-control drops to the nearest
*       ENDDO statement, in effect forcing the loop to repeat.
*       If all three entries (key, cost and sellprice) are good, the program
*       negates the NOGOOD condition, and loops out, to break the cycle.
*       With this coding in place, in case of errors a bell will sound, and
*       the operator will see a message always on the same area of the
*       screen. After all, "user-friendliness" is the name of the game.
   APPEND BLANK
   REPLACE PART WITH MPART;
           COST WITH MCOST;
           SELLPRICE WITH MSELL
   REPLACE ONHAND WITH MONHAND;
           ONORDER WITH MONORDER;
           USAGE WITH MUSAGE;
           LEAD WITH MLEAD
ENDDO
*                       END  OF  PGME
```

The Difference Between FIND and SEEK

In Program E we made use of the macro FIND &MPART. This statement would translate to FIND P1 or FIND P2, and so on depending on the value in the memory variable MPART.

If you recall, only a character memory variable can be used as a macro. Now suppose your master file was indexed on a numeric field, such as SALARY, and your data entry procedure had the same kind of check for duplicates as we saw earlier. The operator's entry for SALARY would be stored in a numeric memory variable, and the FIND command thus cannot be used to check for a duplicate entry. This is where the SEEK command comes in.

If the operator's entry is in a numeric memory variable called MSAL, then SEEK MSAL would be your command to find an existing key with the same value as the value found in MSAL. Please note that you *do not* specify SEEK &MSAL.

To summarize, the FIND command is used against an indexed file to find the contents of character memory variables, while the SEEK command is used against an indexed file to find the contents of numeric memory variables. The FIND command must have the ampersand used in the macro, while the SEEK command must not!

EDITING EXISTING DATA

We can take advantage of format files to generate our own EDIT screens. That is, you can generate a screen layout and supporting program not only to produce the data entry screen, but also to produce the data-edit screen. Now the operator could not only add new records, but could also edit existing data, either sequentially, or at will. He or she could pick and choose the next record or existing data to be edited.

The biggest obvious difference between editing data and adding data is that our format file GET statements should now refer to existing field names from the file in use and not to memory variables. If the GET statements refer to field names, then the GET and READ combination will now not only display (GET) existing data from the current record, but will also automatically replace (GET/READ) the data back into the fields of the current record of information.

Now if we don't need memory variables to be able to change existing data, it follows that we will not need the STORE statements that initialize the memory variables, nor the REPLACE commands that replace the field names of the file with the contents of the memory variables.

PROGRAM F

This program will let us edit records sequentially, without permitting any changes to the key field. The logic is very simple. The program will bring up the first valid (non-deleted) record for edit. The cursor will then be made to skip the part number field, thus ensuring that no changes are made to the key field. Other changes will update the record directly. Now the program will skip to the next valid, nondeleted record and repeat the cycle.

Let us build the format file first. Either make a copy of the previous format file for quick changes or start with the command .MODI COMM LAYOUTF.FMT, as usual.

```
* LAYOUTF.FMT - CALLED FROM PGMF.PRG
* -----------
@ 03,01 SAY DATE()
@ 3,25  SAY 'INVENTORY DATA-EDIT SCREEN'
@ 4,25  SAY '--------------------------'
@ 5,15  SAY 'Edit records sequentially, no changes to key-field'
@ 07,14 SAY '(PgDn/PgUp for forward/backward.   CTRL+W to exit...)'
@ 10,1  SAY 'PARTNUM '
@ 10,12 SAY PART PICTURE    'XXXXX'
@ 12,1  SAY 'COST      ' GET COST PICTURE '99999.99'
@ 14,1  SAY 'SELLPRICE' GET SELLPRICE PICTURE '99999.99'
@ 16,1  SAY 'ONHAND   ' GET ONHAND PICTURE '999'
@ 18,1  SAY 'ONORDER  ' GET ONORDER PICTURE '999'
@ 20,1  SAY 'USAGE    ' GET USAGE PICTURE '99'
@ 22,1  SAY 'LEAD     ' GET LEAD  PICTURE '99'
```

Notice that now, in the GET commands, we are referring to field names from the file in use and not to memory variables. Notice also, that since this program does not check for a duplicate key entry, the format file does not permit any kind of changes to the PART NUMBER field. Notice the SAY parameter for the PART NUMBER field. During data entry, the cursor will come to rest in the COST field, as the first GET field eligible for changes!

Let us now build another command file that will call the format file. This file will be called PGMF.PRG.

```
* PGMF.PRG - EDIT SEQUENTIALLY, NO DUPLICATES CHECK.
* --------
CLEAR
USE INVENTRY [INDEX PARTINDX]
*       Bring the appropriate file into use, with or without the index,
*       depending on your requirement. Note that USE command automatically
*       ignores the leading deleted records in the file, if any, and brings
*       up the first valid, non deleted record under USE. This is because we
*       had specified SET DELE ON in the menu program.
*       If the index is active, the records will be presented to you in the
*       order of the index.. This is the only role played by the index here,
*       since we are not permitting any changes to the key field.
SET FORMAT TO LAYOUTF
EDIT
*       This command activates the format file. Now the operator will see all
*       the outputs of the SAY and GET commands exactly as had been specified
*       in the format-file called LAYOUTF.FMT. That is, the literals and the
*       data from the field names of the current-record will appear on the
*       screen. (The GET commands will get the data to the screen. The
*       built-in READ function of the EDIT command will GET the operator
*       entries back into the same fields of the current record.
*
*       This editing is identical to editing in native mode. The only
*       difference is in the appearance of the screen. You can scroll up and
*       down through the records, just like in the native edit mode. Notice,
*       therefore, that the layout-file provides instructions to the operator
*       on how to go forward/backward through the records, and how to stop
*       the edit function.
SET FORMAT TO
RETURN
*       As explained on previous occasions, you must close the format file
*       before returning to the calling menu.
*                         END  OF  PGMF
```

A Word of Caution

Our next programs will let the operator edit records sequentially or randomly, via either the record number or the PART NUMBER. Changes to the key fields will be permitted. Such programs, which allow the operator to make changes to key values in master files, are always tricky, to say the least. Let us understand what could possibly happen when we allow key values to be changed.

Our format files will refer to the actual field names from the record, and not to any memory variables. This has been discussed in previous sections. The program will, of course, have to use the indexed version of the master file for checking for duplicates.

As an example, assume that upon initiation, the program displays the formatted screen containing data from the first record of the indexed file. The operator makes changes to the data, and also, unfortunately, decides to change the key field value! As soon as the SET FORMAT TO <filename> and the READ commands have been executed, the first record has already been updated, and in effect, since the key value was changed, the record appears in a different location, as per the index! In fact, even if the new key value was the duplicate of another key, the SET FORMAT TO LAYOUTG and the READ combination has already logically repositioned the new record after the existing record with the same key.

Somehow, the program must be made to start with, say, the first (indexed) record, keep a pointer to that current record, accept the changes to data and key values, check the key for duplicates through the FIND command, reposition the new record if a valid key has been entered, flag an error if a duplicate key has been entered, and still retain its position on the current record, and so on, and so on. In other words, we are going to be looking at a slightly complicated program. Nothing will be introduced here that we have not already covered, and liberal comments will be thrown in, for your understanding. However, programs that allow key-values to be changed are always a challenge.

Again, let us remember that *programming is an art, not a science*, and the solutions provided here are by no means the only possible solutions to the problem.

PROGRAM G

Program G will let you edit records sequentially via record numbers, permit changes to (indexed) key fields, and check for duplicates.

The logic of this program will be as follows: First it will display the first valid (non-deleted) record and accept changes to all fields. The changes to the non-key fields will be accepted immediately in the actual record, but any changes to the key field will be placed in a memory variable. Then the program will use the FIND command against the indexed file to see if the key exists. If it does, the program will bring the record back to the screen with the error message. This will be repeated until the operator quits or enters a valid key field.

If a valid key change is entered, the program goes back to the current record, replaces the key field with the change, and then skips to the next valid (nondeleted) record, to repeat the cycle.

The format file has the following lines:

```
* LAYOUTG.FMT - CALLED FROM PGMG.PRG
* -----------
@ 03,01 SAY DATE()
@ 3,30 SAY 'INVENTORY DATA-EDIT SCREEN'
@ 4,30 SAY '--------------------------'
@ 5,25 SAY 'Sequential edit, with duplicates-check.'
@ 07,23 SAY '(Enter  CTRL-W  or  PgDn, to go forward...)'
@ 08,1 SAY 'PARTNUM ' GET MPART PICTURE '!!!!!!'
@ 10,1 SAY 'COST     ' GET COST PICTURE '99999.99'
@ 12,1 SAY 'SELLPRICE' GET SELLPRICE PICTURE '99999.99'
@ 14,1 SAY 'ONHAND   ' GET ONHAND PICTURE '999'
@ 15,35 SAY MWARN
@ 16,1 SAY 'ONORDER  ' GET ONORDER PICTURE '999'
@ 18,1 SAY 'USAGE    ' GET USAGE PICTURE '99'
@ 20,1 SAY 'LEAD     ' GET LEAD PICTURE '99'
@ 23,25 SAY 'MORE (Y/N) ?'  GET MMORE PICTURE 'X'
```

Note: The biggest change now is in the fact that the operator entry for the PART NUMBER key field will go into a memory variable and will not directly update the key field of the current record. Obviously, this is done since the operator entry for the key value must be edited first, for uniqueness, before it can be accepted in the master file. Note also that all entries into the part number field will be accepted in uppercase only, for the sake of uniformity of data.

The calling program for this purpose is Program G (PGMG.PRG).

```
* PGMG.PRG - EDIT SEQUENTIALLY, WITH DUPLICATES CHECK
* ---------
CLEAR
USE INVENTRY INDEX PARTINDX
STORE ' ' TO MWARN
STORE 'Y' TO MMORE
DO WHILE .NOT. EOF() .AND. MMORE = 'Y'
*       Once again, the USE statement starts out with the first valid, non-
*       deleted record in the file.
*
*       Start a loop. For as long as it is not the end-of-file, and the
*       operator wants to proceed (has not altered the MMORE variable),
*       perform the next steps continuously.
   STORE STR(RECNO(),8) TO MCURRENT
*       We want to keep track of the current record we are working on. The
*       reason is that we will have to check the operator's entry for a
*       unique key value, using the FIND command. However, during the working
*       of the FIND command, the record-pointer moves all over the place, and
*       we lose our position in the data-base.
*       So we store the current record number, not as is (a numeric), but
*       in its string version. Note also, that the use of the 8 implies
*       that I have made the humble presumption that you will not have more
*       than 1 million records in your file.
*       The string requirement will be explained later. For now, we have
*       captured the current record number in the MCURRENT variable, which is
*       now a character variable.
   STORE PART TO MPART,REALPART
*       I also want to store the PART NUMBER of the current record into a
*       variable called MPART and REALPART. I need it in MPART since MPART
*       is the variable defined in the layout file, and I need to see what
*       part number I am working on, on the screen. I need it in REALPART
*       since the entry in MPART will be corrupted as soon as the operator
*       enters new data in the part number field.
*       I now want to display the current record for as long as the operator
*       keeps entering invalid key values in the PART NUMBER field.
   STORE .T. TO NOGOOD
   DO WHILE NOGOOD
      SET FORMAT TO LAYOUTG
      READ
      STORE ' ' TO MWARN
*       Force a condition called NOGOOD which implies just that - an invalid
*       entry by the operator - and force the layout to come up for the
*       first time. As soon as operator entries have been read in, clear out
*       the variable called MWARN.
   IF UPPER(MPART) = UPPER(REALPART)
      STORE .F. TO NOGOOD
```

```
            LOOP
         ENDIF
*        Never assume that the operator will make an entry in the part-number
*        field. If the operator did not make any entry in the part-number
*        field, then the value in MPART has not changed (compare it to the
*        variable REALPART). Obviously, if the key-field has not changed
*        we don't need to check for any duplicates, and so we negate the
*        NOGOOD condition (everything is good), and loop out, through to the
*        ENDDO statement. Now the loop will be broken, and program control
*        will pick up after the ENDDO statement.
*        If, however, MPART is not equal to REALPART, then the operator did
*        make some change in the part-number field, so we have to check for
*        duplicates.
         FIND &MPART
         IF FOUND()
             STORE 'DUPLICATE KEY!' TO MWARN
             ? CHR(7)
             &MCURRENT
             LOOP
*        Try and FIND the value entered by the operator. If we have a problem,
*        store the 'duplicate key' error message, ring a bell at the console,
*        obtain position back at the "current record"(!), and loop out.
*        To explain the &MCURRENT command: If the value in MCURRENT was the
*        number 45, then during execution, &MCURRENT translates to the command
*        .45 !  You may recall from earlier pages that the easiest way to
*        position yourself at any record is simply to enter the record-number
*        at the dot prompt. So &MCURRENT will automatically position you to
*        the record number contained in the MCURRENT variable.
*        You obviously recognize the use of the &MCURRENT as a macro, and
*        hence the necessity of converting the current record number into a
*        string variable. Only string variables can be used as macros.
*        So the net effect of the above commands is that if the operator makes
*        a key change, dBASES uses the FIND command to check on the validity
*        of the entry, confirms a duplicate key, sets up the error message
*        with a beep , repositions you back to the current record, and brings
*        up the screen layout again, so the operator is aware of the error.
*        If, however, no duplicate was sensed, then the entry was a unique
*        key-change, so it has to be accepted.
         ELSE
             &MCURRENT
             REPLACE PART WITH MPART
             STORE .F. TO NOGOOD
         ENDIF
      ENDDO
*        If no duplicate was sensed, we still need to move back to our current
*        record position (remember, the FIND command plays havoc with the
*        current record pointer). Having moved back into position, we must now
*        replace the key field of the current record with what the operator
*        had keyed into the MPART variable. Obviously, once we have replaced
*        the existing key value with a valid change, we have to negate the
*        NOGOOD condition, and loop back. At this point, the looping cycle
*        breaks, and program control picks up after the ENDDO statement.
*        So program control will reach this point either if:
*        (1) the operator did not make any change to the key field, or if
*        (2) the operator made a valid, non duplicate key change.
      SKIP
   ENDDO
```

```
*         The program will now skip to the next good record, and head back into
*         the big loop. It will continue this until it is either the end-of-
*         file, or an operator request not to continue (by altering the memory-
*         variable called MMORE to any character other than a 'Y').
'SET FORMAT TO
RETURN
*         Close the format file, as usual, before returning to the main menu
*         program.
*                           END  OF  PGMG
```

Note: It is important to understand the significance of the SKIP command when a change has been made to a key field. Suppose, for now, that we have five records in the inventory file, with key values P1, P2, P3, P4, and P5. When indexed, P1 will be record #1, P2 will be record #2, and so on. Now let us say I run the above program and bring up record #1 on the screen, and without altering anything in it, I go on to record #2. Now in record #2, I change the key value to P6. As soon as I do the PgDn to have my changes accepted, the valid change will be accepted, but the record pointer will now move to a new position as the last record in the file. So the SKIP command will not bring up record #3, but will reach the end-of-file, and so will take me back to the main menu!

By the same token, if I bring up record #4 on the screen and change its key value to P11, I will get record P2 as the next record, since logically P11 is positioned between P1 and P2. (Remember that PART NUMBER is a character field, so here we have character evaluations, not numeric evaluations!) This repositioning of the record when you alter the contents of a key field is obviously essential to keep the index in sync with the actual keys.

If it were required that, after the key value of P1 was changed to P6, P2, rather than the record following the new key as specified by the index, must be displayed, it can be done. This would, however, require some complexity in the programming, and I have opted not to burden you with this, for now.

PROGRAM H

Program H will let you edit records randomly via record numbers, make changes to key fields, and check for duplicates. The logic of the program is as follows. It first displays a miniscreen asking the operator to enter a record number for editing. It makes sure that record number is within the range of records in the file, and that record is not already a deleted record. If the requested record is either outside the range of record numbers or a deleted record, it displays the appropriate message and stays on the miniscreen. This is repeated, until the operator either quits or provides a valid record number.

When a valid number is provided, the program brings the appropriate record to the screen, accepts operator entries, and determines whether or not the key has been changed. If it hasn't been, the program accepts the other changes to the record and goes back to the miniscreen, asking for the next choice of record number. If the record key has been changed, the program checks the change for uniqueness, and either accepts or rejects the change. If the change is rejected, it brings the same record up on the screen again, as we have seen before.

The format file, LAYOUTH.FMT, looks like this:

```
* LAYOUTH.FMT - CALLED FROM PGMH.PRG
* -----------
@ 03,01 SAY DATE()
@ 3,28  SAY 'INVENTORY DATA-EDIT SCREEN'
@ 4,28  SAY '--------------------------'
@ 5,20  SAY 'Random edit on record-numbers, with dup-checks'
@ 8,1   SAY 'CURRENT RECORD'
@ 8,20  SAY RECNO() PICT '9999999'
@ 10,1  SAY 'PARTNUM ' GET MPART PICT '!!!!!!'
@ 11,1  SAY 'COST     ' GET COST PICTURE '99999.99'
@ 12,1  SAY 'SELLPRICE' GET SELLPRICE PICTURE '99999.9'
@ 13,1  SAY 'ONHAND   ' GET ONHAND PICTURE '999'
@ 14,1  SAY 'ONORDER  ' GET ONORDER PICTURE '999'
@ 15,1  SAY 'USAGE    ' GET USAGE PICTURE '99'
@ 16,1  SAY 'LEAD     ' GET LEAD PICTURE '99'
@ 19,30 SAY MWARN
```

The calling-program, PGMH.PRG, will look like this:

```
* PGMH.PRG - EDIT RANDOMLY ON RECORD-NUMBERS WITH DUP. CHECKS.
* ---------
USE INVENTRY INDEX PARTINDX
*      We need the indexed file for a subsequent check for a duplicate key.
DO WHILE .T.
    CLEAR
    STORE 0 TO MNEXT
    @ 01,01 SAY DATE()
    @ 01,20 SAY 'RANDOM EDIT ON RECORD-NUMBERS, WITH DUP.-CHECKS.'
    @ 10,01 SAY 'Enter record-number for edit ' GET MNEXT PICT ;
'9999999'
    @ 12,01 SAY 'Touch <cr>, to exit.....'
*      Start an infinite loop, clear the screen, define MNEXT to hold the
*      record number entered by the operator, provide the operator an option
*      to escape, and wait for the response.
    READ
    IF MNEXT = 0
        RETURN
    ENDIF
*      If the operator seeks an escape and makes no entry in MNEXT, the
*      variable will remain at the initialized value of zero, so the program
*      returns to the main menu.
    IF MNEXT > RECCOUNT()
        @ 20,01 SAY 'YOU ONLY HAVE '+STR(RECCOUNT(),7) +'   RECORDS IN YOUR ;
FILE.....Touch <cr>...'
        ? CHR(7)
        WAIT ' '
        LOOP
    ENDIF
*      If MNEXT was not left at value zero, the operator made an entry, so
*      we check to see if the record number entered was within the range of
```

```
*       the file. If not, we put out the error message, then loop back into
*       the main stream, to repeat the process.
*       If the range check is good, we now check to see if the record number
*       that was requested points to a deleted record.
     STORE STR(MNEXT,7) TO MNEXT
     &MNEXT
*       Convert the numeric variable MNEXT into a character variable for use
*       as a macro, then move the current record pointer to the requested
*       record number. Please note that in this case the pointer will move to
*       the specified record, even if the record is a deleted record (!) and
*       you have specified "SET DELE ON" ! So you will have to check for the
*       deleted record condition.
     IF DELETED()
        @ 20,10 SAY 'The record is already deleted !       Touch ;
<CR>...'
        ? CHR(7)
        WAIT ''
        LOOP
     ENDIF
*       If the record is deleted, put out the message, then loop back into
*       the main stream.
*       If the record is good, program control moves to the next statement.
     STORE PART TO MPART,REALPART
*       Store PART to MPART and REALPART memory variables. The reasons for
*       this were outlined in the previous program.
     STORE ' ' TO MWARN
     STORE .T. TO BADKEY
     DO WHILE BADKEY
        SET FORMAT TO LAYOUTH
        READ
*       Force the layout to come up for the first time, with the requested
*       record. Now check for key changes, if any.
        STORE ' ' TO MWARN
        IF UPPER(MPART) # UPPER(REALPART)
*       If there is a key change, try and find the new key in the file.
           FIND &MPART
           IF FOUND()
              STORE 'DUPLICATE KEY !' TO MWARN
              ? CHR(7)
              &MNEXT
              LOOP
*       If a duplicate was found, put out the error message, 'beep' the
*       console, move the pointer back to the current-record, and loop,
*       to bring the record format back again to the screen.
           ELSE
              &MNEXT
              REPLACE PART WITH MPART
           ENDIF
        ENDIF
        STORE .F. TO BADKEY
     ENDDO
*       If the key change is not a duplicate, go again to the current record,
*       replace the part number value with what the operator had entered,
*       and drop out of the IF statements.
*       If program control reaches this point, either the operator did not
*       change the key field, or the change was for a unique key value.
*       Now the BADKEY condition will be negated, which will force the inner
*       loop to end, and the outer loop will once again ask the operator for
```

```
*       the next record number to be edited.
     SET FORMAT TO
ENDDO
RETURN
*       Close the format file, between the times you get out of the inner
*       loop and into the outer. This way, the format file remains closed,
*       if the operator decides not to continue.
*                        END  OF  PGMH
```

PROGRAM I

Program I will let you edit records randomly via part numbers, permit changes to key fields, and check for duplicates.

The logic of this program will be as follows: First it displays a miniscreen, asks for a part number, and uses the FIND command against the indexed file to see if the part number exists. Note that under normal conditions, the FIND command will find deleted records, but in the menu itself we have specified SET DELE ON, and so the FIND command will ignore all deleted records. We will not have to program for a check of deleted records, as was done in the previous program.

As long as the part number requested does not exist, the miniscreen keeps floating up again. If a good part number is entered, the program will display the record and accept all changes. Changes to the non-key fields will be updated in the record immediately, but changes to the key field, if any, will be placed into a memory variable, for checking for duplicates.

If the key change is a duplicate, the program goes back to the current record, displays it with the error message, and waits for another entry. If the key change is unique, the program goes back to the current record, replaces the key field with the new entry, and displays the miniscreen again, to continue the process.

The screen layout file, as usual, looks like this:

```
* LAYOUTI.FMT - CALLED FROM PGMI.PRG
* ------------
@ 3,30  SAY 'INVENTORY DATA-EDIT SCREEN'
@ 4,30  SAY '--------------------------'
@ 5,22  SAY 'RANDOM EDIT ON PART-NUMBERS, WITH DUP-CHECK'
@ 08,1  SAY 'PARTNUM  ' GET MPART PICTURE '!!!!!!'
@ 10,1  SAY 'COST     ' GET COST PICTURE '99999.99'
@ 11,1  SAY 'SELLPRICE' GET SELLPRICE PICTURE '99999.99'
@ 12,1  SAY 'ONHAND   ' GET ONHAND PICTURE '999'
@ 13,1  SAY 'ONORDER  ' GET ONORDER PICTURE '999'
@ 14,1  SAY 'USAGE    ' GET USAGE PICTURE '99'
@ 15,1  SAY 'LEAD     ' GET LEAD PICTURE '99'
@ 21,30 SAY MWARN
```

The calling program, PGMI.PRG, will be as follows:

```
     The calling program (PGMI.PRG) will be as follows:
```

```
* PGMI.PRG - EDIT RANDOMLY ON PART-NUMBERS, WITH DUP. CHECKS.
* --------
USE INVENTRY INDEX PARTINDX
DO WHILE .T.
```

```
        CLEAR
        @ Ø1,Ø1 SAY DATE()
        @ Ø1,18 SAY 'EDIT RANDOMLY ON PART-NUMBERS, WITH DUP-CHECK'
        STORE '      ' TO MSTART
        @ 10,Ø1 SAY 'ENTER PART-NUMBER TO EDIT  ' GET MSTART PICT 'XXXXXX'
        @ 12,Ø1 SAY 'Touch <cr>, to exit.....'
        READ
*          Start an infinite loop. Ask for a starting part number, provide an
*          escape route, and read the operator's entry.
        IF MSTART = '          '
           RETURN
        ENDIF
*          If the operator escapes, return to the main menu. If the operator
*          makes any entry on the screen, check the entry for a valid part
*          number.
        FIND &MSTART
        IF .NOT. FOUND()
           @ 20,15 SAY 'NO SUCH PART-NUMBER KEY !    Touch <cr>'
           ? CHR(7)
           WAIT ''
           LOOP
        ENDIF
*          Try and find the part number in the indexed file. If the part number
*          is not found, go back into the loop, asking for another part number.
*          If the program can find the part number, proceed with the next few
*          commands. Note that at this stage, since the part number is found,
*          the current record pointer is positioned at the "found" record !
        STORE PART TO MPART,REALPART
*          Save the part number for future use.
        STORE ' ' TO MWARN
        STORE .T. TO NOGOOD
        DO WHILE NOGOOD
           SET FORMAT TO LAYOUTI
           READ
           STORE ' ' TO MWARN
*          Start off with the NOGOOD condition, to force the found record to the
*          screen for the first time. Accept all operator changes. Changes to
*          non-key fields will update the fields directly. The change to the
*          part number field, if any, will go into the variable MPART.

           IF UPPER(MPART) ≠ UPPER(REALPART)
              FIND &MPART
              IF FOUND()
                 STORE 'DUPLICATE KEY !' TO MWARN
                 ? CHR(7)
                 FIND &REALPART
                 LOOP
*          If the part number key has been altered, try and find the new key
*          value. If we have a duplicate key entry, store the error message,
*          beep the console, go back to the current record, and loop out, so
*          that this record appears on the screen again.
              ELSE
                 FIND &REALPART
                 REPLACE PART WITH MPART
              ENDIF
           ENDIF
*          Since the key change was a valid one, go back to the current record,
*          and replace the key field value with the changed value.
*          If program control reaches this point, either the operator did not
```

311

```
*      change the key field, or the change was for a unique key value.
*      Now the NOGOOD condition will be negated, which will force the inner
*      loop to end, and the outer loop will once again ask the operator for
*      the next record number to be edited.
       STORE .F. TO NOGOOD
    ENDDO
    SET FORMAT TO
ENDDO
RETURN
*                                    END  OF  PGMI
```

PROGRAM J

Program J will let us delete records randomly on record numbers. The logic of the program is as follows: It first displays a miniscreen asking the operator for the starting record number. It then makes sure that the record number is within the range of the file and identifies a valid, nondeleted record. If either condition is not satisfied, the program displays the appropriate error message and loops through the miniscreen again.

If the record number is that of a valid, nondeleted record, the program displays the record, so the operator can see the data in the record, and asks for confirmation of the delete function for that record! Only if the operator responds with a Y will the record be deleted. After the delete (or immediately if the operator decides not to go ahead with the delete) the miniscreen comes up again, asking for the next record number.

The delete function permits no changes to any of the fields, when the record is brought up for viewing and confirmation of the delete.

The layout file is as follows:

```
* LAYOUTJ.FMT - CALLED FROM PGMJ.PRG
* -----------
@ 01,01 SAY DATE()
@ 1,28  SAY 'INVENTORY DELETE SCREEN'
@ 2,28  SAY '-----------------------'
@ 3,23  SAY 'Random delete on record-numbers:'
@ 06,20 SAY 'C O N F I R M   T H E   D E L E T E  !    (Y/N) ;
?' GET MCONFIRM PICT 'X'
@ 07,20 SAY '                                        -'
@ 08,01 SAY 'Record #:'
@ 08,12 SAY RECNO() PICT '9999999'
@ 10,1  SAY 'PARTNUM '
@ 10,12 SAY PART
@ 11,1  SAY 'COST    '
@ 11,12 SAY COST
@ 12,1  SAY 'SELLPRICE'
@ 12,12 SAY SELLPRICE
@ 13,1  SAY 'ONHAND  '
@ 13,12 SAY ONHAND
@ 14,1  SAY 'ONORDER '
@ 14,12 SAY ONORDER
@ 15,1  SAY 'USAGE   '
@ 15,12 SAY USAGE
@ 16,1  SAY 'LEAD    '
@ 16,12 SAY LEAD
```

Note that there will be no updating taking place, since we have only SAY commands in our format file layout. The cursor will stop in the field that asks for a confirmation of the delete, for the current record.

The program code will be as follows:

```
* PGMJ.PRG - DELETE RANDOMLY ON RECORD-NUMBERS
* --------
USE INVENTRY
DO WHILE .T.
   CLEAR
   STORE 0 TO MNEXT
   @ 01,01 SAY DATE()
   @ 01,20 SAY 'RANDOM DELETE, VIA RECORD-NUMBERS:'
   @ 10,01 SAY 'Enter record-number for delete ' GET MNEXT PICT ;
'9999999'
   @ 12,01 SAY 'Touch <cr>, to exit.....'
   READ
   IF MNEXT = 0
      RETURN
   ENDIF
*       Start an infinite loop. Clear the screen, ask the operator for the
*       record number to be deleted, provide for an escape route, and read
*       the entry. If the operator escapes, return to the main menu.
   IF MNEXT > RECCOUNT()
      @ 20,01 SAY 'YOU ONLY HAVE '+STR(RECCOUNT(),7) +'   RECORDS IN YOUR ;
FILE.....Touch <cr>...'
      ? CHR(7)
      WAIT ' '
      LOOP
   ENDIF
*       If the operator did not escape, then if the requested record number
*       is beyond the range of the file, put out the appropriate error
*       message, and loop back.
   STORE STR(MNEXT,7) TO MNEXT
   &MNEXT
*       Convert MNEXT into a character variable, then position the
*       record pointer at the requested record number.
   IF DELETED()
      @ 20,17 SAY 'RECORD IS ALREADY DELETED  !   Touch <cr>...'
      ? CHR(7)
      WAIT ''
      LOOP
   ENDIF
*       If the record is already deleted, put out an error message, and loop
*       back, asking again for a record number.
   STORE ' ' TO MCONFIRM
   SET FORMAT TO LAYOUTJ
   READ
   IF UPPER(MCONFIRM) = 'Y'
      DELE
   ENDIF
   SET FORMAT TO
ENDDO
*       If the record number is that of a valid record, send the record up
*       on the screen, asking the operator to confirm the delete request.
*       Only if the operator enters a 'Y' will the record be deleted. Notice
```

313

```
*        the DELE command, without any parameters. That deletes the "current"
*        record. After deletion, or if the operator decides against deleting
*        the record, the end of the loop will send up the miniscreen again,
*        asking for the next record number to be deleted.
                            END  OF  PGMJ
```

PROGRAM K

Program K will let you delete records randomly via part numbers. The logic of the
program will be as follows. First it displays a miniscreen, asking for a part number
to be deleted. Using the FIND command, it checks to see if the part number exists.
If it does not, the program loops back to the miniscreen. If the part number exists,
the program displays the record, asks the operator to confirm the delete, and if necessary, performs the delete. With or without the delete, the miniscreen will come up again,
asking for the next part number to be deleted.

The layout file will, as in the previous case, not have any GET statements; that
is, the record to be deleted cannot be changed in any way.

```
* LAYOUTK.FMT - CALLED FROM PGMK.PRG
* ------------
@ Ø1,Ø1 SAY DATE()
@ 1,28  SAY 'INVENTORY DELETE SCREEN'
@ 2,28  SAY '-----------------------'
@ 3,25  SAY 'Random delete on part-numbers:'
@ Ø6,2Ø SAY 'C O N F I R M   T H E   D E L E T E  !    (Y/N) ;
?' GET MCONFIRM PICT 'X'
@ Ø7,2Ø SAY '
@ Ø8,Ø1 SAY 'Record #:'
@ Ø8,12 SAY RECNO() PICT '9999999'
@ 1Ø,1  SAY 'PARTNUM '
@ 1Ø,12 SAY PART
@ 11,1  SAY 'COST     '
@ 11,12 SAY COST
@ 12,1  SAY 'SELLPRICE'
@ 12,12 SAY SELLPRICE
@ 13,1  SAY 'ONHAND   '
@ 13,12 SAY ONHAND
@ 14,1  SAY 'ONORDER  '
@ 14,12 SAY ONORDER
@ 15,1  SAY 'USAGE    '
@ 15,12 SAY USAGE
@ 16,1  SAY 'LEAD     '
@ 16,12 SAY LEAD
```

The program code will be as follows:

```
* PGMK.PRG - DELETE RANDOMLY ON PART-NUMBERS
* --------
USE INVENTRY INDEX PARTINDX
DO WHILE .T.
    CLEAR
    STORE '        ' TO MPART
    @ Ø1,Ø1 SAY DATE()
    @ Ø1,2Ø SAY 'RANDOM DELETE, VIA PART-NUMBERS:'
```

```
     @ 10,01 SAY 'Enter part-number for delete ' GET MPART PICT ;
'XXXXXX'
     @ 12,01 SAY 'Touch <cr>, to exit.....'
     READ
     IF MPART = '      '
        RETURN
     ENDIF
*    Use the indexed file, ask the operator for the part number to be
*    deleted, provide an escape route and read the response. If the
*    operator escapes, return to the main menu.
     FIND &MPART
     IF .NOT. FOUND()
        @ 20,17 SAY 'NO SUCH PART-NUMBER FOUND  !   Touch <cr>...'
        ? CHR(7)
        WAIT ''
        LOOP
     ENDIF
*    If the operator makes any entry, check to see if that part number
*    exists. If not, send up the message and loop back, asking for the
*    next part number.
     STORE ' ' TO MCONFIRM
     SET FORMAT TO LAYOUTK
     READ
     IF UPPER(MCONFIRM) = 'Y'
        DELE
     ENDIF
     SET FORMAT TO
ENDDO
*    If the part number exists, send up the record to the screen, and
*    check the operator's response. The operator either confirms or
*    rejects the deletion. With or without deleting the record,
*    program control will go back to the miniscreen again, asking for
*    the next record key to be deleted.
*                           END  OF  PGMK
```

As a general rule of thumb, if you provide options to delete records, you must always allow for confirmation of the delete, providing a default of no delete. At such times, never permit any changes to any field of the record. This will help ensure data-integrity, in case the operator backs out of the delete operation.

PROGRAM L

Program L will let you scan records sequentially via record numbers, either forward or backward, starting with any selected record number. No changes will be permitted during the scan.

The layout file, containing only SAY clauses, is as follows:

```
* LAYOUTL.FMT - CALLED FROM PGML.PRG
* ------------
@ 01,01 SAY DATE()
@ 1,28  SAY 'INVENTORY SCAN SCREEN'
@ 2,28  SAY '---------------------'
@ 05,20 SAY 'F - Forward      R - Reverse      X - Exit  ' GET MOPTION ;
        PICT 'X'
@ 08,01 SAY 'Record #:'
```

```
@ 08,12 SAY RECNO() PICT '9999999'
@ 10,1  SAY 'PARTNUM '
@ 10,12 SAY PART
@ 11,1  SAY 'COST    '
@ 11,12 SAY COST
@ 12,1  SAY 'SELLPRICE'
@ 12,12 SAY SELLPRICE
@ 13,1  SAY 'ONHAND  '
@ 13,12 SAY ONHAND
@ 14,1  SAY 'ONORDER '
@ 14,12 SAY ONORDER
@ 15,1  SAY 'USAGE   '
@ 15,12 SAY USAGE
@ 16,1  SAY 'LEAD    '
@ 16,12 SAY LEAD
```

The program lines are as follows:

```
* PGML.PRG - SCAN SEQUENTIALLY ON RECORD-NUMBERS
* ---------
USE INVENTRY [INDEX PARTINDX]
*      Note that the use of the index is optional. If the index is active,
*      you merely scan the records in the order of the index.
DO WHILE .T.
    CLEAR
    STORE 0 TO MNEXT
    @ 01,01 SAY DATE()
    @ 01,20 SAY 'SEQUENTIAL SCAN, VIA RECORD-NUMBERS:'
    @ 10,01 SAY 'Enter record-number to start scan: ' GET MNEXT PICT ;
'9999999'
    @ 12,01 SAY 'Touch <cr>, to exit.....'
    READ
*      Ask the operator for a starting record number, provide an escape
*      route, and read the operator's entry.
    IF MNEXT = 0
        RETURN
    ENDIF
*      If the operator escapes, return to the main menu.
    IF MNEXT > RECCOUNT()
        @ 20,01 SAY 'YOU ONLY HAVE '+STR(RECCOUNT(),7) +'    RECORDS IN YOUR ;
FILE.....Touch <cr>...'
        ? CHR(7)
        WAIT ' '
        LOOP
    ENDIF
*      If the selected record number is beyond the range of the file, give
*      out the error message and loop back for the next record number.
    STORE STR(MNEXT,7) TO MNEXT
    &MNEXT
    IF DELETED()
        @ 20,15 SAY 'RECORD IS ALREADY DELETED !!       Touch   <cr>....'
        ? CHR(7)
        WAIT ''
        LOOP
    ENDIF
*      If the record is within the range, move the pointer to the record
*      (with the &MNEXT macro command) and check if the record is already
```

```
*          deleted. If so, provide the error message, and loop back, asking for
*          the next record number.
        STORE ' ' TO MOPTION
        DO WHILE UPPER(MOPTION) ≠ 'X' .AND. .NOT. BOF() .AND. .NOT. EOF()
            STORE ' ' TO MOPTION
            SET FORMAT TO LAYOUTL
            READ
*          If the record is a valid record in all respects, bring up the record
*          to the screen. The screen displays the record, but will not permit
*          changes to the record. An entry field on the screen wants the
*          operator to enter either F for forward scanning, R for reverse
*          scanning, or X to exit scanning.
            IF UPPER(MOPTION) = 'X'
                LOOP
            ENDIF
            IF UPPER(MOPTION) = 'F'
                SKIP
                LOOP
            ELSE
                IF UPPER(MOPTION) = 'R'
                    SKIP -1
                    LOOP
                ENDIF
            ENDIF
        ENDDO
    SET FORMAT TO
ENDDO
*          If you notice the DO WHILE... statement for this loop, the scanning
*          will proceed until the operator enters an X, or the operator attempts
*          scanning outside of the range of the file. The BOF() function is the
*          "beginning of file" function. The DO WHILE...states: "Do the loop
*          for as long as the operator has not entered an X, and it is not the
*          beginning of the file, and it is not the end of the file".
*          The forward and reverse "skip" will automatically ignore deleted
*          records, since we had SET DELE ON in the main menu.
*                              END  OF  PGML
```

PROGRAM M

Program M will let you scan records sequentially in the order of the part number key, instead of in record number sequence. The logic is similar to that of the previous program. We will display a miniscreen, asking for the record key to begin scanning on. The program will check the key for validity, and if incorrect, will display the miniscreen again, asking for the correct start key. When a good key is provided, it brings up the record to the screen, permitting no changes, and gives the operator an option to move foreward or backward or to exit. The record-key index is used, so the records appear in part number sequence.

The layout file, for this program is as follows:

```
* LAYOUTM.FMT - CALLED FROM PGMM.PRG
* ------------
@ 01,01 SAY DATE()
@ 1,28   SAY 'INVENTORY SCAN SCREEN'
@ 2,28   SAY '---------------------'
@ 05,20 SAY 'F - Forward      R - Reverse      X - Exit   ' GET ;
```

```
MOPTION PICT 'X'
@ 08,01 SAY 'Record #:'
@ 08,12 SAY RECNO() PICT '9999999'
@ 10,1  SAY 'PARTNUM '
@ 10,12 SAY PART
@ 11,1  SAY 'COST       '
@ 11,12 SAY COST
@ 12,1  SAY 'SELLPRICE'
@ 12,12 SAY SELLPRICE
@ 13,1  SAY 'ONHAND   '
@ 13,12 SAY ONHAND
@ 14,1  SAY 'ONORDER  '
@ 14,12 SAY ONORDER
@ 15,1  SAY 'USAGE    '
@ 15,12 SAY USAGE
@ 16,1  SAY 'LEAD     '
@ 16,12 SAY LEAD
```

The calling program is as follows:

```
* PGMM.PRG - SCAN SEQUENTIALLY ON PART-NUMBERS
* --------
USE INVENTRY INDEX PARTINDX
DO WHILE .T.
    CLEAR
    STORE '       ' TO MPART
    @ 01,01 SAY DATE()
    @ 01,20 SAY 'SEQUENTIAL SCAN, VIA PART-NUMBERS:'
    @ 10,01 SAY 'Enter part-number to start scan:  ' GET MPART PICT ;
'XXXXXX'
    @ 12,01 SAY 'Touch <cr>, to exit.....'
    READ
*       Start a loop. Ask the operator for a starting record-key, provide an
*       escape route, and read the response. Note that the indexed file has
*       to be brought into play.
    IF MPART = '       '
        RETURN
    ENDIF
*       If the operator escapes, return to the main menu.
    FIND &MPART
    IF .NOT. FOUND()
        @ 20,17 SAY 'NO SUCH PART-NUMBER FOUND  !    Touch <cr>...'
        ? CHR(7)
        WAIT ''
        LOOP
    ENDIF
*       If the operator makes any entry, try and find the entry as a part
*       number key. If no such key exists, provide the error message, and loop
*       back to the mini screen, asking for a valid key.
    STORE ' ' TO MOPTION
    DO WHILE UPPER(MOPTION) # 'X' .AND. .NOT. BOF() .AND. .NOT. EOF()
        SET FORMAT TO LAYOUTM
        STORE ' ' TO MOPTION
        READ
*       When a valid key has been provided, the FIND command has already
*       moved the record pointer to the required record. Bring this record
*       up on the screen, and read the operator's entry for the scanning
*       option (forward or reverse or exit).
```

318

```
            IF UPPER(MOPTION) = 'X'
               LOOP
            ENDIF
            IF UPPER(MOPTION) = 'F'
               SKIP
               LOOP
            ELSE
               IF UPPER(MOPTION) = 'R'
                  SKIP -1
                  LOOP
               ENDIF
            ENDIF
         ENDDO
         SET FORMAT TO
      ENDDO
*     Depending on the operator's request, the scanning moves either
*     forward or reverse in the order of the index, that is, in part-
*     number sequence. An X will break the scan process, as will a
*     beginning-of-file or end-of-file condition, as specified in
*     the DO WHILE..... statement.
*     The SKIPs will automatically ignore deleted records.
*                         END  OF  PGMM
```

PROGRAM N

I am providing Program N as a kind of utility, in case you had been entering new data or editing existing data without too much regard to checking for duplicate key values, and you now find yourself with sufficient duplicate records as to make a physical, manual check quite inappropriate.

The following program will scan your indexed file for records that have duplicate values in the key field and delete those records. The first record, of any series of duplicate records, will be assumed to be the correct one and retained. The others will be flagged as deleted. As you can imagine, this is quite a simple program.

```
* PGMN.PRG  -  DELETE DUPLICATE RECORDS IN INVENTORY FILE
* ---------
CLEAR
@ 01,01 SAY DATE()
@ 01,21 SAY 'REMOVING DELETED RECORDS FROM INVENTORY FILE'
@ 02,21 SAY '--------------------------------------------'
@ 10,21 SAY 'WORKING......Please wait.....'
*     Although this kind of program does not need to produce any screen
*     output per se, it is always a good idea to let the operator know what
*     is going on. It is very disconcerting to an operator to select an
*     option, have a blank screen come back, hear noises as the computer
*     does its task, and not have some kind of reassurance that the
*     master file is not being dismantled record by record.
STORE 0 TO COUNTER
*     I want to keep a count of the number of records that were flagged
*     as deleted, and so this memory variable is set up.
USE INVENTRY INDEX PARTINDX
*     You will need the indexed version of the file, to check for other
*     duplicate keys. In the indexed version, note that all duplicates
*     of any key will appear together.
STORE '        ' TO MPART
```

```
*       Define a variable called MPART, 6 characters wide. We will need this
*       for subsequent comparison purposes.
DO WHILE .NOT. EOF()
*       Start this process, and go through to the end of the file.
    IF PART ≠ MPART
*       For the very first record in the inventory file, the above comparison
*       will result in FALSE, since we have a valid part number in the first
*       record, and MPART is blank, having just been defined.
        STORE PART TO MPART
        SKIP
        LOOP
*       The first part number will enter MPART, and program control will skip
*       to the next indexed record in the file, then loop back to the
*       DO WHILE... statement. If the next part number is not the same as
*       the value in MPART, we will store this next part-number into MPART,
*       and skip to the next record, and loop back. As long as different
*       part numbers are sensed in subsequent records, we will store these
*       to MPART, skip ahead to the next record and loop back for the
*       comparison.
    ELSE
        DELE
        STORE COUNTER+1 TO COUNTER
        SKIP
*       If we find a match on keys between the record in hand and the one
*       in the MPART variable, we know we have a duplicate, with the
*       original being the one in the MPART variable, and the duplicate
*       being the current record. So we delete the current record, add to
*       our counter, and then skip to the next record, and head back into
*       the loop for similar comparisons.
    ENDIF
ENDDO
@ 15,21 SAY STR(COUNTER,7)+'  Records Deleted.    Touch <CR>....'
WAIT ''
RETURN
*       At the end of file, we put out, on the screen, a literal specifying
*       the total number of records that were deleted. The WAIT command
*       permits the operator to see the outcome, be reassured that all is
*       well, and any key entry will then return program control to the main
*       menu again.
                        END  OF  PGMN
```

To highlight a point seen before, if SET DELE (is) ON, then the FIND command
will automatically ignore deleted records, but if you position yourself at a record through
the use of the record number (in the form of a macro, if you recall), then regardless
of the setting of SET DELE ON/OFF, you will have to program a check for the deleted-
record condition and bypass the deleted record.

The last few programs—those that enable you to APPEND data using your own
formats, and to EDIT existing data either sequentially or randomly using your own
formats, both options either with or without a check for duplicate keys in key fields—
round off the basic, important options users require of any system.

To emphasize a point made before, the previous menu system was an overkill, for
the purpose of learning about some of the options available. You need to pick and choose
those options most suited to a particular application.

As you can see from the preceding pages, writing a menu system involves the following tasks:

Writing the menu program itself
Writing the subprograms that the menu transfers control to
Writing the screen formats that the subprograms refer to
Writing the report formats that the subprograms may refer to

You can, of course, come up with any number of functions for a menu system. Only the very real factors of time, system-requirements, and hardware limitations will be the constraints restricting you from giving free rein to your imagination.

Once again, programming is an art, not a science, and you should feel free to invent your own routines for doing exotic things with your computer and with dBASE.

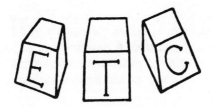

11. Additional
Tips and Techniques

I n this chapter, I will explain some more programming concepts that you will find useful. These include the areas of combining multiple files, editing multiple files simultaneously, providing password protection, enhancing screen outputs, enhancing print outputs in report programs, providing for the automatic execution of the menu program, debugging your programs, doing table look-ups, determining whether any number or variable is odd or even, providing multiple DO..WHILE conditions, and accepting variable inputs.

COMBINING MULTIPLE FILES

When we studied the DISPLAY and the REPORT feature of dBASE, we learned how we could obtain a display or a report from multiple databases, by designating our files as *active* and *nonactive*, and using the SET RELATION TO command. We can use a similar setup, along with our knowledge of programming, to extend this ability to combine multiple files and produce other files, using only two work areas.

When we specify active and nonactive files to dBASE, it maintains separate and distinct current record pointers for each database. By using the SELECT statements, we can alternate the active status between databases, each time picking up where we left off in that database.

Our scenario is as follows: suppose you have an inventory master file, with PART as the key field. Let us suppose there are two other master files that have, among other fields, a PART key field, so you can tie one master file to any of the others. Obviously, each master file has some pieces of information not found in any of the others. It is our task to combine a master file record with its various counterparts to produce another file having in its structure all the fields we would like to see together. Our presumption is that all the files are indexed on their key fields. The input files have the following structure:

Inven1 file : PART COST DESC
Inven2 file : PART CGC
Inven3 file : PART ONHAND

The required output file structure is PART COST DESC CGC ONHAND. This file is called Inven4

We shall proceed as follows: starting with the first record in the Inven1 file, we will store the PART, COST, and DESC into memory variables. Now we will SELECT Inven2 in the second work area and try to FIND a record with the same key as the PART from Inven1. If successful, we store the CGC field of that record into a memory variable. Now we redesignate Inven3 as the file in the second work area and repeat the FIND command. If successful, we store the ONHAND field from that record into a memory variable.

Having stored all the items we want for any one PART into the memory variables (which, of course, may still be blank), we now designate our output file as the file in the second work area, and proceed with the APPEND BLANK command to create a new record of data, the details of which we have covered before.

The program has been provided below.

```
* COMBINE.PRG  -  TO COMBINE DATA FROM SEVERAL FILES, INTO ONE.
* ~~~~~~~~~~~
CLEAR
@ 01,01 SAY DATE()
@ 01,33 SAY 'COMBINING FILES'
@ 02,33 SAY '~~~~~~~~~~~~~~~'
SELE 1
USE INVEN1
*      This file,INVEN1,does not necessarily have to be indexed. If it is
*      indexed, the output-file records will be created in the indexed-order
*      of this file. However, the other (secondary) files will have to be
*      indexed, since we will be using the FIND command against these
*      files.
DO WHILE .NOT. EOF()
   STORE PART TO MPART
   STORE COST TO MCOST
   STORE DESC TO MDESC
   STORE '   ' TO MCGC
   STORE 0 TO MONHAND
*      Do while it is not the end of file, for INVEN1. Store the fields of
*      this record into memory variables, and blank/zero out the memory
*      variables that will be used to store data from the other 2 files.
   SELE 2
   USE INVEN2 INDEX PT2INDX
   FIND &MPART
   IF FOUND()
```

```
         STORE CGC TO MCGC
      ENDIF
*        Use INVEN2 with the index active, and find a record with the same key
*        value as obtained from INVEN1. If the record can be found, store the
*        CGC value into the predefined memory variable. The idea of pre-
*        defining the variable is that if a matching record could not be
*        found, the variable remains blank.
      USE INVEN3 INDEX PT3INDX
      FIND &MPART
      IF FOUND()
         STORE ONHAND TO MONHAND
      ENDIF
*        Using the same technique, if a matching record can be found in the
*        INVEN3 file, store the ONHAND value into the predefined variable.
*        At this point, we have taken the first record out of INVEN1, and
*        tried to obtain a PART match on records from the two other files.
*        Now we can use the data in the variables to create the output record
*        in INVEN4. At this point, we are still in work area-2.
      USE INVEN4
      APPE BLANK
      REPL PART WITH MPART COST WITH MCOST DESC WITH MDESC ;
           CGC WITH MCGC ONHAND WITH MONHAND
      SELE 1
      SKIP
ENDDO
*        Create a new record of information in INVEN4, then SELE 1 again so
*        INVEN1 is our active file again, skip to the next record in the
*        active file, and repeat the process.
CLEAR ALL
RETURN
*        Don't forget the CLEAR ALL command, else the file names will still
*        remain open. Unless closed, you will not be able to USE any file with
*        the format USE <filename>.
*        Using the above format, you can combine any number of files that
*        share some commonality (such as PART NUMBER), using only two work
*        areas.
                     END  OF  COMBINE.PRG
```

EDITING MULTIPLE FILES SIMULTANEOUSLY

So far we have seen how we can relate multiple files (either on the basis of record numbers or on the basis of a key field) and DISPLAY or REPORT data from these files. Now we will extend our understanding of relating multiple files to the edit scenario.

We are going to be using the same four files we have seen earlier, INVEN1, INVEN2, INVEN3, and INVEN4, for this section. Assume, for now, that INVEN1 is going to be our primary or controlling file once again, and the other files will be linked to this file. Note also that an ONORDER field has been added to INVEN4.

I am going to design a screen format for this editing, and I will ask to GET fields from all the files. The only difference this time around will be that the field name from the primary file will be mentioned as is, while the field names from the supporting files will have the file-name prefix attached to them.

The following format of the layout file will be used:

```
* EDITM.FMT - EDITING MULTIPLE FILES SIMULTANEOUSLY.
* ~~~~~~~~~
@ 01,01 SAY DATE()
@ 01,21 SAY 'EDITING DATA FROM 4 FILES, SIMULTANEOUSLY'
@ 02,21 SAY '~~~~~~~~~~~~~~~~~~~~~~~~~~~~~~~~~~~~~~~~~~~'
@ 04,15 SAY 'CTRL+C - Forward      CTRL+R - Reverse      CTRL+W, to
exit.....'
@ 07,01 say 'PART-NUMBER    ' GET PART PICT '!!!!!!'
@ 07,50 SAY 'COST           ' GET COST PICT '999'
@ 09,01 SAY 'DESC           ' GET DESC PICT '!!!!!!!!!!!!!!!!!!!!!!!'
@ 09,50 SAY 'CGC            ' GET INVEN2->CGC PICT 'XXX'
@ 11,01 SAY 'ONHAND         ' GET INVEN3->ONHAND PICT '999'
@ 11,50 SAY 'ONORDER        ' GET INVEN4->ONORDER PICT '999'
```

Since our assumption is that INVEN1 is to be our controlling file, notice that the GET fields for PART, COST, and DESC are defined as is, while the GET field for the CGC, ONHAND, and ONORDER fields coming in from the nonactive files are all prefixed with the appropriate filenames!

When this format file is activated, as long as the relationship has been correctly set, you will be able to see the data from all files, and you can edit the data directly.

The actual program to define the relationships and activate the format file follows:

```
* EDITM.PRG - TO EDIT DATA FROM 4 DATABASES, SIMULTANEOUSLY
* ~~~~~~~~~      SET RELATION TO RECORD-NUMBERS.
SELE 1
USE INVEN1
SELE 2
USE INVEN2
SELE 3
USE INVEN3
SELE 4
USE INVEN4
*      The above commands assign the files to their respective work areas.
SELE 1
SET RELATION TO RECNO() INTO INVEN2
SELE 2
SET RELATION TO RECNO() INTO INVEN3
SELE 3
SET RELATION TO RECNO() INTO INVEN4
*      The above commands define the relationships, to record numbers.
SELE 1
*      The above command designates the INVEN1 file as the active file.
SET FORMAT TO EDITM
EDIT
*      Activate the layout file, so that the EDIT command performs editing
*      in this format, not the normal edit format.
CLOSE ALL
RETURN
*      Remember to deactivate the relationship, when done.
*                         END OF EDITM.PRG
```

You understand that if the relationship was to be set on the basis of the key field (PART NUMBER), only the program would change, with the format file remaining exactly as has been defined. The program that would be required to set relationships to the part number key field follows:

```
* EDITM.PRG - TO EDIT DATA FROM 4 DATA BASES, SIMULTANEOUSLY
* ~~~~~~~~~    SET RELATION TO PART-NUMBERS.
USE INVEN2
INDEX ON PART TO PINDX2
USE INVEN3
INDEX ON PART TO PINDX3
USE INDEX4
INDEX ON PART TO PINDX4
*      The above commands index the files to be linked to the primary file.
SELE 1
USE INVEN1
SELE 2
USE INVEN2 INDEX PINDX2
SELE 3
USE INVEN3 INDEX PINDX3
SELE 4
USE INVEN4 INDEX PINDX4
*      The above commands assign all files to their work areas.
SELE 1
SET RELATION TO PART INTO INVEN2
SELE 2
SET RELATION TO PART INTO INVEN3
SELE 3
SET RELATION TO PART INTO INVEN4
*      The above commands set up the relationships on the key fields.
SELE 1
*      The above command designates INVEN1 as the controlling file.
SET FORMAT TO EDITM
EDIT
CLOSE ALL
RETURN
*      The above commands will activate the format file, the editing process
*      will proceed, and you will see the fields from all the files, as
*      specified by the format file.
*                    · END OF EDITM.PRG
```

PROVIDING PASSWORD PROTECTION

As an enhancement to your main menu, you can provide instructions that ask the operator for a password before the menu will come up to the screen. The instructions will also ensure that the password entry is not displayed on the screen.

I will provide the menu program with the enhancements thrown in, towards the beginning of the menu. The rest of the menu, where specified, is identical to what you have seen before. The extra coding has been highlighted.

```
* MENU.PRG - INVENTORY CONTROL MENU, FOR PROGRAMS FOR THE BOOK
* ~~~~~~~~
CLEAR ALL
SET TALK OFF
SET BELL OFF
SET DELE ON
```

```
*                      PASSWORD PROTECTION BEGINS
STORE .T. TO BADENTRY
DO WHILE BADENTRY
   CLEAR
   @ 01,01 SAY DATE()
   @ 01,28 SAY 'INVENTORY CONTROL SYSTEM'
   @ 02,28 SAY '~~~~~~~~~~~~~~~~~~~~~~~~~'
   @ 10,12 SAY 'Please enter a PASSWORD......Touch <cr> to ;
exit.....'
   @ 12,35
*      Force an entry into a loop for the first time, and ask the operator
*      for a password. The command @ 12,35 only positions the cursor at
*      the appropriate location for accepting the password. As usual, you
*      also provide an escape route.
   SET ESCAPE OFF
   SET EXACT ON
   SET CONSOLE OFF
*      With SET ESCAPE OFF, the operator cannot use the ESC key to abort the
*      program. The SET EXACT ON ensures that if, very coincidentally, the
*      operator enters the leading characters only, out of the entire pass-
*      word, as opposed to entering the complete password, dBASE should not
*      find an "equal" match ! With this feature, for example, if the pass-
*      word is ARMSTRONG, then an entry of ARM will not find a match.
*      The SET CONSOLE OFF ensures that the operator entry will not be
*      echoed to the screen.
   ACCEPT TO MPASS
*      The ACCEPT command waits for the operator's entry which will be put
*      into the memory variable called MPASS.
   SET CONSOLE ON
*      Once the password has been accepted, we must re-activate the console.
   IF MPASS = ' '
      SET ESCAPE ON
      SET EXACT OFF
      RETURN
   ENDIF
*      If the operator did not provide any password, the program will reset
*      ESCAPE and EXACT to their default conditions, and then return to the
*      dot prompt.
   IF MPASS # 'DAX       '
      @ 15,20 SAY 'Incorrect password.....Touch <cr>....'
      WAIT ''
      LOOP
   ENDIF
   STORE .F. TO BADENTRY
ENDDO
*      If the operator did make an entry for password, we check to see if
*      was equal to <whatever you want the password to be>. I have chosen
*      DAX as my password. If the entry does not match the password, we
*      provide the error message, and loop back  for another attempt.
*      If the password matches, make sure that the program negates the
*      BADENTRY condition, so program control can break the loop, and
*      proceed with the rest of the menu program.
*                      PASSWORD PROTECTION ENDS
STORE ' ' TO ERRMSG
DO WHILE .T.
   CLEAR
   ?? DATE()
   ?? "                    INVENTORY CONTROL MENU"
```

```
  ? "                     ~~~~~~~~~~~~~~~~~~~~~"
  TEXT
                       etc, etc, etc, etc,
  *             END  OF  MENU (PASSWORD) PROGRAM
```

ENHANCING SCREEN LAYOUTS

We can incorporate a touch of pizazz into our screen formats by using the screen's *inverse/color video option.* The condition to be satisfied is, obviously, that your particular terminal supports inverse/color video.

Most CRTs can support the following types of visual displays: normal (regular) and special (inverse, blinking, low intensity, graphic, etc.). When you want the display to change from one type to another, you have to initiate a color code that informs the hardware of your intentions. If you have a monochrome monitor, the color code will produce the inverse video effect, in varying shades of foreground, background, and border.

We will revisit our menu program first, to make a slight change in the logic. The change will be the addition of color and the highlighting of erroneous input.

This time around, while I have shown the entire menu program again, I will limit the explanation to the color enhancement, and the additional entries will be highlighted.

```
* MENU.PRG ~ INVENTORY CONTROL MENU.
* ~~~~~~~~~
CLEAR ALL
SET TALK OFF
SET BELL OFF
SET DELE ON
STORE 'SET COLOR TO R*/W' TO HILITE
STORE 'SET COLOR TO B/W' TO COLOR
STORE 'SET COLOR TO     ' TO NORMAL
*      The program does the usual housekeeping first. Now the program stores
*      three SET commands into memory variables, named to reflect the action
*      of each SET command. At the appropriate places in the program lines
*      of code, I will flip the screen's color, depending on whether or not
*      an error needs to be highlighted or a normal action is performed.
*      Obviously, I will use the above variables as macros, for this task.
*                       PASSWORD PROTECTION BEGINS
&COLOR
*      This is a macro command, and the effect is identical to your entering
*      the SET COLOR TO B/W command at this line of code. The effect of this
*      command is to flip the screen into what I want as the operating mode,
*      blue letters on a white background.
STORE .T. TO BADENTRY
   DO WHILE BADENTRY
   CLEAR
   @ 01,01 SAY DATE()
   @ 01,28 SAY 'INVENTORY CONTROL SYSTEM'
   @ 02,28 SAY '~~~~~~~~~~~~~~~~~~~~~~~~~'
   @ 10,12 SAY 'Please enter a PASSWORD......Touch <cr> to exit.....'
   @ 12,35
   SET ESCAPE OFF
   SET EXACT ON
   SET CONSOLE OFF
   ACCEPT TO MPASS
```

```
      SET CONSOLE ON
      IF MPASS = ' '
          SET ESCAPE ON
          SET EXACT OFF
          &NORMAL
          CLEAR
*         If the operator decides to escape at the time the password is
*         requested, I want to flip the screen back to its normal, non-color
*         mode of operation, namely, white lettering on a black background,
*         and clear the screen before I return to the dot-prompt.
          RETURN
      ENDIF
      IF MPASS # 'DAX      '
          &HILITE
*         This will set color to red lettering on a white background. Since the
*         background of the screen was white to begin with (blue letters on a
*         white background), the error message will stand out in red, the more
*         so since it will also be blinking. You can remove the blinking, by
*         altering the macro defined up front,without the asterisk, SET COLOR
*         TO R/W will produce red on white, without the blinking.
*
          @ 15,20 SAY 'Incorrect password.....Touch <cr>....'
          WAIT ''
          &COLOR
*         Always set the screen back to its usual operating mode, once an
*         error has been highlighted. If required, the second time around
*         another error will again flip the screen back to the error mode.
*         But you have to ensure that every screen is switched back to its
*         usual operating mode, else the error tends to remain even when there
*         is no error In this case, I have elected the normal mode to be
*         blue lettering on a white background.
          LOOP
      ENDIF
      STORE .F. TO BADENTRY
  ENDDO
*                            PASSWORD PROTECTION ENDS
  STORE ' ' TO ERRMSG
  DO WHILE .T.
      CLEAR
      ?? DATE()
      ?? "                    INVENTORY CONTROL MENU"
      ? "                     ~~~~~~~~~~~~~~~~~~~~~~"
      TEXT


      A   -   LIST      items of inventory below a stated level
      B   -   LIST      items of inventory in danger of run-out
      C   -   FULL      inventory report
      D   -   ADD       more records into the inventory file
      E   -   ADD       more records - with duplicates-check
      F   -   EDIT      sequentially - no changes to key-field
      G   -   EDIT      sequentially - with duplicates check
      H   -   EDIT      randomly on record-numbers - with duplicates check
      I   -   EDIT      randomly on part-numbers - with duplicates check
      J   -   DELETE    randomly on record-numbers
      K   -   DELETE    randomly on part-numbers
      L   -   SCAN      sequentially on record-numbers
      M   -   SCAN      sequentially on part-numbers
      N   -   REMOVE    (delete) duplicate records from inventory file
```

```
              O  ⌐   EXIT     from this menu
        ENDTEXT
        ?
        ?
        IF ERRMSG # ' '
             &HILITE
  *          After the menu is sent to the screen, the program checks to see if
  *          there is any error message waiting in the ERRMSG memory variable. If
  *          so, then the screen will be placed into a highlight mode (red over
  *          white), and so the error will appear in red blinking letters.
  *          Obviously, only the error message will blink, not the whole screen,
  *          since the highlighting is in effect only from the position of the
  *          cursor  and beyond.
        ENDIF
        ? '                     '+ERRMSG
        ?
        &COLOR
  *          As always, flip the screen back to usual operating environment once an
  *          error message has been sent. If necessary, the error message will
  *          again be generated.
        WAIT '                          Option  ? ' TO ACTION
        STORE ' ' TO ERRMSG
        IF UPPER(ACTION) = 'A'
             DO PGMA
        ENDIF
        IF UPPER(ACTION) = 'B'
             DO PGMB
        ENDIF
        IF UPPER(ACTION) = 'C'
             DO PGMC
        ENDIF
        IF UPPER(ACTION) = 'D'
             DO PGMD
        ENDIF
        IF UPPER(ACTION) = 'E'
             DO PGME
        ENDIF
        IF UPPER(ACTION) = 'F'
             DO PGMF
        ENDIF
        IF UPPER(ACTION) = 'G'
        DO PGMG
        ENDIF
        IF UPPER(ACTION) = 'H'
             DO PGMH
        ENDIF
        IF UPPER(ACTION) = 'I'
             DO PGMI
        ENDIF
        IF UPPER(ACTION) = 'J'
             DO PGMJ
        ENDIF
        IF UPPER(ACTION) = 'K'
             DO PGMK
        ENDIF
        IF UPPER(ACTION) = 'L'
             DO PGML
        ENDIF
```

```
        IF UPPER(ACTION) = 'M'
           DO PGMM
        ENDIF
        IF UPPER(ACTION) = 'N'
           DO PGMN
        ENDIF
        IF UPPER(ACTION) = 'O'
           &NORMAL
           CLEAR
*          When the operator wants to stop running the system, this option will
*          go into effect. At this point, we want normal mode (white letters
*          on a black background), before we clear the screen and return to
*          the dot-prompt.
           RETURN
        ENDIF
        IF ACTION < 'A'    .OR.  UPPER(ACTION) > 'O'
           STORE 'INVALID !!     RE-ENTER, OR EXIT !' TO ERRMSG
           ? CHR(7)
        ENDIF
ENDDO
*                        END  OF  MENU  COLOR  ENHANCEMENT
```

You realize, of course, that you did not have to define the color codes as macro functions, since you could have spelled out the SET COLOR TO <parameters> command at the appropriate places in the menu. However, the very definite advantage of the above method becomes apparent when you want to change a color code. For example, suppose you decide on a different color code when the program encounters an error situation. Now, only one line of code needs to be changed (the line where the macro is defined), instead of the individual multiple lines, and you will have made the change effective across the entire program!

I will now provide another example using one of the programs from the menu. I will show you a version of Program G enhanced with the color codes. As in the previous case, only the changes have been highlighted.

```
* PGMG.PRG - EDIT SEQUENTIALLY, WITH DUPLICATES CHECK
* --------
STORE 'SET COLOR TO R/W,R/BG' TO HILITE
STORE 'SET COLOR TO B/W,N/BG' TO COLOR
&COLOR
*       Define the color macros. Notice that I now have a double combination
*       as follows:  For highlighting an error, I have R/W,R/BG. That is, I
*       want red on white for standard display and red on cyan for inverse
*       display.
*       For my normal operating mode, I have specified B/W,N/BG. That is,
*       program G will provide me with a formatted screen where the normal
*       lettering will appear as blue on white, and the inverse video
*       portion will appear as black on cyan. I want normal lettering in a
*       blue-on-white combination, in keeping with the main menu, since
*       program G will be initiated from the main menu.
*       Notice that I ensure the usual operating mode color as soon as I
*       have entered program G.
CLEAR
USE INVENTRY INDEX PARTINDX
STORE ' ' TO MWARN
STORE 'Y' TO MMORE
```

```
DO WHILE .NOT. EOF() .AND. MMORE = 'Y'
    STORE STR(RECNO(),8) TO MCURRENT
    STORE PART TO MPART,REALPART
    STORE .T. TO NOGOOD
    DO WHILE NOGOOD
        SET FORMAT TO LAYOUTG
        READ
        &COLOR
*       Always go back to usual operating mode, after a read command. This
*       point has been discussed before.
        STORE ' ' TO MWARN
        IF UPPER(MPART) = UPPER(REALPART)
            STORE .F. TO NOGOOD
            LOOP
        ENDIF
        FIND &MPART
        IF .NOT. EOF()
            STORE 'DUPLICATE KEY!' TO MWARN
            ? CHR(7)
            &MCURRENT
            &HILITE
*           On error, force the screen into a highlighted mode of operation
*           so the colors come out as explained earlier.
            LOOP
        ELSE
            &MCURRENT
            REPLACE PART WITH MPART
            STORE .F. TO NOGOOD
        ENDIF
    ENDDO
    SKIP
ENDDO
SET FORMAT TO
RETURN
*                         END  OF  PGMG
```

A word of cheer to the users of monochrome monitors is called for here. By trying out various experiments using different combinations of letters, you will hit upon that specific combination you would like to use for normal, enhanced, and border display. The color codes will produce varying shades of intensity, and these will serve to highlight errors.

Another enhancement that will doll-up any screen is provided here. dBASE provides you with the ability to draw boxes on the screen, either in single or double line format.

```
. @ <row1>,<col1> TO <row2>,<col2>          <cr>
```

The above command will draw a single-line box originating at the row (1) and column (1) specified, and spanning through to row (2) and column (2).

```
. @ <row1>,<col1> TO <row2>,<col2> DOUBLE          <cr>
```

This command will provide a double-lined box.

Note: Row2 must be greater than Row1, and Col2 must be greater than Col1. In other words, dBASE can only draw the box from top to bottom, and left to right.

Using the above command as a program line of code, you can draw any size box you want and then place any literals in the box. You can also have overlapping boxes, if you like. The following short program will provide three overlapping boxes in double lines, with the "I like it!!" phrase appearing in the center of the third box. In each case, you first set the color, then clear the area, and then draw the box.

```
* FRAMES.PRG ~ A SHORT EXAMPLE.
* ~~~~~~~~~~~
CLEAR
SET COLOR TO R/BG
*      This will set the color of the monitor to a sky~blue background, for
*      whatever is to follow subsequently. For now, I have chosen the red
*      foreground, so my first box will be drawn in red, on a sky~blue
*      background.
@ 01,01 CLEAR TO 10,30
*      This clears the block to a sky~blue background.
@ 01,01 TO 10,30 DOUBLE
*      The double lines are now in red, on the blue background!
SET COLOR TO W/R
@ 03,15 CLEAR TO 15,50
*      Note the above command. Since the second box has to overlay a portion
*      of the first box, the appropriate amount of space is cleared out.
*      The above form of the @~~CLEAR will clear the specified portion of
*      the screen to a red background.
@ 03,15 TO 15,50 DOUBLE
*      This will now provide a white double~lined box on a red background.
SET COLOR TO B/G
@ 10,25 CLEAR TO 23,79
@ 10,25 TO 23,79 DOUBLE
*      Clear the required amount of space to a green background, then make a
*      double~lined box in blue.
SET COLOR TO R/W
@ 17,47 SAY 'I LIKE IT !!'
*      Print the literal in red, on a white background, in the middle of the
*      third box which is a blue box on a green background.
SET COLOR TO
*      This will reset the color to normal mode, black on white.
*                      E N D   O F   F R A M E S
```

Please keep in mind that while color monitors help to enhance display outputs, not every user likes to stare at multicolored patches for several hours at a time.

ENHANCING PRINTED OUTPUTS FROM REPORT PROGRAMS

We have seen in an earlier chapter how you can write your own report program in any format you want. Basically, it takes a few @—-SAY statements, formatted the way you want to see the literals and items of data on the report. In this case, I had taken the approach that you were going to be designing a report to be printed on *blank* paper.

The complexity of the programming required becomes apparent if you have to write a report program to generate preprinted forms. For example, you may require a program to pull off Blue Cross/Blue Shield forms, for a billing operation in a medical or dental office. Now, the question of horizontal or vertical spacing becomes important; the form-length may change depending on the preprinted form used; and you may want to provide some kind of boldface type, underscores, or fancy (elongated) print in the body of the report.

This section of the book is geared towards explaining to you exactly how you can use dBASE to control your printer to achieve the special format and printing mentioned. I suggest you keep a close eye on this, for it is quite interesting.

The first item to be covered is that of a *dot-matrix* printer. If you don't have a dot-matrix printer, you cannot obtain some of the fancy (elongated) print mentioned earlier. So I will assume that you have a dot-matrix printer in your collection of hardware.

You may recall from an earlier chapter, that the output of the ? command normally goes to the screen. For example, the command: ? 'I like dBASE' <cr> will work as follows: First a carriage-return line-feed will take place on the screen; that is, the cursor will move to the next line on the screen, and then the literal will be displayed exactly where the cursor is positioned. The command ?? 'I like dBASE' <cr> works almost identically, except that there is no carriage-return line-feed taking place before the literal is output. The literal is displayed exactly where the cursor happens to be located at the time the command is executed. We had used the ?? command in the main menu, if you recall.

If you have .SET PRINT ON, then the output of the ? and ?? commands will go to the printer!!

Now, apart from sending field names and literals to the printer for printing, we can also send control codes to the printer, asking the printer to perform some kind of exotic action on the subsequent data to follow. We send these codes to the printer through the use of the .SET PRINT ON and ? or ?? commands. The control codes go through first; then the data follows. This means that you can have different printer actions on different sections of data.

At the time you send these codes to the printer, you must .SET CONSOLE OFF; otherwise these codes also tend to get translated on the screen, producing unintelligible characters that only serve to clutter up the screen. Besides, you may have a message on the screen that tells the operator to set up such-and-such form for printing, and you don't want these control codes crawling all over the screen.

The following lines of code are from a program I wrote to control the printer. The data spell out the different effects on the printouts. The control codes have been explained in the form of comments. Please note that there is no guarantee that a certain sequence of control codes will work for your printer. While there seems to be a great deal of standardization, I did come across some discrepancies when comparing control codes for three different printers. Your dot-matrix printer manual is the final authority on the specific working of a control-code sequence.

```
* PRINTER.PRG - TO TEST OUT PRINT SETTINGS
* ~~~~~~~~~~~
SET CONSOLE OFF
SET PRINT ON
*       Console must be off, else the control codes get translated on the
*       screen, which you definitely don't want.
*       The SET PRINT ON is the command that activates the printer to receive
*       the outputs of the ?? command (to follow).
*       RESET ALL PRINTER CONTROL CODES
?? CHR(27)+CHR(64)
*       SET THE TOP-OF-FORM
?? CHR(27)+CHR(53)
*       SET FORM LENGTH TO N LINES
*       FORMAT:   ?? CHR(27)+CHR(67)+CHR(N)
?? CHR(27)+CHR(67)+CHR(40)
*       You should always reset printer codes when starting a new form,
*       for obvious reasons. The TOP-OF-FORM position and the FORM-LENGTH
*       need to be spelled out, up front, so that a subsequent command in the
*       program to FORM-FEED (or EJECT) to a new form will cause the printer
*       to bring up another form to the identical corresponding position of
*       the first form.
*       It should be noted that the starting position of the first form
*       rules the subsequent starting positions of all other forms. This
*       starting position is wherever the operator positions the first form.

******************************************
*                                        *
*       START PRINTING ANY DATA YOU WANT  *
*                                        *
******************************************
SET DEVICE TO PRINT
*       This command will ensure that the outputs of all @-~-SAY commands
*       go to the printer.
*       SET PRINT AT 10 CPI
?? CHR(27)+CHR(80)
@ 01,10 SAY 'THIS IS 10 CPI PRINT'
*       SET PRINT AT 12 CPI
?? CHR(27)+CHR(77)
@ 02,10 SAY 'THIS IS 12 CPI PRINT'
*       SET PRINT AT 17 CPI
?? CHR(27)+CHR(15)
@ 03,10 SAY 'THIS IS 17 CPI PRINT'
*       SET PRINT BACK TO 10 CPI
?? CHR(27)+CHR(80)
*       SET LINE SPACING AT N/72 OF AN INCH
*       FORMAT:   ?? CHR(27)+CHR(65)+CHR(N)
?? CHR(27)+CHR(65)+CHR(24)
@ 04,10 SAY 'THIS IS LINE DENSITY AT 3 LINES PER INCH'
*       USING THE ABOVE OPTION, IT IS VERY EASY TO SET THE NEXT
*       LINE LOCATION FOR PRINTING !
*       SET EMPHASIZED MODE, AT 10 CPI ONLY
?? CHR(27)+CHR(69)
@ 05,10 SAY 'THIS IS EMPHASIZED MODE'
*       REMOVE EMPHASIZED MODE
?? CHR(27)+CHR(70)
```

```
*       SET COMPRESSED MODE ~ (SAME EFFECT AS 17 CPI MODE)
?? CHR(27)+CHR(143)
@ 06,10 SAY 'THIS IS COMPRESSED MODE'
*       REMOVE COMPRESSED MODE
?? CHR(18)
*       SET DOUBLE~STRIKE MODE
?? CHR(27)+CHR(71)
@ 07,10 SAY 'THIS IS DOUBLE~STRIKE MODE'
*       REMOVE DOUBLE~STRIKE MODE
?? CHR(27)+CHR(72)
*       SET ELONGATED MODE
?? CHR(27)+CHR(87)+CHR(1)
@ 08,10 SAY 'THIS IS ELONGATED MODE'
*       REMOVE ELONGATED MODE
?? CHR(27)+CHR(87)+CHR(2)
*       SET ELONGATED MODE, WITH DOUBLE~STRIKE MODE
?? CHR(27)+CHR(87)+CHR(1)+CHR(27)+CHR(71)
@ 09,10 SAY 'THIS IS ELONGAGED~WITH~DOUBLE~STRIKE MODE'
*       REMOVE ELONGATED MODE WITH DOUBLE~STRIKE MODE
?? CHR(27)+CHR(87)+CHR(2)+CHR(27)+CHR(72)
*       SET UNDERLINE MODE
?? CHR(27)+CHR(45)+CHR(1)
@ 10,15 SAY 'THIS IS UNDERSCORE MODE'
*       REMOVE UNDERLINE MODE
?? CHR(27)+CHR(45)+CHR(2)
*       FORM~FEED, TO THE TOP OF THE "NEXT" FORM
?? CHR(12)
*       RESET ALL PRINTER CODES
?? CHR(27)+CHR(64)
SET DEVICE TO SCREEN
SET PRINT OFF
SET CONSOLE ON
*       At the end of the printout, remember to SET DEVICE TO SCREEN so the
*       output of all subsequent @~~~SAYs go to the screen, and SET PRINT
*       OFF, so the outputs of subsequent ? and ?? commands go to the
*       screen, and, of course, SET CONSOLE ON (activate the console)
*       again.
```

You now have the ability to select horizontal spacing, vertical spacing, different print formats (emphasized, compressed, elongated, double strike, underscored, and so on), and you can define any length of form necessary. Dot-matrix printers can do much more than what has been outlined here, of course, and your printer manual will list all the other options available.

Is it necessary to have these codes in every print program we write? The answer is no, since the sequence of codes can be placed into memory variables once and saved in a memory file! These variables can then be executed, as macro commands for every subsequent program! For example, you could store these control codes to memory variables:

```
STORE '?? CHR(27)+CHR(64)' TO RESET
STORE '?? CHR(27)+CHR(53)' TO TOF
STORE '?? CHR(27)+CHR(67)+CHR(40)' TO FORMLEN
STORE '?? CHR(27)+CHR(80)' TO CPI10
STORE '?? CHR(27)+CHR(77)' TO CPI12
```

```
         STORE '?? CHR(27)+CHR(15)' TO CPI17
         STORE '?? CHR(27)+CHR(65)+CHR(24)' TO SPACING
         STORE '?? CHR(27)+CHR(87)+CHR(1)' TO ELONGATE
         STORE '?? CHR(12)' TO FORMFEED
```

The above STORE commands have set up several memory variables with commands pertaining to printer-control functions. The names of the variables reflect the action of the command. That is, RESET resets all printer controls, and TOF is the top-of-form command, and so on. Having created the variables, we can now store them all together in a memory file on our disk, so that they are always available in future to any program.

.SAVE TO PRINTER   \<cr\>

This command will save all memory variables present at the time in memory (we shall assume that the above variables are present) into a file called PRINTER.MEM. This is a *memory-file*, a file that contains only memory variables and their contents. You may, of course, provide any name you want for the memory file. The name PRINTER only serves to remind us that this memory file contains printer-control commands.

At the time the printer controls are required, in any program, you can issue the command **RESTORE FROM PRINTER ADDITIVE** \<cr\> This command will reload all the memory variables from PRINTER.MEM into memory, so they can now be invoked as macros. The ADDITIVE parameter ensures that other, existing memory variables are left intact. See the following example:

```
* PRINT.PRG - TO TEST OUT MACROS, FOR PRINTER-CONTROLS
* --------
SET TALK OFF
SET CONSOLE OFF
SET PRINT ON
RESTORE FROM PRINTER ADDITIVE
*      The SET commands are required, as explained in the previous section.
*      The "restore" command now makes all the memory variables available
*      in memory.
&RESET
*      This will reset all prior printer-controls.
&TOF
*      This will set the current setting of the form as the top-of-form.
&FORMLEN
*      This will define the length of the form as 40 lines, at the current
*      line-density setting.
SET DEVICE TO PRINT
*      Now the output of the @---SAY commands will go to the printer.
*      I will presume that you will be able to understand the other macros,
*      for setting characters at 10, 12 or 17 lines per inch,  for setting
*      vertical line spacing (density),  for character-elongation, or for
*      form-feed. Obviously, at the appropriate places, you should also
*      include the code to reset the printer controls.
&CPI10
@ 01,10 SAY 'THIS IS 10 CPI PRINT'
&CPI12
```

```
@ 02,10 SAY 'THIS IS 12 CPI PRINT'
&CPI17
@ 03,10 SAY 'THIS IS 17 CPI PRINT'
&SPACING
@ 04,10 SAY 'XXXXX  THIS LINE AND THE NEXT ONE SHOULD PRINT AT 3 PER INCH'
@ 05,10 SAY 'YYYYY  THIS LINE AND THE ONE ABOVE SHOULD PRINT AT 3 PER INCH'
&CPI10
&ELONGATE
@ 06,10 SAY 'THIS IS ELONGATED MODE'
&FORMFEED
@ 01,10 SAY 'THIS SHOULD PRINT AT THE TOP~OF~PAGE'
@ 02,10 SAY ' '
*        The last instruction above is a dummy instruction, to ensure that the
*        last line of print leaves the print~buffer, for the printer. This is
*        highly advisable for most printers.
&RESET
SET DEVICE TO SCREEN
SET PRINT OFF
SET CONSOLE ON
RETURN
*                              END   OF   PRINT
```

One point, I am sure, must have come to your mind. We have explored how you can control the report format when you write your own report program. But you can do the same thing (on a limited scale, though) when you are pulling off a report with the built-in REPORT FORM command of dBASE.

Let us say you want to pull off the dBASE report in compressed print. Simply provide the compressed-print code to the printer, before you invoke the dBASE report, and the entire report comes off in compressed print. Don't forget to reset the printer to the normal print mode, at the end of the report. An example follows:

```
* SAMPLE PROGRAM ~ TO PULL OFF A DBASE REPORT, IN COMPRESSED MODE
* ~~~~~~~~~~~~~~~
SET CONSOLE OFF
SET PRINT ON
* SET COMPRESSED MODE ON
?? CHR(27)+CHR(15)

USE INVENTRY
REPO FORM RPTA TO PRINT NOEJECT FOR PART = 'P1'

* RESET PRINTER CODES
?? CHR(27)+CHR(64)

SET PRINT OFF
SET CONSOLE ON
RETURN
*                      END   OF   SAMPLE   PROGRAM
```

THE AUTOMATIC EXECUTION OF THE MENU PROGRAM

In a previous section of the book, I outlined how you could predefine various SET commands, so that as soon as dBASE is loaded, it executes these before presenting you with the dot prompt. Remember that MS-DOS (the operating system) first loads itself, then checks the root directory for CONFIG.SYS and executes any commands there, and then checks the root directory for AUTOEXEC.BAT and executes any commands there. If one of the commands in the AUTOEXEC.BAT file is dBASE, then MS-DOS automatically loads dBASE into memory and hands over control to it. Now dBASE searches the current directory for CONFIG.DB (configure dBASE) and executes any commands there. This is the file in which I suggested you may want to keep the SET commands.

Now let us look at a slight variation. Since we have already placed the required SET commands at the start of the menu program, let us replace the SET commands of the CONFIG.DB file with only one statement. That statement is **COMMAND = DO MENU**

Now the sequence of execution will be as follows: MS-DOS will load itself, and then, in response to the AUTOEXEC.BAT file, will load dBASE; dBASE will read and execute the single statement in the file CONFIG.DB. In effect, as soon as dBASE has loaded, it will execute the command: DO MENU! Now, the user has merely to turn on the system, and within a few seconds he or she will be presented with a colorful menu on the screen, running under control of dBASE. This is user-friendliness at its best!

> **P.S.** It would have been user-friendliness at its best. Unfortunately, this latest version of dBASE (PLUS v. 1.0) provides a copyright notice that causes a 10-second delay. You can either wait out the delay or touch <cr> to continue on to the menu program. Nevertheless, the above suggestion would make the menu come up automatically, when the system has been powered on.

By way of information, there is another variation of this method, that provides the identical end-result. In the AUTOEXEC.BAT file, the command dBASE could be replaced with **dBASE MENU**. Now the word menu becomes a parameter of the dBASE command, and in effect, dBASE will load and will DO MENU automatically, totally bypassing the reading of the CONFIG.DB file. Either way, the end result is the same.

DEBUGGING YOUR PROGRAMS

The programmer, who has written a completely bug-proof program of any substance at the first sitting, has not lived. You can train yourself to reduce the number of logic errors you make through practice, but the probability of error is high. So always be prepared to do some debugging of your programs, before they will perform to expectation. dBASE provides a few good tools for debugging, and I will explain these now.

Option 1. The command .SET ECHO ON tells dBASE to echo to the screen, each instruction from your program as it executes. Unfortunately, it does not tell dBASE to slow down at the same time, so the net result is that the instructions in a specific logic path taken by program control are displayed as rapidly as dBASE can execute them.

So we have to use another instruction, to slow things down. The command .SET STEP ON tells dBASE to proceed a step at a time. With a combination of SET ECHO ON and SET STEP ON, you can now follow each instruction as it executes.

Now as each instruction executes, a copy of the instruction comes up on the screen, followed by the message: "Type any key to step—ESC to cancel," and dBASE waits for you. When you touch any key to continue, the next instruction comes to the screen, followed again by the same message.

If your program produced intermediate results on the screen or worked with screen layouts, then this process of debugging clutters up the screen with too much information. You can SET DEBUG ON, so that from now, a copy of the executing instruction and the message from dBASE are sent to the printer, so the screen displays exactly what you would have seen normally, except in slow motion. This final combination of SET ECHO ON, SET STEP ON, and SET DEBUG ON lets you follow each executing instruction on the printer, while also letting you see the results, if any, of the execution on the screen. This way you can see exactly which section of program code is executed and why.

Option 2. Sometimes you want to be able to concentrate only on a certain section of the code, ignoring another section that has been successfully debugged. You can, of course, make another copy of your program, remove what you don't need, and proceed with the remaining portion of the program. There is, however, a much easier way of telling dBASE to ignore one or more sections of your code. All program statements between an IF .F. and an ENDIF will always be automatically ignored! For example, if in the menu program you want to "remove" the option checks for programs G, H, and I, without physically removing the lines of code, you can always use this code:

```
IF .F.
        IF UPPER(ACTION) = 'G'
        DO PGMG
        ENDIF
        IF UPPER(ACTION) = 'H'
            DO PGMH
        ENDIF
        IF UPPER(ACTION) = 'I'
            DO PGMI
        ENDIF
ENDIF
```

Now this section of code will not execute. You can use this technique to limit dBASE's execution to certain sections of your program.

Option 3. You can also make use of dBASE's ability to suspend program execution at any selected point in your program. The command SUSPEND, as a separate line of code anywhere in the body of the program, will pass control back to you at the level of the dot prompt. At this point, dBASE informs you ". Do suspended." You can now check the contents of memory variables for useful debugging information such as totals and counters and thus see what is happening in the program. When you want to pass control back to the program at the point of suspension, you simply enter: .RESUME <cr>, and the program carries on with the instruction after the SUSPEND. If you did not want to resume with program execution, you could use the CANCEL or RETURN commands.

At the time you SUSPEND program execution, you have the ability of releasing one or more memory variables, before resuming, to see the effect of this on the logic of the program. For example, .RELE MTOWN,MORG <cr> will release the memory variables MTOWN and MORG. You can, of course, also create memory variables through the STORE command.

> **Note:** When the program execution has been suspended, you cannot alter the program itself. Trying to use the MODIFY COMMAND command on the program will produce the "File is already open" message from dBASE. To alter the program itself, you have to either RESUME program execution through to completion, or use CANCEL or RETURN.

Option 4. If you are tearing your hair out trying to find which specific statement of a program is causing the program to abend, you could use the following simple trick. Define a variable, say, ABC, as PUBLIC, then store different values in ABC at different places in the program.

```
PUBLIC ABC
. . . .
STORE 1 TO ABC
. . . .
STORE 2 TO ABC
. . . .
Etc
```

When the program abends, the variable ABC will be available in memory, and the command ? ABC <cr> will provide the value in ABC, giving you a very direct pointer to the abending statement. In the above example, for instance, if the value in ABC is 1, then I know that it abended at the statement just after the STORE 1 to ABC line. (The presumption here is that you had the STORE statement placed after each line in a suspected group of lines in the program.)

Option 5. Finally, you can make use of the PUBLIC declaration to check the contents of memory variables for useful debugging information. If you remember, memory variables generated in a called module are not available to the calling module automatically. They have to be declared as PUBLIC before they can be generated in the called module and made available to the calling program. So a combination of PUBLIC and SUSPEND in the calling program can let you inspect the contents of memory variables generated at the called program level.

To inspect the contents of memory variables, you can either display memory through the DISP MEMO command or display the contents of individual memory variables, as for example, by typing . ? MTOWN <cr>.

TABLE LOOKUPS

Suppose we have the following scenario. From each record in a file, you have a code that represents one of nut/bolt/screw/bit/drill/tap/die. You are writing a report program, to your own required format, and you have to translate each code (01, 02, etc.) into one of the above items. That is, a code of 01 should result in NUT on the report, and so on.

One way of doing this is writing several IF statements. For example:

```
IF CODE = '01'
    @ XX,YY SAY 'NUT'                (where XX,YY are any coordinates)
ENDIF
IF CODE = '02'
    @ XX,YY SAY 'BOLT'
ENDIF                  etc, etc, etc.
```

If you had twenty such items, you could write twenty IF statements. However, I want you to note the following single command that will do this kind of decoding for you. To use the command, you must have two tables set up in memory, as follows:

.STORE '01   02   03   04   05   06   07' TO MCODE
.STORE 'NUT   BOLT   SCREWBIT   DRILLTAP   DIE ' TO MITEM

Notice that there is a one-to-one correspondence between the arguments (the codes) and the functions (the items). That is, each argument and each function is built to take exactly five locations in memory.

Let us say that our program now reads a record and obtains the code 03 from the field called CODE. This code has to be translated into the word SCREW.

The following command provides a means for this kind of table lookup:

@ XX,YY SAY SUBSTR(MITEM,AT(CODE,MCODE),5)

where XX and YY are any screen or printer coordinates.

As you remember, to substring a character string you can use this format:

SUBSTR(name-of-string,start-location,number-of-locations)

(For example: SUBSTR(TOWN,2,3)

So the above statement, translated, can be shown as:

@ XX,YY SAY SUBSTR(MITEM,AT(CODE,MCODE),5)

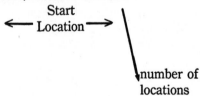

Start
←— Location —→

number of
locations

In the above example, the start location has been provided through the use of the AT function. Read the start location function as: "At the location where we can find the CODE value, in the variable called MCODE."

While this may sound a bit complicated, let us work through the logic. As we mentioned before, suppose we obtained the value 03, in the field called CODE. Where can we find 03 in the variable MCODE? We can find it starting in the eleventh location of MCODE. (Remember that each argument was built to take five character positions.) So the above expression translates itself too:

@ XX,YY SAY SUBSTR(MITEM,11,5).

The substring of MITEM, starting at the eleventh location, for five locations, is the word SCREW.

The key factor here is that the two tables for the arguments and the functions are similar. In this case, each element in each table was defined as five positions wide.

The advantage of this method is that you can avoid writing 20 IF statements, if the occasion called for decoding any one of 20 items. The disadvantage is that if you had to decode any one of 200 items, this method would not be feasible on account of the size of the tables.

Obviously, in such situations, you can always fall back upon the process of indexing. Suppose you built up a dBASE file containing two fields, one with the code and the other with the translation of the code. An inventory file with part number and part description would be a good example. If you enter data into this file, then regardless of the size of the file, you can always index this file on part number sequence. Now using the FIND command, you can always provide a code (the part number) and have dBASE FIND the record, and so pull off the part description. In this case, you have used the indexed file as one giant table, and indexing has helped in the table lookup. Depending on the number and size of the elements in the tables, you may prefer to either hard-code the tables in the program and use the AT function as shown, or build a separate file and use indexing and the FIND command to help with table lookup.

DETERMINING WHETHER A VALUE IS ODD OR EVEN

You can use the INT (integer) function to help make a quick determination if a number, memory variable, field, or expression is a numerical odd or even.

If a number is even, the integer-value of the number divided by two will be the same as the number divided by two; that is, a number is even if INT(NUMBER/2) = NUMBER/2

Example 1: INT(20/2) = 10
20/2 = 10.00

Since 10(.00) = 10.00, the number 20 is even.

Example 2: INT(23/3) = 7
23/3 = 7.67 (rounded to 2 decimals)

Since 7(.00) is not equal to 7.67, the number 23 is odd.

Suppose you want to write a report with even-numbered pages on the left-hand side and odd-numbered pages on the right-hand side. One way of doing it would be by placing the following lines of code at the appropriate place in the report program:

```
ccccccccc
ccccccccc
STORE PAGENO+1 TO PAGENO
IF INT(PAGENO/2) = PAGENO/2        && THAT IS, EVEN-NUMBER
    @ LINECNT,01 SAY 'PAGE  ' + LTRIM(STR(PAGENO,4))
ELSE
    @ LINECNT,68 SAY 'PAGE  ' + LTRIM(STR(PAGENO,4))
ENDIF
```

Another way would be to make use of the Immediate-IF instruction:

```
ccccccccc
ccccccccc
STORE PAGENO+1 TO PAGENO
@ LINECNT,IFF((INT(PAGENO/2)=PAGENO/2),01,68) ;
SAY 'PAGE  ' + LTRIM(STR(PAGENO,4))
```

In the line

@ LINECNT,IIF((INT(PAGENO/2) = PAGENO/2), 01,68) SAY '. . . blah . . . blah'

←—— COLUMN SPECIFICATION ——→

the column specification is done through the immediate-if statement, which should be read as: "If PAGENO is even, give me an 01; otherwise give me a 68. The 01 or the 68 now becomes the column specification. Thus, if PAGENO is even, the above statement translates to:

@ LINECNT,01 SAY 'PAGE' + LTRIM(STR(PAGENO,4))

If PAGENO is odd, the above statement translates to:

@ LINECNT,68 SAY 'PAGE' + LTRIM(STR(PAGENO,4))

MULTIPLE DO WHILE . . . CONDITIONS

Here is the scenario. I display the following screen for the operator, and I provide a default of ALL.

```
Start processing from which PART NUMBER  ?     ALL
                                               ccc

(Enter part-number to process, or blank out to exit. Touch <cr>)
```

The screen clearly asks the operator to put in either a specific part number, take the default, or blank out the field to negate this option.

In my program, I will have to come up with some kind of multiple condition. After all, depending on the operator's entry, either I start at the top of the file and DO WHILE .NOT. EOF( ), or I start at the specific part number provided, and DO WHILE <the

344

same part number keeps presenting itself>!

So I employ the following technique to trap the required condition. In the same program in which I ask for the operator entry, I have the following lines of code. I will assume that the operator's entry goes into a memory variable called MPART. This value may be blank, may contain the word ALL, or may contain a specific part number.

```
IF MPART = ' '
   RETURN
ENDIF
*      If the operator backed-off by entering even one blank, return to the
*      calling program, if any, else return to the dot prompt.
IF MPART = 'ALL'
   STORE 'GO TOP' TO PLACE
   STORE '.NOT. EOF()' TO COND
ELSE
   STORE TRIM(MPART) TO MPART
   STORE 'FIND &MPART' TO PLACE
   STORE 'PART=MPART .AND. .NOT. EOF()' TO COND
ENDIF
*      The above commands store certain literals in memory variables,
*      depending on the operator's response.
USE <master-file> INDEX <anyname>
&PLACE
DO WHILE &COND
*      If the operator had left the default "ALL" intact, the above macros
*      would translate to:
*                        USE <master-file> INDEX <anyname>
*                        GO TOP
*                        DO WHILE .NOT. EOF()
*      If the operator had responded with a part number, the above macros
*      would translate to:
*                        USE <master-file> INDEX <anyname>
*                        FIND &MPART
*                        DO WHILE PART=MPART .AND. .NOT. EOF()
*      So regardless of which entry is placed by the operator, you can
*      provide for the execution of any one of multiple conditions, using
*      "macro-power" as shown above. Note that we have used one macro to
*      put another in place.
*      Note that this (incomplete) program was only intended to serve as
*      a guide to this technique. Our presumption for the above FIND command
*      is that the FIND is successful.
```

A BUG IN dBASE?

While the above technique was completely workable in previous versions of the dBASE software, I found out the hard way that under some situations this technique crashes.

For example, suppose you programmed the code as above, and the macros have correctly placed the appropriate literals. The condition, therefore, has been correctly set, and we have a good DO WHILE ... ENDDO loop. If there is any other DO statement within this loop, and if this DO statement causes an overflow on the screen to the next screen, the above setup fails at the time the logic asks to stop looping!

There are many occasions when you could have DO loops within DO loops, and this bug is, of course, not acceptable. I will show you a workaround, presently. I presented the above technique to you because I know it works in previous versions, and I am sure that later versions will have corrected this *anomaly*, as ASHTON TATE likes to call these little bugs.

The Workaround for this Bug

```
IF MPART = ' '
   RETURN
ENDIF
IF MPART = 'ALL'
   GO TOP
   DO WHILE .NOT. EOF()
ELSE
   STORE TRIM(MPART) TO MPART
   FIND &MPART
   DO WHILE PART=MPART .AND. .NOT. EOF()
ENDIF
*    Note that the above IF..ELSE..ENDIF logic has set the correct
*    DO..WHILE condition !  Now you can have your regular program
*    statements, and at the end, have the ENDDO statement in support of
*    this DO...WHILE.
...............
...............     (regular program statements)
...............
ENDDO
```

You could extend this technique to any number of conditions you want to specify in the DO..WHILE statement.

ACCEPTING VARIABLE INPUTS

This section emphasizes something you have already covered. I want the following option in a program. I want to be able to ask the operator for any number of leading characters of a company name, and I want to be able to present the first company in my file matching the characters input by the operator. I can use the ACCEPT command for this purpose:

ACCEPT 'Enter any number of characters for a company name' TO MCOMPANY

As you recall, the way the ACCEPT command works is to display the literal and wait for a response; the response enters the memory variable called MCOMPANY. Now the important point is that the ACCEPT command creates a variable-length variable. So the length of the variable is dependent on the number of characters input by the operator. If the operator decides to back-out, the length of the variable is 0.

If the operator makes an entry, the program should use the indexed version of the master file, and try to FIND the MCOMPANY variable in the file.

```
IF LEN(MCOMPANY) = Ø
   RETURN
ENDIF
USE COMPANY INDEX COMPNDX
FIND &MCOMPANY
IF .NOT. FOUND()
```

```
    (display an error message on the screen)
ELSE
    (bring up the record on the screen)
ENDIF
```

The ACCEPT command is one way of accepting variable-length inputs. Suppose, however, you were using the @...SAY...GET combination of commands to display messages and obtain operator inputs:

```
STORE SPACE (15) TO MCOMPANY
@ 10,10 SAY 'Enter the company name' GET MCOMPANY PICT
'XXXXXXXXXXXXXXX'
READ
```

The above combination will define the memory variable and display the message; the cursor will wait in the GET field for the operator input. Suppose the operator enters the letters XER, in an attempt to bring up XEROX as the company, to the screen. If you now try:

```
USE COMPANY INDEX COMPNDX
FIND &MCOMPANY
```

you will never find a match on the above! The reason is that in your file you don't have any company name such as 'XER—that is, XER followed by trailing spaces!

This problem arises because the memory variable has already been predefined as having a length of 15 characters! However, you can always do the following:

```
STORE TRIM(MCOMPANY) TO MCOMPANY
FIND &MCOMPANY
```

you can strip off the trailing blanks, in effect redefining the memory variable to a new length that depends on the number of characters input by the operator! Now the result will be the characters 'XER' in the (new) memory variable called MCOMPANY, and the above FIND will work, provided, of course, you have a XEROX in your file.

Please keep in mind this simple technique of using the TRIM function to convert a fixed-length variable into a variable-length one.

A FINAL WORD OF CAUTION ON THE FIND COMMAND

I have always found INDEXing and the FIND command to be of paramount importance in the development of systems, since FIND provides such instant access to records. Therefore, I would like to leave you with some words of wisdom on the usage of the FIND command.

Ensure that you do not accidentally touch the space bar after you enter the FIND command. For instance, using the ^ character to represent the space character, if you enter

```
FIND &MPART^
```

dBASE will never find anything!

If this fact is overlooked, you could spend several hours trying to debug a program.

There is an anomaly I would have brought to your attention much earlier, except that it does not apply to the inventory system we have seen so far. However, this anomaly is a very serious bug, and you need to be made aware of how drastically it might affect your computerized application.

Suppose you had designed a Dental Practice Management system, and one of your master files is the transaction file. This file contains information on every procedure performed on any patient and is indexed on patient id number. That is, all the procedures performed on a specific patient will appear together.

To obtain the dollar amount of procedures performed on any one patient, you would do the following:

USE the indexed-version of the transaction file
FIND a specific patient id
IF FOUND( )
> you would then accumulate all the procedure charges from all transactions for this patient id, for as long as the patient id remained the same, and it was not the end-of-file.
ENDIF

The statement IF FOUND( ) is the all-important one, since, if you can find at least one transaction for this patient id, you would go about accumulating the procedure charges. If the IF FOUND( ) test fails, then this patient has no pending transactions in the transaction file.

Suppose our patient in question had 10 procedures performed and has run up a bill for two hundred dollars. When you run your query program (based on the pseudocode shown above), your program correctly shows the dollar balance. Now, the next day, you run your program again, and your program tells you that your patient suddenly owes you nothing! That is, the program is unable to find a single transaction out of the 10 transactions that you know are present in the file! In effect, the IF FOUND( ) statement comes up with a logical FALSE, indicating that no transactions could be found for this id number.

And here is the (massive) bug in this version of dBASE III PLUS. What has actually happened is that if the very first transaction is deleted, whatever the reason, the IF FOUND( ) test fails, and is unable to detect the presence of the other remaining transactions, thereby forcing your program to the invalid conclusion that there are no outstanding procedure charges for this patient! Obviously, this can have very serious consequences in any business application.

In reality, dBASE does indeed position itself correctly to the first active record (the second physical record from the set of records), but it is only the FOUND( ) test that fails, and returns a logical false, thereby creating the problem.

We did not encounter this problem in our inventory-file system, since we only have a single record for each part number. The bug comes into play only when multiple records for the same entity (person, part number, etc.) are involved, and the very first such record is deleted.

Here is the work-around for this bug. Instead of testing for the presence of the record through IF FOUND( ), you should use, instead, IF .NOT. EOF( ); that is, our pseudocode would state:

USE the indexed version of the transaction file
FIND a specific patient id
IF .NOT. EOF( )
    you would then accumulate all the procedure charges from all transactions for this patient id, for as long as the patient id remained the same, and it was not the end-of-file.
ENDIF

If a record can be found, it is not the end-of-the-file, and you should use this test for checking for the presence of any transaction. This test accurately indicates the presence of other, active transactions, even if the very first one is deleted.

SUMMARY

Well, this is it! If you have managed to digest all this material, you can consider yourself adequately prepared to face the world of data processing, using dBASE III PLUS as your tool-kit.

If I were to try and sum it all up, I would reach the conclusion that dBASE-III PLUS is a very powerful database management system, and to take maximum advantage of it you must sit down and study it. This, of course, is true of any piece of software that provides the same amount of power and flexibility as dBASE III PLUS.

It is now up to you to build upon the tools you have learned so far, and, of course, check the (voluminous) dBASE technical manuals for the rest of the commands and functions. The material you have absorbed so far will help you understand any dBASE commands or functions not explicitly covered in this book.

Appendix A explains the directory structure maintained by DOS, and also explains what happens when you power-on, or reset the system.

Appendix B is a listing of all the programs in the book, without, of course, all the comments and explanations thrown in.

Appendix A
The Directory
Structure in DOS

Before we plunge into the explanation of the directory structure as created by DOS, a brief look at the FORMAT command is needed.

On your DOS disk(ette), you have the DOS system programs, and the DOS utility programs. One of these utilities is called FORMAT.COM, and its sole purpose in life is to help you *format* (*initialize*, or *prepare*) input/output mediums such as floppy diskettes or hard disks, making them suitable for subsequent reads and writes.

All input/output mediums require this initial preparation once, after which they can be used as long as they can last physically. I will use the word disk to mean either a floppy diskette or a hard disk.

The process of formatting involves the writing out of track and sector addresses on the face of the disk, and at the same time, erasing all other information, if any, from the disk. These track/sector addresses are now called *system data*, and will subsequently help DOS in writing out and reading in *user data* to and from the disk.

Draw a parallel to the avenues and streets of New York City. Using the grid of the avenues and streets, you can find your way around the city—you hope. DOS uses the grid of the track and sector addresses to locate user files and/or available data space.

Please note that formatting a disk that was already in use will result in a clean slate! That is, you will lose all information that was previously stored on the disk! The end result of formatting is a disk that contains system data only! The term system data refers to the track and sector addresses, and to other reserved areas as we shall see.

The formatting of a disk should be done only once, and unless several read/write errors are encountered, the disk should never need formatting again. Handled with care, disks should last for several years, but assuming that a disk failure will not happen to you is asking for trouble. Always keep backup copies of all your important work.

When a disk has been formatted, apart from the track and sector addresses written on the disk, a certain amount of space is set aside for subsequent use by DOS. This space is required for holding the names and locations (via track and sector addresses) of the files that will subsequently be created on the disk. This space is called the *root directory* space and is always under the control of the operating system.

Conceptually, a disk that contains three files can be shown as follows:

```
┌─────────────────────────────────────────────────────────────────┐
│ FILEA.COM | FILEB.COM | FILEC.COM | ....|....|....|...           │ ──────→  ROOT
│ ═══════════════════════════════════════════════════════         │          DIRECTORY
│ XXXXXXXXXXXXXX|       |YYYYYYYYYYYYY|       |ZZZZZZZ|             │          SPACE
│ ──────────────────    ─────────────────     ───────────         │
│                        (USER AREA)                               │
└─────────────────────────────────────────────────────────────────┘
```

where

XXXXXXXX	represents the contents of the file called FILEA.COM
YYYYYYYY	represents the contents of the file called FILEB.COM
ZZZZZZZZ	represents the contents of the file called FILEC.COM

The names of the files are in the directory, while the actual contents of the files, which could be several thousand characters of information, are in the *user area* of the disk.

The actual locations (starting and ending track/sector locations) of the files are kept in another part of the disk called the *file allocation table* (FAT), and the directory contains pointers into the FAT for each filename in the directory. So, indirectly, the directory provides information on file locations.

If you have the disk structure as shown above, then it stands to reason that the operating system can never permit you to have two files with the same names on the disk. If you already have a name FILEA.TXT in the directory, an attempt to create another file called FILEA.TXT on the same disk will either result in the original file being *over written* (!) or result in a warning message from the system. This depends on the utility program you are using to create the new file. In the final analysis, you can only have unique filenames in a directory.

This presents a problem of sorts. Suppose for now that you are a contract programmer, designing several applications. You want to design a DENTAL system, a MEDICAL system, a TELEMARKETING system, and so on, all on the same physical medium, a high-capacity hard disk.

Since you will want to design very user-friendly menu-driven systems, you will have, in your DENTAL system, a main program that brings up a menu, from which the user makes a selection. You want to name this program MENU.PRG.

Keeping the above description of the directory space in mind, this would mean that you could not have a menu program called MENU.PRG for the MEDICAL system! As a programmer, you want to be very consistent in naming your files; otherwise the sheer number of files to be created in heavy systems would lead to a chaotic mess of filenames! In most programming situations, it is essential to be able to have multiple files with the same names!

DOS provides you with the ability to have multiple files with the same names. It does this by allowing you to maintain separate *paths* on the disk. These separate paths are called *subdirectories*.

In the example, you can create a subdirectory called DENTAL, and all program files and data files for the dental system can be stored in this path (subdirectory) of files collectively called DENTAL. You can then create a subdirectory called MEDICAL, and all program and data files for this medical system, regardless of the names of these files, can be made to belong to the MEDICAL subdirectory. You can then do the same for any other system you want to develop.

This means that you can have several programs called MENU.PRG, one in each subdirectory. Obviously, in any one subdirectory, you must have unique names for the files in that subdirectory.

A conceptual view of a disk that has multiple "systems" built on it could be as follows:

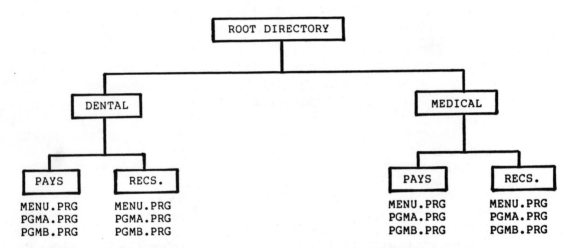

We have shown two subdirectories on the disk, DENTAL and MEDICAL. Each subdirectory has two subdirectories, PAYS (for Payables) and RECS (for Receivables). Each subdirectory at this level has a few program and data files in it. Note that the names of the files are common, across subdirectories.

Note that we always use the word *subdirectory*, regardless of the level of the subdirectory. Also, the words *directory* and *subdirectory* are used interchangeably. That is, a subdirectory at the fifth level of depth could also be referred to as a directory. The actual name of the directory (explained later) will serve to identify the level of depth.

The main directory is called the *root directory*, and is created as soon as a disk is formatted. Directories created under the root are called subdirectories. You can have any number of subdirectories, and subdirectories can have any number of subdirectories, to any level of depth. The only restriction in all this is the amount of disk space available to you.

CREATING SUBDIRECTORIES

I will assume that you are working off the hard disk called drive C; however, the following explanation applies equally well to the floppy disk in drive A. I will also assume that you have DOS on the hard disk, and that you have just loaded the system. It has prompted you for the date and time, and you have responded.

At this point in time, the system comes up with: C>. This means that DOS is now hooked into the C drive and is asking you something to the effect: "What next?"

The system maintains a directory pointer, and the pointer is currently at the root level. That is, your conceptual system, with only the root directory, looks like this:

I now want to Make (a new sub-) Directory at this root level. So I type in the following:

C>MD PROJECTS   <cr>   (The command MD means "Make Directory")

At this point, the new subdirectory has been created, and the setup looks like this:

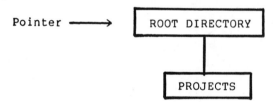

Notice that the pointer is still at the root-level! Making a directory does not change the position of the pointer.

I now want to change my directory-pointer position to the PROJECTS level, since it is my intention to create some subdirectories under the PROJECTS subdirectory. To Change (the) Directory pointer, I enter:

C>CD PROJECTS   <cr>

At this point, the setup looks like this:

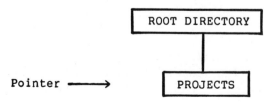

Suppose I want to find out exactly where I am positioned in the directory hierarchy. In other words, suppose I want to Check (the) Directory. I enter:

C>CD   <cr>

DOS responds with: C:\PROJECTS

Note the following points:

    1. The command CD without any parameters means "Check Directory," not "Change Directory!"

    2. The back-slash character [\] refers to the ROOT DIRECTORY. When DOS responds with \PROJECTS, it is telling you that you are at ROOT-PROJECTS, that is, at the PROJECTS subdirectory under the ROOT directory.

    3. The response C:\PROJECTS obviously means that DOS is informing you that you are pointing at PROJECTS under ROOT on the C:drive.

The last statement is important to understand! DOS is providing you with two pieces of information. DOS is telling you that your default drive is the C:drive (that is, DOS is currently hooked into the C:drive). DOS is also telling you that the default (or current) directory is ROOT-PROJECTS!

Since I am now at the PROJECTS level, I want to Make Directorys within PROJECTS. I want to create one called DB3PLUS, for use of my dBASE III PLUS software. So I type in:

C>MD DB3PLUS   <cr>   (MD means "Make Directory")

Now the setup looks like this:

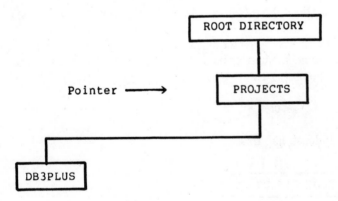

Notice that the pointer is still at the PROJECTS level. Making Directories does not change the pointer position. Changing Directories will change the pointer position.

I now want to make two more subdirectories, DENTAL and MEDICAL, for other subsystems. So I type in:

```
C>MD DENTAL          <cr>
C>MD MEDICAL         <cr>
```

The setup now looks like this:

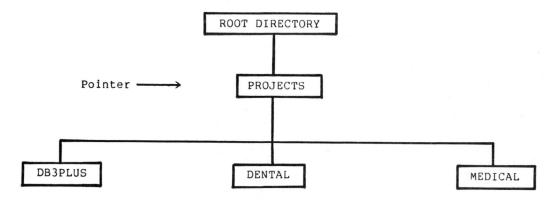

Since I am already positioned at PROJECTS, to make DB3PLUS the current directory, I must enter:

```
C>CD DB3PLUS         <cr>
```

The setup now looks like this:

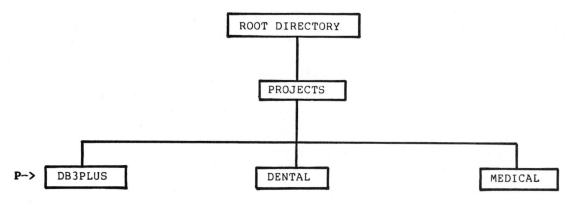

The pointer is now at the DB3PLUS directory.
If at this time I want to check my position; that is, Check the Directory, I enter:

```
C>CD        <cr>
```

DOS responds with: C:\PROJECTS\DB3PLUS. That is, DOS is informing me that
my current directory is DB3PLUS under PROJECTS under ROOT, and my default
drive is the C:drive.

To move the pointer directly to the ROOT directory, whatever the current directory may be, I enter:

```
C>CD \          <cr>
```

I am asking to Change Directory to backslash. If you remember, backslash is the symbol for the ROOT directory. This command will move the pointer back to the root level. The subdirectories created so far, will, of course, remain intact on the disk.

Regardless of where I was positioned in a directory hierarchy, to get to the DB3PLUS level under PROJECTS under ROOT, I can issue the command:

```
CD \PROJECTS\DB3PLUS          <cr>
```

The above command asks DOS to change the position of the directory pointer directly to: ROOT- - - >PROJECTS- - - >DB3PLUS!

Note that the specification \PROJECTS\DB3PLUS is called a *path*. The very first backslash in a path refers to the ROOT level. The other backslashes are only used as separators for the subdirectory names.

To refer to a filename in a specific subdirectory, use the same setup described above. For example, suppose you want to create a file called MYLETTER under \PROJECTS\DB3PLUS. When your word processor asks you for the filename, you must specify \PROJECTS\DB3PLUS\MYLETTER!

Note that DOS knows that PROJECTS and DB3PLUS are subdirectory names, while MYLETTER is not a subdirectory name (not having been created as such), and so it assumes that MYLETTER is a file to be created in the specified hierarchy.

One of the requirements of the dBASE III PLUS installation procedure is that you make a specific subdirectory the default directory to receive the dBASE software, and you make the A:drive the default drive.

Since we have already defined the subdirectory structure, regardless of where we are positioned now, if I want to make DB3PLUS the current subdirectory to receive the dBASE software, I must enter:

```
C>CD \PROJECTS\DB3PLUS          <cr>
```

Now, to make the A:drive the default drive, I must enter:

```
C>A:          <cr>
```

The above command tells DOS that from now on, my A:drive is the default drive, unless otherwise instructed. From now on, you will see the A> symbol on the screen, unless you change the drive designation again to C:.

Please note, at this point, that any reference to the C:drive will automatically reference the DB3PLUS subdirectory, since the directory pointer for the C:drive still points to this subdirectory, and any reference to the A:drive will reference the root directory of the A:drive, since we have not specifically changed the level there! That is, the A:drive is now our default drive, and C:\PROJECTS\DB3PLUS is our default directory on the C:drive.

In case you want to delete a subdirectory, whatever the reason, you will have to ensure that it is an empty subdirectory, before you can delete the subdirectory name. There must not be any files in the subdirectory to be deleted.

Suppose you want to delete the DENTAL subdirectory. First you position yourself at that level, and then you delete all the files within the directory, as follows:

```
C>CD \PROJECTS\DENTAL        <cr>
```

The above command has positioned the pointer to the DENTAL level.

```
C>DEL *.*        <cr>
```

The above DOS command asks to DELETE all the files under the current (DENTAL) directory. DOS now provides a warning message: "Are you sure (y/n)?", and waits for your response. The default is NO. Only if you touch Y, will all the files be deleted.

At this point, all the files from DENTAL have been deleted, but the pointer is still at DENTAL. To delete the directory called DENTAL, you have to be at any position other than the DENTAL level.

```
C>CD ..        <cr>
```

Note the above command. You are asking to change (the) directory position to one previous level! The two-dots (..) mean *one previous level*. Now the pointer is at the PROJECTS level; that is PROJECTS is the current directory. You can now delete the DENTAL directory, as follows:

```
C>RD DENTAL        <cr>
```

The above command asks to remove (the) directory. After the execution, you no longer have the DENTAL directory, and the pointer continues pointing to the PROJECTS directory.

Let us see another way of deleting a directory. Suppose, for now, that I also want to delete the MEDICAL directory. Since I am currently at PROJECTS, I will move down to MEDICAL, so I can delete all the files there.

```
C>CD MEDICAL        <cr>
C>DEL * *        <cr>
```

At this point, I have deleted all the files from the MEDICAL directory, and the pointer is still at MEDICAL. Now, I have to be positioned at any other level except for the MEDICAL level (since I want to remove that directory), so suppose I back off to the ROOT level.

```
C>CD \          <cr>
```

At this point, I am back at the ROOT level. Now to remove the directory called
MEDICAL:

```
C>RD \PROJECTS\MEDICAL          <cr>
```

After execution, the MEDICAL directory is no longer around, and ROOT is still
the current directory.

HOW DOS LOADS ITSELF

The preceding discussion gave you an understanding of DOS directory structures, and
presented methods of creating and deleting directories from a disk. However, some
more of the working environment needs to be set up, before dBASE will function. This
working environment will be appreciated better when you have gained an understanding of what is involved when DOS loads, or *boots*.

At power-up or reset, DOS loads itself, and also loads a special file called COM-
MAND.COM. This file contains all the DOS *internal commands*, and the *command in-
terpreter*; without this file, DOS cannot function. If you don't already have this file on
your disk, you need to copy it from the original DOS system disks received with the
hardware.

If you don't know how to run the COPY command, I have to (regretfully) refer
you to the DOS manuals.

DOS now searches the ROOT directory for a file called CONFIG.SYS, and executes any commands there. For example: CONFIG.SYS may contain the following
statements:

```
FILES = 20
BUFFERS = 15
```

These statements inform DOS that a total of 20 files could be kept open at one time,
and a total of 15 input/output *buffers* should be maintained in memory. Some programs
such as dBASE, WordStar, and Lotus require these statements in the CONFIG.SYS
file. If you are working with a high-capacity hard disk, you may want BUFFERS = 20
instead of 15.

DOS now searches the ROOT directory for a file called AUTOEXEC.BAT, and
executes any commands there. For example, AUTOEXEC.BAT could contain the following:

```
CLS
CD \PROJECTS\DB3PLUS
DBASE
CLS
CD \
```

If this file exists, DOS will execute the commands listed there, as follows: DOS will first Clear the Screen (CLS), then Change Directory to the subdirectory called DB3PLUS under PROJECTS, and having made that the current directory, will execute the software called DBASE. At this point in time, you will be in dBASE, and will continue running dBASE until you type in quit.

When you quit from dBASE, the above *batch* file takes over again, at the instruction after DBASE. That is, on quitting from dBASE, DOS will Clear the Screen again (CLS), and then Change-Directory back to the ROOT level, presenting you, once again, with the C> symbol.

If DOS cannot find the AUTOEXEC.BAT file in the ROOT directory, it will present the Date and Time prompts on the screen, followed by the C> sign, asking "What next?"

Please understand that the AUTOEXEC.BAT file merely facilitates the execution of dBASE or any other software from within a specific subdirectory. This file is not essential to the running of dBASE. However, the CONFIG.SYS file, with its FILES and BUFFERS statements is essential to the running of dBASE.

To create the CONFIG.SYS (essential) and AUTOEXEC.BAT (optional) files on the ROOT directory, proceed as follows. Load DOS, and get to the C> prompt. Now do the following procedure:

**C>CD ** `<cr>`		This ensures that you are at the ROOT.
C>COPY CON: CONFIG.SYS `<cr>`		At this point, you are asking to copy from the console, a file called CONFIG.SYS. The cursor moves to the next line, and waits for you to type in whatever statements you would like in the file. So you now type in:

FILES = 20
BUFFERS = 15

(On this line, type in Ctrl-Z, and you will find yourself back to the C> prompt.)

At this point, you will have created the CONFIG.SYS file in the ROOT directory of the C:drive.

During keyboard entry, if you realize you have made a typo on one or more lines, wrap up the process via Ctrl-Z and start again at the COPY command, in effect writing over the previous incorrect or incomplete file called CONFIG.SYS.

Use the identical process for creating the AUTOEXEC.BAT file, if required. Take greater care during keyboard entry here, since there is more to retype, if an error is made.

A pictorial representation of the directory structure, with the CONFIG.SYS and

AUTOEXEC.BAT files, and the DB3PLUS subdirectory would be as follows:

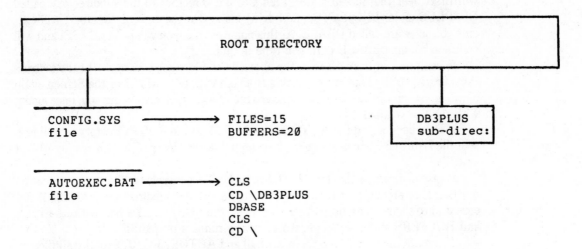

Having defined the CONFIG.SYS file and the AUTOEXEC.BAT file, if required, on the ROOT directory, and having set up the subdirectory in which dBASE will be subsequently loaded, you are now ready to continue reading where you left off in the description of the installation process.

Appendix B
The Programs

This appendix contains all the programs you will find in the book, without the detailed comment lines. I have shown extra heading comments to highlight what the program does. This will make comprehension easier, since there are no comments in the program listings.

```
* PGM1A.PRG - PROGRAM EXAMPLE 1 - a sequential program, no logic involved.
* ----------
CLEAR
USE PERSNL
INDEX ON TOWN TO TINDX
LIST
WAIT
CLEAR
INDEX ON ORG TO OINDX
LIST
WAIT


* PGM1B.PRG - PROGRAM EXAMPLE 1 - A sequential program.
* ----------                      Note the use of the '' after
*                                 the WAIT statement.
*
CLEAR
USE PERSNL
INDEX ON TOWN TO TINDX
LIST
WAIT ''
```

```
CLEAR
INDEX ON ORG TO OINDX
LIST
WAIT ''
```

```
* PGM2.PRG - PROGRAM EXAMPLE 2 - A sequential program - no logic involved.
* --------
CLEAR
USE PERSNL
SORT ON TOWN TO TSORT
SORT ON ORG TO OSORT
SORT ON EMP_NUM TO ESORT
*
USE TSORT
REPORT FORM RPT1 TO PRINT
*
USE OSORT
REPORT FORM RPT2 TO PRINT
*
USE ESORT
REPORT FORM RPT3 TO PRINT
*
USE
*
DELE FILE TSORT.DBF
DELE FILE OSORT.DBF
DELE FILE ESORT.DBF
```

```
* PGM3A.PRG - A decision command file - Accept operator input, read the
* ---------                            first record, and compare, and give
*                                      "good" or "bad" response.
*
CLEAR
ACCEPT 'Please enter a town name     ' TO MTOWN
USE PERSNL
IF UPPER(TOWN) = UPPER(MTOWN)
    @ 15,1Ø SAY 'GOOD'
ELSE
    @ 15,1Ø SAY 'Too Bad, Try Again'
ENDIF
```


```
* PGM3B.PRG - A decision command file - Obtain operator input, read the
* ---------                            first record, compare, and inform
*                                      why "good" or "bad".
*
CLEAR
ACCEPT 'Please enter a town name     ' TO MTOWN
USE PERSNL
IF UPPER(TOWN) = UPPER(MTOWN)
    @ 1Ø,15 SAY 'GOOD'
ELSE
    @ 1Ø,15 SAY 'THE TOWN WAS NOT'
```

```
      @ 10,35 SAY MTOWN
      @ 12,15 SAY 'IT WAS'
      @ 12,35 SAY TOWN
   ENDIF
```

```
* PGM4.PRG - A repetition command file - Obtain operator input, compare
* --------                               with each record, and give "good"
*                                        or "bad" response.
CLEAR
ACCEPT 'Please enter a town name    ' TO MTOWN
CLEAR
USE PERSNL
DO WHILE .NOT. EOF()
   IF UPPER(TOWN) = UPPER(MTOWN)
      @ 15,10 SAY 'GOOD'
   ELSE
      @ 15,10 SAY 'TOO BAD, TRY AGAIN'
   ENDIF
   WAIT ''
   @ 15,10
   SKIP
ENDDO
CLEAR
@ 15,10 SAY "HOW'S THAT, FOLKS !"
```

```
* PGM5A.PRG - A practical program - Obtain operator input, list all records
* ---------                         that match using DISPLAY command.
*
CLEAR
ACCEPT 'PLEASE ENTER AN ORGANISATION NAME     ' TO MORG
CLEAR
USE PERSNL
DISP    EMP_NUM,EMP_NAME,SALARY    FOR    UPPER(ORG) = UPPER(MORG)
WAIT ''
CLEAR
@ 15,10 SAY "HOW'S THAT, FOLKS !"
```

```
* PGM5B.PRG - A practical program - Obtain operator input, list all records
* ---------                         that match using a DO LOOP. Record-
*                                   numbers that don't qualify also list
*                                   out.
CLEAR
ACCEPT 'PLEASE ENTER AN ORGANISATION NAME     ' TO MORG
CLEAR
USE PERSNL
DO WHILE .NOT. EOF()
   IF UPPER(ORG) = UPPER(MORG)
      DISP EMP_NUM,EMP_NAME,SALARY
   ENDIF
   SKIP
ENDDO
WAIT ''
CLEAR
@ 15,10 SAY "HOW'S THAT, FOLKS !"
```

```
* PGM5C.PRG - A practical program - Same as above, except for the use of
* ---------                          the SET TALK OFF statement. No more
*                                    extraneous verbage from dBASE.
*
SET TALK OFF
CLEAR
ACCEPT 'PLEASE ENTER AN ORGANISATION NAME      ' TO MORG
CLEAR
USE PERSNL
DO WHILE .NOT. EOF()
   IF UPPER(ORG) = UPPER(MORG)
      DISP EMP_NUM,EMP_NAME,SALARY
   ENDIF
   SKIP
ENDDO
WAIT ''
CLEAR
@ 15,10 SAY "HOW'S THAT, FOLKS !"


* PGM5D.PRG - A practical program - Ensure only one heading line for the
* ---------                          display.
SET TALK OFF
CLEAR
ACCEPT 'PLEASE ENTER AN ORGANISATION NAME      ' TO MORG
CLEAR
USE PERSNL
DO WHILE .NOT. EOF()
   IF UPPER(ORG) = UPPER(MORG)
      DISP EMP_NUM,EMP_NAME,SALARY
      SET HEADING OFF
   ENDIF
   SKIP
ENDDO
WAIT ''
CLEAR
@ 15,10 SAY "HOW'S THAT, FOLKS !"
SET HEADING ON
```

```
* PGM6.PRG - Extending the logic with more variables - Two ACCEPTs used.
* --------
SET TALK OFF
CLEAR
ACCEPT 'Please enter a town-name       ' TO MTOWN
CLEAR
ACCEPT 'Now please enter an organisation-name ' TO MORG
CLEAR
USE PERSNL
DO WHILE .NOT. EOF()
   IF UPPER(TOWN) = UPPER(MTOWN) .AND. UPPER(ORG) = UPPER(MORG)
      DISP EMP_NUM,EMP_NAME,SALARY
      SET HEADING OFF
   ENDIF
   SKIP
ENDDO
WAIT ''
```

```
CLEAR
@ 10,15 SAY "HOW'S THAT, FOLKS !"
SET HEADING ON
```

```
* PGM7.PRG - Accepting numeric input - Difference between ACCEPT and INPUT.
* --------
SET TALK OFF
CLEAR
ACCEPT 'Please enter a town name       ' TO MTOWN
CLEAR
INPUT   'Now please enter the SALARY  ' TO MSAL
CLEAR
USE PERSNL
DO WHILE .NOT. EOF()
   IF UPPER(TOWN) = UPPER(MTOWN) .AND. SALARY < MSAL
      DISP EMP_NAME,ORG,DT_OF_HIRE
      SET HEADING OFF
   ENDIF
   SKIP
ENDDO
WAIT ''
CLEAR
@ 10,15 SAY "HOW'S THAT, FOLKS !"
SET HEADING ON
```

```
* PGM8.PRG - Providing a record count.
* --------
SET TALK OFF
STORE 0 TO COUNTER
CLEAR
ACCEPT 'Please enter a town name       ' TO MTOWN
CLEAR
INPUT   'Now please enter the SALARY  ' TO MSAL
CLEAR
USE PERSNL
DO WHILE .NOT. EOF()
   IF UPPER(TOWN) = UPPER(MTOWN) .AND. SALARY < MSAL
      DISP EMP_NAME,ORG,DT_OF_HIRE
      SET HEADING OFF
      STORE COUNTER+1 TO COUNTER
   ENDIF
   SKIP
ENDDO
WAIT ''
CLEAR
@ 10,15 SAY 'NUMBER OF MATCHING RECORDS'
@ 10,45 SAY COUNTER
SET HEADING ON
```

```
* PGM4A.PRG - A repetition command file, with timing loop - Can be used in
* ---------                              in place of the indefinite WAIT.
*
CLEAR
SET TALK OFF
ACCEPT 'PLEASE ENTER A TOWN NAME    ' TO MTOWN
CLEAR
USE PERSNL
DO WHILE .NOT. EOF()
   IF UPPER(TOWN) = UPPER(MTOWN)
      @ 15,10 SAY 'GOOD'
   ELSE
      @ 15,10 SAY 'TOO BAD, TRY AGAIN'
   ENDIF
   STORE 0 TO COUNTER
   DO WHILE COUNTER < 100
      STORE COUNTER+1 TO COUNTER
   ENDDO
   @ 15,10
   SKIP
ENDDO
CLEAR
@ 15,10 SAY "HOW'S THAT, FOLKS !"
```

```
* PGM9A.PRG - Providing averages.
* ---------
SET TALK OFF
STORE 0 TO RECCNT,TOTSAL
CLEAR
ACCEPT 'Please enter a town name       ' TO MTOWN
CLEAR
INPUT  'Now please enter the SALARY  ' TO MSAL
CLEAR
USE PERSNL
DO WHILE .NOT. EOF()
   IF UPPER(TOWN) = UPPER(MTOWN) .AND. SALARY < MSAL
      DISP EMP_NAME,ORG,DT_OF_HIRE
      SET HEADING OFF
      STORE RECCNT+1 TO RECCNT
      STORE TOTSAL+SALARY TO TOTSAL
   ENDIF
   SKIP
ENDDO
WAIT ''
CLEAR
@ 10,15 SAY 'NUMBER OF MATCHING RECORDS'
@ 10,45 SAY RECCNT
@ 12,15 SAY 'TOTAL SALARY'
@ 12,45 SAY TOTSAL
@ 14,15 SAY 'AVERAGE SALARY'
@ 14,45 SAY TOTSAL / RECCNT
SET HEADING ON
```

```
* PGM9B.PRG - Providing averages - Ensure that you do not divide by zero !
* ---------
SET TALK OFF
STORE 0 TO RECCNT,TOTSAL
```

```
CLEAR
ACCEPT 'PLEASE ENTER A TOWN NAME        ' TO MTOWN
CLEAR
INPUT   'NOW PLEASE ENTER SALARY        ' TO MSAL
CLEAR
USE PERSNL
DO WHILE .NOT. EOF()
   IF UPPER(TOWN) = UPPER(MTOWN) .AND. SALARY < MSAL
      DISP EMP_NAME,ORG,DT_OF_HIRE
      SET HEADING OFF
      STORE RECCNT+1 TO RECCNT
      STORE TOTSAL+SALARY TO TOTSAL
   ENDIF
   SKIP
ENDDO
WAIT ''
CLEAR
@ 10,15 SAY 'NUMBER OF MATCHING RECORDS'
@ 10,45 SAY RECCNT
@ 12,15 SAY 'TOTAL SALARY'
@ 12,45 SAY TOTSAL
IF RECCNT > 0
   @ 14,15 SAY 'AVERAGE SALARY'
   @ 14,45 SAY TOTSAL / RECCNT
ENDIF
SET HEADING ON
```

```
* PGM10.PRG - Calling other programs - Passing program control, via "DO".
* ----------
PUBLIC MTOWN,MORG
SET TALK OFF
CLEAR
DO ACCEPTS
CLEAR
USE PERSNL
DO WHILE .NOT. EOF()
   IF UPPER(TOWN) = UPPER(MTOWN) .AND. UPPER(ORG) = UPPER(MORG)
      DISP
      SET HEADING OFF
   ENDIF
   SKIP
ENDDO
SET HEADING ON


* ACCEPTS.PRG - CALLED FROM PGM10.PRG
* -----------
ACCEPT 'Please enter a town name       ' TO MTOWN
CLEAR
ACCEPT 'Now please enter an org. name  ' TO MORG
RETURN
```

```
* PGM11.PRG - Nested IF statements - Make them indented, so you can match
* ---------                          the IF with the ENDIF, ensuring
*                                    logical accuracy.
*
SET TALK OFF
CLEAR
USE PERSNL
DO WHILE .NOT. EOF()
    IF UPPER(TOWN) = 'ROCH'
        @ 10,15 SAY 'ROCHESTER'
    ELSE
        IF UPPER(TOWN) = 'WEB'
            @ 10,15 SAY 'WEBSTER'
        ELSE
            IF UPPER(TOWN) = 'FAIR'
                @ 10,15 SAY 'FAIRPORT'
            ELSE
                @ 10,15 SAY 'NEITHER: ROCH/WEB/FAIR'
            ENDIF
        ENDIF
    ENDIF
    WAIT ''
    @ 10,15
    SKIP
ENDDO
```

```
* PGM12.PRG - The "CASE" approach - Can be used in place of the IF..ELSE..
* ---------                         ENDIF approach.
*
SET TALK OFF
CLEAR
USE PERSNL
DO WHILE .NOT. EOF()
    DO CASE
        CASE    UPPER(TOWN) = 'ROCH'
                @ 10,15 SAY 'ROCHESTER'
*
        CASE    UPPER(TOWN) = 'WEB'
                @ 10,15 SAY 'WEBSTER'
*
        CASE    UPPER(TOWN) = 'FAIR'
                @ 10,15 SAY 'FAIRPORT'
*
        OTHERWISE
                @ 10,15 SAY 'NEITHER: ROCH/WEB/FAIR'
    ENDCASE
    WAIT ''
    @ 10,15
    SKIP
ENDDO
```

```
* PGM13.PRG - Report Program - Writing your own report program, providing
* ---------                    all the necessary logic to select records
*                              and format the display.
*
SET TALK OFF
CLEAR
```

```
      PUBLIC MTOWN,MORG,LINECNT
      DO ACCEPTS
      CLEAR
      SET DEVICE TO PRINT
      DO HDR
      STORE Ø TO TOTSALARY,RECORDCNT
      USE PERSNL
      DO WHILE .NOT. EOF()
         IF UPPER(TOWN) = UPPER(MTOWN) .AND. UPPER(ORG) = UPPER(MORG)
            @ LINECNT,1Ø SAY EMP_NUM
            @ LINECNT,25 SAY EMP_NAME
            @ LINECNT,43 SAY DT_OF_HIRE
            @ LINECNT,58 SAY SALARY
            STORE RECORDCNT+1 TO RECORDCNT
            STORE TOTSALARY+SALARY TO TOTSALARY
            STORE LINECNT+1 TO LINECNT
            IF LINECNT > 55
               DO HDR

            ENDIF
         ENDIF
         SKIP
      ENDDO
      STORE LINECNT+3 TO LINECNT
      @ LINECNT,1Ø SAY 'SALARY TOTAL'
      @ LINECNT,25 SAY TOTSALARY
      STORE LINECNT+1 TO LINECNT
      @ LINECNT,1Ø SAY 'TOTAL RECORDS'
      @ LINECNT,25 SAY RECORDCNT
      STORE LINECNT+1 TO LINECNT
      IF RECORDCNT > Ø
         @ LINECNT,1Ø SAY 'AVG. SALARY:'
         @ LINECNT,25 SAY (TOTSALARY/RECORDCNT)
      ENDIF
      @ LINECNT+3,1Ø SAY ' '
      SET DEVICE TO SCREEN


      * ACCEPTS.PRG - CALLED FROM PGM1Ø.PRG
      * -----------
      ACCEPT 'Please enter a town name        ' TO MTOWN
      CLEAR
      ACCEPT 'Now please enter an org. name  ' TO MORG
      RETURN


      * HDR.PRG - CALLED FROM PGM13
      * -------
      EJECT
      @ Ø1,Ø1 SAY DATE()
      @ Ø1,28 SAY 'REPORT AS OF MARCH 3Ø, 1986'
      @ Ø2,Ø1 SAY TIME()
      @ Ø2,28 SAY '----------------------------'
      @ Ø5,1Ø SAY 'EMP_NUMBER'
      @ Ø5,25 SAY 'EMP_NAME'
      @ Ø5,43 SAY 'DT/HIRE'
      @ Ø5,6Ø SAY 'SALARY'
      STORE 8 TO LINECNT
      RETURN
```

```
* MENU.PRG - INVENTORY CONTROL MENU - main controlling program, which sends
* --------                            up a menu on the screen, accepts a
*                                     response, then executes necessary
*                                     program
*
*
*                     CHECK OPTION - LENGTHY PROCESS
*
CLEAR ALL
SET TALK OFF
SET BELL OFF
SET DELE ON
STORE ' ' TO ERRMSG
DO WHILE .T.
   CLEAR
   ?? DATE()
   ?? "                    INVENTORY CONTROL MENU"
   ? "                    ---------------------"
   TEXT

      A  -   LIST    items of inventory below a stated level
      B  -   LIST    items of inventory in danger of run-out
      C  -   FULL    inventory report
      D  -   ADD     more records into the inventory file
      E  -   ADD     more records - with duplicates-check
      F  -   EDIT    sequentially - no changes to key-field
      G  -   EDIT    sequentially - with duplicates check
      H  -   EDIT    randomly on record-numbers - with duplicates check
      I  -   EDIT    randomly on part-numbers - with duplicates check
      J  -   DELETE  randomly on record-numbers
      K  -   DELETE  randomly on part-numbers
      L  -   SCAN    sequentially on record-numbers
      M  -   SCAN    sequentially on part-numbers
      N  -   REMOVE  (delete) duplicate records from inventory file
      O  -   EXIT    from this menu
   ENDTEXT
   ?
   ?
   ? '                         '+ERRMSG
   ?
   WAIT '                         Option  ?  ' TO ACTION
   STORE ' ' TO ERRMSG
   IF UPPER(ACTION) = 'A'
      DO PGMA
   ENDIF
   IF UPPER(ACTION) = 'B'
      DO PGMB
   ENDIF
   IF UPPER(ACTION) = 'C'
      DO PGMC
   ENDIF
   IF UPPER(ACTION) = 'D'
      DO PGMD
   ENDIF
   IF UPPER(ACTION) = 'E'
      DO PGME
   ENDIF
   IF UPPER(ACTION) = 'F'
      DO PGMF
   ENDIF
```

```
                IF UPPER(ACTION) = 'G'
                   DO PGMG
                ENDIF
                IF UPPER(ACTION) = 'H'
                   DO PGMH
                ENDIF
                IF UPPER(ACTION) = 'I'
                   DO PGMI
                ENDIF
                IF UPPER(ACTION) = 'J'
                   DO PGMJ
                ENDIF
                IF UPPER(ACTION) = 'K'
                   DO PGMK
                ENDIF
                IF UPPER(ACTION) = 'L'
                   DO PGML
                ENDIF
                IF UPPER(ACTION) = 'M'
                   DO PGMM
                ENDIF
                IF UPPER(ACTION) = 'N'
                   DO PGMN
                ENDIF
                IF UPPER(ACTION) = 'O'
                   RETURN
                ENDIF
                IF ACTION < 'A'   .OR.  UPPER(ACTION) > 'O'
                   STORE 'INVALID !!     RE-ENTER, OR EXIT !' TO ERRMSG
                   ? CHR(7)
                ENDIF
             ENDDO
```

```
* MENU.PRG - INVENTORY CONTROL MENU, FOR PROGRAMS FOR THE BOOK
* --------
*
*                       CHECK OPTION - CASE APPROACH, instead of the nested
*                                      IF approach.
*
*
CLEAR ALL
SET TALK OFF
SET BELL OFF
SET DELE ON
STORE ' ' TO ERRMSG
DO WHILE .T.
   CLEAR
   ?? DATE()
   ?? "                    INVENTORY CONTROL MENU"
   ? "                    ----------------------"
   TEXT
```

```
        A  -  LIST     items of inventory below a stated level
        B  -  LIST     items of inventory in danger of run-out
        C  -  FULL     inventory report
        D  -  ADD      more records into the inventory file
        E  -  ADD      more records - with duplicates-check
        F  -  EDIT     sequentially - no changes to key-field
        G  -  EDIT     sequentially - with duplicates check
        H  -  EDIT     randomly on record-numbers - with duplicates check
        I  -  EDIT     randomly on part-numbers - with duplicates check
        J  -  DELETE   randomly on record-numbers
        K  -  DELETE   randomly on part-numbers
        L  -  SCAN     sequentially on record-numbers
        M  -  SCAN     sequentially on part-numbers
        N  -  REMOVE   (delete) duplicate records from inventory file
        O  -  EXIT     from this menu
   ENDTEXT
   ?
   ?
   ? '                  '+ERRMSG
   ?
   WAIT '                              Option  ?  ' TO ACTION
   STORE ' ' TO ERRMSG
   DO CASE
      CASE UPPER(ACTION) = 'A'
           DO PGMA
      CASE UPPER(ACTION) = 'B'
           DO PGMB
      CASE UPPER(ACTION) = 'C'
           DO PGMC
      CASE UPPER(ACTION) = 'D'
           DO PGMD
      CASE UPPER(ACTION) = 'E'
           DO PGME
      CASE UPPER(ACTION) = 'F'
           DO PGMF
      CASE UPPER(ACTION) = 'G'
           DO PGMG
      CASE UPPER(ACTION) = 'H'
           DO PGMH
      CASE UPPER(ACTION) = 'I'
           DO PGMI
      CASE UPPER(ACTION) = 'J'
           DO PGMJ
      CASE UPPER(ACTION) = 'K'
           DO PGMK
      CASE UPPER(ACTION) = 'L'
           DO PGML
      CASE UPPER(ACTION) = 'M'
           DO PGMM
      CASE UPPER(ACTION) = 'N'
           DO PGMN
      CASE UPPER(ACTION) = 'O'
           RETURN
      OTHERWISE
           STORE 'INVALID !!     RE-ENTER, OR EXIT !' TO ERRMSG
           ? CHR(7)
   ENDCASE
ENDDO
```

```
* MENU.PRG - INVENTORY CONTROL MENU, FOR PROGRAMS FOR THE BOOK
* --------
*
*                          CHECK OPTION - QUICK PROCESS for checking for
*                                         operator input. Requires knowledge
*                                         of $-function, and macros.
*
CLEAR ALL
SET TALK OFF
SET BELL OFF
SET DELE ON
STORE ' ' TO ERRMSG
DO WHILE .T.
   CLEAR
   ?? DATE()
   ?? "                   INVENTORY CONTROL MENU"
   ? "                   ----------------------"
   TEXT

      A  -   LIST     items of inventory below a stated level
      B  -   LIST     items of inventory in danger of run-out
      C  -   FULL     inventory report
      D  -   ADD      more records into the inventory file
      E  -   ADD      more records - with duplicates-check
      F  -   EDIT     sequentially - no changes to key-field
      G  -   EDIT     sequentially - with duplicates check
      H  -   EDIT     randomly on record-numbers - with duplicates check
      I  -   EDIT     randomly on part-numbers - with duplicates check
      J  -   DELETE   randomly on record-numbers
      K  -   DELETE   randomly on part-numbers
      L  -   SCAN     sequentially on record-numbers
      M  -   SCAN     sequentially on part-numbers
      N  -   REMOVE   (delete) duplicate records from inventory file
      O  -   EXIT     from this menu
   ENDTEXT
   ?
   ?
   ? '                     '+ERRMSG
   ?
   WAIT '                           Option  ?  ' TO ACTION
   STORE ' ' TO ERRMSG
   IF UPPER(ACTION) = 'O'
      RETURN
   ENDIF
   IF UPPER(ACTION) $('ABCDEFGHIJKLMN')
      STORE 'PGM'+UPPER(ACTION) TO CHOICE
      DO &CHOICE
   ELSE
      STORE 'INVALID !!     RE-ENTER, OR EXIT !' TO ERRMSG
      ? CHR(7)
   ENDIF
ENDDO
```

```
* PGMA.PRG - REPORT ITEMS WITH ONHAND BELOW STATED LEVEL
* --------
CLEAR
@ 01,01 SAY DATE()
@ 01,21 SAY 'REPORT OF INVENTORY BELOW A STATED LEVEL'
@ 07,01 SAY "Enter inventory-level for which status is required"
```

```
@ 10,20 SAY 'Touch  <CR>, to exit......'
STORE 0 TO LEVEL
@ 18,20 SAY 'Your entry:  ' GET LEVEL PICT '999'
READ
IF LEVEL = 0
   RETURN
ENDIF
*
CLEAR
USE INVENTRY INDEX PARTINDX
REPORT FORM RPTA FOR ONHAND < LEVEL
WAIT
RETURN


* PGMAA.PRG  -  USING THE NULL VARIABLE IN PGMA.
* ----------
CLEAR
?? DATE()
?? '               REPORT OF INVENTORY BELOW A STATED LEVEL'
?
?
?
?
? 'What is the minimum inventory level for the status report '
?
? '                    Touch  <CR>,  to  exit.....'
?
?
ACCEPT '                   Your entry ?   '  TO LEVEL
*
*
IF LEN(LEVEL) = 0
   RETURN
ENDIF
*
*
IF LEVEL < '0' .OR. LEVEL > '9'
   RETURN
ENDIF
*
CLEAR
USE INVENTRY INDEX PARTINDX
REPORT FORM RPTA FOR ONHAND < VAL(LEVEL)
WAIT
RETURN


* PGMAB.PRG - REPORT ITEMS WITH ONHAND BELOW STATED LEVEL
* ----------
*
*          ENHANCEMENT WITH SPECIAL HEADER
*
*
CLEAR
@ 01,01 SAY DATE()
@ 01,21 SAY 'REPORT OF INVENTORY BELOW A STATED LEVEL'
@ 07,01 SAY "Enter inventory-level for which status is required"
@ 10,20 SAY 'Touch  <CR>, to exit......'
STORE 0 TO LEVEL
@ 18,20 SAY 'Your entry:  ' GET LEVEL PICT '999'
```

374

```
READ
IF LEVEL = Ø
   RETURN
ENDIF
*
STORE STR(LEVEL,3) TO LEVEL
*
CLEAR
USE INVENTRY INDEX PARTINDX
REPORT FORM RPTA FOR ONHAND < VAL(LEVEL) ;
        HEADING 'REPORT FOR ONHAND LESS THAN &LEVEL'
WAIT
RETURN
```

```
* PGMB.PRG - LIST ITEMS IN DANGER OF STOCK RUNOUT
* ---------
CLEAR
USE INVENTRY INDEX PARTINDX
REPORT FORM RPTB    FOR ONHAND <= USAGE * (LEAD + 10)
WAIT
RETURN
```

```
* PGMC.PRG - FULL INVENTORY REPORT
* ---------
CLEAR
USE INVENTRY INDEX PARTINDX
REPORT FORM RPTC
WAIT
RETURN
```

```
* LAYOUTD.FMT - CALLED FROM PGMD.PRG
* -----------
@ Ø2,Ø1 SAY DATE()
@ 2,25  SAY 'INVENTORY SYSTEM DATA-ENTRY SCREEN'
@ 3,25  SAY '----------------------------------'
@ 4,25  SAY 'Adding more records into inventory:'
@ 6,26  SAY 'PgUp/PgDn for Forward/Backward'
@ Ø8,5  SAY 'PART-NUM ' GET  PART      PICTURE 'XXXXX'
@ 10,5  SAY 'COST     ' GET  COST      PICTURE '99999.99'
@ 12,5  SAY 'SELLPRICE' GET  SELLPRICE  PICTURE '99999.99'
@ 14,5  SAY 'ONHAND   ' GET  ONHAND  PICTURE '999'
@ 16,5  SAY 'ONORDER  ' GET  ONORDER PICTURE '999'
@ 18,5  SAY 'USAGE    ' GET  USAGE   PICTURE '99'
@ 20,5  SAY 'LEAD     ' GET  LEAD    PICTURE '99'
@ 23,15 SAY 'Leave the screen blank, and <CR>, to exit.....'

* PGMD.PRG - ADD RECORDS TO INVENTORY, NO DUPLICATES CHECK
* ---------
CLEAR
USE INVENTRY INDEX PARTINDX
```

```
SET FORMAT TO LAYOUTD
APPEND
SET FORMAT TO
RETURN
```

```
* LAYOUTE.FMT - CALLED FROM PGME.PRG
* -----------
@ 02,01 SAY DATE()
@ 2,28  SAY 'INVENTORY DATA-ENTRY SCREEN'
@ 3,28  SAY '---------------------------'
@ 4,20  SAY 'Adding new records, with duplicates-check'
@ 6,1   SAY 'Enter the following items of information:'
@ 08,1  SAY 'PARTNUM  ' GET MPART PICTURE '!!!!!!!'
@ 10,1  SAY 'COST     ' GET MCOST PICTURE '99999.99'
@ 12,1  SAY 'SELLPRICE' GET MSELL PICTURE '99999.99'
@ 14,1  SAY 'ONHAND   ' GET MONHAND PICTURE '999'
@ 16,1  SAY 'ONORDER  ' GET MONORDER PICTURE '999'
@ 18,1  SAY 'USAGE    ' GET MUSAGE PICTURE '99'
@ 20,1  SAY 'LEAD     ' GET MLEAD PICTURE '99'
@ 22,10 SAY 'LEAVE PART-NUMBER FIELD BLANK, AND  ctrl-W,  TO EXIT.'
@ 08,50 SAY MWARN


* PGME.PRG - ADD MORE RECORDS, WITH DUPLICATES-CHECK
*
CLEAR
USE INVENTRY INDEX PARTINDX
DO WHILE .T.
   STORE '       ' TO MPART
   STORE 0 TO MCOST,MSELL,MONHAND,MONORDER,MUSAGE,MLEAD
   STORE ' ' TO MWARN
   STORE .T. TO NOGOOD
   DO WHILE NOGOOD
      SET FORMAT TO LAYOUTE
      READ
      STORE ' ' TO MWARN
      IF MPART = '       '
         SET FORMAT TO
         RETURN
      ENDIF
*
      FIND &MPART
      IF FOUND()
         STORE 'DUPLICATE KEY !' TO MWARN
         ? CHR(7)
      ELSE
         STORE .F. TO NOGOOD
      ENDIF
   ENDDO
   APPEND BLANK
   REPLACE PART WITH MPART;
           COST WITH MCOST;
           SELLPRICE WITH MSELL
   REPLACE ONHAND WITH MONHAND;
           ONORDER WITH MONORDER;
           USAGE WITH MUSAGE;
```

ENDDO

```
*  PGME.PRG - ADD MORE RECORDS, WITH DUPLICATES-CHECK - An enhancement to
*                              also check for valid entries in other
*                              (non-key) fields.
*
*
*                   ENHANCED WITH MORE EDIT CHECKS
*
CLEAR
USE INVENTRY INDEX PARTINDX
DO WHILE .T.
   STORE '        ' TO MPART
   STORE Ø TO MCOST,MSELL,MONHAND,MONORDER,MUSAGE,MLEAD
   STORE ' ' TO MWARN
   STORE .T. TO NOGOOD
   DO WHILE NOGOOD
      SET FORMAT TO LAYOUTE
      READ
      STORE ' ' TO MWARN
      IF MPART = '        '
         SET FORMAT TO
         RETURN
      ENDIF
*
      FIND &MPART
      IF .NOT. EOF()
         STORE 'DUPLICATE KEY !' TO MWARN
         ? CHR(7)
         LOOP
      ENDIF
      IF MCOST < 1Ø .OR. MCOST > 15
         STORE 'INVALID COST !' TO MWARN
         ? CHR(7)
         LOOP
      ENDIF
      IF MSELL < 2Ø .OR. MSELL > 25
         STORE 'INVALID SELL-PRICE !' TO MWARN
         ? CHR(7)
         LOOP
      ENDIF
      STORE .F. TO NOGOOD
   ENDDO
   APPEND BLANK
   REPLACE PART WITH MPART;
           COST WITH MCOST;
           SELLPRICE WITH MSELL
   REPLACE ONHAND WITH MONHAND;
           ONORDER WITH MONORDER;
           USAGE WITH MUSAGE;
           LEAD WITH MLEAD
ENDDO
```

```
* LAYOUTF.FMT - CALLED FROM PGMF.PRG
* -----------
@ 03,01 SAY DATE()
@ 3,25  SAY 'INVENTORY DATA-EDIT SCREEN'
@ 4,25  SAY '-------------------------'
@ 5,15  SAY 'Edit records sequentially, no changes to key-field'
@ 07,14 SAY '(PgDn/PgUp for forward/backward.    CTRL+W to exit...)'
@ 10,1  SAY 'PARTNUM '
@ 10,12 SAY PART PICTURE   'XXXXXX'
@ 12,1  SAY 'COST      ' GET COST PICTURE '99999.99'
@ 14,1  SAY 'SELLPRICE' GET SELLPRICE PICTURE '99999.99'
@ 16,1  SAY 'ONHAND   ' GET ONHAND PICTURE '999'
@ 18,1  SAY 'ONORDER  ' GET ONORDER PICTURE '999'
@ 20,1  SAY 'USAGE    ' GET USAGE PICTURE '99'
@ 22,1  SAY 'LEAD     ' GET LEAD  PICTURE '99'


* PGMF.PRG - EDIT SEQUENTIALLY on record-numbers, NO DUPLICATES CHECK.
* --------
CLEAR
USE INVENTRY
SET FORMAT TO LAYOUTF
EDIT
SET FORMAT TO
RETURN
```

```
* LAYOUTG.FMT - CALLED FROM PGMG.PRG
* -----------
@ 03,01 SAY DATE()
@ 3,30  SAY 'INVENTORY DATA-EDIT SCREEN'
@ 4,30  SAY '-------------------------'
@ 5,25  SAY 'Sequential edit, with duplicates-check.'
@ 07,23 SAY '(Enter  CTRL-W  or  PgDn, to go forward...)'
@ 08,1  SAY 'PARTNUM  ' GET MPART PICTURE '!!!!!!'
@ 10,1  SAY 'COST     ' GET COST PICTURE '99999.99'
@ 12,1  SAY 'SELLPRICE' GET SELLPRICE PICTURE '99999.99'
@ 14,1  SAY 'ONHAND   ' GET ONHAND PICTURE '999'
@ 15,35 SAY MWARN
@ 16,1  SAY 'ONORDER  ' GET ONORDER PICTURE '999'
@ 18,1  SAY 'USAGE    ' GET USAGE PICTURE '99'
@ 20,1  SAY 'LEAD     ' GET LEAD PICTURE '99'
@ 23,25 SAY 'MORE (Y/N) ?'  GET MMORE PICTURE 'X'


* PGMG.PRG - EDIT SEQUENTIALLY on record-numbers, WITH DUPLICATES CHECK
* --------
CLEAR
USE INVENTRY INDEX PARTINDX
STORE ' ' TO MWARN
STORE 'Y' TO MMORE
DO WHILE .NOT. EOF() .AND. MMORE = 'Y'
    STORE STR(RECNO(),8) TO MCURRENT
    STORE PART TO MPART,REALPART
    STORE .T. TO NOGOOD
    DO WHILE NOGOOD
        SET FORMAT TO LAYOUTG
        READ
```

```
                STORE ' ' TO MWARN
                IF UPPER(MPART) = UPPER(REALPART)
                    STORE .F. TO NOGOOD
                    LOOP
                ENDIF
                FIND &MPART
                IF FOUND()
                    STORE 'DUPLICATE KEY!' TO MWARN
                    ? CHR(7)
                    &MCURRENT
                    LOOP
                ELSE
                    &MCURRENT
                    REPLACE PART WITH MPART
                    STORE .F. TO NOGOOD
                ENDIF
            ENDDO
            SKIP
        ENDDO
        SET FORMAT TO
        RETURN
```

```
* LAYOUTH.FMT - CALLED FROM PGMH.PRG
* -----------
@ 03,01 SAY DATE()
@ 3,28  SAY 'INVENTORY DATA-EDIT SCREEN'
@ 4,28  SAY '--------------------------'
@ 5,20  SAY 'Random edit on record-numbers, with dup-checks'
@ 8,1   SAY 'CURRENT RECORD'
@ 8,20  SAY RECNO() PICT '9999999'
@ 10,1  SAY 'PARTNUM ' GET MPART PICT '!!!!!!!'
@ 11,1  SAY 'COST     ' GET COST PICTURE '99999.99'
@ 12,1  SAY 'SELLPRICE' GET SELLPRICE PICTURE '99999.9'
@ 13,1  SAY 'ONHAND  ' GET ONHAND PICTURE '999'
@ 14,1  SAY 'ONORDER ' GET ONORDER PICTURE '999'
@ 15,1  SAY 'USAGE   ' GET USAGE PICTURE '99'
@ 16,1  SAY 'LEAD    ' GET LEAD PICTURE '99'
@ 19,30 SAY MWARN


* PGMH.PRG - EDIT RANDOMLY ON RECORD-NUMBERS WITH DUP. CHECKS.
* --------
USE INVENTRY INDEX PARTINDX
*
DO WHILE .T.
    CLEAR
    STORE 0 TO MNEXT
    @ 01,01 SAY DATE()
    @ 01,20 SAY 'RANDOM EDIT ON RECORD-NUMBERS, WITH DUP.-CHECKS.'
    @ 10,01 SAY 'Enter record-number for edit ' GET MNEXT PICT '9999999'
    @ 12,01 SAY 'Touch <cr>, to exit.....'
    READ
    IF MNEXT = 0
        RETURN
    ENDIF
    IF MNEXT > RECCOUNT()
        @ 20,01 SAY 'YOU ONLY HAVE '+STR(RECCOUNT(),7) +'   RECORDS IN YOUR ;
FILE.....Touch <cr>...'
```

```
          ? CHR(7)
          WAIT ' '
          LOOP
      ENDIF
*
*

      STORE STR(MNEXT,7) TO MNEXT
      &MNEXT
      IF DELETED()
          @ 20,10 SAY 'The record is already deleted !    Touch ;
<CR>...'
          ? CHR(7)
          WAIT ''
          LOOP
      ENDIF
*
      STORE PART TO MPART,REALPART
*
*
*    AT THIS POINT, WE HAVE A GOOD STARTING RECORD-NUMBER
*
*

      STORE ' ' TO MWARN
      STORE .T. TO BADKEY
      DO WHILE BADKEY
          SET FORMAT TO LAYOUTH
          READ
          STORE ' ' TO MWARN
          IF UPPER(MPART) # UPPER(REALPART)
              FIND &MPART
              IF FOUND()
                  STORE 'DUPLICATE KEY !' TO MWARN
                  ? CHR(7)
                  &MNEXT
                  LOOP
              ELSE
                  &MNEXT
                  REPLACE PART WITH MPART
              ENDIF
          ENDIF
          STORE .F. TO BADKEY
      ENDDO
      SET FORMAT TO
ENDDO
RETURN
```

```
* LAYOUTI.FMT - CALLED FROM PGMI.PRG
* -----------
@ 3,30  SAY 'INVENTORY DATA-EDIT SCREEN'
@ 4,30  SAY '--------------------------'
@ 5,22  SAY 'RANDOM EDIT ON PART-NUMBERS, WITH DUP-CHECK'
@ 08,1  SAY 'PARTNUM  ' GET MPART PICTURE '!!!!!!'
@ 10,1  SAY 'COST     ' GET COST PICTURE '99999.99'
@ 11,1  SAY 'SELLPRICE' GET SELLPRICE PICTURE '99999.99'
@ 12,1  SAY 'ONHAND   ' GET ONHAND PICTURE '999'
@ 13,1  SAY 'ONORDER  ' GET ONORDER PICTURE '999'
@ 14,1  SAY 'USAGE    ' GET USAGE PICTURE '99'
```

```
      @ 15,1  SAY 'LEAD        ' GET LEAD PICTURE '99'
      @ 21,30 SAY MWARN

      * PGMI.PRG - EDIT RANDOMLY ON PART-NUMBERS, WITH DUP. CHECKS.
      * ---------
      USE INVENTRY INDEX PARTINDX
      DO WHILE .T.
         CLEAR
         @ 01,01 SAY DATE()
         @ 01,18 SAY 'EDIT RANDOMLY ON PART-NUMBERS, WITH DUP-CHECK'
         STORE '       ' TO MSTART
         @ 10,01 SAY 'ENTER PART-NUMBER TO EDIT  ' GET MSTART PICT 'XXXXXX'
         @ 12,01 SAY 'Touch <cr>, to exit.....'
         READ
         IF MSTART = '      '
            RETURN
         ENDIF
         FIND &MSTART
         IF .NOT. FOUND()
            @ 20,15 SAY 'NO SUCH PART-NUMBER KEY !    Touch <cr>'
            ? CHR(7)
            WAIT ''
            LOOP
         ENDIF
      *
      *
         STORE PART TO MPART,REALPART
         STORE ' ' TO MWARN
         STORE .T. TO NOGOOD
         DO WHILE NOGOOD
            SET FORMAT TO LAYOUTI
            READ
            STORE ' ' TO MWARN
            IF UPPER(MPART) # UPPER(REALPART)
               FIND &MPART
               IF FOUND()
                  STORE 'DUPLICATE KEY !' TO MWARN
                  ? CHR(7)
                  FIND &REALPART
                  LOOP
               ELSE
                  FIND &REALPART
                  REPLACE PART WITH MPART
               ENDIF
            ENDIF
            STORE .F. TO NOGOOD
         ENDDO
         SET FORMAT TO
      ENDDO
      RETURN
```

```
      * LAYOUTJ.FMT - CALLED FROM PGMJ.PRG
      * -----------
      @ 01,01 SAY DATE()
      @ 1,28  SAY 'INVENTORY DELETE SCREEN'
      @ 2,28  SAY '-----------------------'
      @ 3,23  SAY 'Random delete on record-numbers:'
      @ 06,20 SAY 'C O N F I R M   T H E   D E L E T E  !    (Y/N)
      ?' GET MCONFIRM PICT 'X'
```

```
@ Ø7,2Ø SAY '                          _'
@ Ø8,Ø1 SAY 'Record #:'
@ Ø8,12 SAY RECNO() PICT '9999999'
@ 1Ø,1  SAY 'PARTNUM '
@ 1Ø,12 SAY PART
@ 11,1  SAY 'COST     '
@ 11,12 SAY COST
@ 12,1  SAY 'SELLPRICE'
@ 12,12 SAY SELLPRICE
@ 13,1  SAY 'ONHAND  '
@ 13,12 SAY ONHAND
@ 14,1  SAY 'ONORDER '
@ 14,12 SAY ONORDER
@ 15,1  SAY 'USAGE   '
@ 15,12 SAY USAGE
@ 16,1  SAY 'LEAD    '
@ 16,12 SAY LEAD


* PGMJ.PRG - DELETE RANDOMLY ON RECORD-NUMBERS
* ---------
USE INVENTRY
DO WHILE .T.
   CLEAR
   STORE Ø TO MNEXT
   @ Ø1,Ø1 SAY DATE()
   @ Ø1,2Ø SAY 'RANDOM DELETE, VIA RECORD-NUMBERS:'
   @ 1Ø,Ø1 SAY 'Enter record-number for delete ' GET MNEXT PICT '9999999'
   @ 12,Ø1 SAY 'Touch <cr>, to exit.....'
   READ
   IF MNEXT = Ø
      RETURN
   ENDIF
   IF MNEXT > RECCOUNT()
      @ 2Ø,Ø1 SAY 'YOU ONLY HAVE '+STR(RECCOUNT(),7) +'   RECORDS IN YOUR ;
FILE.....Touch <cr>...'
      ? CHR(7)
      WAIT ' '
      LOOP
   ENDIF
*
   STORE STR(MNEXT,7) TO MNEXT
   &MNEXT
   IF DELETED()
      @ 2Ø,17 SAY 'RECORD IS ALREADY DELETED  !   Touch <cr>...'
      ? CHR(7)
      WAIT ''
      LOOP
   ENDIF
   STORE ' ' TO MCONFIRM
   SET FORMAT TO LAYOUTJ
   READ
   IF UPPER(MCONFIRM) = 'Y'
      DELE
   ENDIF
   SET FORMAT TO
ENDDO
```

```
* LAYOUTK.FMT - CALLED FROM PGMK.PRG
* -----------
@ 01,01 SAY DATE()
@ 1,28  SAY 'INVENTORY DELETE SCREEN'
@ 2,28  SAY '-----------------------'
@ 3,25  SAY 'Random delete on part-numbers:'
@ 06,20 SAY 'C O N F I R M   T H E   D E L E T E   !    (Y/N)
?' GET MCONFIRM PICT 'X'
@ 07,20 SAY '                                          _'
@ 08,01 SAY 'Record #:'
@ 08,12 SAY RECNO() PICT '9999999'
@ 10,1  SAY 'PARTNUM '
@ 10,12 SAY PART
@ 11,1  SAY 'COST    '
@ 11,12 SAY COST
@ 12,1  SAY 'SELLPRICE'
@ 12,12 SAY SELLPRICE
@ 13,1  SAY 'ONHAND  '
@ 13,12 SAY ONHAND
@ 14,1  SAY 'ONORDER '
@ 14,12 SAY ONORDER
@ 15,1  SAY 'USAGE   '
@ 15,12 SAY USAGE
@ 16,1  SAY 'LEAD    '
@ 16,12 SAY LEAD


* PGMK.PRG - DELETE RANDOMLY ON PART-NUMBERS
* --------
USE INVENTRY INDEX PARTINDX
DO WHILE .T.
   CLEAR
   STORE '      ' TO MPART
   @ 01,01 SAY DATE()
   @ 01,20 SAY 'RANDOM DELETE, VIA PART-NUMBERS:'
   @ 10,01 SAY 'Enter part-number for delete ' GET MPART PICT 'XXXXXX'
   @ 12,01 SAY 'Touch <cr>, to exit.....'
   READ
   IF MPART = '      '
      RETURN
   ENDIF
   FIND &MPART
   IF .NOT. FOUND()
      @ 20,17 SAY 'NO SUCH PART-NUMBER FOUND !   Touch <cr>...'
      ? CHR(7)
      WAIT ''
      LOOP
   ENDIF
   STORE ' ' TO MCONFIRM
   SET FORMAT TO LAYOUTK
   READ
   IF UPPER(MCONFIRM) = 'Y'
      DELE
   ENDIF
   SET FORMAT TO
ENDDO
```

```
* LAYOUTL.FMT - CALLED FROM PGML.PRG
* -----------
@ 01,01 SAY DATE()
@ 1,28  SAY 'INVENTORY SCAN SCREEN'
@ 2,28  SAY '---------------------'
@ 05,20 SAY 'F - Forward      R - Reverse      X - Exit  ' GET ;
PICT 'X'
@ 08,01 SAY 'Record #:'
@ 08,12 SAY RECNO() PICT '9999999'
@ 10,1  SAY 'PARTNUM '
@ 10,12 SAY PART
@ 11,1  SAY 'COST      '
@ 11,12 SAY COST
@ 12,1  SAY 'SELLPRICE'
@ 12,12 SAY SELLPRICE
@ 13,1  SAY 'ONHAND    '
@ 13,12 SAY ONHAND
@ 14,1  SAY 'ONORDER   '
@ 14,12 SAY ONORDER
@ 15,1  SAY 'USAGE     '
@ 15,12 SAY USAGE
@ 16,1  SAY 'LEAD      '
@ 16,12 SAY LEAD

* PGML.PRG - SCAN SEQUENTIALLY ON RECORD-NUMBERS
* ---------
USE INVENTRY
DO WHILE .T.
    CLEAR
    STORE 0 TO MNEXT
    @ 01,01 SAY DATE()
    @ 01,20 SAY 'SEQUENTIAL SCAN, VIA RECORD-NUMBERS:'
    @ 10,01 SAY 'Enter record-number to start scan:  ' GET MNEXT PICT ;
'9999999'
    @ 12,01 SAY 'Touch <cr>, to exit.....'
    READ
    IF MNEXT = 0
        RETURN
    ENDIF
    IF MNEXT > RECCOUNT()
        @ 20,01 SAY 'YOU ONLY HAVE '+STR(RECCOUNT(),7) +'    RECORDS IN YOUR ;
FILE.....Touch <cr>...'
        ? CHR(7)
        WAIT ' '
        LOOP
    ENDIF
    STORE STR(MNEXT,7) TO MNEXT
    &MNEXT
    IF DELETED()
        @ 20,15 SAY 'RECORD IS ALREADY DELETED !!      Touch <cr>....'
        ? CHR(7)
        WAIT ''
        LOOP
    ENDIF
    STORE ' ' TO MOPTION
    DO WHILE UPPER(MOPTION) # 'X' .AND. .NOT. BOF() .AND. .NOT. EOF()
        STORE ' ' TO MOPTION
        SET FORMAT TO LAYOUTL
        READ
        IF UPPER(MOPTION) = 'X'
```

```
            LOOP
         ENDIF
         IF UPPER(MOPTION) = 'F'
            SKIP
            LOOP
         ELSE
            IF UPPER(MOPTION) = 'R'
               SKIP -1
               LOOP
            ENDIF
         ENDIF
      ENDDO
      SET FORMAT TO
ENDDO
```

```
* LAYOUTM.FMT - CALLED FROM PGMM.PRG
* -----------
@ 01,01 SAY DATE()
@ 1,28  SAY 'INVENTORY SCAN SCREEN'
@ 2,28  SAY '---------------------'
@ 05,20 SAY 'F - Forward     R - Reverse     X - Exit  ' GET ;
MOPTION PICT 'X'
@ 08,01 SAY 'Record #:'
@ 08,12 SAY RECNO() PICT '9999999'
@ 10;1  SAY 'PARTNUM '
@ 10,12 SAY PART
@ 11,1  SAY 'COST    '
@ 11,12 SAY COST
@ 12,1  SAY 'SELLPRICE'
@ 12,12 SAY SELLPRICE
@ 13,1  SAY 'ONHAND  '
@ 13,12 SAY ONHAND
@ 14,1  SAY 'ONORDER '
@ 14,12 SAY ONORDER
@ 15,1  SAY 'USAGE   '
@ 15,12 SAY USAGE
@ 16,1  SAY 'LEAD    '
@ 16,12 SAY LEAD


* PGMM.PRG - SCAN SEQUENTIALLY ON PART-NUMBERS
* --------
USE INVENTRY INDEX PARTINDX
DO WHILE .T.
   CLEAR
   STORE '      ' TO MPART
   @ 01,01 SAY DATE()
   @ 01,20 SAY 'SEQUENTIAL SCAN, VIA PART-NUMBERS:'
   @ 10,01 SAY 'Enter part-number to start scan:  ' GET MPART ;
PICT 'XXXXXX'
   @ 12,01 SAY 'Touch <cr>, to exit.....'
   READ
   IF MPART = '      '
      RETURN
   ENDIF
   FIND &MPART
   IF .NOT. FOUND()
      @ 20,17 SAY 'NO SUCH PART-NUMBER FOUND  |   Touch <cr>...'
      ? CHR(7)
```

```
        WAIT ''
        LOOP
     ENDIF
     STORE ' ' TO MOPTION
     DO WHILE UPPER(MOPTION) # 'X' .AND. .NOT. BOF() .AND. .NOT. EOF()
        SET FORMAT TO LAYOUTM
        STORE ' ' TO MOPTION
        READ
        IF UPPER(MOPTION) = 'X'
           LOOP
        ENDIF
        IF UPPER(MOPTION) = 'F'
           SKIP
           LOOP
        ELSE
           IF UPPER(MOPTION) = 'R'
              SKIP -1
              LOOP
           ENDIF
        ENDIF
     ENDDO
     SET FORMAT TO
ENDDO


* PGMN.PRG   -  DELETE DUPLICATE RECORDS IN INVENTORY FILE
* --------
*
*
CLEAR
@ 01,01 SAY DATE()
@ 01,21 SAY 'REMOVING DELETED RECORDS FROM INVENTORY FILE'
@ 02,21 SAY '--------------------------------------------'
@ 10,21 SAY 'WORKING......Please wait.....'
STORE 0 TO COUNTER
USE INVENTRY INDEX PARTINDX
STORE '        ' TO MPART
DO WHILE .NOT. EOF()
    IF PART # MPART
       STORE PART TO MPART
       SKIP
       LOOP
    ELSE
       DELE
       STORE COUNTER+1 TO COUNTER
       SKIP
    ENDIF
ENDDO
*
*
@ 15,21 SAY STR(COUNTER,7)+'   Records Deleted.    Touch <CR>....'
WAIT ''
RETURN
```

```
* COMBINE.PRG  -  TO COMBINE DATA FROM SEVERAL FILES, INTO ANOTHER ONE.
* -----------
*
*
CLEAR
@ 01,01 SAY DATE()
@ 01,33 SAY 'COMBINING FILES'
@ 02,33 SAY '---------------'
SELE 1
USE INVEN1
DO WHILE .NOT. EOF()
   STORE PART TO MPART
   STORE COST TO MCOST
   STORE DESC TO MDESC
   STORE '   ' TO MCGC
   STORE 0 TO MONHAND
*
   SELE 2
   USE INVEN2 INDEX PT2INDX
   FIND &MPART
   IF FOUND()
      STORE CGC TO MCGC
   ENDIF
   USE INVEN3 INDEX PT3INDX
   FIND &MPART
   IF FOUND()
      STORE ONHAND TO MONHAND
   ENDIF
*
   USE INVEN4
   APPE BLANK
   REPL PART WITH MPART COST WITH MCOST DESC WITH MDESC;
      CGC WITH MCGC ONHAND WITH MONHAND
   SELE 1
   SKIP
ENDDO
CLEAR ALL
RETURN
```

```
* EDITM.FMT - EDITING MULTIPLE FILES SIMULTANEOUSLY.
* ----------
@ 01,01 SAY DATE()
@ 01,21 SAY 'EDITING DATA FROM 4 FILES, SIMULTANEOUSLY'
@ 02,21 SAY '~~~~~~~~~~~~~~~~~~~~~~~~~~~~~~~~~~~~~~~~~~~'
@ 04,15 SAY 'CTRL+C - Forward      CTRL+R - Reverse      CTRL+W, to
exit.....'
@ 07,01 say 'PART-NUMBER  ' GET PART PICT '!!!!!!'
@ 07,50 SAY 'COST         ' GET COST PICT '999'
@ 09,01 SAY 'DESC         ' GET DESC PICT '!!!!!!!!!!!!!!!!!!!!!!!!'
@ 09,50 SAY 'CGC          ' GET INVEN2->CGC PICT 'XXX'
@ 11,01 SAY 'ONHAND       ' GET INVEN3->ONHAND PICT '999'
@ 11,50 SAY 'ONORDER      ' GET INVEN4->ONORDER PICT '999'
```

387

```
* EDITM.PRG - TO EDIT DATA FROM 4 DATA-BASES, SIMULTANEOUSLY
* ---------     SET RELATION TO RECORD-NUMBERS.
*
*
SELE 1
USE INVEN1
SELE 2
USE INVEN2
SELE 3
USE INVEN3
SELE 4
USE INVEN4
*
*
SELE 1
SET RELATION TO RECNO() INTO INVEN2
SELE 2
SET RELATION TO RECNO() INTO INVEN3
SELE 3
SET RELATION TO RECNO() INTO INVEN4
*
*
SELE 1
*
SET FORMAT TO EDITM
EDIT
CLOSE ALL
RETURN
```

```
* EDITM.PRG - TO EDIT DATA FROM 4 DATA-BASES, SIMULTANEOUSLY
* ---------     SET RELATION TO PART-NUMBERS. The screen layout for this
*                                              program is the same as for the
*                                              previous program.
*
*
SELE 1

USE INVEN1
SELE 2
USE INVEN2
SELE 3
USE INVEN3
SELE 4
USE INVEN4
*
*
SELE 1
SET RELATION TO PART INTO INVEN2
SELE 2
SET RELATION TO PART INTO INVEN3
SELE 3
SET RELATION TO PART INTO INVEN4
*
*
```

```
    SELE 1
    *
    SET FORMAT TO EDITM
    EDIT
    CLOSE ALL
    RETURN
```

```
* MENUA.PRG - INVENTORY CONTROL MENU, FOR PROGRAMS FOR THE BOOK
* ----------
*                   PASSWORD PROTECTION.
*
CLEAR ALL
SET TALK OFF
SET BELL OFF
SET DELE ON
*
*
*                                   PASSWORD PROTECTION BEGINS
*
*
STORE .T. TO BADENTRY
DO WHILE BADENTRY
    CLEAR
    @ Ø1,Ø1 SAY DATE()
    @ Ø1,28 SAY 'INVENTORY CONTROL SYSTEM'
    @ Ø2,28 SAY '------------------------'
    @ 1Ø,12 SAY 'Please enter a PASSWORD......Touch <cr> to exit.....'
    @ 12,35
    SET ESCAPE OFF
    SET EXACT ON
    SET CONSOLE OFF
    ACCEPT TO MPASS
    SET CONSOLE ON
    IF MPASS = ' '
        SET ESCAPE ON
        SET EXACT OFF
        RETURN
    ENDIF
    IF MPASS # 'DAX        '
        @ 15,2Ø SAY 'Incorrect password.....Touch <cr>....'
        WAIT ''
        LOOP
    ENDIF
    STORE .F. TO BADENTRY
ENDDO
*
*
*                                   PASSWORD PROTECTION ENDS
*
*
STORE ' ' TO ERRMSG
DO WHILE .T.
    CLEAR
    ?? DATE()
    ?? "                    INVENTORY CONTROL MENU"
    ? "                    ----------------------"
```

```
      TEXT

        A  -  LIST     items of inventory below a stated level
        B  -  LIST     items of inventory in danger of run-out
        C  -  FULL     inventory report
        D  -  ADD      more records into the inventory file
        E  -  ADD      more records - with duplicates-check
        F  -  EDIT     sequentially - no changes to key-field
        G  -  EDIT     sequentially - with duplicates check
        H  -  EDIT     randomly on record-numbers - with duplicates check
        I  -  EDIT     randomly on part-numbers - with duplicates check
        J  -  DELETE   randomly on record-numbers
        K  -  DELETE   randomly on part-numbers
        L  -  SCAN     sequentially on record-numbers
        M  -  SCAN     sequentially on part-numbers
        N  -  REMOVE   (delete) duplicate records from inventory file
        O  -  EXIT     from this menu
      ENDTEXT
      ?
      ?
      ? '                    ' + ERRMSG
      ?
      WAIT '                          Option  ? ' TO ACTION
      STORE ' ' TO ERRMSG
      IF UPPER(ACTION) = 'A'
         DO PGMA
      ENDIF
      IF UPPER(ACTION) = 'B'
         DO PGMB
      ENDIF
      IF UPPER(ACTION) = 'C'
         DO PGMC
      ENDIF
      IF UPPER(ACTION) = 'D'
         DO PGMD
      ENDIF
      IF UPPER(ACTION) = 'E'
         DO PGME
      ENDIF
      IF UPPER(ACTION) = 'F'
         DO PGMF
      ENDIF
      IF UPPER(ACTION) = 'G'
         DO' PGMG
      ENDIF
      IF UPPER(ACTION) = 'H'
         DO PGMH
      ENDIF
      IF UPPER(ACTION) = 'I'
         DO PGMI
      ENDIF
      IF UPPER(ACTION) = 'J'
         DO PGMJ
      ENDIF
      IF UPPER(ACTION) = 'K'
         DO PGMK
      ENDIF
      IF UPPER(ACTION) = 'L'
```

```
               DO PGML
         ENDIF
         IF UPPER(ACTION) = 'M'
               DO PGMM
         ENDIF
         IF UPPER(ACTION) = 'N'
               DO PGMN
         ENDIF
         IF UPPER(ACTION) = 'O'
               RETURN
         ENDIF
         IF ACTION < 'A'    .OR.   UPPER(ACTION) > 'O'
               STORE 'INVALID !!     RE-ENTER, OR EXIT !' TO ERRMSG
               ? CHR(7)
         ENDIF
   ENDDO
```

```
* MENUB.PRC - INVENTORY CONTROL MENU, FOR PROGRAMS FOR THE BOOK
* ----------
*              Adding color to the menu, using macro-statements.
*
CLEAR ALL
SET TALK OFF
SET BELL OFF
SET DELE ON
STORE 'SET COLOR TO R*/W' TO HILITE
STORE 'SET COLOR TO B/W' TO COLOR
STORE 'SET COLOR TO     ' TO NORMAL
*
*
*                         PASSWORD PROTECTION BEGINS
*
*
&COLOR
STORE .T. TO BADENTRY
DO WHILE BADENTRY
   CLEAR
   @ 01,01 SAY DATE()
   @ 01,28 SAY 'INVENTORY CONTROL SYSTEM'
   @ 02,28 SAY '------------------------'
   @ 10,12 SAY 'Please enter a PASSWORD......Touch <cr> to exit.....'
   @ 12,35
   SET ESCAPE OFF
   SET EXACT ON
   SET CONSOLE OFF
   ACCEPT TO MPASS
   SET CONSOLE ON
   IF MPASS = ' '
      SET ESCAPE ON
      SET EXACT OFF
      &NORMAL
      CLEAR
      RETURN
   ENDIF
   IF MPASS # 'DAX      '
      &HILITE
      @ 15,20 SAY 'Incorrect password.....Touch <cr>....'
      WAIT ''
```

```
         &COLOR
         LOOP
      ENDIF
      STORE .F. TO BADENTRY
ENDDO
*
*
*                            PASSWORD PROTECTION ENDS
*
*
STORE ' ' TO ERRMSG
DO WHILE .T.
      CLEAR
      ?? DATE()
      ?? "                    INVENTORY CONTROL MENU"
      ? "                    -----------------------"
      TEXT


      A  -  LIST    items of inventory below a stated level
      B  -  LIST    items of inventory in danger of run-out
      C  -  FULL    inventory report
      D  -  ADD     more records into the inventory file
      E  -  ADD     more records - with duplicates-check
      F  -  EDIT    sequentially - no changes to key-field
      G  -  EDIT    sequentially - with duplicates check
      H  -  EDIT    randomly on record-numbers - with duplicates check
      I  -  EDIT    randomly on part-numbers - with duplicates check
      J  -  DELETE  randomly on record-numbers
      K  -  DELETE  randomly on part-numbers
      L  -  SCAN    sequentially on record-numbers
      M  -  SCAN    sequentially on part-numbers
      N  -  REMOVE  (delete) duplicate records from inventory file
      O  -  EXIT    from this menu
      ENDTEXT
      ?
      ?
      IF ERRMSG # ' '
         &HILITE
      ENDIF
      ? '                        '+ERRMSG
      ?
      &COLOR
      WAIT '                    Option  ? ' TO ACTION
      STORE ' ' TO ERRMSG
      IF UPPER(ACTION) = 'A'
         DO PGMA
      ENDIF
      IF UPPER(ACTION) = 'B'
         DO PGMB
      ENDIF
      IF UPPER(ACTION) = 'C'
         DO PGMC
      ENDIF
      IF UPPER(ACTION) = 'D'
         DO PGMD
      ENDIF
      IF UPPER(ACTION) = 'E'
         DO PGME
```

```
          ENDIF
          IF UPPER(ACTION) = 'F'
              DO PGMF
          ENDIF
          IF UPPER(ACTION) = 'G'
          DO PGMGA
          ENDIF
          IF UPPER(ACTION) = 'H'
              DO PGMH
          ENDIF
          IF UPPER(ACTION) = 'I'
              DO PGMI
          ENDIF
          IF UPPER(ACTION) = 'J'
              DO PGMJ
          ENDIF
          IF UPPER(ACTION) = 'K'
              DO PGMK
          ENDIF
          IF UPPER(ACTION) = 'L'
              DO PGML
          ENDIF
          IF UPPER(ACTION) = 'M'
              DO PGMM
          ENDIF
          IF UPPER(ACTION) = 'N'
              DO PGMN
          ENDIF
          IF UPPER(ACTION) = 'O'
              &NORMAL
              CLEAR
              RETURN
          ENDIF
          IF ACTION < 'A'    .OR.   UPPER(ACTION) > 'O'
              STORE 'INVALID !!       RE-ENTER, OR EXIT !' TO ERRMSG
              ? CHR(7)
          ENDIF
      ENDDO
```

```
* PGMGA.PRG - EDIT SEQUENTIALLY, WITH DUPLICATES CHECK
* ----------
*
*                    COLOR ENHANCEMENT for PGMG.PRG
*
*
STORE 'SET COLOR TO R/W,R/BG' TO HILITE
STORE 'SET COLOR TO B/W,N/BG' TO COLOR
&COLOR
CLEAR
USE INVENTRY INDEX PARTINDX
STORE ' ' TO MWARN
STORE 'Y' TO MMORE
DO WHILE .NOT. EOF() .AND. MMORE = 'Y'
STORE STR(RECNO(),8) TO MCURRENT
STORE PART TO MPART,REALPART
```

```
        STORE .T. TO NOGOOD
        DO WHILE NOGOOD
           SET FORMAT TO LAYOUTG
           READ
           &COLOR
           STORE ' ' TO MWARN
           IF UPPER(MPART) = UPPER(REALPART)
              STORE .F. TO NOGOOD
              LOOP
           ENDIF
           FIND &MPART
           IF .NOT. EOF()
              STORE 'DUPLICATE KEY!' TO MWARN
              ? CHR(7)
              &MCURRENT
              &HILITE
              LOOP
           ELSE
              &MCURRENT
              REPLACE PART WITH MPART
              STORE .F. TO NOGOOD
           ENDIF
        ENDDO
        SKIP
ENDDO
SET FORMAT TO
RETURN
```

```
* FRAMES.PRG - TO PRODUCE COLOR-FRAMES ON THE SCREEN.
* ----------
CLEAR
SET COLOR TO R/BG
@ 01,01 CLEAR TO 10,30
@ 01,01 TO 10,30 DOUBLE
*
SET COLOR TO W/R
@ 03,15 CLEAR TO 15,50
@ 03,15 TO 15,50 DOUBLE
*
SET COLOR TO B/G
@ 10,25 CLEAR TO 23,79
@ 10,25 TO 23,79 DOUBLE
*
SET COLOR TO R/W
@ 17,47 SAY 'I LIKE IT !!'
SET COLOR TO
RETURN
```

```
* PRINTER.PRG - TO TEST OUT PRINT SETTINGS - Comments are retained, here.
* -----------
SET CONSOLE OFF
SET PRINT ON
*
*
*     RESET ALL PRINTER CONTROL CODES
?? CHR(27)+CHR(64)
*
```

```
*
*       SET THE TOP-OF-FORM
?? CHR(27)+CHR(53)
*
*
*       SET FORM LENGTH TO 12 LINES
?? CHR(27)+CHR(67)+CHR(12)
*
*
*******************************************
*                                         *
*       START PRINTING ANY DATA YOU WANT  *
*                                         *
*******************************************
*
*
SET DEVICE TO PRINT
*
*
*       SET PRINT AT 10 CPI
?? CHR(27)+CHR(80)
@ 01,10 SAY 'THIS IS 10 CPI PRINT'
*
*
*       SET PRINT AT 12 CPI
?? CHR(27)+CHR(77)
@ 02,10 SAY 'THIS IS 12 CPI PRINT'
*
*
*       SET PRINT AT 17 CPI
?? CHR(27)+CHR(15)
@ 03,10 SAY 'THIS IS 17 CPI PRINT'
*
*
*       SET PRINT BACK TO 10 CPI
?? CHR(27)+CHR(80)
*
*
*       SET LINE SPACING AT N/72 OF AN INCH
?? CHR(27)+CHR(65)+CHR(24)
@ 04,10 SAY 'THIS IS LINE DENSITY AT 3 LINES PER INCH'
*
*
*       USING THE ABOVE OPTION, IT IS VERY EASY TO SET THE "NEXT"
*               LINE LOCATION. IN EFFECT, YOU HAVE A "VERTICAL TAB"
*               SETTING.
*
*
*       SET EMPHASIZED MODE, AT 10 CPI ONLY
?? CHR(27)+CHR(69)
@ 05,10 SAY 'THIS IS EMPHASIZED MODE'
*
*
*       REMOVE EMPHASIZED MODE
?? CHR(27)+CHR(70)
*
*
*       SET COMPRESSED MODE - (SAME AS 17 CPI MODE)
?? CHR(27)+CHR(143)
```

```
@ 06,10 SAY 'THIS IS COMPRESSED MODE'
*
*
*      REMOVE COMPRESSED MODE
?? CHR(18)
*
*
*      SET DOUBLE-STRIKE MODE
?? CHR(27)+CHR(71)
@ 07,10 SAY 'THIS IS DOUBLE-STRIKE MODE'
*
*
*      REMOVE DOUBLE-STRIKE MODE
?? CHR(27)+CHR(72)
*
*
*      SET ELONGATED MODE, AT CURRENT CPI
?? CHR(27)+CHR(87)+CHR(1)
@ 08,10 SAY 'THIS IS ELONGATED MODE'
*
*
*      REMOVE ELONGATED MODE
?? CHR(27)+CHR(87)+CHR(2)
*
*
*      SET ELONGATED MODE, WITH DOUBLE-STRIKE MODE
?? CHR(27)+CHR(87)+CHR(1)+CHR(27)+CHR(71)
@ 09,10 SAY 'THIS IS ELONGATED-WITH-DOUBLE-STRIKE MODE'
*
*
*      REMOVE ELONGATED MODE WITH DOUBLE-STRIKE MODE
?? CHR(27)+CHR(87)+CHR(2)+CHR(27)+CHR(72)
*
*
*      SET UNDERLINE MODE
?? CHR(27)+CHR(45)+CHR(1)
@ 10,15 SAY 'THIS IS UNDERSCORE MODE'
*
*
*      REMOVE UNDERLINE MODE
?? CHR(27)+CHR(45)+CHR(2)
*
*
*      FORM-FEED, TO THE TOP OF THE "NEXT" FORM
?? CHR(12)
*
*
*      RESET ALL PRINTER CODES
?? CHR(27)+CHR(64)
*
*
SET DEVICE TO SCREEN
SET PRINT OFF
SET CONSOLE ON
RETURN
```

```
* PRINT.PRG - TO TEST OUT MACROS, FOR PRINTER-CONTROLS
* ----------
SET TALK OFF
SET CONSOLE OFF
SET PRINT ON
STORE '?? CHR(27)+CHR(64)' TO RESET
STORE '?? CHR(27)+CHR(53)' TO TOF
STORE '?? CHR(27)+CHR(67)+CHR(12)' TO FORMLEN
STORE '?? CHR(27)+CHR(80)' TO CPI10
STORE '?? CHR(27)+CHR(77)' TO CPI12
STORE '?? CHR(27)+CHR(15)' TO CPI17
STORE '?? CHR(27)+CHR(65)+CHR(24)' TO SPACING
STORE '?? CHR(27)+CHR(87)+CHR(1)' TO ELONGATE
STORE '?? CHR(12)' TO FORMFEED
*
*
&RESET
&TOF
&FORMLEN
SET DEVICE TO PRINT
&CPI10
@ 01,10 SAY 'THIS IS 10 CPI PRINT'
&CPI12
@ 02,10 SAY 'THIS IS 12 CPI PRINT'
&CPI17
@ 03,10 SAY 'THIS IS 17 CPI PRINT'
&SPACING
@ 04,10 SAY 'XXXXX   THIS LINE AND THE NEXT ONE SHOULD PRINT AT 3 ;
PER INCH'
@ 05,10 SAY 'YYYYY   THIS LINE AND THE ONE ABOVE SHOULD PRINT AT ;
3 PER INCH'
&CPI10
&ELONGATE
@ 06,10 SAY 'THIS IS ELONGATED MODE'
&FORMFEED
@ 01,10 SAY 'THIS SHOULD PRINT AT THE TOP-OF-PAGE'
@ 02,10 SAY ' '
*
*
*
&RESET
SET DEVICE TO SCREEN
SET PRINT OFF
SET CONSOLE ON
RETURN
```

Index

user data, 350
user-friendliness, 273

V

VAI function, 68
value function, 68
values
  odd and even, 343
variable

memory, 247
null, 282
variables
  extending logic with, 256
variables inputs
  accepting, 346
versions
  earlier, 14
vertical formats, 207
  totals in, 216

W

WHILE parameter, 60, 124
WHILE parameter for reports, 221
work area, 39
wrap around, 194
write operation, 5

Z

ZAP command, 105

Other Bestsellers From TAB

Other Bestsellers From TAB